He has been called America's greatest ex-president, a man who lost the White House after one term but went on to become a respected spokesman for peace and human rights.

Burton Kaufman's book on the Carter years was hailed as the best account of his administration. This new edition probes more deeply into Jimmy Carter's approach to the presidency and the issues that he faced, placing his tenure in that office more squarely in the context of the fundamental changes taking place in America while he served. It features more information on his foreign and environmental policies and expanded coverage of his personal background—both his upbringing and naval career—along with insights into his wife's activist role.

Drawing on Carter's previously unavailable Handwriting File, as well as on new oral histories and Carter's own books, Burton and Scott Kaufman show the ways in which Carter had the opportunity—but failed—to be a successful transitional president for the Democrats. They argue that by the fall of 1978 he had become a more effective leader than during the first part of his presidency but could not undo his earlier mistakes and continued to make seriou errors of political judgment.

Weighing achievements such as the Alaskan Lands Bill with shortcomings such as disarray within the White Hous and strained relations with Congress, the authors re-examine the world events

The Presidency of
JAMES EARL
CARTER JR.

AMERICAN PRESIDENCY SERIES

Clifford S. Griffin, Donald R. McCoy, and Homer E. Socolofsky, Founding Editors

George Washington, Forrest McDonald
John Adams, Ralph Adams Brown
Thomas Jefferson, Forrest McDonald
James Madison, Robert Allen Rutland
James Monroe, Noble E. Cunningham Jr.
John Quincy Adams, Mary W. M. Hargreaves
Andrew Jackson, Donald B. Cole
Martin Van Buren, Major L. Wilson
William Henry Harrison & John Tyler, Norma Lois Peterson
James K. Polk, Paul H. Bergeron
Zachary Taylor & Millard Fillmore, Elbert B. Smith
Franklin Pierce, Larry Gara
James Buchanan, Elbert B. Smith
Abraham Lincoln, Phillip Shaw Paludan
Andrew Johnson, Albert Castel
Rutherford B. Hayes, Ari Hoogenboom
James A. Garfield & Chester A. Arthur, Justus D. Doenecke
Grover Cleveland, Richard E. Welch Jr.
Benjamin Harrison, Homer B. Socolofsky & Allan B. Spetter
William McKinley, Lewis L. Gould
Theodore Roosevelt, Lewis L. Gould
William Howard Taft, Paolo E. Coletta
Woodrow Wilson, Kendrick A. Clements
Warren G. Harding, Eugene P. Trani & David L. Wilson
Calvin Coolidge, Robert H. Ferrell
Herbert C. Hoover, Martin L. Fausold
Harry S. Truman, Donald R. McCoy
Dwight D. Eisenhower, Chester J. Pach Jr. & Elmo Richardson
John F. Kennedy, Second Edition, Revised, James N. Giglio
Lyndon B. Johnson, Vaughn Davis Bornet
Richard Nixon, Melvin Small
Gerald R. Ford, John Robert Greene
James Earl Carter Jr., Burton I. Kaufman
George Bush, John Robert Greene

The Presidency of
JAMES EARL
CARTER JR.

SECOND EDITION, REVISED

Burton I. Kaufman
and Scott Kaufman

UNIVERSITY PRESS OF KANSAS

Published by the University Press of Kansas (Lawrence, Kansas 66045),
which was organized by the Kansas Board of Regents and is
operated and funded by Emporia State University, Fort Hays State University,
Kansas State University, Pittsburg State University, the University of Kansas,
and Wichita State University

Library of Congress Cataloging-in-Publication Data
Kaufman, Burton Ira.
The presidency of James Earl Carter, Jr. / Burton I. Kaufman and
Scott Kaufman. — 2nd ed., rev.
p. cm. — (American presidency series)
Includes bibliographical references and index.
ISBN 0-7006-1470-2 (cloth : alk. paper) — ISBN 0-7006-1471-0 (pbk. : alk. paper)
1. United States—Politics and government—1977–1981.
2. Carter, Jimmy, 1924–   I. Kaufman, Scott, 1969–   II. Title. III. Series.
E872.K38   2006
973.926092—dc22
[B]
2006013434

British Library Cataloguing-in-Publication Data is available.

Printed in the United States of America

10 9 8 7 6 5 4 3 2 1

For Diane

CONTENTS

CONTENTS

A photograph section appears following page 140.

FOREWORD

The aim of the American Presidency Series is to present historians and the general reading public with interesting, scholarly assessments of the various presidential administrations. These interpretive surveys are intended to cover the broad ground between biographies, specialized monographs, and journalistic accounts. As such, each is a comprehensive work that draws on original sources and pertinent secondary literature, yet leaves room for the author's own analysis and interpretation.

Volumes in the series present the data essential to understanding the administration under consideration. Particularly, each book treats the then-current problems facing the United States and its people and how the president and his associates felt about, thought about, and worked to cope with these problems. Attention is given to how the office developed and operated during the president's tenure. Equally important is a consideration of the vital relationships between the president and his staff, the executive officers, Congress, foreign representatives, the judiciary, state officials, the public, political parties, the press, and influential private citizens. The series is also concerned with how this unique American institution—the presidency—was viewed by the presidents, and with what results.

All this is set, insofar as possible, in the context not only of contemporary politics but also of economics, international relations, law, morals, public administration, religion, and thought. Such a broad approach is necessary because a presidential administration is more than the elected and appointed officers composing it; its work often reflects the major problems, anxieties, and glories of the nation. In short, the authors in this series strive to recount and evaluate the record of each administration and to identify its distinctiveness and relationships to the past, its own time, and the future.

The General Editors

PREFACE TO
THE SECOND EDITION

In the more than ten years since the first edition of this book was published, there has been a resurgent interest in presidential biography and in the study of the presidency. Best-selling biographies of Presidents George Washington, John Adams, Abraham Lincoln, John F. Kennedy, and Lyndon Johnson indicate the renewed public interest in presidential biography.[1] There have also been important new studies and evaluations of the presidency by such highly respected historians, political scientists, and journalists as Lewis L. Gould, Robert Dallek, Fred Greenstein, Stephen Graubard, Eric Alterman, Bob Woodward, E. J. Dionne Jr., David Gergen, and Stephen Skowronek.[2]

Although there is no overarching theme to these works, there are clusters of commonality. One is that presidential leadership matters; that for all the emphasis historians and political scientists place on cultural, social, economic, and bureaucratic forces, leadership from the Oval Office has consequences that extend long beyond an incumbent's term as president. Another is that presidents, especially in recent years, have engaged in lies, deception, cover-ups, and evasions that have come back not only to haunt them but also to harm the nation.

A third theme that in many ways conflicts with the first two is the constraints placed on a president because of forces and developments beyond his control, not the least of which have been shifts in ideological or political outlook. In this analysis, which emphasizes patterns that cut across periods and de-emphasizes notions of periodization, such as the premodern and modern presidency, presidents caught in the transition from one dominant political outlook to another have generally not been successful. They have been torn between trying to respond to the interests that elected them and the dynamics of an emerging new electorate. The finest example of this mode of analysis is Stephen Skowronek's *The Politics Presidents Make*, and he uses the presidency of Jimmy Carter to illustrate his point. Of the Carter presidency Skowronek writes: "Carter had diagnosed a political regime in deep trouble, one that would have to alter radically the way it worked in order to meet the problems of the day. Yet he came to power to rejuvenate that regime rather than to repudiate it, to save it rather than destroy it. As the order-affirming and order-shattering dimensions of this project had virtually the same referents, Carter convened a politics in which he could not win for winning."[3]

Skowronek's analysis of the Carter presidency is not entirely new. As commented on in the first edition of this book, defenders of the Carter administration have made the point that anyone entering the White House in 1977 would have faced a herculean task in responding to the constraints placed on the new administration. Among these were the recent experience of the Vietnam War and the Watergate scandal, a breakdown of the historically strong party system, cracks in the congressional system of seniority, and the appearance of hundreds of political action committees, all of which weakened the power of the presidency. Along with these developments was a rejection of modern-day liberalism and a movement toward more conservative political, social, and cultural values, beginning as early as 1964 with the Republican nomination of Barry Goldwater and culminating in the Reagan revolution of the 1980s. It was this transition in values and outlook that, more than any other change, in Skowronek's view, compromised the power of the Oval Office during Carter's presidency.

In this second edition of *The Presidency of James Earl Carter Jr.* we are cognizant of the point Skowronek has argued so well. We probe more deeply into Carter's approach to the presidency and place the office he held within the context of the fundamental changes taking place during his time in the White House. We also discuss in more detail, for example, the importance of the president's southern rural upbringing, his naval career, and his early forays into politics, as well as the influence of his parents and his commanding officer in the nuclear submarine program, Admiral Hyman Rickover. We examine more deeply the reform movement on Capitol Hill, beginning in the 1960s and accelerating in the 1970s, that made the legislative process more open and democratic but also more difficult for a president to navigate. We pay more attention to the social and cultural upheaval of the 1970s that historian Bruce J. Schulman so ably described.[4] We deal at greater length with one of the most notable achievements of the Carter presidency—environmental legislation culminating in the Alaskan Lands Bill of 1980, which, as some critics rightfully pointed out, did not receive adequate attention in the first edition. Finally, we note the influential role of Rosalynn Carter in her husband's administration and the controversy she bred with respect to what a First Lady's proper role should be.

At the same time, we remain convinced that presidents matter and that no presidency is doomed or destined for success from the start. Surely this point is underscored by the abundant literature already noted. Indeed, in his *Why Americans Hate Politics*, columnist and commentator E. J. Dionne suggests that Jimmy Carter represented a "lost opportunity" for modern-day liberalism, the Democratic Party, and, indeed, the United States. Accepting the proposition that the United States was going through a transition from the New Deal liberalism that had dominated the nation's politics since the 1930s to the conservative movement that has been ascendant since the election of Ronald Reagan in 1980, Dionne places much of the blame for the demise of modern-day liberalism on the indulgent demands of the liberals themselves. But he also maintains that, having won the election in 1976 as an outsider from the South not beholden to the traditional Washington and liberal Democratic establishments, Carter had an opportunity to save liberalism from itself and from the growing conservative movement in the nation by creating a new American center. Recognizing the demands imposed by traditional liberal constituencies and the shift toward the political Right already under way when Carter entered the White House in 1977, Dionne nevertheless faults the thirty-ninth president for not possessing the requisite political skills to change the course of American politics or, in Skowronek's terms, to be a successful transitional president. "In the end," Dionne writes, "it was a bad case of unrequited politics: Liberals never appreciated what Carter had done for their coalition; Carter never appreciated what the coalition had done for him."[5]

Accepting Dionne's premise about a "lost opportunity" during the Carter presidency, we argue that the essential elements of a message that might have had broad appeal to the American public and helped create a new American center within the Democratic Party were inherent in Carter's legislative programs and policies. We also maintain that, by the fall of 1978, Carter had become a more effective leader than he had been during his early presidency. Finally, we acknowledge that in his last two years in office, the president was often the victim of economic and political developments at home and abroad, including an inflation aggravated by oil shortages and rising energy prices and the Iranian revolution and hostage crisis over which he had little or no control.

At the same time, we argue that Carter could not simply undo the mistakes of his first twenty months in office, that he continued to make serious errors of political judgment, and that at least some of the problems of his last two years in office were of his own making. We also note the political disarray within the White House during much of Carter's administration, in part because of a poor transitional process, in part because of Carter's refusal to appoint a chief of staff at the beginning of his administration, and in part because of a lack of White House control over the cabinet; not until the middle of his administration did Carter attempt to address the latter two problems. We conclude, however, that Carter's most serious failure as president was his inability to put together a coherent message or offer the American people a direction and vision on which to build a strong base of support and ensure his success as a transitional president.

Although we follow the format of the first edition by alternating chapters on domestic and foreign policy, we also made substantial changes to the chapters on foreign policy. We examine, for example, Carter's human rights policy in significantly greater detail. We explore the bureaucratic infighting over human rights within the administration, and we discuss how the administration's position on human rights changed as the White House gave greater emphasis to security issues, particularly after 1979. We examine in more detail the issue of arms control, incorporating materials from the Soviet Union that recently became available. We also argue that the conflict between Secretary of State Cyrus Vance and National Security Adviser Zbigniew Brzezinski was even more profound than described in the first edition. Finally, we discuss a number of important matters not covered in the first edition, such as the issue of nuclear nonproliferation as it pertained to West Germany, Japan, and Pakistan; the Mariel boatlift from Cuba; and the so-called Koreagate scandal, which had important foreign policy and domestic implications.

Throughout the chapters on foreign policy, we acknowledge again the important foreign policy accomplishments of the Carter administration, such as the Panama Canal treaties and the Camp David accords, both of which represented agreements his predecessors had failed to achieve. The president also normalized relations with the People's Republic of China and made human rights a permanent component of U.S. foreign policy and the United States a symbol of support for victims of repression throughout the world.

We argue, however, that these accomplishments were tempered by many of the same problems that bedeviled Carter's domestic policies. For example, the administration's normalization of relations with China without warning Congress in advance—considered justified by the White House in order to avoid leaks—only worsened already strained relations with Capitol Hill. The president also had difficulty prioritizing, thereby making it hard to focus the administration's energy on one or a few goals.

Similarly, at times, Carter seemed not to understand the difficulty of implementing the policies he sought to carry out, as in the case of human rights or nuclear nonproliferation. Taken together with the Vance-Brzezinski dispute, many of these same problems caused confusion among observers at home and abroad as to what the administration's foreign policy goals were. As in the case of domestic policy, they also resulted in a failure by President Carter to develop an overall foreign policy concept to which the American people might have lent their strong support, and which might have made him a successful transitional president.

We finish the book with a detailed examination of Carter's postpresidential years. We note that he has continued to advance his own agenda, including fighting poverty and disease and promoting world peace, even when his actions and outspoken views have been criticized by some political pundits or have angered his successors in the White House. Yet his reputation has continued to grow; this may say something about what Americans have come to expect of their former chief executives.

ACKNOWLEDGMENTS

First, thanks go to the staff of the Carter Library for their assistance in preparing the revised edition of this book. They were always ready to answer questions, locate materials, and keep us updated on recently released collections. Scott would specifically like to thank the archivists for inviting him to one of their annual Christmas parties, where he had a wonderful time.

Our colleagues at Miami University of Ohio and Francis Marion University were very supportive of our academic endeavors. Scott in particular would like to express his appreciation to Francis Marion for reducing his teaching load during the spring 2005 semester, thereby giving him much-needed time to complete his portions of this work. In addition, we would like to thank Miami's Western College and Department of History, the Francis Marion University History Department, and the Francis Marion Foundation for their financial support.

We are deeply appreciative of the assistance and encouragement of the editors of the American Presidency Series. Fred Woodward of the University Press of Kansas was very patient with us as we worked to complete the revised edition and astonishingly quick in sending us his comments.

Finally, we would like to thank our family members—Diane, wife and mother, and Heather, daughter and sister—for their love and support.

1

★ ★ ★ ★ ★

WHAT MAKES JIMMY RUN?

Jimmy Carter is a southerner, an engineer, an agribusinessman, and a politician. He is not a nuclear physicist, a populist, or even a dirt farmer, as he and his followers have sometimes claimed. He is a Southern Baptist and an evangelical but not a fundamentalist. He is deeply religious but not theological. He can be—and most of the time is—courteous, compassionate, and gracious, but he can also be—and frequently has been—sarcastic, short-tempered, calculating, and opportunistic. He is a person of deep moral conviction and principle; at the same time, during his career, he has often been devious and politically pragmatic. He is highly intelligent, introspective, and thoughtful, but he is not ideological, philosophical, or conceptual. His successful quest for the White House was made possible by the news media, but he was not an especially effective media candidate. He is, in other words, an individual whose personality and career are replete with contradictions and inconsistencies. For that reason, the people who voted for him in 1976 probably did so more as an act of faith and a measure of hope than as a statement of their abiding commitment to him or to the programs he espoused.

The future president was born on 1 October 1924 in Plains, Georgia, a community of about 500 people in the southwestern part of the state about 190 miles west of Savannah and 120 miles south of Atlanta. The oldest of four children, he was the first president to be born in a hospital. He grew up on the family's 350-acre farm in Archery, a predominantly black community a few miles from Plains. His father, Earl, was a successful local businessman and farmer who owned a considerable amount of real estate and operated a warehouse and brokerage in peanuts. His mother, Lillian Gordy, was a registered nurse. Jimmy also had two sisters—Gloria, born in 1926, and Ruth, born in 1929—and a much younger brother, Billy, born in 1937, when Jimmy was already a teenager.

Carter had a typical childhood for a white youngster growing up in the rural South whose father was a successful but by no means wealthy member of the community. A loyal supporter of the Talmadge dynasty that dominated Georgia politics and an ardent foe of the New Deal, Earl believed totally in the southern system of segregation, but he treated his black workers with respect and dignity. Lillian, who often cared for African Americans when other health providers would not, was more liberal in her racial views. The family home, a shotgun cottage set back about 50 feet from the dirt road on which it fronted, was comfortable. Jimmy had his own room, and there was even a dirt tennis court next to the house. But until he was eleven years old, there was no indoor plumbing, electricity, or telephone. The bathroom was the outdoor privy. When the family wanted to listen to the radio, they used a battery. Most of their food was homegrown. Electricity finally reached Archery when Jimmy was thirteen.

Most of Jimmy's neighbors were poor blacks who lived in run-down cabins. Poverty surrounded him. The locals either worked for the nearby Seaboard Airline Railroad or were sharecroppers or field hands on his father's land. On Sundays he attended the Plains Baptist Church, which, like all social institutions in the South, was segregated. But once a year his family would be invited by one of his neighbors, Bishop William Decker Johnson, to attend services at St. Mark African Methodist Episcopal Church.

Carter's playmates as a young boy were the black youngsters who lived nearby. They hunted, trapped, explored, and fished together and played at one another's houses. He often ate and slept at their homes, and for much of the time, while his mother was working, he was brought up by a young black woman, Rachel Clark, whose husband, Jack, was foreman of Earl Carter's farmhands. Rachel would live to see Carter become president.

Occasionally Jimmy and his closest black friend, A. D. Davis, would get on the local train and go to nearby Americus to see a movie together. But his friend would have to sit in a separate section of the train and in the balcony of the theater reserved for blacks only. "I don't remember ever questioning the mandatory racial separation, which we accepted like breathing or waking up in Archery every morning," Carter later recalled.[1]

Carter did not become aware of the full system of southern segregation until he was about fourteen years old, when, as was southern custom, he continued with his schooling but his black friends did not. Wanting to be on the varsity basketball team and having an interest in girls, he developed closer ties with the white community. Commenting on the separation that developed between him and his black friends, he later wrote: "We still competed equally while on the baseball field, fishing, or working in the field, but I was not reluctant to take advantage of my new stature by assuming on occasion, the authority of my father. Also, we were more inclined to go our separate ways if we had an argument, since I was increasingly involved with my white friends in Plains."[2]

Like other youngsters of the rural South, Jimmy had his daily chores, the worst of which, he recalled, was mopping cotton with a mixture of arsenic and molasses to kill the dreaded boll weevil. The mixture attracted flies and other insects and left his jeans so stiff that they remained standing by themselves when he took them off at night. Often he would have to put on the same pair of jeans the next day. He also disliked taking buckets of drinking water as much as two miles from the spring where the water was drawn to the workers in the fields during the hot Georgia summers.

In contrast to his toleration of his daily chores, Carter was obsessed with hunting and fishing. It was not only the outdoors and the challenges of the two sports he loved, but also the opportunity to be with his father, whom he adored. In many respects, his father had a more rounded personality than the future president. If Earl's views on race were circumscribed by the rigid system of southern segregation, if his conservative economic and political views were those of a successful farmer and businessman who despised being told by the Roosevelt administration that he had to kill his young hogs and limit his cotton acreage in order to raise agricultural prices, and if he was a devout Southern Baptist and deacon of his church, these aspects of his life defined only the more conservative and circumspect side of his personality. By all accounts, he was outgoing, fun loving, athletic, and surrounded by friends. He played baseball as well as tennis, had a regular poker game on Friday nights, enjoyed a few drinks, and went dancing on Saturday nights with Lillian. He took regular vacations, usually to a city with a major league baseball team to see the sport he and Lillian loved so much.

Lillian was more unconventional than her husband. Although she never quite crossed the bounds of traditional southern mores—she was never, for example, a foe of segregation or a champion of civil rights—she tried their outer limits. Not only did she provide free health care to the black community, but when the Harvard-educated son of Bishop Johnson came to visit, Lillian would meet him at the front door and entertain him in her living room, something that was normally not done in the South. As a working mother, she was not always home, and when she had free time, she preferred reading to household or maternal chores. She also had an entrepreneurial spirit, supplementing her nursing salary with the harvesting and sale of pecans from the family's abundant pecan trees.

3

It would be easy to overemphasize the formative impact of Jimmy's upbringing on his later political career and presidency. Certainly it had an important bearing. Jimmy's father was a stern disciplinarian who worked his son hard and expected him to be obedient and follow the golden rule. President Carter's own commitment to hard work and sense of discipline can clearly be traced to the father he worshipped, and so can his love of outdoor sports and the environment. Even as a young boy, Carter was also a fledging fiscal conservative. Under his father's influence, he bagged and sold peanuts in Plains during the summer, earning as much as a dollar a day during the weekdays and several times that on Saturdays. He invested the money he earned, first buying cotton for five cents a pound when prices were depressed and then selling it when prices went up; he then used that money to buy houses in Plains, which he rented. He also earned a reputation early in life as a tightwad, once refusing to loan his cousin Hugh Carter the price of a movie ticket.

From his mother and one of his high school teachers, Julia Coleman, Carter also developed a lifelong commitment to learning and a love of reading, which was carried on even at the supper table. President Carter's concern for the poor and the underprivileged and his commitment to racial and gender equality were unquestionably influenced by his surroundings as a boy and by his mother's work with African Americans. The importance of faith in Carter's life can be traced back to the fact that he came from a devoutly religious family and was expected to attend Sunday school and services on Sundays as well as the summer revival meetings held just before harvest time. Most important, Carter's personal sense of self-confidence and commitment to doing what he believed was right, regardless of its political consequences, which characterized his entire presidency, was traceable to the fact that his upbringing was a rooted one—rooted in a mentoring father, nurturing and loving parents, and a sense of place and certitude.

That said, the formative elements of Carter's later political career and presidency were not so much his rural childhood but rather what came after he left Plains. After all, Carter's quest since boyhood was to escape the red clay of Georgia, not to embrace it. In terms of personality, he fit neither the gregarious mode of his father nor the curmudgeon-like qualities of his mother. Nor was there anything in his boyhood that set him apart from other relatively privileged and bright children of the rural South or hinted at a political career. Even in physical appearance, he was good-looking but not strikingly so. He stood just 5 feet, 6 inches tall at the end of his senior year in high school (he would grow 3 inches over the next year) and weighed about 130 pounds; his only memorable features were his pale blue eyes and broad, toothy smile. Indeed, convention, rather than a lack of it, characterized Carter's younger years.

Finishing high school in 1941, Carter spent the next two years boning up on his science background at Georgia Southwestern College and then the Georgia Institute of Technology before being admitted to the U.S. Naval Academy, which had been his goal since he was six years old. The challenge of his studies at Georgia Tech and the discipline he endured at the academy had a lasting impact on him, forcing him to focus his attention and leaving him with a determination to achieve and a sense of vulnerability he had never experienced before. He also turned inward, becoming a very private person. Rushing through accelerated wartime courses, he worked hard, excelled in his studies, and received high grades, finishing sixtieth out of a class of 822. Aside from his good academic record, however, there was little else that made him stand out at the academy; indeed, he made few friends, and most of his classmates did not even remember him.

After graduating from Annapolis in 1946, Jimmy married Rosalynn Smith, who was also from Plains and a good friend of Ruth Carter. Although they had known each other since childhood, they did not begin to date until after Jimmy returned home from Annapolis. Like Jimmy, Rosalynn had set high standards for herself, graduating from high school as class valedictorian. She also shared Jimmy's desire to see more of the world beyond Plains.

Carter spent the next seven years in the navy. His first assignment was as radar officer on the USS *Wyoming*, an old battleship that was decommissioned a year later. In 1951 he was assigned to what he regarded as "the finest Navy billet available to any officer of [his] rank—the development of the first atomic submarine." Before he received the assignment, he had to be screened by the person responsible for the navy's atomic submarine program, Captain (and later Admiral) Hyman Rickover, a brilliant but demanding officer. As the lengthy interview was ending, Rickover asked the junior officer whether he had done his best at Annapolis. After reflection, Carter said that he had not, to which Rickover countered, "Why not?" The interview had a profound and lasting impact on Carter. "Why Not the Best?" would be the theme of his drive for the presidency and the title of his campaign autobiography. Carter saw Rickover's question as a challenge that demanded an ongoing process of self-examination.[3]

Rickover accepted the young officer into his program and put him to work on the *Sea Wolf,* one of the prototypes of the nuclear submarine. Rickover always remained bigger than life for Carter, a figure who would haunt him long after he left the navy. In 1970 he sent his former superior an invitation to attend his inauguration as governor of Georgia, and the admiral had to ask one of his aides who Carter was. But Carter remembered well his experiences as one of Rickover's junior officers. During his campaign for president, the Democratic nominee wrote to the admiral that if he were elected president, and if it was "within the bounds of military/political propriety," he would like to have Rickover's views on a number of matters. As president, Carter also made it clear to his staff that he was to see any letters or memorandums from Rickover and would personally respond to his telephone calls.[4]

The two men were soul mates in many ways. The qualities that Rickover displayed as a naval officer and that Carter so admired were the same qualities that helped define Carter's approach to his presidency. Rickover was a loner who never cared much for the social life of the navy or of the Washington, D.C., establishment. He had seemingly inexhaustible energy. He approached problem solving through a mastery of detail. He was not prone to compromise. He demanded excellence. He micromanaged. He believed that self-fulfillment meant something more than material gain and that he served some singular purpose other than his own ambitions. Accordingly, he was prepared to skirt ordinary chains of command or conventional political processes. "Admiral Rickover had a profound effect on my life—perhaps more than anyone except my own parents," the former president later wrote.[5]

Moving in 1952 to Schenectady, New York, where the *Sea Wolf's* reactor was being built, Lieutenant Carter took classes at Union College in reactor technology and nuclear physics; although these were accelerated, one-semester, noncredit courses, they provided the basis for his later claim that he had been trained as a nuclear physicist. Carter's future now seemed settled. He was a seasoned submariner and lieutenant senior grade, working on the latest submarine technology under the direction of an exacting and sometimes even abrasive superior for whom he had the greatest respect and admiration. He had been selected to be chief engineer of the *Sea Wolf* when it put to sea. He was also the father of three children—John "Jack" William, born in 1947; James Earl "Chip" Carter III, born in April 1950; and Donald Jeffrey, born in August 1952. Both he and Rosalynn loved the navy life—the work, the experiences, the camaraderie that existed among the officers. He would therefore pursue his career in the navy.

Then word came from Plains that Jimmy's father was dying, and his life abruptly changed. Since leaving Annapolis, he and Earl had drifted apart, finding that they had less and less in common. Jimmy's occasional contact with blacks at the academy and as a naval officer, and then in the claustrophobic confines of the submarine, where blacks and whites were forced to work closely together, made his views on race liberal to the point that he could not discuss the issue with his father. Jimmy was saddened by the lack of rapport with his father. Having grown up with a robust sense of family and home, he sometimes felt that he had deserted his roots to follow his own ambitions. After his father's death, Carter went through a type of midlife crisis. "I began to think about the relative significance of his life and mine," Carter remarked. "He was an integral part of the community, and had a wide range of varied but interrelated interests and responsibilities. He was his own boss, and his life was stabilized by the slow evolutionary change in the local societal structure." The more he compared his life with his father's, the more convinced he became that his father's way was the more satisfying one. In 1953 he, Rosalynn, and their three boys came home to Plains to stay.[6]

During his seven years in the service, Carter had proved that he was a good officer—intelligent, resourceful, able to carry out difficult assignments with a minimum of direction. As part of Rickover's team, he had also dealt frequently and effectively with government officials. Yet there was no indication that he was on the fast track to high command. He had not seen service in the Korean War, and his fellow officers had not singled him out as a leader of men. Indeed, he tended to be more aloof than most officers, usually rushing home to his family as soon as he was off duty. Perhaps that is why Carter had so few regrets about leaving the navy once he made the decision to resign. "I had only one life to live," he recalled, "and I wanted to live it as a civilian, with a potentially fuller opportunity for varied public service."[7]

Jimmy's first years back in Plains were difficult as he and Rosalynn tried to readjust to rural living and rebuild his father's faltering warehouse peanut business during one of Georgia's worst droughts. But things soon improved, for the drought of 1954 was followed by the rains of 1955 and a bumper peanut crop. Jimmy became skilled at raising peanuts, and after a few years, his business was prospering. Active in community affairs and serving as a deacon of the Plains Baptist Church, he had become by 1960 one of Plains's most respected business and civic leaders.

Although Carter had shown little interest in politics to this point, he came from a politically active family. Earl Carter had served on the Sumter County School Board and had been elected to the state legislature the year before he died. Jimmy got his first taste of politics when he also became a member and then chairman of the county school board. As a board member, he visited both the black and the white schools in the county, and what he saw had a lasting impact on him. His views in support of integration, which had already been influenced by his career in the navy, became more fixed. By no means was he prepared to champion integration, but there is little doubt that he was appalled by what he learned about the black schools. In addition, he would have nothing to do with the blatantly racist White Citizen's Council, even when he was approached about joining the organization and lost business when he refused to do so. "The books were those that had been declared too worn for use in the white schools," he later recounted about his visit to the black schools. "Classes were held in various places, including Sunday school classrooms of black churches and even private homes. For some reason, my most vivid memory is of large teenage boys trying to sit on chairs designed for children of kindergarten age."[8]

As his business flourished, Carter had more time for outside interests. When some of his friends encouraged him to run for office, he needed little persuasion. The ambition that had made him so determined and competitive was still a driving force of his personality. In this sense, public office was another of Carter's quests for greater achievement, but it is undeniable that he also had a real commitment to civic duty.

In his first bid for public office, Carter chose to run for a seat in the Georgia Senate in 1962. His initiation into elective politics was characterized by exceptional energy and enthusiasm, typical of all his campaign efforts. As in future races, he made personal character—his compared with that of his opponents—the central campaign issue. It was "an amateurish and whirlwind" effort, Carter later remarked. He lost the primary by 139 votes, but believing that he had been cheated out of the nomination by a county political boss, he hired Charles Kirbo, a brilliant trial lawyer in one of Atlanta's leading law firms, to challenge the election results. Kirbo was able to persuade a superior court judge that a ballot box in one of the precincts had been tampered with. The judge declared the entire vote from that precinct invalid, thereby changing the outcome of the primary from defeat to victory for the thirty-seven-year-old peanut farmer from Plains. In the general election in November, Carter won by a comfortable margin. Kirbo became his closest friend and adviser, even though the Atlanta lawyer never held public office.

Carter's campaign for the senate had a profound impact on the way he looked at politics. He was especially offended by the gerrymandering, cronyism, and special interests that were part of Georgia politics. "Later as governor and then president," he wrote in a book about his senatorial campaign, "I was continually reminded by national and world events of these earliest days of my political life and the similar challenges that still confront people everywhere who search for justice, truth, human rights, and governments in which they can have confidence."[9]

Carter served two terms in the state senate, from 1963 to 1966. He was an industrious and hardworking legislator, and he established a record as a moderate progressive who supported "good government" measures and educational reform, lashed out at lobbyists for special interests, and stressed the importance of caring for the poor, the underprivileged, and the underrepresented in government. By 1964 a Georgia newspaper poll named Carter as one of the state's most influential legislators. Spurred to seek higher office, the next year he announced that he was running for governor.

Virtually unknown outside his own district, Carter conducted a grueling gubernatorial campaign, even by Georgia standards. At first not taken seriously by most political pundits, his candidacy appeared increasingly more viable as he traveled through the state meeting an estimated 300,000 Georgians. On the eve of the election, he fully expected to be in a runoff against either former governor Ellis Arnall or Lester Maddox, a restaurant owner who had gained national notoriety for defying integration by standing in the doorway of his establishment holding an ax handle. The next morning, however, Carter learned that he had finished a close third. Rather than being satisfied that he had gone from being practically unknown to almost winning a runoff spot, he was devastated and fell into a deep depression that was lifted only by the solace he found as a born-again Christian.

Although religion had always been an important part of his daily life, Carter had not been devout. At age eleven he had announced that he had accepted Jesus Christ as his personal savior, but religion was not at the core of his existence. Now Carter went through a second experience of conversion, and his renewed Christian faith only intensified his commitment to public service. He never thought that his faith provided unerring answers to contemporary problems, but he was more convinced than ever that his purpose was to serve God's will, which he interpreted as serving humanity. He also accepted theologian Reinhold Niebuhr's aphorism that "the sad duty of politics is to establish justice in a sinful world." As a result, his secular sense of public duty became firmly wedded to a gospel of service based on his strong religious convictions.

At peace with himself and convinced that he had good work to do, Carter decided to run for governor again in 1970 and to win, whatever the cost. The result was a campaign that even he and his advisers would later regret. To defeat governor Carl Sanders, his chief opponent in the Democratic primary, Carter appealed to segregationist and white supremacist elements in the state. He spoke out against busing, visited a segregated private academy, and said that he would welcome a meeting with Alabama's openly racist governor George Wallace. In the primary runoff, Carter easily beat Sanders and then went on to an overwhelming victory in the general election in November.

Unquestionably, the campaign was not one of Carter's finest moments. He had acted with a ruthlessness that belied the basic principles he believed in and was inexcusable even on grounds of the ends justifying the means. Yet the governor-elect also owed his election to hard work. For almost four years he had crisscrossed the state, delivering more than 1,800 speeches to almost any group that invited him. He pored over old

Georgia budgets to master state finances and developed an extensive mailing list of anyone he met who might support his candidacy. Although Carter's fourth child and first daughter, Amy, was still a toddler—she was born in 1967—Rosalynn joined him on the campaign trail. He also expanded his group of advisers and consultants to include Jody Powell, a graduate student at Emory University who became his chauffeur and personal confidant, and Stuart Eizenstat, a young Atlanta attorney and recent Harvard Law School graduate who became his issues coordinator. Already on board were Hamilton Jordan, who, as a student at the University of Georgia, had worked on Carter's gubernatorial campaign in 1966 and quickly became one of his shrewdest political advisers, and Charles Kirbo. These four formed the nucleus of the so-called Peanut Brigade, which would play a prominent role in the Carter White House.

Considering his campaign pitch, almost no one could anticipate that, as governor, Carter would promote racial moderation and become known as a reform leader, yet that is precisely what happened. In his inaugural address in January, Carter surprised his listeners by promising to steer Georgia into a new era of racial equality and economic and social justice, and in fact, he achieved an impressive list of reforms. During his tenure, the number of black state employees increased from 4,850 to 6,684 as a result of his efforts. Carter established a special commission to improve services for the mentally and emotionally handicapped and authorized 111 new community mental health centers. He worked successfully for environmental protection; for tax, welfare, and judicial reform; and for consumer protection—all programs that would receive similarly high priority during the Carter presidency. He also instituted the practice of "zero-base budgeting," a system requiring an annual review of budgetary priorities as a means of promoting and measuring efficiency.

However, Carter's main goal as governor was to reorganize state government to improve its operation and cost-effectiveness. A reorganization measure easily passed the state assembly but ran into considerable opposition in the senate. Carter responded by throwing the full weight of his office behind the legislation, making it a test of his authority as governor. The results were inconclusive. Although the senate passed the bill, it authorized only the preparation of a reorganization plan, not its implementation. In the months that followed, Carter appointed teams of experts and prominent citizens to design a set of proposals that he could then submit to the legislature for its approval. Meeting regularly with these groups, the governor impressed them with his mastery of detail and his management skills. To win public support for reorganization, he initiated a massive media campaign orchestrated by Gerald Rafshoon, an Atlanta advertising executive who became another member of the Peanut Brigade.

At times Carter was his own worst enemy, committing many of the same strategic and tactical mistakes he would make as president. For example, he unnecessarily antagonized powerful state officials by attempting to turn the battle over reorganization into a morality play in which he was the guardian of the public welfare and his opponents were tools of special-interest groups. He compounded his mistake by resisting efforts at compromise and coalition building when the reorganization proposal was finally submitted to the Georgia General Assembly. Yet Carter did succeed in getting most of his programs passed by the legislature. Although many aspects of the plan were more cosmetic than corrective—for example, it eliminated agencies that never met or consolidated agencies without cutting back their expenditures—the overall outcome was a more effective, efficient, and responsive state government than had existed before.

By the end of his second year in office, Carter had earned a solid record of achievement. He appeared to typify a new group of southern governors known for their moderate racial views and progressive response to economic and social change in the South. Indeed, as early as May 1971, *Time* magazine featured Carter on its cover as the representative of this new political leadership in the South. "Soft-voiced, assured, looking eerily like John Kennedy from certain angles," *Time* reported, "Carter is a man as contradictory as Georgia itself, but determined to resolve some of its paradoxes."[10] Indeed, Carter *was* a man of opposites. His consummate personal ambition was linked to a compelling sense of public purpose; though spiritually content and eminently successful in nearly everything he did, Carter was not complacent but driven. His cousin Hugh Carter, who served as majority leader of the state senate when Jimmy was governor, later framed the question, "What made Jimmy run?" He concluded that Jimmy ran because he perceived himself as a "lay missionary" who saw only harmony between his own ambition and his larger spiritual and political purposes.[11]

So it was that in 1972, after only two years as Georgia's governor, Carter turned his attention to the nation's top political prize—the White House. The Georgian made his decision to run for president following Richard Nixon's overwhelming defeat of Senator George McGovern in November. Even though he was virtually unknown outside of Georgia, he was encouraged to seek the 1976 Democratic nomination by Hamilton Jordan and Dr. Peter Bourne, a psychiatrist who headed Georgia's drug-abuse program. They recognized what more seasoned politicians had missed: the significance of the change in the nominating process, and the shift in the nation's political temper.

Jordan and Bourne realized that McGovern had won his party's nomination because the guidelines for selecting delegates had been revised to provide for a more democratic selection process and for proportional representation of minorities and women at national conventions. To ensure compliance with these standards, a record number of states were filling their slates through direct primaries. Whereas only fifteen states had held primaries in 1952, in 1972 there were twenty-one, and by 1976 there would be at least thirty. This meant that the nomination would increasingly be determined at the ballot box, not by the party's hierarchy. If Carter could build momentum by winning some of the early primaries, his advisers reasoned that he could win the nomination.

Jordan and Bourne also sensed a real advantage in the fact that Carter was a political outsider and not part of the Washington establishment. By the early 1970s a wave of cynicism had surged over much of the country, manifested as widespread distrust of politics and politicians. The reasons for this feeling were complex, but it arose in part from a growing conviction that politicians had failed to deal with the great issues confronting the nation over the past ten years—war, poverty, increasing inflation, and economic stagnation. McGovern had been able to capitalize on this anti-Washington sentiment, and Carter's advisers believed that he could do the same.

Jordan explained all this to Carter in a seventy-two-page memorandum he wrote in 1972 outlining a strategy for victory in 1976. "Perhaps the strongest feeling in this country today," he told Carter, "is the general distrust of government and politicians at all levels. The desire and thrust for strong moral leadership in the nation was not satisfied with the election of Richard Nixon."[12] Brilliantly conceived, Jordan's brief became the blueprint for Carter's campaign. In fact, the only major difference between Jordan's recommendations and the strategy adopted was Carter's decision to enter as many primaries as possible instead of running in a carefully chosen few, as Jordan had advised. "Our strategy was simple," Carter later recalled: "Make a total effort all over the country."[13]

Beginning in January 1973 with a talk before the National Press Club, Carter threw himself into the presidential race with all the intensity and diligence that had marked his previous campaigns. For the next two years he traveled throughout the country meeting people, shaking hands, appearing on television, and holding news conferences. To gain more foreign policy exposure, he joined the Trilateral Commission, a private international organization founded by David Rockefeller of the Chase Manhattan Bank; its purpose was to promote closer ties among the United States, Europe, and Japan and create greater worldwide economic stability.

Wherever he traveled, Carter remained intentionally vague on the issues—stating publicly, for example, that he could not support an antiabortion constitutional amendment (already a heated campaign issue) but allowing that he might back a "national statute" limiting abortions. Similarly, in foreign affairs he declared that the policy of détente with the Soviet Union had gone too far, without explaining how much too far. On only a few matters did he take a firm stand, favoring strict enforcement of antitrust laws, enactment of gun control legislation, and welfare reform. He also stressed the need to reorganize the federal bureaucracy, following the state of Georgia's lead.

The emphasis, however, was on values. Government, Carter said, had to measure up to the honesty and integrity, the love and compassion, the idealism and heroism of the American people. He talked about his own character and career as a successful farmer and businessman, a dedicated family man, a military officer and veteran, a trained engineer and nuclear scientist, and an efficient and progressive state governor. In this way he was able to project himself differently—but effectively—to a variety of constituencies across a broad political spectrum.

Since Carter's message was about the failure of government to be worthy of the character and principles of the American people, he would benefit by the fallout from the Watergate scandal and Richard Nixon's subsequent resignation in August 1974. But the most important early development benefiting the Carter candidacy was the decision by Massachusetts senator Edward "Ted" Kennedy in September 1974 to take himself out of the presidential race. Carter's advisers had acted on the assumption that Kennedy would run and had the best chance of getting the Democratic nomination. The senator's withdrawal thus opened the way for other aspirants, more liberal than Carter, to vie for the nomination. If the liberal vote were divided among a number of candidates—most notably senators Birch Bayh of Indiana and Henry Jackson of Washington, former senator Fred Harris of Oklahoma, and congressman Morris Udall of Arizona—Carter could co-opt the political center and compete for the political Right and Left of the party. He could also appear to be a progressive alternative to George Wallace, who, though now confined to a wheelchair, had announced his candidacy for president in November 1975 and remained a wild card in the campaign.

Just as Jordan had hypothesized, Carter won the Democratic nomination after key victories in the caucuses and early primaries. His first breakthrough came in January 1976 in Iowa, where he won 27.6 percent of the vote, more than twice that of his nearest rival, Birch Bayh. Although less than 10 percent of registered Democrats had actually participated in the Iowa caucuses, and the largest bloc of votes went not to Carter but to uncommitted delegates, the news media declared Carter the winner; this gave him the momentum he needed to win next month in New Hampshire, which held the first election of the primary season. Soon Carter's face was appearing on the covers of *Time* and *Newsweek*, and he was being widely touted as the front-runner in the race for the Democratic nomination.

Even so, Carter's victory in the 9 March Florida primary was just as crucial as his successes in Iowa and New Hampshire. The contest was largely between Carter and Wallace, since the other candidates, except for Jackson, chose to sit out the primary, believing that the state was Wallace country. Between New Hampshire and Florida, Carter had suffered a major defeat in the Massachusetts primary, where he had finished a poor fourth. If he lost in Florida, he would probably be through as a serious candidate. But if he beat Wallace in the South, his claim to be the moderate southern alternative to the Alabama governor would still be viable, and his strategy of running as a centrist candidate acceptable to the mainstream of the Democratic Party would be justified.

Carter's plan worked brilliantly. He finished with 34.3 percent of the primary vote in Florida, compared with Wallace's 30.6 percent and Jackson's 23.9 percent. As *Time* reported, Carter "dominated the center on the issues, had the best organization and had the broadest appeal of all the candidates." He won large majorities among voters under age twenty-five, blue-collar workers, and Democrats identifying themselves as liberals. "I don't see anybody who can beat me," Carter said after the primary, "but I see a lot of hard political scraps ahead."[14] In the weeks that followed, Carter easily beat Wallace in Illinois and North Carolina, but he lost badly in the New York primary in April and beat Udall by less than 5,000 votes in Wisconsin. Because Jackson and Udall had not run in Illinois, Carter had yet to demonstrate that he could succeed against strong opposition in a northern industrial state. Pennsylvania, the site of the next major primary, became the proving ground.

Before the campaign in Pennsylvania, Carter made one of his few serious blunders of the primary season by telling reporters that he had "nothing against" an ethnic community "trying to maintain the ethnic purity of their neighborhoods." As he explained later, what he meant to say was that he was opposed to using the power of the federal government to "artificially" change the ethnic character of a neighborhood, but that he would not condone discrimination against any family wishing to move into the neighborhood. However, the phrase "ethnic purity" captured the attention of the press and made the headlines. Soon Carter was being loudly criticized by black leaders such as the Reverend Jesse Jackson of Chicago, who called Carter's views "a throwback to Hitlerian racism," and Mayor Richard Hatcher of Gary, Indiana, who referred to Carter as a "Frankenstein monster with a Southern drawl."[15]

For two days Carter refused to retract his statement, insisting that it had been taken out of context. Only after considerable coaxing from Rosalynn did he finally acknowledge his mistake, stating at a news conference in Philadelphia that he too had been bothered by the word "purity." This was enough to mollify most black leaders. Detroit mayor Coleman Young said that Carter's apology was "satisfactory" and that the whole matter had been a "phony issue." Other black leaders concurred.[16]

One of the intriguing questions about the campaign is how a rural southern white candidate could enjoy such support from blacks. In Florida, Carter had received 70 percent of the black vote; in North Carolina, 90 percent. Even in his Massachusetts defeat he had led the other candidates in the nearly all-black Boston neighborhood of Roxbury. Part of the explanation for Carter's appeal in such states as Florida and North Carolina was that blacks there would have backed almost anyone against Wallace. In addition, as governor of Georgia, he had opened the doors of state government to many more black employees and had made the important gesture of putting a portrait of Martin Luther King Jr. in the rotunda of the state capitol. As a result, he had gained the strong support of such respected black leaders as Martin Luther King Sr. and Atlanta congressman Andrew Young. Deputy campaign coordinator Ben Brown, one of 19 blacks on Carter's paid staff of 200, also had close connections with influential blacks throughout the country who were able to mobilize black voters on Carter's behalf. Finally, evangelical blacks could relate to Carter's own religious background and to his call for a national renewal of spiritual values.

Accordingly, Carter was able to carry the black vote in Pennsylvania by a substantial margin. He also managed to sway a large number of blue-collar workers, despite Henry Jackson's endorsement by Pennsylvania's powerful labor leaders. Together, these groups gave Carter the victory he needed in a northern industrial state. After the loss in Pennsylvania, Jackson announced his withdrawal from the race; meanwhile, Hubert Humphrey, who had been considering entering the campaign, said in a press conference that he would not actively seek the nomination. New polls showed that voters considered Carter the strongest possible Democratic candidate and that he would defeat President Gerald Ford by as much as 10 percent.

Carter's decision to participate in every primary, combined with party rules that awarded delegates on a basis proportional to a candidate's vote, now worked to his advantage. Although he actually lost most of the remaining primaries, including major ones in California and New Jersey, to latecomers Senator Frank Church of Idaho and Governor Edmund Brown of California, he managed to win at least one election every primary Tuesday. Thus, he was able to maintain his political pace and pick up enough delegates, even in the states he lost, to ensure his nomination when the Democrats held their convention in July.

Carter had performed a political miracle. In 1972, when he had announced to his mother that he was going to run for president, Lillian had responded, "President of what?" In winning his party's nod, Carter had pursued George McGovern's route of four years past—running actively in as many primaries as possible, avoiding the formal Democratic Party structure, and relying instead on thousands of volunteers throughout the primary campaigns. He had also finessed his opponents by appealing to all sectors of the party, liberals as well as conservatives, by focusing on unobjectionable values instead of specific issues and exploiting the nation's anti-Washington mood.

A revolt against Washington was what the election was all about. American voters, most polls showed, felt that government was far too meddlesome and intrusive, that it was unmovable and overbureaucratized, and that it was out of touch with the American people and insensitive to their ability to manage their own affairs. Disgruntled Americans sought new ideas, fresh faces, and a style of leadership predicated on openness, truthfulness, and public responsiveness. Indeed, morality was the emerging keynote of the campaign—a desire to restore a sense of purpose, trust, fairness, and civic responsibility to American life. Carter understood the national mood perfectly, and he attacked Washington in a positive way, emphasizing not so much what was wrong in the nation's capital as the power of the American people to set things right, appealing not to their cynicism but to their idealism.

By the time of the Democratic National Convention in July, Carter's nomination was a foregone conclusion. He won on the first ballot when Ohio's 132 votes put him over the top. As his running mate he selected Senator Walter Mondale of Minnesota, a liberal Washington insider who could balance the ticket and heal any rifts left over from the campaign. Opposing them were Gerald Ford, who won the Republican nomination in August after a close battle with former California governor Ronald Reagan, and Ford's vice presidential nominee, Senator Robert Dole of Kansas.

The election seemed Carter's to win. In contrast to the Democrats, the Republicans remained badly split between moderates who had backed Ford and conservatives who had supported Reagan. The polls indicated, moreover, that although Americans appreciated Ford's honesty and personal character and thought that he had restored integrity to the office of the president, they still had serious doubts about his competence. Even Ford's own campaign plan acknowledged that "the President has not shown the capability of causing a sharp increase in his approval rating for a sustained period of time."[17]

Realizing that voters generally had a positive image of Carter but found him obscure on the issues, Ford's advisers decided to hammer away at that vagueness. The Democratic candidate defined "trust of the people in government" as the campaign's major issue, and Ford responded by accusing Carter of "fuzziness." The Republican strategy soon began paying dividends. In August, Carter had a 15 percent lead over Ford, but by the beginning of September it was clear that the gap was closing fast. Carter's uninspiring rhetoric helped fuel the Republican critique. Yale historian C. Van Woodward marveled at "Carter's remarkable propensity . . . for fusing contradictions and reconciling opposites," remarking that "the result was an unusual assortment of unified ambiguities and ambiguous unities." Political commentators Rowland Evans and Robert Novak suggested that the Democratic candidate was "allergic to all efforts at eloquence."[18] Polls conducted by the Ford campaign showed that the Republican candidate was gaining ground in southern states, including Texas, Louisiana, Mississippi, Virginia, and North Carolina. Another poll revealed that although Carter still had a six- to eight-point lead over Ford in California, his support was "soft."

The last two weeks of September and the first week of October were a disaster for Carter. First he was heckled by angry anti-abortionists over his opposition to a constitutional amendment banning abortion. Then he displeased pro-abortion forces by modifying his position, telling a group of Catholic bishops that although he would not support an anti-abortion amendment, he would not oppose one either. His statement merely added credence to another of Ford's claims—that Carter flip-flopped on the issues.

Carter's meeting with the bishops had been intended to dispel Catholic concerns about his born-again Christianity. During his campaign, the Democratic candidate had neither hidden his deep religious faith nor harped on it. Nevertheless, it had become an issue. All the polls indicated that Carter would do well among the nation's 30 million white evangelical Protestants but that his support was weak among traditionally Democratic Catholics, who feared fundamentalist intolerance. Compounding the religious rift was the displeasure of urban, ethnic Catholics at Carter's efforts to reach out to blacks. As a result, many Catholics indicated that they would stay home on election day or vote Republican.

Of more immediate importance to the Carter campaign than Catholic disaffection, however, was public reaction to the Democratic candidate's interview in *Playboy*, in which he used risqué language and said that he had "committed adultery in [his] heart many times." The story exposed him to ridicule and raised questions about his judgment in granting the interview in the first place and then using such terms as "screw" and "shacks up." Prospects dimmed further for Carter after his poor showing in the first televised debate with Ford, which was held in Philadelphia on 23 September. Although neither candidate was particularly impressive, Ford appeared composed and in charge of the evening—less discursive, more articulate, better able to project himself to the television audience, and more on the offensive than Carter, frequently accusing Carter of being evasive in his responses or a big spender. A *New York Times*/CBS poll four days later showed that by a margin of 37 percent to 24 percent, the respondents named Ford the winner of the debate; the remaining 39 percent expressed no opinion or thought the debate was a draw.

By the end of September, the impulse toward victory had clearly shifted from Carter to Ford. Dick Cheney, one of the president's campaign strategists, informed Ford on 30 September that the latest polls showed him "closing the gap in the South." A member of the White House staff, Doug Bailey, commented that the "President's major opportunity to win the election" was the second debate, set for 6 October in San Francisco."[19] The first encounter had concentrated on the domestic economy, but the second would cover foreign policy and defense issues. Ford staffers expected the second debate to be the trump card of the president's campaign. Ford would characterize his foreign policy as one of peace through strength. Because of the military might of the United States and its allies, his administration had been able to lower the level of tension with the Soviet Union. In fact, as a result of his policies, the danger of war in central Europe had been greatly reduced, Berlin was no longer a source of constant friction, and limitations had been placed on the size of the Soviet nuclear arsenal. All this would make the president appear the more statesmanlike of the two candidates.[20]

The plan backfired. Predictably, Carter was much more aggressive in the second debate, accusing Ford of showing "an absence of leadership and an absence of a grasp of what this country is and what it ought to be." Ford countered by charging that his Democratic opponent would cut the defense budget by $15 billion (actually, Carter had proposed a $5 billion to $7 billion cut). But then Ford made what proved to be the great gaffe of the campaign. In response to a question about eastern Europe, he said that there was "no Soviet domination of eastern Europe, and there never will be under a Ford administration."

The query about eastern Europe was not unexpected. Anticipating that it would be raised at some point in the debate, the president's staff had carefully prepared a response for him. "The peoples of Europe," he was supposed to say, "have a right to freedom and national independence, and the United States has not, and will not abandon them." However, in longhand, Ford had added the following note to the briefing materials he had received: "No Soviet sphere of influence in eastern Europe. Agreement borders cannot be changed by force." Apparently, Ford had simply misread or misinterpreted the information provided by his staff.[21]

Ford's mistake disrupted the momentum of his campaign and brought an abrupt halt to his improved showing in the polls. A survey conducted immediately after the debate found a majority of voters still planning to vote for Ford over Carter (54 percent versus 36 percent). But as reporters pressed Ford to clarify his remarks, which were now blazoned in the headlines, the seriousness of his blunder became apparent. In another poll conducted the following night, Carter was *leading* Ford by almost the same percentage (54 percent to 37 percent) he had been trailing the president a day earlier. Democrats (although not Carter) had argued that Ford was not smart enough to be president, and his gaffe about eastern Europe seemed to prove that. Moreover, his remarks cost him heavily among ethnic Catholics, many of whom still had families in eastern Europe.[22]

Ford's comments also galvanized Carter's candidacy. The Democratic challenger stayed permanently on the offensive, even accusing the president of being "brainwashed" on eastern Europe. In his third and final debate with Ford on 22 October at Williamsburg, Virginia, Carter seemed more quick-witted and sharper than the president, who appeared distraught and agitated. Although Ford made no great errors, almost all observers agreed that Carter had outperformed him.

Even so, the race was not over yet. Ford had defused his blunder over eastern Europe somewhat by acknowledging his mistake. What he had meant to say, he remarked, was that he would not concur in Soviet domination of the region. In addition, the fuzziness label still worked with great effectiveness. During a whistle-stop train ride through Illinois, Ford said of Carter, "He wavers, he wanders, he wiggles, and he waffles and he shouldn't be President of the United States." The president hammered away at this theme with some success for the remainder of the campaign, assisted by the specter of the infamous *Playboy* interview.

As election day drew near, the polls indicated a virtual dead heat between the two candidates. On the morning of the election, the Harris poll placed Carter ahead by 1 percentage point; the Gallup poll had him trailing by the same amount. The candidates' own surveys showed that neither of them had generated much excitement or aroused intense loyalty among the voters. The "vast number of voters," commented Jerald ter Horst, a Ford campaign staffer, "have looked at the two men and see no practical difference." Indeed, if there was a consensus in the country, it was that these two candidates were not the best the parties had to offer the voters.

As the polls predicted, the election proved to be one of the closest in the nation's history. Carter won with about 41 million popular votes (50.1 percent) to Ford's 39 million (48 percent). In the electoral contest, Carter received 297 to Ford's 240. However tiny his margin of victory, the once obscure former governor of Georgia had beaten all the odds by running against Washington. The question now was whether he could make a smooth transition from political outsider to presidential helmsman.

2

★ ★ ★ ★ ★

TRANSITION AND HONEYMOON

At first glance, it appeared that Jimmy Carter had won the presidency by restoring the old political coalition established by Franklin Roosevelt forty years earlier but crumbling since the 1950s. Like Roosevelt, Carter carried the South as well as the big industrial cities of the North and upper Midwest. For the first time in almost twenty-five years, Democrats captured every southern and border state except Virginia. Organized labor, which had deserted the Democratic Party in the presidential election of 1972, went strongly Democratic in 1976 and handed Carter about 62 percent of its vote. Blacks also turned out in record numbers to support the Democratic candidate, casting five out of every six of their ballots for him. Without the union and black vote, Carter would have lost the election.

In several respects, however, Carter's coalition bore little resemblance to Roosevelt's. In the 1930s, for example, it was a white South that had supported FDR, since most blacks were disenfranchised then. But in 1976 it was the black South that made the difference for Carter. The majority of white southerners voted for Ford, although not as many as had supported Republicans in 1968 and 1972. Similarly, both union and nonunion labor had voted for Roosevelt; in 1976 nonunion workers voted for Ford (52 percent) over Carter (48 percent). Finally, Roosevelt had enjoyed stronger support from Catholics than Carter did.

Indeed, in an election in which Carter defeated Ford by a margin of less than 2 percent, the president-elect owed a good part of his victory to Republican crossovers. For example, he had solid backing from professional and business groups, particularly among younger voters, whose members typically cast their ballots for Republicans. Even more important, he cut into normally Republican terrain in rural Protestant areas. Although Ford garnered a higher percentage of the Catholic vote than had historically been given to Republican candidates, he could not match Carter's gains among rural Protestants. This was especially true in the South, where pride in a native son blended with shared religious beliefs to reduce the majorities that Republicans had won among white voters in earlier presidential elections. Together with the black vote, a return of white southerners to the Democratic Party assured Carter of a larger share of the vote (54 percent) than any Democratic candidate had received since 1948—and twice George McGovern's share four years earlier.

Carter's inroads were not limited to the South. His ethical convictions and religious passion had great national appeal, especially among fellow evangelical Protestants. Although many Americans, especially religious minorities, found his publicly stated commitment to Christian principles worrisome, many others were attracted to his call for a spiritual reawakening after a decade in which the integrity and morality of the nation's political leaders had come under fire.

The nature of Carter's victory had important implications for his presidency. In the first place, Carter lacked a political mandate from the American people. Not only had the election been close, but a record number of voters, apparently unimpressed with either of the two major candidates, had not cast their ballots. Only in the Deep South was voter turnout larger than in 1972. And different constituencies expected different things from the president-elect. Professional people tended to be economic conservatives, while blacks were more likely to put economic growth—especially jobs—and civil rights ahead of other concerns. Similarly, younger voters were generally more interested in such issues as the environment and quality of life than were older voters, who turned their attention to matters involving health and Social Security. Organized labor, which had conducted a massive get-out-the-vote campaign, had its own agenda for the new president, which included a broad program of social welfare legislation and measures to stimulate the economy. Given Carter's narrow victory and his ambiguous platform, each of these constituencies could—and did—take credit for his election. They also anticipated his unequivocal support for their particular interests, even when they conflicted with one another or with Carter's own legislative proposals.

There were already several indications that the new president would have trouble persuading Congress to approve his programs. Although Democrats maintained their two-to-one majority in the House and their three-to-two majority in the Senate, most of the House members had assumed office since 1972, and nearly one-fifth of the senators were newly elected. Because Carter had campaigned as much against the Washington establishment as against the Republican Party, few members of the new Congress felt politically obligated to him. Lawmakers gained and held office more by building personal organizations than by being staunch Democrats or Republicans. In addition, recent institutional changes on Capitol Hill limited the authority of hitherto powerful committee chairmen while augmenting that of more junior subcommittee heads.

Strong personal rivalries among leading Democrats in the House and Senate complicated the problem of party loyalty. Just before Carter took office, a bitter battle for House majority leader had pitted Philip Burton of California against Richard Bolling of Missouri and Jim Wright of Texas. Although Wright emerged the winner, Burton and Bolling had been the favorites going into the voting. Burton, as head of the Democratic Caucus, had spearheaded the reform movement in the House; Bolling, another reformer and one of the intellectuals of the House, despised the coarse and abrasive lawmaker from California. That Wright, the underdog in the contest, emerged the winner was due to the fact that Bolling was eliminated in a second round of balloting and the presumptive Speaker of the House, Thomas "Tip" O'Neill, quietly lobbied against Burton, whom he disliked and distrusted. But almost as soon as he lost to Wright, Burton began planning to challenge him again in the 96th Congress (1979–1980). In the Senate, Henry Jackson of Washington, chairman of the Energy Committee, frequently battled with Russell Long of Louisiana, chairman of the Finance Committee, who openly acknowledged his commitment to protecting his state's oil interests. Both Democrats were skillful lawmakers well versed in the art of hardball politics. So was majority leader Robert Byrd of West Virginia, who was a master of the arcane rules of the Senate and highly protective of its prerogatives. Taken together, the structural changes and interpersonal rivalries on Capitol Hill meant that Carter faced an increasingly independent, divided, and even intractable Congress and a decline in the cohesiveness of the legislative process.

The flip side of a more assertive Congress was an increasingly encumbered presidency. As early as 1960, Harvard University professor Richard Neustadt had written that presidential power to reverse policy direction was limited by political and bureaucratic barriers and scarce resources. In response to the Vietnam War, the Watergate scandal, and charges of an "imperial presidency," Congress enacted legislation in the 1970s that further circumscribed the authority of the Oval Office. For example, the War Powers Act of 1973, approved over President Richard Nixon's veto, curtailed the president's power to engage in military action abroad without congressional consent; that same year, Congress banned funds for combat activities in Indochina. In 1974 Congress responded to Nixon's attempts to impound appropriated funds by passing legislation forcing him to release the funds. This was part of a larger overhaul of the entire budgetary procedure—including the establishment of new House and Senate budget committees and a Congressional Budget Office—intended to give Congress greater control over government spending. In the meantime, in response to Nixon's support for repressive governments abroad, lawmakers passed resolutions calling for the denial of economic or military aid to nations violating human rights. Between 1975 and 1976 Congress added teeth to those resolutions, passing laws requiring the president to curtail economic and military assistance to repressive regimes.

Congress's determination to redress what it considered an imbalance between the executive and legislative branches of government posed a formidable challenge for the incoming president. Indeed, to some observers, there was a fundamental question as to just how governable the United States was when Carter entered the White House. In 1974 the National Academy of Public Administration and the Committee for Economic Development cosponsored a three-day conference, attended by some of the nation's leading authorities on the presidency, to discuss the problems associated with governing the nation. Their final report contained more than 140 recommendations for improving the institutional relationships among the Oval Office, Congress, the press, the federal bureaucracy, state and local governments, the major political parties, and the public. "A president confronts a splintered and shell-shocked nation," commented Ernest S. Griffith of the Library of Congress in summarizing the conference's suggestions.[1]

The next year, political scientist Thomas E. Cronin published a highly praised volume on the state of the presidency in which he asserted that the American public expected more than the president could deliver in terms of making the nation a better place to live. The presidency was an "under-defined institution" constitutionally and historically, and the American people seemed to want a strong and effective chief executive who was also open and democratic. Yet these worthy objectives were not always compatible. The public also longed for leadership but was skeptical of the nation's leaders. Indeed, Cronin pointed to a fundamental dilemma of the presidency: "A president will always have too much power for the realization of that cherished ideal—government by the people—yet never enough to solve all the problems we expect him to solve." In addition, he is "asked to represent the unrepresented and the under-represented, yet he [is] expected to be responsive to the electoral majority."[2]

Paradoxically, though, the 1970s represented the end of what historian Bruce L. Schulman called the "great American ride" and a revolt against most forms of authority, including governmental authority. Carter had run on an anti-Washington campaign, but the revolt against authority ran much deeper than that. The counterculture, so often identified with the 1960s, actually burgeoned in the 1970s, represented in every manner from long, shaggy hair to outrageous fashions and challenges to traditional sexual mores. Alongside this counterculture were a libertarian ethic, a renewed faith in the marketplace, the evangelical Christian movement that Carter had successfully tapped into, and a renascent conservative political movement—all manifested in Ronald Reagan's nearly successful bid for the Republican presidential nomination as well as Carter's own campaign for president.[3]

Another complication for Carter was the widely held perception that he was inexperienced. Even his own advisers acknowledged his image problem, in part the result of a campaign that had been more about style than substance; the upshot was that most Americans still did not know where he stood on the issues. According to all the polls, the public's greatest concern was the state of the economy. Despite a drop in the inflation rate from about 12 percent in 1974 to around 6 percent by the end of 1976, the economy remained sluggish. The nation's output of goods and services (the gross national product [GNP]) had risen at an annual rate of only 3 percent during the last three months of 1976, the lowest since the spring of 1975. Unemployment also stood at a high 7.8 percent of the workforce; to lower that figure, economists estimated that the GNP would have to grow at an annual rate of at least 4 percent.

The media, which had helped invent Carter as a national figure, posed another obstacle to his presidency. The press had become more assertive in its investigatory role since the Watergate affair, and the image projected by the president even became the topic of late-night television. As historian Lewis L. Gould observed, "presidential celebrity" became "a major element of the modern presidency and a long-term weakness as well." Parodies of Gerald Ford's alleged clumsiness, despite the fact that he was a physically fit former athlete, helped undermine his stature as president. During the campaign, a discernible hostility developed between the press corps covering Carter and the candidate, with reporters pressing him for specifics on his vague policy proposals and noting that he tailored his message differently for white and black audiences.[4]

Disturbing demographic trends also confronted Carter as he prepared to take office. In 1976 the United States was a nation of about 215 million people, with 158 million living in urban areas with populations of 50,000 or more. The fastest growing segment of the population was the elderly. Since 1970 the number of children under age ten had declined by 5.5 million, while the size of the population aged sixty-five and over had grown by 3 million, or 14.8 percent; more than 10 percent of the population was now in this age group. These statistics meant rapidly rising costs for Social Security and health care. The number of people living below the poverty level also continued to grow, from 11.2 percent in 1974 to 12.5

percent in 1976, and a staggering 50 percent of all black female heads of households fell into this category. Overall, the nation's social safety net was distended by tremendous strains.

The United States was also a nation on the move—mostly to the Sun Belt. The population of the thirteen states of the West and the sixteen states of the South had grown by about 9 percent over the last five years, compared with a 2 percent growth for the rest of the nation. Similarly, most urban centers of the North and East had either declined in population or increased only marginally; the fifteen fastest growing metropolitan areas were in Florida, Texas, Arizona, and Colorado. These population shifts contributed to a deepening blight in the nation's oldest and largest cities and an ongoing erosion of the traditional power base of the Democratic Party. Paralleling the urban trauma was the havoc inflicted on the environment. Natural habitats for wildlife continued to shrink as a result of such activities as drainage projects and subdivisions of western lands for mining and logging. Three million acres of farmland and 4 billion tons of topsoil were being lost each year as a result of urbanization, flooding, and wind and water erosion.

Finally, the political nation was moving toward what Harvard University professor Samuel H. Beer later referred to as a "new and destructive pluralism"—that is, a society of organized groups bound together by common goals, represented by professional lobbyists, and relying on public authority to support or actively promote their private interests. As Beer described this development, the centralizing tendencies of a burgeoning federal bureaucracy were being offset by the fragmentation inherent in specialized knowledge, economic and political differences, and growing tolerance of social and cultural diversity. Within the multitude of groups arising out of this process, it was difficult to build lasting coalitions based on shared views of public policy. Leaders of these groups looked to Washington for leadership and direction and were aggrieved when Washington fell short. But they were concerned more with problem solving than with matters of public philosophy and national purpose.[5]

Yet the institutional and demographic developments that Carter faced were not entirely dismal. The American people were better educated, held down more white-collar jobs, and took home higher salaries than ever before. Between 1970 and 1976 the number of high school students increased from 14.4 million to 15.8 million, or 8.9 percent, and the number of college students rose from 7.1 million to 9.7 million, or 26.8 percent. During this same period the number of white-collar workers increased by about 3 percent each year, while the number of blue-collar workers decreased by about the same amount. In addition, median family income nearly doubled between 1970 and 1976 (although, because of inflation, this represented only about a 3 percent gain in real purchasing power).

Despite the Vietnam War, the Watergate scandal and other evidence of corruption in high government places, and the revolt against authority in the 1970s, surveys also showed that Americans retained their faith in the nation's basic institutions and were anxious to "feel good about things" again. Although the president was beleaguered and some of the president's authority had diminished, he still wielded enormous power in terms of setting the nation's agenda and priorities and marking its direction. "The promise of the American presidency may have been oversold, overstated, and stretched beyond reality," Cronin observed in 1975, "but denying the importance and the need for presidential leadership would be to overstate the case, as well as misleading." Finally, the American people tended to see the president-elect as a potentially stronger and more decisive leader than President Ford had been. Carter would bring a new way of doing business to the government; he would be a practical "anti-politician" truly concerned about doing something for the "average person."[6]

Even on Capitol Hill there were circumstances that augured well for the incoming Democratic president. Over the past fifty years, conservative southern Democrats and northern Republicans in the House had combined to defeat legislation sponsored by more liberal Democratic presidents. But since 1958, southern Democrats had been losing their seats to Republicans, while outside the South, mostly liberal Democrats had replaced Republicans. Meanwhile, the changes spearheaded by the Democratic Caucus, which included limiting the power of committee chairmen, had actually increased the authority of the top Democratic leadership. This was especially true for the Speaker, who was now in charge of committee assignments and had the exclusive right to appoint the powerful Rules Committee, which controlled the flow of legislation onto the House floor. As presidential scholar Nelson Polsby noted, "Congressional reform devolved not only downward . . . but also upward," and the outcome was "an increased potential for favorable results for any President willing to work with the congressional leadership in establishing legislative priorities and strategies."[7]

The president-elect's pollster, Pat Caddell, explained many of these demographic and structural developments to Carter in a fifty-five-page postmortem on the election. He also warned Carter of some of the political obstacles that awaited him, including opposition on Capitol Hill from such Democrats as Edward Kennedy, George McGovern, and Morris Udall—all of whom Caddell described as "traditional Democrats . . . in many ways . . . as antiquated and anachronistic a group as are conservative Republicans." Although he advised Carter to seek good relations with these liberals, he also recommended that the Democratic National Committee (DNC) be "'Carterized' and made a political wing of the

White House" and that the president use the DNC "to reward supporters [and] co-opt adversaries." As for the economic issues confronting the new administration, he told Carter not to handle them by "resort[ing] to old Democratic dogmas," which, he said, no longer appealed to younger and more prosperous voters. Instead, he urged the new president to "devise a context that [was] neither traditionally liberal nor traditionally conservative" but rather that cut "across traditional ideology." Indeed, Caddell was concerned almost as much with questions of ideology and the administration's long-term plans for the country as he was with more pressing economic and political matters.

Yet Caddell's lengthy report was flawed in several important aspects. First, although he believed that, to succeed, the new president would have to provide an "articulated vision" of where the country was going, he failed to offer Carter any sense of what that vision should be or what ideological perspective should guide his leadership. He also ignored such fundamental considerations as the interests and priorities of the congressional leadership, and although he encouraged Carter to focus his attention on legislative issues that would have "the greatest impact on the public," he never articulated these issues for the president or placed them in the context of long-range goals. Nevertheless, Carter digested the report carefully, described it as "excellent," and ordered that it be read by his other political advisers. In fact, the legislative and political course that the new president pursued was the one Caddell had laid out for him.[8]

Soon after his primary victory in Pennsylvania, Carter had followed the recommendation of Jack Watson, a young attorney who had worked for him in Georgia as chairman of the Department of Human Resources, and established a policy planning organization to prepare for his transition from candidate to president should he win in November. Over the summer and fall, a group headed by Watson produced a series of briefing books and option papers on the issues most likely to confront an incoming Carter administration; they were transmitted to Carter at the end of October—a week before the election. The most important of these was a paper on the budget, in which the transition team asserted that it was possible to fulfill campaign promises of holding government spending down and balancing the budget by fiscal year 1981. In fact, the writers projected a budget surplus in 1981 of $52 billion.

Like the Caddell postmortem, however, the budget memorandum was deficient in several respects. First, it made light of the fact that achieving a $50 billion to $60 billion budget surplus by 1981, even under optimal economic conditions, would require a policy of fiscal restraint that was certain to cause confrontation with liberal Democrats on Capitol Hill. Second, it assumed a 5.5 percent to 6 percent annual growth in GNP and a decline in the inflation rate from 6 percent to 5 percent by 1981.

Even Charles Schultze, Carter's chairman-designate of the Council of Economic Advisers (CEA), conceded that these goals were "optimistic."[9]

Besides drafting policy papers for a Carter presidency, the Watson group concerned itself with staffing the new administration, and its involvement in this process provided an early insight into a recurring problem of the Carter administration: weak or conflicting delegation of authority. Although the Watson team reviewed the résumés of thousands of potential Carter appointees, the president-elect never gave it exclusive responsibility for staffing. As a result, much of its work was duplicated in a separate operation at the DNC. Making matters worse, Hamilton Jordan wanted to be in charge of White House personnel. When Watson submitted a transition budget giving Jordan only one staff member, Jordan exploded, accusing Watson of trying to undercut him. The president-elect was finally forced to intervene. On 15 November he announced that Jordan would assume primary responsibility for presidential appointments, in effect, stripping Watson of much of his power.

Selection of cabinet and other high administration officials also proceeded slowly, in part because Carter insisted on lengthy review procedures, including consideration of at least one minority and one woman for each cabinet-level post. For more than three weeks the president-elect remained virtually sequestered in his home in Plains, examining dossiers and checking references for each key position within the new administration. Not until December, exactly one month after the election, did he announce his first appointments. He named his close friend, Atlanta banker Bert Lance, as director of the Office of Management and Budget (OMB) and chose former defense official Cyrus Vance as secretary of state. A week later he selected the chief executive of the Bendix Corporation, Michael Blumenthal, as treasury secretary and decided on Washington congressman Brock Adams as secretary of transportation. Other appointments soon followed: former budget director Charles Schultze as chairman of the CEA; Columbia University professor Zbigniew Brzezinski as national security adviser; Harold Brown, president of the California Institute of Technology, as secretary of defense; Georgia congressman Andrew Young as ambassador to the United Nations; and Idaho governor Cecil Andrus as secretary of the interior. But not until the beginning of January, when Carter named Theodore Sorensen, former aide to President John F. Kennedy, as director of the Central Intelligence Agency (CIA) and former defense secretary James Schlesinger as his presidential assistant for energy, were all the top positions in the Carter administration finally filled. Of the newly elected presidents since 1952, Carter was the slowest in choosing his cabinet.

The problems caused by the long delay in selecting cabinet and White House personnel cannot be overemphasized. As a number of eminent presidential scholars have pointed out, the first few months of an incoming administration can set the tone for much of what follows. Stephen Hess of the Brookings Institution, who advised Carter during the transition, suggested that as a "handy rule of thumb," an incoming administration should have its White House staff in place by Thanksgiving and its cabinet secretaries announced by Christmas.[10]

Many of these same scholars have made another point—one that Carter's close friends and advisers Charles Kirbo and Bert Lance, as well as other administration officials, recognized later: the need for a chief of staff. Kirbo thought that one of Carter's biggest mistakes as president was not appointing Jack Watson (Kirbo's law partner) as chief of staff immediately upon taking office. Although Kirbo appreciated the role that Hamilton Jordan and press secretary Jody Powell had played in getting Carter elected, he believed that they were still "young boys that hadn't fully developed." Jordan, he rightly thought, lacked both the interest and the attention to detail required by the position. Kirbo believed that Watson would have made an excellent chief of staff and described him as the best young lawyer his firm had ever developed as a partner. He later regretted not pushing harder to convince the president to appoint Watson, but he had been afraid of jeopardizing his effectiveness in the new administration by promoting his former partner over someone like Jordan, who was much closer to the incoming president and was also known as a tough political infighter.[11]

Carter was willing to have Kirbo or Jordan serve as chief of staff, even though the concept of a keeper of the gate, inherent in the position, was contrary to the president-elect's desire to give senior staff and cabinet members ready access to the Oval Office. But Jordan, who understood his limitations as an administrator, did not want the job, and Kirbo turned the offer down, believing that he could not afford the financial sacrifice involved in giving up his law practice and moving his family to Washington.[12]

The incoming president did not offer the job to anyone else. Perhaps because of Jordan's influence, Carter had reservations about Watson, who would have liked the position of chief of staff but never exerted as much influence as did other members of the senior staff. As for appointing someone other than one of his inner circle of advisers from Georgia, Carter believed that it would have been "improper [and] inconsistent to bring an outsider in as a leader of all these people who had been with me since I was a young politician."[13]

Instead of having a strong chief of staff to control and regulate the vital arteries of communication between the Oval Office and the rest of the administration—as had H. R. Haldeman during the Nixon administration and, to a lesser extent, Richard Cheney and Donald Rumsfeld during the

Ford administration—Carter announced a "spokes-in-the-wheel" system for his White House staff, intending to give his cabinet secretaries direct access to him. But without a chief of staff, who would ultimately be responsible for running the White House? For delegating authority? For protecting the president's time and energy? For watching over the flow of paper to and from the Oval Office? Decisions on these and similar structural questions had not been made when Carter took the oath of office on 20 January.

In assembling his administration, the president-elect made a concerted effort to appoint blacks and women to high government positions, as he had promised during the campaign. It proved to be a harder task than he expected, however, because several prominent blacks, including mayors Thomas Bradley of Los Angeles and Coleman Young of Detroit, declined offers to join the Carter team. But he was eventually able to persuade two women to join his cabinet: Patricia Harris (who was also black), a former dean of Howard Law School, as secretary of housing and urban development, and Duke University vice president Juanita Kreps as commerce secretary.

Carter was less successful in opening the administration door to Washington outsiders. Among his cabinet appointments, only Ray Marshall, a University of Texas economist named as Carter's secretary of labor, could be regarded as a genuine newcomer to Washington. Most of the other "unknowns" were fellow Georgians who were already being referred to by some as the "Georgia Mafia." In addition to Bert Lance, the new faces included Hamilton Jordan as chief staff aide and the president's most trusted adviser; Jody Powell as press secretary; Stuart Eizenstat as head of the Domestic Policy Staff, responsible for providing Carter with options on major domestic policy issues; Jack Watson as cabinet secretary; and Atlanta judge Griffin Bell as attorney general.

Aside from these Georgians and a few others, the top positions in the Carter administration, including the three most important posts—state, defense, and treasury—went to individuals with considerable Washington experience. Vance was a former secretary of the army and deputy secretary of defense under presidents Kennedy and Johnson and a successful Washington lawyer; he epitomized the Washington establishment. Brown had also served under Kennedy and Johnson, first as director of research at the Pentagon and then as secretary of the air force. Blumenthal had served from 1961 to 1967 as deputy assistant secretary of state for economic affairs and as chairman of the U.S. delegation to the Kennedy round of tariff negotiations at Geneva.

In picking his cabinet, the president isolated himself from the diversity of viewpoints that might have better informed his leadership and furnished the White House with a broader perspective. As it was, he chose

Vance, Brown, Blumenthal, and most of the rest of his cabinet-level officials not because they were original thinkers, grand strategists, or innovative planners but because he respected their managerial talents, believed they would be skilled negotiators, felt they could be relied on for sound advice, and thought they would follow instructions from the Oval Office. Although he surrounded himself with valued subordinates in good management style, Carter had spent so much time choosing his administration that he had neglected executive policy planning; nor, as a manager, had he implemented efficient procedures or delegated authority along clearly established organizational lines.

For a politician who had been remarkably successful in defying the odds by winning the White House, Carter also displayed lapses in political judgment. His appointment of Griffin Bell as attorney general stirred up a hornet's nest because of Bell's decisions in earlier desegregation cases and his membership in two segregated social clubs. The transition team at the Department of Justice had warned the president-elect of the outcry that would follow Bell's nomination and had recommended that he choose someone who was more "respected by responsible minority leaders." But Carter refused even to meet with civil rights leaders to discuss the appointment.[14]

Ten weeks after the election, Carter remained a veiled figure. During the campaign he had often been referred to as a Populist—a voice of the people outside the mainstream of American politics who promised to rid Washington of its entrenched leadership, seek justice for the common people, and eradicate concentrations of political and economic power. In reality, the new president was closer to the Progressives than the Populists, attempting to make government more competent and more rational. Like the Progressives of the early twentieth century, he stood for responsible and efficient government, spoke out against vested interest groups, and talked about the importance of subordinating self-interest to a broader national interest. Similarly, he assumed that those who opposed his programs acted from selfish motives rather than from their own perception of the public good. Thus he was loath to compromise on what he regarded as matters of principle. Envisioning himself as a trustee of the public welfare, he also perceived one of his major tasks as president to be that of arousing the public conscience. But he was not a social reformer seeking fundamental changes. Trained as an engineer, he emphasized solving problems rather than articulating a public philosophy. As a result, when the new administration undertook a vast array of initiatives in its first few months in office, it did so without any well-articulated sense of direction or long-term objective.

From the time Carter assumed office on 20 January, he was warned by his own White House staff to proceed slowly and set priorities in de-

veloping his legislative program. But the president ignored these admonitions. "Everybody has warned me not to take on too many projects so early in the administration, but it's almost impossible for me to delay something that I see needs to be done," he noted in his diary a week after taking office.[15]

As a result, Carter presented the 95th Congress with a legislative docket whose passage would have taxed the political skills of any president, much less one as unfamiliar with Washington's modus operandi as Carter. Among the proposals he submitted to the new Congress during his first six months in office were cuts in water projects, a measure to establish an agency for consumer affairs, executive reorganization authority, programs of urban and welfare reform, an ethics in government bill, changes in Social Security, hospital cost containment legislation, a bill to create a Department of Energy, and a comprehensive energy program.

Of the programs Carter sent to Capitol Hill, however, none was more important than a package designed to stimulate the sluggish economy by giving all citizens a $50 tax rebate, cutting corporate taxes by $900 million, and allocating modest increases in public works and other job-creating programs. The president's plan underscored a shift in his economic philosophy. During the campaign Carter had defined the most serious economic problem facing the nation as the high rate of unemployment. Yet as president-elect and newly installed president, he emphasized the need to avoid a reacceleration of the inflation rate, largely through budgetary restraint. When his domestic policy adviser Stu Eizenstat sent him a proposed package of legislation just four days after he took the oath of office, Carter's only handwritten comment was "Hold line on budget."[16]

The administration's program reflected Carter's own admitted fiscal conservatism. On other issues, such as civil rights, the environment, and "helping people overcome handicaps to lead fruitful lives," he claimed to be "quite liberal," but this proved to be an untenable dichotomy. Carter's stance raised real questions about achieving "liberal" ends through "conservative" means—for example, could he help people overcome handicaps without greater fiscal expenditures? Politically, it challenged powerful elements within Carter's own party, who denied that liberal ends could be reached by conservative means without distorting those ends—for example, if his proposals defined "handicaps" so as to exclude people lacking basic job skills.[17]

The response to Carter's economic package exposed the dissonance within Democratic ranks. Reaction ranged from mixed to negative, with the sharpest attacks coming from groups that had mobilized behind Carter during the campaign. The U.S. Conference of Mayors said that his proposals did not do enough to help the cities. Seeking a much larger package, including a $30 billion public works program for 1977 alone, the

AFL-CIO called the plan "a retreat from the goals we understand President-elect Carter to have set during last year's election campaign." Although Carter worked hard on Capitol Hill to sell his ideas, lawmakers were highly critical of the administration for relying too heavily on a tax refund to stimulate the economy instead of bringing down the unemployment rate by creating more public-sector jobs. Yielding to the criticism that a rebate given to high-income taxpayers had no real economic benefit, the administration agreed to limit the refund to people with incomes of less than $30,000. However, the basic suspicion persisted that such tax measures would not be enough to energize the economy.[18]

By March 1977 organized labor was in open rebellion against the administration, not only because it disliked Carter's economic stimulus package but also because it had not received White House backing on a number of other issues, including an increase in the minimum wage from $2.30 to $3.00 an hour. Labor leaders were also disappointed that the president had given only lukewarm support to a common situs picketing bill, which would have allowed a union striking against a single subcontractor to shut down an entire construction site. According to Lane Kirkland, secretary-treasurer of the AFL-CIO, Carter had simply failed to keep his campaign promises to "working people."[19]

Contrary to Kirkland's contention, Carter was neither unmindful of nor unsympathetic to labor's interests. But his primary concern was with the unorganized, bottom rung of the labor market rather than the more highly paid union members. In addition to agreeing to a more modest, twenty-cent increase in the minimum wage, he took a strong stand against a proposed "split" that would have set a lower minimum for employees not covered by federal minimum wage laws before 1966 (primarily service and farm workers and individuals in the retail and wholesale trades). "The differential hurts the most vulnerable workers," he told Eizenstat. Despite the support of most of his economic advisers, the proposal was still unacceptable to him.[20]

Carter also had difficulties in his relations with Capitol Hill. In December the president-elect had come to Washington to confer with President Ford and leaders of the new Congress. In a private conversation with Carter, House Speaker Tip O'Neill lectured him on the need to separate the rhetoric of the campaign from the reality of the legislative process. But according to O'Neill, "Carter didn't seem to understand." On the contrary, Carter told the Massachusetts congressman that, as governor of Georgia, he had taken his message to the people when the state legislature had blocked him; if, as president, he faced a similar situation with Congress, he would not hesitate to employ the same methods. He later repeated that statement to a group of lawmakers, telling them, "I can talk to your constituents easier than you can."[21]

The new president also provoked many lawmakers when, immediately after he took office, he honored a campaign promise to pardon Vietnam War draft evaders. Republican senator Barry Goldwater of Arizona was enraged and described Carter's action as "the most disgraceful thing that a President has ever done." His nomination of Theodore Sorensen to head the CIA also caused considerable consternation. Because Sorensen had registered for the draft as a conscientious objector and had admitted to removing classified information without authorization while working at the Kennedy White House, even liberal Democrats opposed his appointment. Foreseeing certain defeat in the Senate, the president withdrew the nomination—but only after the whole episode had turned very nasty, warning of things to come.[22]

Nowhere was the early conflict between the White House and Capitol Hill more evident than in the flap over Carter's announcement at the end of February 1977 that he was targeting a number of dam and water projects (his so-called hit list) for possible elimination in the fiscal year 1978 budget. Again, his action arose from a campaign pledge—this time, to end waste and pork-barrel projects in the federal government. Unfortunately for Carter, pork-barrel politics had been sacrosanct on Capitol Hill for many decades. Lawmakers also viewed the hit list as further evidence of the president's political indifference to Congress. Even Carter acknowledged that his new administration had sometimes "inadvertently" given Congress cause for complaint by not conferring with the congressional leadership.[23]

By April, Congress and the president were at loggerheads over the water projects. Although Carter modified his hit list by dropping some items and adding others, and although he promised to meet with lawmakers "to establish a dialogue and close cooperation in this issue," he was determined to excise the remaining projects. "Prepare dam project statement listing those which will be eliminated or cutback," he instructed Eizenstat. "In every case, itemize objections in strongest terms." Congress responded by soundly defeating (252 to 143) an administration-sponsored amendment to cut $100 million of funding for water projects from the budget.[24]

Relations between the president and lawmakers on Capitol Hill became even more strained after Carter announced unexpectedly on 14 April that he was rescinding his administration's proposal for a $50 tax rebate. The president had intended the measure as a one-time expedient to energize the economy, but since the economic picture continued to improve after he took office, there seemed less need for it. Nevertheless, the decision to drop the tax rebate angered congressional leaders who had agreed to back the White House despite their own reservations. "It was a little less than fair to those of us who supported it against our better judgment and worked hard to get it passed," complained Al Ullman, chairman of the House Ways and Means Committee.[25]

By early spring, therefore, Carter had already alienated many groups that had been instrumental in his election and whose support he needed if his legislative programs were to succeed. Yet the president remained extremely popular with the American public. Before he took office, his advisers had told him that, as president, he should project himself in the same way he had as a candidate—as a political outsider committed to restoring to government the values that had been the basis of the United States' greatness as a nation. Vice President–elect Walter Mondale also recommended that he present himself as a leader "who is close to the people, who cares about their problems and is determined to give them a government that is courteous, compassionate, and helpful."[26] This advice dovetailed nicely with Carter's own commitment to an open and accessible administration and to his belief in direct dialogue with the American people as a way of getting public support.

Accordingly, Carter authorized an extensive public-relations campaign after taking office that would portray him as a "citizen-president" and a champion of traditional American values. Breaking with the pomp and circumstance surrounding the presidency, he disposed of most of the White House's fleet of limousines, ended the practice of having "Hail to the Chief" played whenever the president made a public appearance, placed his nine-year-old daughter, Amy, in a predominantly black public elementary school, and carried his own suit bag whenever he traveled.

Carter also approved a "People Program" that included fireside chats, radio call-ins, and town meetings, all designed to show the American people that their president was close to them and to allow him to gauge public opinion without intermediaries.[27] After holding a televised town meeting in Clinton, Massachusetts, on 16 March, the president spent the night at the home of a local family before traveling the next day to Charleston, West Virginia, for a grassroots discussion on energy problems. In addition to this outreach program, Carter insisted on weekly summaries of mail sent to him and the rest of the first family (and became angry at backlogs of unanswered mail), held twice-monthly press conferences, and even opened cabinet meetings to press coverage.

Furthermore, Carter placed great emphasis on what he had referred to during the campaign as "federalism," or shared decision making between Washington and local government. He encouraged regional and local advisory groups and regional meetings sponsored by federal officials. He also urged his cabinet to maintain close contact with governors, mayors, and other local officials. At the White House work got under way on a new urban and regional policy that included federal-local and public-private partnerships in urban development programs.

All this had great appeal for a nation whose people, according to commentator Hugh Sidey, were "looking for smaller dimensions [and] for more simplicity in their lives." Carter's popularity was reflected in the polls. A Gallup survey taken at the end of April gave Carter a 71 percent approval rating, while a Harris poll gauged the rating four points higher, at 75 percent.[28]

The president wielded his popularity to win congressional authorization to reorganize sectors of the federal bureaucracy. What made this victory so impressive was that it was achieved over the strong opposition of lawmakers who objected to the legislation's carte blanche, since it allowed Carter to revamp the executive branch without seeking Congress's preliminary approval. Even so, the first three months of the Carter administration were characterized more by brisk activity than by actual accomplishments. Besides developing a new urban development program based on Carter's concept of federalism, the administration was preparing a major message on the environment. In addition, the president ordered his staff and the cabinet to "be aggressive" in eliminating unnecessary advisory committees, regulations, and other paperwork.[29] He also endorsed proposals for universal voter registration and the establishment of a Consumer Protection Agency, and he named Esther Peterson, a leading proponent of consumer rights recommended by consumer-advocate Ralph Nader, as his special assistant for consumer affairs.

Aside from the economy, the most pressing legislative matter for the president was the nation's worsening energy crisis. Since the 1973 Yom Kippur War, the price of foreign oil had more than doubled, from about $6 to more than $12 a barrel. At the same time, U.S. dependence on foreign oil had risen from about 35 percent of its total supply to more than 50 percent. Virtually every public official, including the president, agreed that unless something was done to curb this energy appetite, the nation's future would be mortgaged to the oil producers of the Middle East.

The brutal winter of 1976–1977 underscored how critical the situation had become. Because of a shortage of natural gas, schools and factories throughout the nation were forced to close. According to White House estimates, by the end of January, as many as 400,000 workers had been laid off for a day or more since November as a result of fuel deficiencies. A number of states even declared energy emergencies. The administration responded to this crisis quickly and decisively. The Interstate Commerce Commission ordered railroads to give priority to oil tank cars and permitted trucks licensed to do business in only one state to cross state lines to deliver fuel. The Federal Energy Administration directed refineries to curtail the production of jet fuel in favor of heating oil. President Carter dramatized his own concern for the plight of the people hardest hit by the freeze by making a quick trip to ice-bound Pittsburgh and then declaring eleven states disaster areas.

In February the White House also asked for emergency authority to deregulate the price of gas piped across state lines. Because interstate gas was regulated at $1.44 per 1,000 cubic feet, but unregulated gas (that is, gas sold within the producing state) sold at $1.90 or more, pipeline companies preferred to sell their gas intrastate. Consequently, gas-producing states had plentiful supplies, while other states faced a fuel emergency. If interstate gas was sold at the market price instead of the regulated price, gas would flow to wherever it was most needed. Congress responded with inordinate speed. On 2 February, just six days after Carter had asked for deregulation authority, lawmakers passed the Emergency Natural Gas Act, giving the president what he wanted.

Meanwhile, the president struggled with the problem of how to get the American people to conserve energy. In his view, there had to be a significant increase in energy costs to discourage waste and to encourage the further development of national energy resources, yet the increase could not be so steep as to throw the nation into recession or even depression. Nor should the oil and gas producers be allowed to make such enormous profits that the American people would reject the program outright. Although the administration attached considerable importance to generating public support for such an energy plan, the actual drafting was done in great secrecy by Carter's energy adviser, James Schlesinger, and a small group of his assistants. The complex strategy they developed contained 113 separate provisions, the most important of which placed a tax on all domestic oil production and a standby gasoline tax each year gasoline consumption exceeded stated targets. The program also imposed a "gas-guzzler" tax on automobiles with low fuel efficiency, penalized heavy industrial users of oil and natural gas, and instituted tax credits and other incentives to encourage conservation. On 18 April the president spoke to the nation on energy, referring to his energy program as the "moral equivalent of war," a theme that had been suggested to him by Admiral Hyman Rickover.[30] Although some pundits later pointed out that the acronym for "moral equivalent of war" was "meow," the public response to his program was overwhelmingly favorable. "For the first time, a strong activist President has seized the initiative on energy," *Newsweek* later commented.[31]

Unfortunately, the energy program had been put together with such total disregard for any review process that it bristled with technical flaws and raised a number of questions, such as the effect of the gas-guzzler tax on the automobile industry, the inflationary impact of the standby gasoline tax, and the costs of converting from oil and natural gas to coal, as mandated by the legislation. Even Blumenthal and Schultze complained about having no opportunity to scrutinize the program. Hence, when the White House finally briefed House and Senate leaders on the plan, administration officials often contradicted one another on specific matters. But the president chose to blame his difficulties on the lobbying power of vested interest groups rather than on problems internal to his administration.

After three months, the Carter White House remained in an organizational tangle, with such fundamental questions as the delegation of authority and the administrative structure of the staff still largely unresolved. Complicating matters was the president's commitment to a form of government in which cabinet members were given an unusual amount of autonomy, including making subcabinet appointments without first clearing them through normal White House and congressional channels. Much of the friction with Capitol Hill came about as a result of this practice. Carter also failed to delineate clearly the authority of agencies whose purview overlapped, such as OMB, CEA, and the Treasury Department. As a result, competing interests often tried to win his support by offering the advice they thought he wanted to hear rather than recommendations worked out after careful deliberation. *"A great premium is placed on anticipating what you want instead of providing you with frank and hard analysis,"* Hamilton Jordan told the president in March.[32]

The president buried himself in an endless flow of paper, distancing himself from his own staff and curtailing his time for thought and reflection. Very little seemed to escape his attention. He sought information on the quantity and cost of ceremonial pens and other presidential mementos, decided that the number of pens given out at signing ceremonies should be limited to four, ordered cutbacks on the number of White House newspaper and magazine subscriptions, complained about the care of the White House and its grounds, and sought an explanation of the White House's "barber shop staffing/pay" situation. He also found time to pen a congratulatory note to actor Sylvester Stallone after watching his film *Rocky*, wrote a kind note to singer Pat Boone after Boone had apologized on a matter having to do with their shared religious beliefs, and instructed his staff to spend more time with their families and involve them as much as possible in the life of the White House.

When Carter first took office, he had anticipated a fifty-five-hour workweek, of which about fifteen hours would be spent reading and responding to the material in his "in box." By April his workweek had grown to about eighty hours, with more than thirty hours given over to paperwork. Consequently, by the time he delivered his energy message, his staff had become overwhelmed by the amount of paper circulating through the Oval Office. "Look, we are trying to do too much," Jody Powell finally told Carter in April, but to little avail.[33]

Undoubtedly, obtaining approval for a comprehensive energy policy would have been grueling for any person in the Oval Office. Opponents of the energy program had begun lobbying against it even before the president addressed the joint session of Congress. Critics denounced the package as being too complex, going too far, not going far enough, and not presenting an accurate picture of the energy industry. Carter might have undercut the opposition to his program by bringing congressional leaders—those who were more in touch with the political pulse on Capitol Hill than the president—into the preparation process and by seeking allies within the energy industry itself.

This is not to say that Carter did not try to establish good relations with Congress. In fact, early in his administration he had Speaker Tip O'Neill and majority leader Robert Byrd over to the private residence for dinner, and he did the same with other congressional leaders. More important, he spent countless hours with small and large groups of lawmakers in formal and less formal meetings, greeting them and explaining his policies to them. As the president correctly remarked after he left office, "Many nights when I was tired and would like to have relaxed, we had a supper for maybe a hundred members of the House and I would spend two hours in the East Room in a town meeting forum describing different elements of either domestic or foreign defense policy, answering their questions and either having Harold Brown or Brzezinski with me, if there was defense or foreign policy."[34] He was also diligent in using the telephone to call congressmen and senators seeking their support on matters of particular importance to him.

When Carter entertained at the White House, however, it took the form of an institutional function rather than personal engagement. He had neither the character nor the inclination to massage the egos of critical lawmakers by sharing a cocktail or engaging in banter with them or taking them into his confidence. He especially disliked participating in what he referred to as the Washington cocktail circuit. Conversely, he was reluctant to use the Oval Office to threaten or intimidate reluctant lawmakers or engage in the type of "in your face" politics and horse trading employed by Lyndon Johnson. As his close friend Bert Lance later remarked, Carter had developed "the idea that as long as he did what he thought was right and that he reached that decision based on what was in the best interest of the people . . . then those other things would fall into line."[35] Viewing himself as a trustee of the nation's welfare who had to keep his administration above the political fray and conduct it according to his perception of the national interest, he refused to engage in the type of power brokering that had been utilized by successful presidents since at least Woodrow Wilson.

There are certain parallels between Wilson and Carter that permit a highly instructive comparison. Both leaders were progressive southerners and devout Christians who believed in the gospel of service and considered political office a form of ministry. In contrast to Carter, however, Wilson had a clear sense of purpose. He also had a better grasp of the attainable and a better understanding of the negotiable and the expendable. Unalterably committed to certain basic values, Wilson could be cunning and devious in achieving his aims, but he understood that flexibility and compromise on specific issues did not entail the repudiation of fundamental principles. Hence, he managed to get Congress to pass a program of economic and social legislation that ranks his administration as one of the most productive in the nation's history.

Although Carter was by no means unaware of the realities of American politics and public life, in contrast to Wilson, his progressive mentality seemed to blind him to the fact that the special interests he assailed were a reflection of the pluralistic nature of American politics—that there was not a single constituency but an array of them, with often conflicting but legitimate interests. To rally support for his programs, he needed to be a creative and flexible leader with a well-articulated sense of purpose that commanded broad respect. This latter requirement, in particular, would pose a stumbling block throughout his four years in office.

3
★ ★ ★ ★ ★

MORALITY AND FOREIGN POLICY

Although President Carter undertook a full agenda of domestic initiatives in his early months in office, he also devoted considerable attention to matters of foreign policy. Indeed, there were some striking similarities between his handling of foreign policy and his management of domestic affairs. In both cases he was determined to play a dominant role, proposed a number of bold new measures, angered constituencies that had helped elect him, failed to understand at times the complexity of the initiatives he proposed, and tried to do too much too quickly.

From the time Carter took office, he intended to take charge of his own foreign policy. In accordance with his "spokes-in-the-wheel" system of decision making, his key advisers would have access to him so that they could provide him with information and opinions, but he would make the final decision. Many of those key advisers came from the Trilateral Commission to which Carter belonged. He had come to the commission's attention in 1973 when Zbigniew Brzezinski, a Columbia University professor and the commission's director, decided to include on its roster a state governor from each party. One of Brzezinski's colleagues suggested Carter, noting that the Georgia governor "was making a name for himself on economic issues."[1] Twenty-five of the commission's members received high-level posts in the new administration, including the new secretary of state, Cyrus Vance. Formerly President Lyndon Johnson's deputy secretary of defense, Vance was wary of using military force to resolve disputes, preferring negotiations as the key to peace. In particular, he sought an arms agreement with the Soviet Union, believing that such an understanding would reduce the threat of nuclear war and improve relations between the two superpowers. Although there would always be disagreements between the Kremlin and Washington, Vance rejected the idea of linking arms control to other areas of Soviet behavior.

Carter appointed Brzezinski as his national security adviser. From the very beginning of his administration, Carter was on closer personal terms with Brzezinski than with Vance. Prior to his appointment, Vance had never developed more than an acquaintanceship with Carter; in contrast, Brzezinski had been an adviser to the Georgia governor on foreign policy matters during the campaign. The new national security adviser took a more hard-line attitude toward the Soviet Union than did Vance, believing that it was possible to negotiate with the Kremlin only from a position of strength. Despite his long-standing dislike of former secretary of state Henry Kissinger, Brzezinski demonstrated a preparedness to engage in Kissinger's policy of linkage.

Although Carter realized that Brzezinski did not agree with Vance on key areas of policy, he regarded Brzezinski as a "first rate thinker"— impulsive and sometimes wrongheaded, but possessing the ability to grasp and clarify the fundamental interrelationships of global politics. Distrusting the bureaucracy of the State Department, Carter believed that the National Security Council (NSC) would also furnish a more favorable setting for developing and analyzing strategic concepts. In conducting foreign policy, therefore, Carter would be able to balance the bureaucratized but rationalized professionalism of the State Department with the intellectual ferment of the NSC.

Carter also predicated his foreign policy on open diplomacy and the linkage between morality and power. Influenced by his religious and familial background, the president had a missionary-like impulse to use U.S. influence to change the world in ways that he felt would best achieve peace and stability. One way of reaching that goal was by ending what he regarded as Kissinger's closed and secret diplomacy. "Our Secretary of State simply does not trust the judgment of the American people," he told the Chicago Council on Foreign Relations in March 1976. Moreover, he felt that Kissinger, like other cold war policy makers, had been overly influenced by the fear of communism, which had led the United States to send aid to, and even engage in war to support, authoritarian governments that violated the rights of their own people. As a world power that had long promoted the idea of spreading democracy, Carter contended, it was vital for the United States to eschew its old cold war mentality and adopt a new foreign policy based on morality and the principles of human rights established in the Helsinki Accords of 1975.[2]

The new president had not always felt this way. In 1975 he had criticized the Jackson-Vanik amendment on free emigration from the Soviet Union—a rallying point for human rights activists—as unwarranted interference in Soviet internal affairs. Increasingly, though, he had become disturbed by the policy of realpolitik and the Ford administration's willingness to support anticommunist dictatorships. As a born-again Christian, Carter identified human rights with his own religious beliefs. His campaign strategists also saw human rights as a "no-lose issue" that might even win Carter votes from foreign policy hard-liners because of its implicit attack on the Soviet Union. Beginning with a speech to the B'nai B'rith in September 1976, therefore, Carter made human rights a campaign theme, attacking the Ford administration for its neglect and promising, when in office, to make the United States once more "a beacon of light for human rights throughout the world."[3]

Carter's belief in human rights was linked to other concerns that guided his foreign policy, including poverty and nuclear proliferation. Poverty bred instability, which threatened the international economy and could lead to war if not checked. Spreading political freedom—such as giving representatives of the poor a greater say in the affairs of their countries—could help alleviate the possible dangers presented by poverty. Nuclear proliferation and the spread of atomic weapons posed their own threats to human life. Additionally, the spread of nuclear arms endangered U.S. security by giving enemy states, and possibly even terrorists, access to atomic weaponry.

Addressing the concerns of human rights, poverty, and nuclear proliferation gave Carter additional reason to move away from the language of realpolitik. American power had limits, as demonstrated by the Vietnam War, and it was therefore vital for the United States to recognize that it alone could not remedy the problems of the planet. If solving world problems required the assistance of the Soviet Union and the communist world, so be it. Although by no means naïve about the Soviet Union or the threat it posed to U.S. interests in the world, Carter was convinced that global interdependence had to replace global confrontation with Moscow. By downplaying the ideological and geopolitical differences between the two superpowers and concentrating instead on resolving matters of mutual interest, such as the nuclear arms race, Washington could achieve a more cooperative relationship with Moscow.

Cooperation and the development of a community of nations also became a theme with regard to the United States' allies. Using language similar to that of the Trilateral Commission, Carter declared that the "time has come" for the United States "to seek a partnership between North America, Western Europe, and Japan." Attacking Kissinger for ignoring the western European powers in his effort to improve relations with Moscow, he also argued that "[to] the maximum extent possible," Washington's relations with communist countries "should reflect the combined view of these democracies."[4]

Thus, by the time Carter moved into the White House in January 1977, the general outlines of his foreign policy were fairly well established. Yet problems soon arose over implementation. Some of the difficulties stemmed from the same organizational woes that hampered the administration's domestic agenda. It was not always clear, for example, who spoke for the president before Congress. Carter also complained that he was receiving too many undigested briefings on foreign policy issues. "Get together and from now on give me *one coordinated* briefing book—collected from the myriad sources," he instructed Brzezinski and his staff.[5]

Another difficulty, which also affected Carter domestically, was his managerial style: often he would initiate policy without fully understanding the difficulties of implementing it. The human rights issue was a case in point. In his inaugural address, the president declared that his policy on human rights would be "absolute," suggesting that any nation, whether an ally or not, would face punishment if it did not protect the rights of its people.[6] By the end of the following month, however, Vance declared that a policy of absolutism was not possible. Instead, the administration would take into account how important the target nation was to the United States' security or geopolitical concerns before determining whether to impose some form of punishment. Accordingly, the United States took a cautious approach to countries such as South Korea and Iran, which had repressive governments but were vital to U.S. security interests.[7]

It did not take long for the administration to add other countries to the list of nations it would treat gingerly on the subject of human rights. Having stated as early as May 1977 that he wanted to normalize relations with China, the president avoided pressing that country about its human rights violations so as not to threaten the normalization process. Despite the fact that Carter called Cambodian leader Pol Pot the "worst violator of human rights in the world," he avoided pressing the issue because of Pol Pot's close relationship with China.[8] Zaire's supply of cobalt made the administration careful about pushing that country's leader, Joseph Mobutu, too hard. Although Carter declared in August 1977 his desire to see a resolution of the dispute between London and Dublin over Northern Ireland, he remained sensitive about any initiatives that might upset London. Wariness also directed the White House's dealings with Israel, Egypt, Saudi Arabia, North Yemen, Indonesia, and the Philippines.

As a result of this pragmatic approach to the issue of human rights, the administration directed most of its attention to Latin America. In January 1978 Anthony Lake, head of the State Department's Policy Planning Staff, acknowledged in a memorandum to Secretary of State Vance that the United States had rejected, on human rights grounds, more international financial institution assistance programs aimed at Latin America than at other parts of the world. A number of reasons, "some better than others," wrote Lake, explained why the human rights policy came to focus on Latin America. Among these were the leverage the United States had in the region, the fact that Washington had less of a "security and economic stake" in the Western Hemisphere "than in East Asia or the Middle East," and the fact Latin American countries were "ideologically disinclined to turn to Moscow."[9]

The matter of aid to other nations brought to light another issue—bureaucratic infighting—that complicated not only the administration's human rights policy but also its entire foreign policy. In April 1977 the NSC ordered the State Department to establish what became the Interagency Group on Human Rights and Foreign Assistance. Also known as the "Christopher Group," because it was chaired by Undersecretary of State Warren Christopher, it included representatives from all the major departments of government as well as the NSC and the Export-Import Bank. Although its stated purpose was to take into account human rights considerations when deciding whether to provide aid to other countries, the group's purview quickly became restricted. Opposition from the Defense, Commerce, and Treasury Departments succeeded in removing a number of programs from the group's coverage, including military assistance, security supporting assistance, Titles I and II of the Food for Peace Program, the International Monetary Fund, the International Fund for Agricultural Development, and Commodity Credit Corporation export credits.

The end result was that the Christopher Group soon found its review procedures limited largely to aid from the multilateral development banks (MDBs): the World Bank, the Asian Development Bank, the African Development Bank, and the Inter-American Development Bank. The White House failed to take any action to overcome the bureaucratic infighting that limited the Christopher Group's purview or to enhance its ability to use the MDBs effectively. According to Caleb Rossiter, a staff consultant for the Arms Control and Foreign Policy Caucus, American representatives to the MDBs "cast negative votes as instructed, but it was little more than a pro forma exercise. No serious efforts were made to build the voting coalitions with other member nations that were necessary to ensure the defeat of loans to human rights violators."[10]

Meanwhile, the promotion of human rights threatened the relationship that Carter hoped to develop with the Soviet Union. There is no question that the president wanted to carry on the policy of détente; he said as much to Soviet leader Leonid Brezhnev six days after moving into the White House. But his human rights initiative actually helped détente's opponents, such as the Committee on the Present Danger (CPD).

Formed in 1976, the CPD argued that détente jeopardized the United States' ability to confront the aggressive worldwide designs of the Soviet Union. Its membership included a number of highly influential Democrats who questioned why the president would believe that it was possible to establish cordial relations with a nation that he himself had denounced as repressive.

The president's advisers also falsely believed that he could speak out against Soviet infringements of human rights without alarming Moscow. "Surely the Soviets are sophisticated enough to understand that the domestic flexibility we need to make progress in other areas is enhanced by our position on human rights," Jody Powell told the president in February 1977. Carter agreed, reminding news correspondents that he was not singling out the Soviet Union as the only place where human rights were being violated.[11]

It soon became clear, however, that the president and his press secretary were being extremely naïve. The first clash between Washington and Moscow over human rights occurred only a week after Carter took office. In a public statement, the Department of State accused Czechoslovakia of violating the 1975 Helsinki agreements by harassing a group of Czechoslovakian intellectuals who were demanding domestic reforms. Two days later it issued another statement calling the Soviet dissident Andrei Sakharov "an outspoken champion of human rights" and warning the Soviets that any effort to "intimidate" him would "conflict with accepted international standards of human rights." Carter even sent a personal note to Sakharov, pledging his support for human rights worlwide.[12]

The Soviets were infuriated. In their view, the Carter administration had violated an unwritten agreement between the two superpowers not to comment on each other's internal affairs. The State Department broadsides also represented the first time that Washington had publicly condemned an eastern European country for not abiding by the Helsinki agreements. Meanwhile, Moscow had already decided to step up its efforts to block contact between dissident leaders in the East and their sympathizers in the West. As Soviet ambassador to the United States Anatoly Dobrynin met with Vance to protest Carter's letter to Sakharov, the Soviets intensified their repression of political dissidents, making a point of arresting such leading critics as Alexander Ginsburg and Yuri Orlov. Rumors circulated in Washington that they would be deported to the West along with Sakharov.

Ignoring the growing strain in Soviet-American relations, the White House mounted a diplomatic offensive to win a new arms reduction agreement with Moscow. With the SALT I treaty set to expire in October, the Soviets were also anxious to resume arms limitation talks, which had been stalled since 1974 when Ford and Brezhnev agreed at Vladivostok to impose a ceiling of 2,400 strategic missile launchers on both their countries. Carter did not like that accord. Rather than reducing existing stockpiles, it only created parity at a level beyond which neither nation would build. A new generation of Soviet intercontinental ballistic missiles (ICBMs) with enormous warheads and greatly improved accuracy also worried him.

The situation also concerned lawmakers on Capitol Hill, including Henry Jackson, one of the Senate's harshest critics of Moscow and the founder of the Coalition for a Democratic Majority, formed in 1972 by Democrats favoring a strong military counter to the Soviet threat. Shortly after Carter's inauguration, Jackson informed the president that he would insist on deep cuts in the Soviets' ICBM and intermediate-range ballistic missile stockpiles as part of any SALT II treaty. The White House realized that Jackson would have a major impact on the ratification of any arms agreement. "Jackson," Vance wrote, "would be a major asset in a future ratification debate if he supported the treaty, and a formidable opponent if he opposed it."[13] Disliking the Vladivostok agreement himself, and hoping to get the support of Jackson and his allies, Carter decided to call for a significant reduction in the nuclear arsenals on both sides. As a fallback position, he was willing to settle for a pact based on the Vladivostok accord but with a ceiling about 10 percent lower.

The White House had ample warning that the Soviets would never accept the comprehensive arms agreement the president wanted. As early as December 1976, Dobrynin had told Carter that Moscow was concerned by the president's feeling that he was not bound by previous agreements with the Kremlin. In early 1977 Carter wrote to Brezhnev that he wanted to sign a SALT II agreement that would include limits on the Soviets' Backfire bomber—which U.S. officials maintained could be modified to strike the United States—but would not include limits on U.S. cruise missiles—relatively inexpensive pilotless drones that could fly at altitudes low enough to escape radar detection; discussion of cruise missiles would be left for subsequent negotiations. Carter also proposed a limit on the number of missiles able to carry more than one warhead (multiple independently targeted reentry vehicles, or MIRVs). Brezhnev replied angrily, stating that any further discussions had to be based on Vladivostok; that before he would discuss MIRV missiles, an agreement on cruise missiles was required; and that since the Backfire had not been brought up in the 1974 talks, it was out of bounds. He notified Carter that these would be the Soviet positions taken in the talks with Vance.[14]

It is not surprising, then, that the Soviets responded bitterly to Vance's opening remarks during his visit to Moscow. Almost all the major cutbacks would be in weapons categories in which the Soviets held an edge; there would be few restrictions on submarines or air-launched weapons, the classes in which the United States had the clear advantage. In addition, both sides would have to cease making improvements in warhead accuracy, again leaving the United States far ahead. What angered the Soviets almost as much as the specifics, however, was the fact that they had been stated publicly. Taken together with Carter's avowed support for Soviet dissidents, Soviet leaders were convinced that the U.S. call for a major reduction in nuclear weapons was part of a duplicitous campaign to embarrass them. They were determined not to be sucked into what they regarded as Washington's ploy. At his first meeting with Vance, Brezhnev rejected the U.S. proposals without offering any counterproposals. He then ended the meeting and canceled the rest of the negotiating sessions scheduled during Vance's visit.

In its first few weeks in office, therefore, the Carter administration had made a muddle of U.S.-Soviet relations. The president and his advisers had tried to impose their values and perspectives on Moscow, and their efforts had backfired. Carter had assumed that the Soviets were just as anxious as he was for arms reductions, but he had miscalculated the effects of his outspoken criticism of the Kremlin and his well-publicized arms proposals on the secretive, even paranoid, Soviet government.

It was true that Carter faced severe constraints in negotiating with the Soviets. There had already been a battle over his nomination of Paul Warnke as the nation's chief arms negotiator, revealing the depth of the opposition in the Senate to any agreement that seemed disadvantageous to the United States. A close friend of Vance, Warnke was widely regarded in Washington as a "dove" on arms control, and his critics feared that he would make too many concessions to the Soviets. Although the president managed to get Warnke confirmed, the closeness of the vote (fifty-eight to forty) indicated the difficulty he would have getting the two-thirds majority needed in the Senate for ratification of a new SALT agreement.

Regardless, Carter had ignored the Kremlin's warnings that it would not accept the arms deal. Had he heeded these signals, he might have put together an agreement that would have stood a better chance of acceptance by the Soviets. The president himself later acknowledged that he had misjudged Moscow's reaction to his campaign for arms control. "Had I known then what I know now about the Soviet Union," he stated, "I would have approached [arms reductions] differently, in a little bit slower fashion and with more preparation before Vance's mission was publicized."[15]

Despite the failure of the first Moscow meeting, both sides were willing to return to the bargaining table. The Soviet Union wanted a formal conclusion to the Vladivostok agreement of 1974, while the United States was under increasing pressure domestically and from its allies to recover some of the ground lost as a result of the March fiasco. In May the arms limitation talks resumed at Geneva, and after three days of negotiations, the two sides reached agreement on the broad outlines of a new SALT II accord that would run through 1985. Reluctantly, Vance accepted the ceiling of 2,400 strategic launchers as the starting point for SALT II. In return, Soviet foreign minister Andrei Gromyko indicated Moscow's readiness to consider paring down each side's strategic arsenals by as much as 10 percent. Vance also agreed to a protocol restraining the development and deployment of U.S. cruise missiles.

Nevertheless, Washington and Moscow remained far apart on the size of any arms reduction and on numerous other specifics. The administration wanted to limit the number of MIRVs on all classes of ICBMs, not just the ones with the heaviest thrust (or throw power), as it had earlier proposed. The Soviets believed that this would unduly benefit the United States, since it had already put multiple warheads on its sea-launched ballistic missiles, while the Soviets had not. Furthermore, the president insisted on including the Backfire in the negotiations, which the Kremlin adamantly refused to do. Therefore, Moscow rejected the proposal.

Carter's human rights campaign also remained a festering sore point in Soviet-American relations. The president had moderated his censure of Soviet violations, but he did not desist entirely. In a commencement address at Annapolis, he criticized Moscow's refusal to tolerate free speech and to grant all Soviet citizens the right to emigrate. To the Kremlin, it appeared that Carter was meddling again. When the president wrote to Brezhnev in June offering to meet with him at a mutually acceptable time and place, the Soviet leader told U.S. ambassador Malcolm Toon that a summit meeting would be possible only after a SALT agreement had been reached. He also took the occasion to deliver an angry, table-thumping attack on Carter's Soviet policy.

By midsummer 1977 relations between the two superpowers had dipped to such a low point that Carter considered it imperative to adopt a more conciliatory posture toward Moscow. In a speech before the Southern Legislative Conference, he emphasized the need for cooperation between the United States and the Soviet Union to bring about a "gentler, freer, more bountiful world." He also noted that the "whole history of Soviet-American relations teaches us that we will be misled if we base our long range policies on the mood of the moment." Even so, Soviet-American dealings remained icy.

Closer to home, Carter was also running into trouble. Determined to move away from the rhetoric of the cold war and to place more emphasis on a North-South dialogue, the president gave more attention to relations with countries in the Western Hemisphere. Mexico was particularly important. Carter understood the significance of that nation to the United

States in terms of both trade and energy resources, and he was worried about Mexico's unstable financial and political situation. In part to restore the financial community's confidence in Mexico, the president invited its president, Jose López Portillo, to be his first state visitor to the White House. The administration, however, infuriated López Portillo when it refused to accept an agreement between Mexico and several U.S. gas companies under which Mexico would sell natural gas to those firms. The Mexican president had ignored the White House's warnings that any agreement between the U.S. companies and Mexico required Washington's approval beforehand. López Portillo never forgave Carter for that decision.

Anxious to promote human rights and spread democracy in the Western Hemisphere, the administration increased its pressure on authoritarian governments in the region—including those of Argentina, Chile, Brazil, Uruguay, Peru, El Salvador, and Nicaragua—through means ranging from private and public diplomacy to cuts in assistance. The leaders of these countries, as well as many conservatives in Congress, such as archconservative Republican senator Jesse Helms of North Carolina, contended that the president was unfairly targeting anticommunist allies. But Carter also angered congressional liberals. In 1977, for instance, the White House successfully fought an attempt by Senator Edward Kennedy to terminate all military and commercial aid to Argentina, including that in the "pipeline" (goods paid for but not yet delivered). Arguing that a carrot-and-stick approach was a better way to alter the attitude of human rights–violating states, the president approved limited military aid to Argentina. His action infuriated Kennedy and other liberals in Congress.

Carter's most serious problem in Latin America, however, involved his decision to cede American control of the Panama Canal and Panama Canal Zone (an area five miles wide on either side of the canal) to Panama by the end of the century. Negotiations on these issues had been going on sporadically since 1964. They had not been a point of contention in the 1976 Democratic primaries, but they had been in the Republican contests. Ronald Reagan had slashed away at Gerald Ford for agreeing to the eventual transfer of the canal and canal zone to Panama. Reagan's stance had struck a responsive chord among the American people, and negotiating a treaty with Panama had become an important issue during the general election. Carter had avoided the question as much as possible, but when queried, he had reiterated his stand against relinquishing U.S. hegemony. "I would never give up complete control or practical control of the Panama Canal Zone," he had commented during the presidential debates.[16]

After the election, however, Carter changed his mind, becoming convinced that turning over the canal to Panama was morally right, that it would enhance the United States' image throughout Latin America, and that gaining Senate ratification of a canal agreement would demonstrate to the American people his willingness and ability to tackle difficult assignments. The president had also been warned by the State Department that if a settlement was not reached with the government of General Omar Torrijos, violence might erupt in Panama, threatening the security of the canal.

U.S. policy toward Panama became the first Latin American issue reviewed by the NSC. On 27 January the council's Policy Review Committee—a body chaired by the secretary of state that coordinated foreign, defense, and international economic matters—recommended that the administration inform Panama of its willingness to negotiate a new treaty. Talks began on 14 February, but they almost broke off because of the United States' insistence on retaining the right to use military force if necessary to keep the canal open. The Panamanians balked at what they regarded as an infringement of their sovereignty. The talks did not resume until May, when the Panamanians agreed to a U.S. proposal for two treaties. The first would transfer control of the canal to Panama after 1999; the second would give the United States an indefinite right to defend the neutrality of the canal, but only against external threats. On this basis, the two sides reached a final agreement in August.

By this time, however, the Panama Canal had become a cause célèbre on Capitol Hill. Lawmakers flooded the White House with letters, some supporting the administration's decision to negotiate with Panama, but most angrily denouncing it. Although Republicans led the charge, many Democrats joined them in accusing Carter of surrendering one of the nation's great treasures. Opinion polls differed substantially over the degree of public opposition to the agreement, but it was clearly significant and well organized.

Meanwhile, Carter had become ensnarled in the enormously complex and seemingly endless Middle East crisis. During the campaign and after the election, he had been warned by his advisers not to get involved in that particular quagmire. But as he later wrote, his concern about Israeli security, the rights of the Palestinians, the possibility of Soviet influence in the region, and the West's dependence on Arab oil led him to ignore their counsel.

Carter's campaign statements on the region had been unexceptional. Very early in his candidacy, he had urged Israel to withdraw from most of the territories it had seized during the Six Days' War of 1967, and he had later endorsed the establishment of a Palestinian state on the West Bank of the Jordan River. But in an obvious effort to court Jewish voters, he increasingly emphasized the importance of strengthening ties with Israel and came out in support of Israel's demands for "defensible borders," a term generally understood to mean continued occupation of the areas taken in 1967. He also stated that he would not recognize the Palestine Liberation Organization (PLO) "or other government entities representing the Palestinians" until he was convinced that they acknowledged Israel's right to exist.[17]

Once in office, however, Carter adopted a different attitude. While declaring that he would "rather commit suicide than hurt Israel," he decided to wield U.S. influence to resolve the Arab-Israeli conflict even if that placed him at odds with Israeli leaders and the American Jewish community. Rejecting the "step-by-step" approach of Kissinger, the president sought a comprehensive settlement to be achieved by reconvening the 1973 Geneva conference. In deciding on this course, he had been influenced by a 1975 Brookings Institution report entitled "Toward Peace in the Middle East." Written with the help of Brzezinski and William Quandt, who was now the NSC's Middle East specialist, the report called for a comprehensive settlement.[18] The recommendation resonated with Carter, who, as a Christian, had a profound interest in the region where Christianity had been born and, as a politician, realized that if his efforts succeeded, he would gain political points at home. It also appealed to his missionary zeal to solve world problems. For Brzezinski and the trilateralists, such a settlement could promote stability in a vitally important but unstable part of the world.

Yet promoting a comprehensive settlement was risky. For one thing, there were logistical problems: it was doubtful that such a complex gathering could even be arranged by year's end. In the meantime, moderate Arabs might not be able to withstand pressure from more radical groups to renew military action against Israel. Egypt would also want to send its own delegation to Geneva to negotiate bilaterally with Israel, while its Arab archrival Syria would hold out for a single Arab delegation to keep Egypt from reaching a separate agreement with the Israelis. But the most intractable problem concerned the status of the PLO at the Geneva conference. Would the PLO try to send its own delegation to Geneva, or would it accept membership in a pan-Arab delegation? More to the point, would Israel permit PLO representation under any circumstances? To explore these issues and prepare the groundwork for a Geneva conference, Carter sent Vance to the Middle East in February 1977.

Vance's efforts did not bear fruit. Initially the White House was optimistic. The secretary found Egyptian president Anwar Sadat, Syrian president Hafiz al-Assad—whom Vance described as "the hardest" of the Arab leaders—and Israeli prime minister Yitzhak Rabin willing to compromise. But that optimism soon faded. Between March and June Carter met with Rabin, Sadat, Crown Prince Fahd of Saudi Arabia, King Hussein of Jordan, and Assad. The talks proved unproductive. Rabin told the president that he would oppose a Geneva conference if the PLO or other Palestinian representatives were present. He also stated that he would not agree to total withdrawal from the West Bank or Golan Heights or permit the establishment of an independent Palestinian state on the West Bank. Discussions with the other leaders did not produce any breakthroughs either.

Meanwhile, relations with Israel began to sour. In March 1977, in a town meeting in Clinton, Massachusetts, Carter made the first of a number of statements favoring a Palestinian homeland. Israeli leaders reacted angrily, believing that the president was trying to impose his own peace settlement on the Middle East. Moreover, with a May election approaching, they were worried that Carter's meeting with Assad would play into the hands of the hard-line Likud Party headed by Menachem Begin.

The president's comments regarding the Palestinians and his courting of the Arab powers also upset American Jewish leaders. They had voted for Carter in November but had done so reluctantly, wary of his avowed evangelical Christianity. To solidify their favor, Carter had Brzezinski and Vice President Walter Mondale meet with them soon after he took office to underscore his continued support for Israel. More important, he strongly supported a measure prohibiting U.S. firms doing business in the Middle East from participating in the Arab trade embargo against Israel.

Although most Jewish leaders appreciated Carter's efforts, the president soon canceled out whatever goodwill he had earned when he blocked the sale of twenty-four Israeli Kfir fighter-bombers with U.S.-manufactured engines to Ecuador. He then followed this decision by proposing to sell Hawk and Maverick missiles to Saudi Arabia. Carter justified his action on the Kfir fighter-bombers as part of his policy of limiting arms sales to third-world countries and tried to mollify his critics on the missiles, including Congressman Benjamin Rosenthal of New York, by stating that the United States' commitment to Israel was "unequivocal." But as Hamilton Jordan later commented, there was "*widespread concern* in the American Jewish community over the President's positions on Israel."[19]

As Rabin and his Labor Party feared, on 18 May Israelis elected Begin prime minister. Carter was shocked. A hard-liner whom *Time* had labeled a "superhawk," Begin referred to the West Bank and Gaza Strip as "liberated territories, part of the land of Israel," and even called the West Bank by its biblical names of Judea and Samaria. In the president's view, Begin's election hardly boded well for the peace process.[20]

On 19 July the new Israeli leader arrived in Washington for two days of meetings with the president. Contrary to his expectations, Carter found Begin to be an intelligent, courteous, and even charming figure who listened attentively both to the president's reassurances that he would not impose a peace plan on Israel and to his objections about the building of Israeli settlements in the occupied territories. In response, the prime minister stated his own desire for a Geneva settlement. He also stressed that all issues were negotiable at Geneva and that the deliberations should be based on United Nations Resolutions 242 and 338, calling for the withdrawal of Israeli troops from the occupied territories in return for Arab recognition of the state of Israel.

The Carter-Begin talks did much to dispel the president's worst fears about Begin's inflexibility. They also helped mend fences between the president and American Jewish leaders. Yet major differences still existed between Begin and the president. The Israeli leader interpreted Resolutions 242 and 338 to mean the withdrawal of Israeli forces from "some" occupied territories; Carter construed the resolutions to mean withdrawal from "all" the territories. Moreover, under no circumstances would Begin give up the West Bank, parley with the PLO, begin talks in Geneva with a combined Arab-Palestinian delegation, agree to a Palestinian homeland, or stop the construction of Israeli settlements in the occupied territories.

U.S.-Israeli tensions increased shortly after Begin returned to Israel, when he announced plans for a large number of new settlements on the West Bank. His pronouncement prompted a sharp exchange between Washington—which had been trying to coax the Arab states to the negotiating table—and Jerusalem over the issue of settlements. These events rekindled earlier concerns among American Jews about the administration's Middle East policy and pushed relations between them and the White House to the breaking point.

Politically and diplomatically, therefore, Carter's Middle East policy was a disaster. No progress had been made toward resolving the crisis, and the president had alienated the Jewish community and lawmakers on Capitol Hill who were sympathetic to Israel. As the president himself later observed, "My own political supporters were coming to see me, groups were meeting with Cy Vance, and stirrings within Congress were becoming more pronounced."[21]

Another battle on Capitol Hill formed around the president's pledge to withdraw U.S. troops from South Korea. Carter's determination on this matter was another legacy of his campaign. Although he favored a buildup of U.S. ground forces in Europe, where Soviet troops outnumbered North Atlantic Treaty Organization (NATO) forces, he saw no useful military purpose for having U.S. troops in Korea, which, he believed, could be better defended with air and logistical support. He also considered the politically repressive government of Park Chung Hee to be morally repugnant. For both these reasons, he promised to start removing U.S. ground forces from Korea soon after taking office.

On 26 January the president announced at a press conference that he intended to carry through with his campaign pledge. The news was not well received by powerful circles in Japan and the United States. The Japanese feared instability on the Korean peninsula and were worried about the implications of the withdrawal in terms of the United States' security commitments to Japan. They were also miffed that they had not been consulted before Carter made his decision. In the United States, the president's announcement drew strong opposition from foreign policy hard-liners and senior military officials who believed that the pullout might encourage North Korea to launch a second invasion of South Korea. In May, General John K. Singlaub, the third ranking army officer in Korea, told the *Washington Post* that, in his view, the removal of 32,000 ground troops from South Korea would lead to war.

Replicating President Harry Truman's firing of General Douglas MacArthur in 1951 for questioning official policy, Carter immediately relieved Singlaub of his command and ordered him home. Critics of the redeployment seized on Singlaub's dismissal as a way of pressuring Carter into reversing his decision. On Capitol Hill, influential Democratic senators such as John Glenn of Ohio, Sam Nunn of Georgia, Henry Jackson of Washington, Daniel Inouye of Hawaii, Hubert Humphrey of Minnesota, and Gary Hart of Colorado joined Republicans in opposing the president. Opinion ran against the plan even within the White House. Of Carter's senior advisers, only Brzezinski approved of the president's resolve. Although Carter refused to budge from his public commitment to take the troops out of Korea, it was clear by the end of the summer that he had dug himself into a hole over the issue. Opposition to troop removal was so great that he wisely deferred implementation, but he had every reason to expect a donnybrook on Capitol Hill should he later go ahead with the withdrawal. As Secretary Vance noted, "Congress continued to hammer home warnings of a political explosion if the withdrawals actually proceeded."[22]

Complicating matters with respect to South Korea was the so-called Koreagate scandal, involving efforts by the South Korean Central Intelligence Agency to use bribes to manipulate U.S. policy. Among the key figures in the scandal was Tongsun Park, who had ties to the Park government. Lawmakers wanted Tongsun Park to come to the United States to testify about what he knew. When President Park refused to extradite him, they threatened to oppose a package of economic and military aid proposed by the White House to compensate South Korea for the withdrawal of U.S. troops. Brzezinski warned Carter in July that to secure support for the compensation package, "the administration will have to mount a very major effort involving the expenditure of significant political capital without any certainty that such an effort can succeed on the

Hill." He concluded that congressional support for keeping the troops in Korea, combined with Koreagate, "may warrant some adjustment of our withdrawal policy."[23]

Loud reverberations from Capitol Hill could also be heard at the White House over Carter's decision to scrap the development of a new class of B-1 bomber. For more than a decade, a fight had raged in Washington over whether to build this new bomber to replace the United States' aging fleet of 330 B-52s, many of which were more than twenty years old. Pentagon planners and others argued that the B-1, which could fly faster (up to 1,320 miles per hour) and lower than the B-52s, was needed to penetrate Soviet air defenses. Opponents of the B-1 argued that the plane was not only outlandishly expensive but also a dinosaur in the age of rocketry.

Over a period of five months, Carter met with Defense Secretary Harold Brown, the Joint Chiefs of Staff, and other defense experts to assess the military value of the bomber. Most Washington observers anticipated that Carter would approve at least some of the 120 B-1s that the air force was requesting. Secretary Brown had supported the plane when he was air force secretary under Lyndon Johnson, and Carter had included the construction of five B-1s in the Defense Department's authorization bill for 1978. Certainly the president gave no indication before June that he intended to cut the entire program.

But that is just what he decided to do. Impressed particularly by his conversations with Brown, who had determined that the B-1 was not cost-effective, Carter stunned reporters at a news conference on the last day of June by announcing that he was discontinuing the production of new weapons systems. The president's move was a courageous one, and he understood that it would generate political flak from the many people who had an economic stake in the huge project and from defense hard-liners and political opponents of the administration. Never before had a president killed so large a program so close to production. Speaker O'Neill congratulated the president for being so bold, remarking that Carter was "the only President who doesn't have to rely on the Pentagon to make his military decisions."[24]

Yet Carter could have served his administration better if he had done something to soften the impact of his announcement on congressional and public attitudes, such as seeking Soviet concessions in return for eliminating the B-1 or simply delaying any action until the conclusion of the SALT talks. As it was, the president indulged in the worst possible timing by cutting the B-1 program two days after the House had rejected a measure to cancel its production. The bomber's proponents charged him with purposely trying to embarrass Congress. They also accused him of failing again to provide for national security.

While Carter was criticized at home for not being firm enough on national defense, Europeans attacked him for being too inflexible in his conduct of foreign affairs. They regarded his policy on human rights as preachy, and they maintained that few nations in the world had spotless records. In addition, many European officials believed that the president was unnecessarily provoking Moscow. West German chancellor Helmut Schmidt, who had openly supported Ford during the election, was especially critical of Carter's foreign policy. He regarded the new president as an amateur who had no experience in foreign affairs and whose advisers had little knowledge of Europe. Brzezinski was the notable exception, but Schmidt blamed the NSC adviser for pushing the administration into what the chancellor considered an unrealistically tough stance toward the Soviets.

In addition, Schmidt felt that the Carter administration too often neglected German concerns. He was upset, for example, that the Pentagon appeared ready to renege on an agreement to buy German Leopold II battle tanks because of their alleged inferiority to U.S. tanks. He also resented the administration's pressure on him to stimulate the German economy as part of a coordinated effort with the United States and Japan to prevent a global recession. He later wrote that Carter and Brzezinski "ignore[d] the interests of America's German allies—there had been nothing like it in German-American relations since the days of Lyndon Johnson's dealings with Ludwig Erhard."[25]

But what irked Schmidt the most was Carter's nuclear nonproliferation policy. In 1968 the United States had signed a nuclear nonproliferation treaty. Even so, the issue of nuclear proliferation remained a secondary concern until the mid-1970s, when India's test of an atomic bomb and President Nixon's proposal to give Egypt and Israel nuclear reactor technology focused much more attention on the issue. Carter, who had a good understanding of atomic power because of his background working on nuclear submarines, made nonproliferation a key component of his campaign. After taking office, he became determined to stop the spread of technology that could allow other countries to develop atomic weapons. He put words into action in February 1977 when he asked Schmidt not to proceed with a $4.7 billion sale to Brazil of a complete nuclear facility, on the grounds that Brazil could use part of the facility to develop its own nuclear weapons capability.

Schmidt refused. He responded that although Germany supported nonproliferation, it was unfair to discriminate against all nations interested in developing nuclear power because of a fear that they might acquire nuclear weapons. Since his proposed transaction with Brazil concerned the peaceful use of nuclear power, he added, it did not violate the treaty. In his view, the administration was trying to force U.S. policy down Bonn's throat without taking into account German sensitivities. In fact, the United States was hardly concerned with multilateral decision making.

Japan felt the same way about the White House's nonproliferation initiative. The Japanese were in the process of building a reprocessing plant at Tokai Mura as part of a program to provide the country with nuclear power, but it needed uranium from the United States to begin operations. Carter opposed Tokyo's plans for Tokai Mura because the reprocessing of uranium produced plutonium, which could be used for the creation of an atomic weapon; moreover, allowing Japan to begin operations at Tokai Mura would encourage other nations to follow suit. Prime Minister Takeo Fukuda persisted, however. He argued, as had Schmidt, that Carter was engaging in discrimination and that since Tokai Mura was to be used for peaceful nuclear purposes, it did not violate the nonproliferation treaty. Furthermore, he warned that failure to begin operations at Tokai Mura could hurt him politically, making it more difficult for him to resolve other problems affecting U.S.-Japanese relations, such as Japan's trade surplus with the United States.

These differences between the United States and its allies overshadowed the London economic summit, which Carter attended in May. There, Carter met with Schdmit, Fukuda, and the other leaders of western Europe and Canada. The press anticipated a donnybrook over such issues as the economy and nonproliferation, but that did not happen. As expected, much of the summit was spent considering ways to deal with the worldwide economic problems of high inflation and unemployment and the rising global trend toward protectionism. Carter and Fukuda also held private discussions on Tokai Mura. By all accounts, the president was a smashing success. He had prepared carefully for the meeting, and he impressed the other leaders at the summit with his grasp of economic issues, his willingness to listen, his easygoing friendliness, his lack of pretension, and his deliberate manner.

Despite this amity, the president continued to bicker with the Europeans and the Japanese. Schmidt and other European leaders maintained their concerns over Carter's human rights policy. French president Valéry Giscard d'Estaing, who was angry with Carter for not revoking the New York Port Authority's ban on the Concorde supersonic airliner, gave a magazine interview in which he accused the president of having "compromised the process of détente" by being clumsy in his dealings with Brezhnev. On 13 July Schmidt came to Washington carrying a message from the leaders of all the Common Market countries urging Carter to moderate his campaign on behalf of human rights. The nonproliferation effort only added to the tension. Germany's proposed sale of the nuclear plant to Brazil remained a bone of contention. As for the Japanese, although Fukuda and Carter discussed Tokai Mura in London, they agreed only that their nations should continue negotiations on the matter. Brzezinski later wrote that "relations with our allies were strained significantly over the nuclear issue."[26]

Carter had hoped to develop a trilateral relationship involving the United States, Japan, and Europe, but as with issues such as human rights, he had failed to grasp the complexities involved. Western Europeans and the Japanese supported human rights and nonproliferation, but they believed that the way the White House promoted those policies showed a lack of understanding of their countries' interests.

The president only added to his difficulties by trying to do too much too fast. He implemented initiatives without taking the time to determine which were most important or how to accomplish them without impeding other goals. William Quandt of the NSC recalled that if Carter "saw a problem he wanted to solve it, and that was all there was to it." He added, "we would send lists to the president and say, 'Here are twenty issues or so that are of concern. . . .Which two or three are most important to you?' and the checklist would come back with a note to do all twenty of them." Quandt concluded, "Carter certainly did not have the inclination or capacity to make the grand strategic trade-offs."[27]

Thus, as fall approached, there was a growing perception, even among Democrats, that the administration's foreign policy was seriously flawed. According to *Time*, "Quite a few members of the mainly Democratic foreign policy establishment are beginning to wonder whether [the president] is really up to the job." As if to confirm this view, former undersecretary of state George Ball observed that the human rights campaign "to some extent . . . had become a stuck needle, getting in the way of things which might be more important in the long run."[28]

Carter's foreign policy, then, was being questioned both at home and abroad, among Democrats as well as Republicans, liberals as well as conservatives. Meanwhile, the president had succeeded in alienating his own constituencies while providing ample ammunition for the opposition to use against him. But all this paled in comparison with the problems he faced on the domestic front, especially a developing scandal involving his close friend and OMB director Bert Lance.

4

★ ★ ★ ★ ★

THE DOG DAYS OF SUMMER
AND FALL

By the fall of 1977, Carter's public approval rating had begun a precipitous decline from which it never recovered. A Harris poll taken in March had given the president a resounding 75 percent rating on his ability to "inspire confidence"; by late September that figure had dropped to 50 percent. Moreover, an NBC poll taken a few weeks later showed that only 46 percent of the people surveyed approved of his performance as president.

Part of the reason for Carter's dramatic drop in the polls was simply that high ratings are normally given to presidents early in their administrations. Indeed, the new president's approval rating after three months in office, though impressive, was not unprecedented. At the same point in their administrations, John F. Kennedy had had a favorable grade of 83 percent; Dwight Eisenhower, 74 percent; and Lyndon Johnson, 73 percent. However, their support was not as soft as Carter's. As chief executive, Carter satisfied the American people but did not motivate them; he sought to awaken the national conscience but was unable to inspire public confidence; he won supporters but did not gain committed followers.

Early spring had gone well enough for Carter. After much difficulty and delay, the White House had been able to negotiate a deal with the House and Senate on the president's hit list of water projects. Like most compromises, this one did not represent a clear victory for either side. Because several of the most expensive and least environmentally sound ventures were still slated for construction, Stu Eizenstat advised the president not to sign the agreement. Even Carter remarked later that he rued the day he had agreed to compromise on "those worthless dam projects." Nevertheless, as a result of his persistence, only half the projects he had targeted for elimination were funded, and appropriations were cut by more than half (from $147 million to $63 million).[1]

Meanwhile, the president could take considerable satisfaction from the fact that the economy appeared to be moving ahead strongly. Despite the severe winter, the rate of economic growth in the first quarter of 1977 was 5.2 percent, and preliminary calculations for the second quarter placed it at 6.4 percent. "This estimate seems more likely to be revised up than down as more data becomes available," CEA chairman Schultze told the president at the end of June. The rates of inflation and unemployment were also down as food prices moderated and more people found jobs.[2]

At the White House the president continued his efforts to reach out to the American people and make his administration and the rest of the federal government more open and accessible. He visited each cabinet department and held question-and-answer sessions with its employees. He allowed NBC to follow him for an entire day, and the coverage was subsequently broadcast nationwide. He met on a regular, twice-a-month basis with newspaper editors from outside Washington. He mandated that the White House Office of Public Liaison, headed by Midge Costanza, "pay particular attention . . . to enhancing communications with groups and interest[s] which traditionally have not had access to the White House, Cabinet, or sub-cabinet levels of government."[3] And he submitted an election reform message in which he called for universal voter registration and public financing of congressional elections.

On Capitol Hill most of Carter's economic stimulus package was winding its way through committee without the tax rebate, which the president had decided to scrap. On 5 May Congress passed a $20.1 billion measure to increase employment through various jobs programs. In June it approved a one-year extension of the Comprehensive Employment and Training Act, under which most federal jobs and training programs operated. The next month it passed yet another bill establishing a number of jobs projects for disadvantaged youth. In addition, lawmakers simplified the tax laws, as the president had requested, and approved a plan for countercyclical aid to help state and local governments avoid cutbacks during economic slowdowns.

Carter could therefore point to a substantial list of accomplishments during his second trimester as president, but his achievements were again clouded by major economic and political uncertainties. In the first place, not all the economic news was good. Foreign trade deficits were growing, and the Commerce Department forecast that business investment for the latter half of 1977 would be sluggish. If that happened,

Schultze admitted that his projections of economic growth for 1977 and 1978 would be too high. Similarly, the Congressional Budget Office reported that although it was possible for the president to meet his goals of reasonably full employment (an unemployment rate near 5 percent) and a balanced budget by 1981, it was unlikely without further measures to stimulate the economy. Eizenstat informed Carter that, in all likelihood, the administration would have to choose between full employment and a balanced budget.

There was never much doubt about which of these two alternatives Carter would favor. The president was committed to reducing inflation and balancing the budget, even if that meant a restrictive fiscal policy, higher levels of unemployment than he preferred, and a limit on new government programs. "There is nothing in your inflation memo involving government spending restraints—future impact of initiating new programs—balancing the federal budget, etc. Why?" he asked Schultze angrily at the end of March.[4]

The president's commitment to reducing inflation by restricting government spending became evident in his proposal for overhauling the nation's labyrinthine system of public welfare. Shortly after his victory, the president-elect had asked Joseph Califano, whom he was considering for secretary of health, education, and welfare (HEW), how fast a welfare reform plan could be developed. Caught off guard and not expecting to be taken literally, Califano responded that it could be ready by 1 May. Much to his alarm, Carter took him at his word, informing his newly appointed cabinet in December that May would be the month for welfare reform. Over the next few weeks, Califano told Carter repeatedly that he needed more time, but the president-elect flatly turned him down.

Misunderstandings over what reform entailed became even more apparent after Carter took office. Califano assumed that welfare reform would involve more money, yet the president meant to keep spending at existing levels. Analysts at HEW and the Labor Department, who were supposed to be working together to develop the legislation, also differed over the best approach to take. HEW officials emphasized the importance of improving the efficiency of existing maintenance programs for welfare recipients and the working poor. Spokesmen from the Labor Department stressed the need to provide more jobs for recipients who could work. Even representatives of welfare recipients were divided as to what modifications were most needed.

By late March HEW had come up with a series of options for reforming the system, ranging from modest administrative changes to a guaranteed annual income for most people on welfare. Califano decided to brief Carter on these options, since the president had not involved himself in the planning process. "I wanted to give him a picture of the existing system and of the problems involved in shaping a reform proposal," the secretary recalled. He also hoped to move back the 1 May deadline and to get an idea of the type of welfare system Carter expected, including the level of funding to which he was prepared to commit.[5]

His meeting with the president on 25 March did not go well. Carter instructed Califano to redesign the whole proposal at current levels of funding. Both Califano and Labor Secretary Ray Marshall, who advocated a program of guaranteed public jobs for the unemployed poor, were keenly disappointed. Marshall even considered not giving the president any zero-cost alternatives, believing them to be unrealistic. Califano sent Carter a ten-point memorandum of reform principles in which he called once more for "funding increments above zero-cost to increase equity and make the package more politically attractive."[6]

Over the next month, officials from HEW and Labor developed three zero-cost reform plans, reflecting their inability to reconcile their differences. One plan featured Marshall's job program; a second, favored by HEW, proposed to replace the existing system of nine separate programs with a so-called negative income tax, or direct cash payments to the poor based strictly on need; and a third, supported by the AFL-CIO, included a jobs program and cash assistance for people who could not work. When Califano met with Carter again on 11 April, he argued that without additional funding, many welfare recipients would be worse off no matter which option the president selected. Carter became irate. "Are you telling me there is no way to improve the present welfare system except by spending billions of dollars?" he asked. "In that case, to hell with it! We're wasting our time." After the president cooled down, however, he told the HEW secretary to come to terms with Marshall and to present him with an outline that he could broadcast on 1 May.[7]

Over the next three weeks, the conflict between the Labor Department and HEW, which had been relatively subdued, became more pronounced as each agency sought to protect its institutional interests. At the same time, representatives of the poor continued to air their own grievances, charging that both HEW's plan for a negative income tax and Labor's proposed jobs program were inadequate. When Califano and Marshall met with the president on 30 April, just one day before his promised announcement on welfare reform, they still had not been able to reach a consensus. Determined to meet his May commitment, Carter resigned himself to a general statement of principles on which welfare reform would be based rather than the presentation of a legislative package, which was now put off until August.

The public bickering and interagency squabbling that characterized this episode left Carter totally frustrated. His mood had become so dark that, toward the end of April, Hamilton Jordan advised him to get away from Washington and relax at Camp David. "If you work all weekend on welfare reform, you will begin the week tired," Jordan told the president. Yet many of the difficulties could be traced back to Carter himself. His unrealistic deadlines were intended to force action, but they gave officials at HEW and the Department of Labor little time to wade through the complexities involved in changing the welfare system—much less to develop a carefully structured program on which there was widespread agreement.[8]

The president had also failed to make the hard choices or provide the guidelines demanded by the type of major overhaul of the welfare system that he wanted. Left unresolved were such fundamental issues as who would be required to work or be excused from work, what would be the minimum level of subsistence for individuals and families, to what extent would the government be expected to provide jobs for the unemployed, and whether the poor would be aided primarily through the negative income tax favored by HEW, the jobs program preferred by the Labor Department, or some combination of the two. Indeed, there was no consideration of whether it was even possible to have a welfare system that was both fair and simple at the same time.

In the final analysis, though, it was Carter's fiscal conservatism, as evidenced by his determination to hold welfare spending to existing levels, that made it virtually impossible for his administration to reach agreement by the 1 May deadline. Because the president demanded only a redistribution of extant resources without indicating who should be helped or hurt under a reallotment, HEW and Labor were unable to reconcile their differences without adversely affecting the constituencies they served, something they were both loath to do.

In August the president finally sent his proposals for welfare reform to Congress. Illustrating his emphasis on the work ethic, Carter's program provided jobs for welfare recipients who could work and a "decent income" for those who could not, such as the disabled and single parents with children. Initial reaction to the plan was overwhelmingly favorable, but as lawmakers and others examined it more carefully, they began to object strongly to some of its provisions. Senator Russell Long and other congressional conservatives expressed alarm at the large number of people who would be added to the welfare rolls. During one of the earlier iterations of the bill, the president had expressed a similar concern.[9] The AFL-CIO claimed that the huge jobs programs paying minimum wage would weaken local labor markets. Welfare advocates decried the scheme's complexity.

Lawmakers also began to raise questions about the proposal's real costs. Although the president had wanted to constrain welfare reform within current budgetary limits, he had agreed over the summer to $2.8 billion in additional spending as a way of supplying more fiscal relief to the states. But to balance the books, the administration had to include in its cost estimates compensatory savings and new revenue sources. Many of the projected offsets, such as savings in extended unemployment insurance and a wellhead tax on oil, were problematic.

By this time, the president had also suffered a major reversal on his farm program, and many of his other legislative proposals, including energy and tax reform, were in trouble as well. A massive grain sale to the Soviet Union in 1972 had wiped out most of the nation's grain surplus accumulated during the 1950s and 1960s. At the same time, droughts, poor harvests, and rising populations in other countries had caused farm prices to soar as demand boomed worldwide for plentiful U.S. agricultural products. As a result, in 1973 Congress had replaced the existing program of high fixed price supports—which, by encouraging overproduction, had created most of the nation's farm surpluses—with a more flexible system of target and loan prices for commodities. Because these prices were considerably below market prices, few expected the government to be back in the business of storing excess grain.

The situation had changed by Carter's inauguration in 1977. A worldwide agricultural recovery, including an unexpected bumper crop in the Soviet Union in 1976, led to tumbling farm prices. By the end of 1976 the price of wheat, which had sold for as much as $5.32 a bushel in February 1974, was selling for only $2.85. An emergency farm bill that would have raised target and loan prices had been vetoed by President Gerald Ford in 1975 on the grounds that it was too expensive and would undermine the existing market-oriented farm policy. This had cost Ford heavily among farmers in the race against Carter. As the new administration assumed office, therefore, farmers' organizations and lawmakers from farm states looked to the new president for relief, warning about an agricultural crisis unless help was forthcoming.

They were sorely disappointed. Although Carter had made the farm crisis a campaign issue, accusing Nixon and Ford of causing farm income to drop and promising new legislation to ensure support prices that were at least equal to the cost of production, he discovered that this promise conflicted with his higher commitment to a balanced budget by 1981. Consequently, the farm program that Secretary of Agriculture Bob Bergland sent to Congress at the end of March contained support prices that were even lower than existing prices.

Not surprisingly, the plan came under heavy fire. In the House Agricultural Committee, chairman Thomas Foley told Bergland that even with an all-out effort, he could muster no more than five of the committee's forty-six votes in favor of the administration's proposal. With his usual candor, Jordan admonished Carter for presenting Congress with such a politically untenable program. "Instead of being considered seriously by the Congress and having an impact on the final outcome of the legislation," he said, "the Administration's position on [price supports] will be discarded and the likelihood is that Congress will come up with a more expensive program than would have been originally acceptable to the various interests if we had come in with a *politically credible proposal.*"[10]

Yielding to the widespread dissatisfaction both inside and outside his administration, Carter agreed on 18 April to accept higher target prices for wheat, corn, cotton, and rice. Although he warned that he would veto any measure that exceeded these supports, the Senate ignored his threat and approved its own, more expensive farm bill by a margin of sixty-nine to eighteen, more than the two-thirds vote needed to override a presidential veto. At first, Carter responded angrily, and at a news conference on 26 May he renewed his veto pledge. But by July, when the House took up the farm bill, there was little question that lawmakers would overwhelmingly approve price supports higher than those the administration wanted.

Aware that the opposition had enough votes to cancel his veto, the president adopted a more conciliatory line and merely urged Senate and House conferees to accept the less costly provisions in the two bills. In the final legislation, which both houses approved in September, the target price of wheat was set at either $3.00 or $3.05 a bushel, depending on the size of the wheat crop. Although the president objected to the expense of the program, he signed the measure into law at the end of September. The administration's original farm bill had a price tag of $1.4 billion per year for crop years 1978 to 1981. By September that figure had jumped to as much as $6.2 billion.

In retrospect, there were several reasons why Carter lost the contest over price supports. First, falling agricultural prices and a near-record grain harvest in the summer of 1977, after a record harvest a year earlier, evoked nationwide sympathy for the plight of farmers. Second, wheat growers and lawmakers from wheat-producing states conducted an enormously successful lobbying effort on behalf of higher target prices; farmers from the Midwest came to Washington by the hundreds to press their case. Further, the farm bill itself was a multifaceted piece of legislation, which allowed ample opportunity for bargaining. Since it also authorized funding for food stamps, lawmakers from the grain-producing states were able to horse-trade with their urban counterparts to win approval for higher prices.

The president, however, also helped undermine his own farm program by failing to give Bergland or anyone else the authority to coordinate farm policy. As a result, the administration continued to bicker internally over the size of the price supports it should recommend. Bergland found himself pitted against CEA chairman Charles Schultze and

OMB director Bert Lance, both of whom favored lower price supports than he did. When Carter's own people were unable to thrash out their differences, it left the president hard-pressed to sell his farm program to Congress. It did not escape the notice of a number of House and Senate members that Bergland's support for the program was lackluster. The hot-tempered chairman of the Senate Budget Committee, Edmund Muskie, was already furious with the White House for changing its mind on the tax rebate, which he had reluctantly agreed to support only to have the White House reverse course without consulting him. He had been willing to fight for a more restrictive farm measure, but now he was totally frustrated with the administration, believing that it was undermining his credibility with his own committee. Even Carter was frustrated, blaming Bergland for what had been his own failure to set firm policy. "I'm disappointed with the way the farm bill costs have apparently skyrocketed," he wrote to Bergland in September. "I'm not able to check USDA figures and thought we were appropriating only minimal increases above our $2 billion limit. Please explain."[11]

Elsewhere on the president's agenda, the combined efforts of Speaker Tip O'Neill and the White House's own lobbying produced a crucial legislative victory in August when most of Carter's energy program was accepted by the House. O'Neill, who regarded passage of the energy package as a test of whether a Democratic president and Congress could work together, short-circuited the regular legislative process by having the program quickly funneled to a forty-member ad hoc Committee on Energy, which he had established. The Speaker also made sure that the majority of the committee's members supported Carter's energy proposals. In this way, he sought to prevent the five volumes of legislation from being carved up and mutilated by the nine House committees and subcommittees that normally would have been responsible for sending the legislation to the House floor. "This bill was going to pit one region of the country against another," O'Neill later explained. "I *had* to get that bill through—and quickly, so that Congress could move ahead on other fronts."[12]

Meanwhile, the White House succeeded in turning back an effort to decontrol the price of natural gas, which was not part of Carter's program but had been broached by House members from energy-producing states. The administration had less success with its proposed standby tax on gasoline, which House members believed was not politically feasible; the measure never resurfaced after being rejected by the Ways and Means Committee. Except for that provision and one for tax rebates to buyers of small cars, which the House thought would amount to a subsidy for foreign imports, Carter's program was approved on 5 August by a vote of 244 to 177.

House passage of the energy plan represented a major coup for Carter, which was made even sweeter by the fact that he had just signed legislation establishing the new Department of Energy. But as both advocates and critics of the president's program realized, the real battle over energy still lay ahead in the Senate, where procedural rules made it easier than in the House for a small group to block legislation or to amend it to death, and where much of the leadership was in the hands of lawmakers from energy-producing states. Because the plan was built around higher taxes to discourage the use of energy, its fate would be determined largely by the Senate Finance Committee and its powerful chairman, Russell Long of Louisiana. Although Long remained closemouthed about his own position on Carter's proposal, it was clear, even to the White House, that the energy industry would get a much more sympathetic hearing before the Senate committee than it had received in the House.

Carter's program for tax reform was also in trouble. The president had made a firm commitment during the campaign to clean up the tax system, which he described as "nothing less than a disgrace." As a candidate and as president-elect, he had promoted three fundamental objectives for tax reform: (1) it must be comprehensive; (2) the result must be a fairer, more progressive tax system; and (3) it must achieve simplification. He called for taxing capital gains at the same rate as ordinary income, eliminating tax shelters, limiting business expense deductions (such as first-class travel and "two martini" lunches), tightening the rules on other tax deductions (such as large charitable gifts), and shifting more of the tax burden from low- and middle-income families to wealthy people and corporations.

One of the changes in the tax code that Carter hoped to accomplish—simplifying and increasing the standard deduction for individual and joint returns—was included in the tax portion of his economic stimulus package, but the president considered this only the first step. As early as February, he had instructed Treasury Secretary Michael Blumenthal to devise an inclusive tax reform and simplification package to be presented to Congress in the fall. But as late as the end of April, Blumenthal was still seeking guidance from the president as to the specifics. In May Blumenthal gave Carter a preliminary outline of his proposal, which contained many of the features the president had wanted, such as discarding preferential treatment for capital gains and placing some restrictions on tax-deductible business expenses. However, the treasury secretary's plan also allowed deductions for many other business expenses and eliminated "double taxation" on corporate income paid out as dividends (by taxing only income and not dividends, both of which were subject to taxes under existing law). In addition, the current schedule of tax rates, which ranged from 14 percent to 70 percent, was changed to one that varied from 13 percent to 50 percent.

At the White House, Stuart Eizenstat reacted angrily to Blumenthal's suggestions. The two men were not on the best of terms. Blumenthal chaired the steering committee of the Economic Policy Group, which had broad authority over virtually every economic issue facing the administration. Eizenstat had never been happy with the oversight power delegated to Blumenthal because it intruded into his own domain as the president's assistant for domestic affairs and head of the White House's Domestic Policy Staff. But Eizenstat objected to the treasury secretary's tax recommendations mainly because he thought they favored the rich and were not based on a complete review of all special tax provisions. *"If you want a really comprehensive review of the tax system with all major issues and options presented to you for decision,"* he told Carter in May, *"you will have to instruct Treasury to that effect."* Carter's chief speechwriter, Jim Fallows, also warned the president of the political damage the proposals might cause. "I am not an expert in taxes," he remarked, "but I believe we should start now to measure this plan against the expectations we have built up."[13]

Following the advice he received from Eizenstat, Fallows, and other White House aides, Carter assumed a more active role in putting together his administration's tax package. He instructed Blumenthal to simplify his plan and make it more progressive. Blumenthal agreed to reduce the tax on the lowest income bracket from 14 percent to 12 percent, rather than the 13 percent he had originally recommended. He also proposed to limit deductible personal interest payments to $10,000 and to tighten business deductions for entertainment. Eizenstat estimated that under the latest version of the reform program, all income classes below $30,000 would bear a smaller share of the total tax burden, and those above $30,000 would shoulder a larger share. But he and Schultze continued to object to the tax breaks given to business.

With the administration itself divided over tax reform and Congress already handling a full docket, the president decided, on the advice of the congressional leadership, to delay sending his tax proposals to Congress until the end of the session. Thus, after a promising start in early summer, by autumn most of Carter's legislative agenda had stalled or was in serious trouble. The president had made an energy bill, welfare reform, and tax reform three of his highest priorities, and all faced an uncertain future.

There were also signs of pending economic woes as the robust economy of the first half of 1977 became increasingly sluggish. The growth rate for the first six months of 1977 had been about 6.8 percent, and Schultze had predicted that this would continue for the entire year. Yet third-quarter growth slowed substantially to around 4 percent. Although

Schultze still thought that the economy would improve in the fourth quarter, he was not as optimistic as he had been. "It appears to us that, in the absence of additional measures to stimulate growth," he told Carter in October, "the rate of expansion will fall well short of our 5 percent target for next year." Inflation, which was still running at around 6 percent, also remained a nagging concern. Contrary to his earlier estimates, Schultze was now forecasting that inflation would continue to hound all the major nations, including the United States.[14]

No problem, however, caused Carter greater grief or did more harm to his presidency in that first year than the scandal resulting from the banking and business practices of his OMB director and close friend Bert Lance. The Lance affair struck at the very foundation of a vulnerable administration. Although Lance was eventually forced to resign his post, Carter's unfailing support of his friend, well beyond the bounds of political prudence, raised questions not only about his political judgment but also about his publicly stated commitment to the highest ethical standards in government. Just as important, Lance's resignation deprived the president of a close friend and the only one of his advisers from Georgia who was near his age, someone with whom he could engage in frank discussions on an almost daily basis and who might have acted as a rudder to a president and an administration whose course often seemed aimless.

Lance and Carter met in 1966 during Carter's first campaign for governor when the burly and amiable north Georgia banker introduced himself to the future president. Although they were polar opposites in many ways, the two men shared common religious interests and became close friends and political allies. As governor, Carter appointed Lance director of the Georgia Department of Transportation. Lance began most workdays by meeting with the governor and often ended the day playing tennis with him. Given his close ties to Lance, it was not surprising that the first person President-elect Carter nominated for a cabinet-level position was Lance. As OMB director, Lance remained close to the president personally as well as officially; they continued to play tennis and talk informally. Being near in age to the president only enhanced Lance's personal relationship with the chief executive. Easily approachable as well as influential, he was one of the more well-liked members of the president's inner circle.

The episode leading to the OMB director's resignation began innocently enough. After his election, Carter directed all his appointees to reveal their financial holdings and to divest themselves of any that might lead to a conflict of interest. In accordance with this policy, the president-elect asked Lance to dispose of his considerable assets in the National Bank of Georgia (NBG), which he had headed, along with the much smaller First National Bank of Calhoun. Lance agreed to place his NBG stock, valued at $3.3 million, in a blind trust, with instructions to the trustee to divest it of all NBG stock by the end of 1977.

However, the value of Lance's NBG holdings began to drop after it was learned that the bank planned to charge off various bad loans, which would affect its ability to continue paying dividends. By July Lance's NBG holdings were worth only $1.7 million; his annual income had also declined. Faced with worsening economic prospects, the OMB director went to Carter for help. After conferring with Charles Kirbo, the president sent a letter to Democratic senator Abraham Ribicoff of Connecticut, chairman of the Senate Governmental Affairs Committee, which had confirmed Lance, asking for an unlimited extension of the 31 December deadline for the stock divestiture.

In addition to his promise to sell his bank stock by the end of the year, Lance had pledged during his confirmation hearings to disqualify himself from participating in any matter involving banking regulation so long as he held NBG stock. Yet reports (which were later confirmed) circulated in Washington that he had met in his OMB office with NBG officials and had written to Senate Banking Committee chairman William Proxmire of Wisconsin against an anti-redlining proposal that would require banks to give priority to the credit needs of their communities in making loans. Even more serious, columnist William Safire accused the OMB director of peddling his political influence to obtain a $3.4 million loan with deferred interest from the First National Bank of Chicago; the *Washington Post* claimed that the loan was made in return for a $200,000 deposit of NBG funds in a non-interest-bearing account. The U.S. Comptroller's Office began an investigation of these charges, Senator Ribicoff summoned Lance before his committee for an explanation, and Senator Proxmire, the only senator to oppose Lance's confirmation, undertook his own probe.

Lance's appearance before the Ribicoff committee failed to produce the fireworks that many Washington observers had anticipated. Denying Safire's charge of a "sweetheart loan," Lance said that he was paying a respectable 0.75 percent above the prime interest rate on the loan. He also maintained that the NBG's account with the First National Bank of Chicago was long-standing and that he had not acted illegally or unethically either before or after being appointed OMB director. That seemed to satisfy the committee, which granted him the extension he sought.

On 18 August comptroller John Heimann released his agency's eagerly awaited report on Lance's banking practices. In a massive 394-page document, Heimann determined that Lance had done nothing illegal. As far as the White House was concerned, that amounted to the OMB director's vindication. At a news conference the president personally announced the report's central conclusion; he then turned to Lance, who

"The referral to justice," Carter's White House counsel, Robert Lipshutz, informed him, "will undoubtedly increase pressure for the appointment of a Special Prosecutor." Both *Business Week* and the *Los Angeles Times* called for Lance to step down, and the *Wall Street Journal* declared that Lance could no longer be effective as budget director.[18]

Carter's visceral reaction to the outcry for Lance's resignation was to stand by his friend. As late as the middle of September he defended Lance before a group of news reporters, saying that the OMB chief was neither dishonest, incompetent, nor unethical. But the pressure to ask for Lance's resignation continued to rise. Hamilton Jordan even flew down to Lance's vacation home on Sea Island, Georgia, during the Labor Day weekend to tell him that the controversy was becoming a huge liability for the president. On Capitol Hill a large and growing number of lawmakers urged Carter to dismiss his friend. Unable to stem the call for Lance's head, the president reluctantly began to back away from his support of the OMB director, acknowledging, for example, that Lance's use of overdrafts was "obviously a mistake." He asked, however, that no final judgment be made until after Lance went before Ribicoff's Governmental Affairs Committee. "Bert would be permanently disgraced if he left office without having some chance to defend himself," the president later commented.[19]

Lance's appearance before the Senate committee on 15 September was his last hurrah. In a two-hour opening statement and then in subsequent testimony carried on national television, the OMB director defended himself well, even putting his accusers on trial. "The basic American principle of justice and fair play has been pointedly ignored by certain members of this committee," he charged. "The rights that I thought that I possessed have, one by one, gone down the drain." By the time the committee adjourned for the weekend, many observers predicted that Lance might yet be able to keep his job.[20]

On Saturday, however, Carter met with Jordan, Vice President Walter Mondale, press secretary Jody Powell, and Kirbo, who had flown up from Atlanta. As the president recorded in his diary, they agreed that Lance had "won a great victory and now should step down." Returning to Washington from Camp David that afternoon, the president called Lance and asked to see him the next morning. He also telephoned majority leader Robert Byrd to get his reaction to Lance's performance. Although Byrd believed that Lance had been "a good, affable, strong witness," he warned that the Lance affair was not going to vanish and that it was doing serious damage to Carter on Capitol Hill. The presidency was more important than any single individual, he said.[21]

After a sleepless night, Carter met Lance in the morning. He congratulated his friend on his appearance before the Governmental Affairs

Committee, saying that his critics had suffered a setback. But he added that the opposition was regrouping, and he strongly suggested that Lance consider resigning. Before deciding, Lance wanted to discuss the situation with his wife, LaBelle, and his attorney, Clark Clifford. After a game of tennis that afternoon, Lance indicated that he planned to resign. "I didn't argue with him," the president recorded in his diary. But on the following day, 21 September, which the president described as "one of the worst days I've ever spent," Lance informed Carter that his wife was convinced that he should stay in office and he was unsure what to do. The president replied that he had made the right decision on the tennis courts, and that afternoon Lance agreed to step down—although LaBelle adamantly opposed his decision and told Carter that he had betrayed his best friend. A few hours later the president announced the resignation to a news conference that had actually been scheduled for earlier in the day.[22]

After the announcement the White House was flooded with telephone calls, telegrams, and letters, most of which, according to Carter, condemned the press and Congress for their relentless attacks on Lance. Even so, there seems little question that the president's support of Lance did irreparable harm to his administration. Even the president later conceded this point. Besides distracting the administration from more pressing domestic and foreign policy matters, the controversy had helped poison relations with Congress and undermined the public's trust in Carter, which he had worked so hard to foster and was so essential to his success as president.

Just as important, Lance's resignation left the president without the one person in his administration who felt comfortable speaking frankly to him and who was able to serve as a bridge between the White House and Capitol Hill and the rest of Washington's influential political and social circle. "If a Senator or somebody called or somebody that he expected to get something out of later on," Charles Kirbo later commented, "he moved right in and he was extra good in that . . . he enjoyed knowing everybody, and he was very skillful at it and would follow up. He had the time and the energy to entertain in meaningful ways."[23] In this way, Lance was able to establish ties and provide a perspective that neither Hamilton Jordan nor Jody Powell nor anyone else close to Carter could do. More than that, even though Jordan, Powell, and even Stuart Eizenstat were like sons to Carter, and he trusted and listened to them, Carter himself described Lance as being like a brother to him, and the feeling was reciprocated. As a result, Lance's forced resignation left a void in the administration that was never filled.

Yet the problems confronting Carter extended beyond Bert Lance. As one reporter correctly observed, that muddle was "only the tip of the iceberg." Although the president had enjoyed some success in both his domestic programs and his conduct of foreign policy, most of his legislative agenda had not been passed, and some of the United States' closest allies were openly expressing reservations about his ability as a world leader. Perhaps even more important, public cynicism about government remained as hardened as ever. "The optimism we saw in December," Pat Caddell told the president in September, "has faded and voters see the past, present, and future as quite similar. They are becoming resigned to the idea that problems like inflation, poverty, and war will be ever with us."[24]

Presidential scholar Richard Neustadt has remarked that "presidential power is the power to persuade."[25] After a promising start, and despite his efforts at outreach, by the fall of 1977 Carter had clearly failed to achieve that essential element of leadership. This was true both among the American people and inside the Washington Beltway. That this was so was not from a lack of trying. In all his major legislative initiatives, Carter had continued to work hard to win congressional support. During the summer, for example, the president had held a series of well-attended White House lawn parties for lawmakers and their families, complete with entertainment for the children. For each high-priority piece of legislation, the White House established an administration task force to coordinate legislative strategy. The congressional liaison office, headed by Frank Moore, kept close tabs on each piece of legislation as it made its way through Capitol Hill. His office even developed a highly sophisticated computer system that kept detailed information on each lawmaker; it was coded in such a way as to allow the White House to respond to a host of different assumptions and variables. The president also continued his standard practices of hosting dinners and suppers with legislative leaders and meetings with groups of lawmakers to explain and answer questions about major legislative initiatives.

Yet President Carter was never able to develop a solid base of dedicated supporters on Capitol Hill. This failure, moreover, was not due to a breakdown of party discipline or loyalty or to a reassertion of congressional authority. What is striking in the relationship between Capitol Hill and the White House, in fact, was the genuine desire by leading Democrats to work with the president and their frustration with White House miscues. Much of this dissatisfaction was directed at Frank Moore and, to a lesser extent, Hamilton Jordan, who were notorious for not responding to telephone calls. But congressional despair ran deeper than that. As early as March, freshman lawmaker Dan Glickman of Kansas, who greatly admired Carter and would later become secretary of agriculture in the Bill Clinton administration, expressed much of the frustration felt by his more senior colleagues. "Your openness and desire for input from the American people," Glickman wrote to the president, "are beautiful examples of making people part of the method of deciding how to do things. I am only suggesting that you allow the same things with all members of Congress. . . . My point is that you need not wait for an important bill or a crisis to occur in order to obtain Members' support."[26] Fast-forward to the summer, and complaints about being ignored or not being taken into the president's confidence were being made by such Senate luminaries as Robert Byrd, Henry Jackson, and Russell Long. All three of these leading lawmakers had considerable egos that needed to be cultivated. But the president refused to take that step.

After Carter left office, Long expressed regrets to his wife, Carolyn, that Carter had not done more to reach out to him. When she reminded him that the president had invited them to a private dinner in September 1977, Long replied that that had not been enough. If the president had approached him in the spirit of trying to reach a mutual accommodation, his relationship with Carter might have been different. But the president never proposed such a deal. "I never knew what I could count on," he commented. "I never knew if I could count on him or not."[27]

Congressional concerns about the White House were usually more specific. One matter that especially riled lawmakers was the administration's ongoing failure to replace Republicans in non-civil-service positions. "The Leadership is beginning to get back comments that if the Administration won't help Members, why should they help the Administration when it comes to votes," Moore warned Carter at the end of July.[28] The president was as frustrated on this matter as Congress was. Time and again he had urged members of his cabinet and other high government officials to replace Republican officeholders with Democrats whenever possible. But, committed to a cabinet form of government, the president too often assumed that his instructions would be carried out without oversight; as a result, he failed to follow up or to castigate those who failed to heed his admonitions. A common theme in the exit interviews and oral histories conducted after Carter left office was his reluctance to discipline recalcitrant members of his administration.

This failure on the president's part pointed to another problem within the administration: the lack of an adequate organizational structure. Even the assignment of offices created problems. Until 1979, when Alonzo McDonald was brought in as White House staff director, the six offices of the congressional liaison group were scattered throughout the West Wing and Executive Office Building on the seventeen-acre White House complex. This created problems of communication. "One of the reasons [the congressional liaison office] could never respond to telephone calls," McDonald later recalled, "was that they could not find out where the calls had come in. They couldn't respond to correspondence because they couldn't know where the correspondence was, and when they found it they didn't know where to send it."[29]

The lack of an adequate organizational structure within the White House underscored yet another problem within the administration: the failure to develop a cohesive legislative program. Again, the president understood the problem. Notwithstanding the enormous legislative agenda he sent to Congress, he sought to set his legislative priorities within some kind of coherent framework. "I've got to tie together four major concepts: a) balanced FY81 budget; b) Energy policy; c) Tax reform; d) Welfare reform," he wrote to energy adviser James Schlesinger at the end of March. "You, Stu [Eizenstat], Mike [Blumenthal], Charlie [Schultze], Bert [Lance] have to work together with me on this. Yours is the first to be addressed. . . . Both I and the person in the street have to see the whole picture."[30] Unfortunately, Carter and his advisers were never able to develop this "whole picture"—not in the first year of his administration or in the three years that followed.

Yet the elements of a coherent policy that might have dealt with Carter's most profound problem as president—how to bridge the transition between the demise of the New Deal coalition and the emerging conservative movement in the United States—were already apparent in who Carter was and in much of what he said and did. The president was an antiestablishment, evangelical Christian who was an implacable foe of interest-group politics. He advocated personal responsibility, morality in public affairs, and the limits of government. He believed that the welfare state discouraged work and the traditional family. He was also pro-life. He talked about making personal sacrifices, reducing the deficit, balancing the budget, and reforming a tax system that he considered a national disgrace. This was the discourse of the growing conservative movement.

At the same time, Carter believed that the federal government still had a major role to play in affording social justice and improving the human condition; in providing jobs for those who could work, assistance for those who could not, and a minimum income for all working Americans; in finding new sources of energy; in ensuring a more equitable and progressive tax system that would provide tax relief for the working class, especially low-income Americans, including an earned income tax credit. This was the discourse of the traditional Democratic coalition and was inherent in his energy program and in his proposals for tax and welfare reform.

To these goals might be added Carter's support for the equal rights amendment, his opposition to a constitutional amendment prohibiting abortion, and a number of other measures on which his administration was already working. These included a new urban policy; reform of the nation's health care system, including hospital cost containment and a program of national health insurance that, at the very least, would insure all Americans against catastrophic illness; a consumer protection agency; deregulation of the airline and other industries to make them more competitive and their services more affordable for American consumers; and legislation to clean up the environment and protect the remaining American wilderness against exploitation.

In short, the basic elements of a coherent policy were already present early in the Carter administration. It might not satisfy the most ardent advocates of limited or limitless government—those of the radical Right or the radical Left—but it might be attractive to a new American center. To succeed in being a transitional president, however, Carter had to be able to articulate this message in a persuasive fashion to the American people and their representatives in Congress. He had to be a leader who could speak with passion and eloquence and stay on message. He had to be intimately engaged in the political process of give-and-take, including agreeing to increased spending in the short term (such as for jobs and job training) to bring about savings in the long term (taking people off welfare rolls). He had to balance his conservative and liberal instincts. He had to refrain from disparaging government and constituent politics even as he presented himself as a "good government" reformer who would provide tangible benefits to the American people. He had to uplift rather than to despair, offer hope rather than the moral equivalent of war. He had to be concerned as much with being a successful communicator as with being a problem solver. In short, he had to articulate a vision that the American people could grab onto and, in the process, develop his own base of loyal followers.

Instead, by the fall of 1977, it appeared to an increasing number of Americans that the outsider from Georgia had been unable to elevate the level at which the affairs of government were being conducted and that his administration was already crumbling from within.

5

★ ★ ★ ★ ★

CAN CARTER COPE?

Although there was a mounting perception among American voters that the still-young Carter administration was in disarray, polls at the end of 1977 indicated that the voters were not yet ready to pass final judgment on the president. When asked for whom they would vote if they could choose again between Carter and Ford, the people surveyed still chose Carter (44 percent) over Ford (41 percent), with 15 percent not sure. These figures compared favorably with Carter's 2 percent margin of victory in 1976 and suggested that voters would elect him by about the same plurality a year later.

But these surveys also revealed a growing sense among the American people that the president had not lived up to his campaign promises and that he was unable to get things done. In particular, respondents doubted whether he could handle inflation and high unemployment, the issues that most concerned them. Only 18 percent of the interviewees in one poll had "a lot" of confidence in the president's ability to deal with the economy, while 23 percent had "practically no" confidence. Voters also complained that the president was trying to do too much at once; that he was trying to do too much by himself; that he had compromised on too many issues; that his staff was insular, inexperienced, uncoordinated, and error prone; and that he had yet to master the art of congressional relations. Although most of these criticisms were not new, they were being stated with increasing frequency, leading more and more Americans to ask, "Can Carter cope?"

Carter's defense of Bert Lance had done him considerable political damage. At the very least, he had displayed an obstinacy and a blind spot regarding his friend that seemed to belie his reputation for cool judgment and high moral standards. But Lance was not the only member of his administration to embarrass Carter or present him with major complications. Also undercutting the president politically was Andrew Young, the United States' first black ambassador to the United Nations. By advocating support for newly emerging nations, openly attacking the apartheid policies of Rhodesia and South Africa, and working on behalf of majority rule in Rhodesia and Namibia, Young was instrumental in gaining African confidence in the United States. But at the same time he created enormous controversy by his uninhibited candor and sometimes reckless remarks—such as his suggestion in a *Playboy* interview that a race war in South Africa would cause whites in the United States "to panic" and attack American blacks, or his comment in the same interview that Soviet dissidents were only a "literary elite who had tasted a little freedom and wanted more." The latter statement in particular caused a public furor. American Jewish leaders and others called the White House demanding that Young apologize for his comments. Although the ambassador tempered his remarks over the next several months, his bluntness continued to rankle many Americans, and there were rumblings that he should be forced to resign.[1]

Conversely, many liberal Democrats complained that Vice President Walter Mondale was not playing the vital role in the administration that had been promised by the president. In reality, this charge was grossly exaggerated. Although Mondale's political liberalism sometimes clashed with Carter's economic conservatism, the vice president quickly became one of the president's closest advisers. He was kept fully informed on all domestic issues by Eizenstat and his staff, and the vice president was one of only four people—along with the president, the secretary of state, and the national security adviser—to have a daily intelligence briefing. Nevertheless, the doubts expressed in the news media about Mondale's influence within the administration, when coupled with the largely negative reporting on Young, raised new accusations that the White House was controlled by the "Georgia Mafia" and further weakened Carter's already tenuous political standing with Congress.

Just how vulnerable the president had become on Capitol Hill was evident when House Speaker Tip O'Neill decided to cancel a pending vote on legislation sponsored by the White House and supported by a coalition of consumer groups to establish a federal office for consumer affairs. Both as governor of Georgia and as a candidate for president, Carter had spoken out on the need to protect the rights of consumers. Although he had not campaigned explicitly for the establishment of a Consumer Protection Agency (CPA), he had allied himself during the campaign with the nation's leading spokesman on behalf of the consumer, Ralph Nader.

On Nader's recommendation he had named Esther Peterson as special assistant for consumer affairs. Explaining to Peterson his plans to establish a CPA, Carter added that he wanted the government to be on the same wavelength as the consumer.

After the administration introduced legislation to establish a CPA, business interests launched an intense and well-funded attack against the measure, leading Peterson to remark that she was "frightened for [her] country after seeing the demonstration of corporate power."[2] Opponents of the agency were able to argue successfully that the establishment of a CPA would merely add another layer of federal regulation. Congressional opposition to the measure remained so strong that O'Neill pulled it off the House calendar the day before it was scheduled for a floor vote.

Peterson later blamed herself for not using her authority as special assistant to the president to push harder for the CPA, especially with the congressional liaison office headed by Frank Moore. "I would have been on the Hill lots more, lobbying what I felt," she remarked. "I was a little reluctant to do that because Frank Moore and I didn't get along too well. . . . I didn't want them to think that I was sticking my nose in their affairs." With the congressional liaison office unenthusiastic about the legislative prospects for a CPA, the president decided not to expend the energy necessary to win its approval.[3]

The president suffered an even more far-reaching defeat when the Senate gutted his energy program and then locked horns with the House in conference committee. In the House the president's energy legislation was contained in one omnibus measure, but in the Senate it was divided among six separate bills. Four were relatively noncontroversial, including one requiring new electric utilities and major industrial plants to burn coal or other fuels instead of oil and natural gas, and another providing $1.02 billion for a broad range of conservation measures. Except for a ban on "gas-guzzling" cars, which the Senate approved in place of the tax passed by the House, this quartet sailed through the upper chamber.

That was not the case with the president's proposals to bring intrastate gas under federal regulation for the first time, thereby rationalizing gas distribution and pricing, and to adjust the price of new natural gas based on the heating equivalent of oil—that is, the same output for the same cost, or about $1.75 for 1,000 cubic feet. Although this represented a significant increase over the current ceiling of $1.46, lobbyists for the oil and gas industry wanted total deregulation of new gas within five years. By a narrow fifty to forty-six vote, the Senate ratified legislation placing a two-year price cap of $2.46 on new gas, after which the price would be fully deregulated.

The Senate also rejected Carter's proposal to raise the price of domestically produced oil to the world price by 1980 through a crude oil equalization or wellhead tax. Opposition to the plan was led by Russell Long, chairman of the Finance Committee. Since the economy of his home state, Louisiana, was dependent on oil and gas, Long had complained from the outset that Carter's energy program did not provide adequate incentives for increasing oil and gas production. Although he was willing to consider a wellhead tax whose revenues would be returned to the oil industry, he was not prepared to accept a plan that involved a rebate to taxpayers. On 21 October Long's committee reported out a bill whose only revenue raiser was an extension of the existing four-cents-per-gallon tax on gasoline. After six days of debate, the full Senate approved the measure.

The president had badly misread the Senate and its differences with the House. At a news conference on 13 October—after the Senate had already voted to deregulate natural gas and the Senate Finance Committee had mangled the tax portions of his program—Carter conceded that "in retrospect it would have helped had [he] had more meetings with the members of the Senate." Even then, he still expected Senator Long to come up with an acceptable energy package on which both houses of Congress could compromise. But the divisions between the House and Senate over the deregulation of natural gas and the imposition of a wellhead tax were so fundamental that they were unable to resolve their disagreements in conference committee. Instead, final action on the energy legislation had to be postponed until the next session of Congress.

Once Congress reconvened in January, the White House was determined to win swift passage of its energy program. Delayed action, Eizenstat told the president, would be "disastrous," since it would divert attention on Capitol Hill from the other economic issues the administration had targeted for 1978. Yet the White House also recognized that it would have to make concessions to oil and gas producers to reach a final agreement. Meeting with reporters in January, Carter declared that passage of his energy legislation would again "be the first order of business . . . the first priority." Because he was willing to strike a bargain, he also predicted that a bill "acceptable to me and to the country . . . will come very early in this session."[4]

There was no quick resolution of the issues that separated the House and Senate, however, and the energy package languished in conference committee. Long made it clear that he and the other Senate conferees would not discuss the tax provisions of the president's program without a compromise on natural gas. As a basis for negotiation, the administration made an offer just before Christmas that kept some controls on natural gas until 1985 but increased producer revenue by $17 billion by raising the ceiling price for newly discovered gas. Later, it even proposed shortening the interim until complete deregulation and increasing the industry's revenue even more. Still, that failed to resolve the legislative impasse.

As hopes for accommodation dimmed, the White House decided to intervene in the negotiations. On 12 April Carter called the conferees to the White House. After meeting for thirteen hours, a small group of House and Senate lawmakers announced that they had reached a shaky compromise that imposed price controls on both interstate and intrastate natural gas, thus creating a unified national market; in return, federal controls on new natural gas would end by 1985. But House members protested the secrecy of the talks, and within a week, the agreement fell apart. Other efforts at compromise also became unglued at the last moment. On 9 May O'Neill threatened for the first time to split up the five-part energy package the House had passed—a move that almost certainly would have killed the unpopular wellhead tax, which the president had described as the centerpiece of his energy program.

During the Senate debate, Eizenstat and James Schlesinger had told the president that, in terms of domestic legislation, his administration's performance would be measured in large part by the outcome of his national energy plan; the president had agreed. With the fate of the package in peril, the administration was in line for a poor evaluation. But criticism of the Carter White House extended beyond any single piece of legislation to the instability within the administration itself. This was illustrated by the next testing ground for the White House—a Supreme Court case involving alleged reverse discrimination against a white applicant, Allan Bakke, who had been denied admission into the University of California Medical School at Davis.

In the decade since the peak of the civil rights movement in the mid-1960s, affirmative action laws had been passed to create avenues of opportunity for minorities (and women) in education and employment. Special programs had been established to ensure minority hiring and job promotion, even over employees with seniority. Colleges and universities encouraged minority applicants and set aside slots for minority students. These developments produced a backlash among some whites who claimed that, as a result of affirmative action programs, they had fallen victim to "reverse discrimination." In 1973 Bakke, a marine veteran who had twice been denied admission to the medical school at Davis, filed suit alleging that the university had discriminated against him by accepting minority students with college grades and aptitude test scores lower than his own, under an affirmative action program that reserved sixteen places for disadvantaged students. After the California Supreme Court upheld his complaint, the regents of the University of California appealed the decision to the U.S. Supreme Court, which agreed to hear the case. Immediately, *Bakke v. Regents of the University of California* became the most important civil rights case since the 1954 *Brown v. Board of Education*, not only pitting proponents against opponents of affirmative action but also dividing advocates between those who supported and those who denounced racial quotas.

Almost any position the White House adopted with respect to the case was bound to alienate one of the administration's traditional constituencies. American Jewish leaders, for example, generally favored affirmative action programs if they were based on goals rather than quotas. Most of organized labor opposed affirmative action entirely, viewing it as a frontal assault on its prized seniority system. The black community supported affirmative action programs, including ones utilizing racial quotas.

The *Bakke* case, therefore, presented Carter with a no-win situation. Almost as soon as the Supreme Court agreed to hear the case, Parren J. Mitchell of the Congressional Black Caucus wrote to Attorney General Griffin Bell and President Carter to urge the Justice Department to file an amicus curiae brief on behalf of the University of California regents. In contrast, the Anti-Defamation League of the B'nai B'rith and other Jewish organizations urged Carter not to intervene. Moreover, Carter himself was ambivalent about affirmative action. As a matter of principle, the president opposed all quotas, whatever their purpose. "I hate to endorse the proposition of quotas for minority groups, for women or for anyone else," he remarked in response to a reporter's question on the *Bakke* case. At the same time, he recognized that previous patterns of racial discrimination might have to be addressed in a way that could be injurious to particular individuals.

In August Bell gave Carter a draft of the Justice Department's brief on the *Bakke* case, which challenged the Davis plan because it established separate admissions procedures for whites and minorities. At the same time, the attorney general tried to reassure the president by telling him and White House counsel Robert Lipshutz that the Justice Department intended to "stand for affirmative action," even though it supported Bakke. As Lipshutz, Eizenstat, and other members of the administration read the document, however, they found its defense of affirmative action equivocal and murky. Although the brief ultimately concluded that some forms of affirmative action were appropriate, it also argued that all racial classifications were "suspect," including "even ostensibly benign classifications." Indeed, it stated that race was "presumptively pernicious as a basis on which to bestow or withhold benefits."[5]

Eizenstat and Lipshutz tore the document apart, warning the president that the brief did "not clearly express this Administration's firm commitment to affirmative action." Instead of asking the Supreme Court to declare the medical school's affirmative action program unconstitutional, the brief should firmly endorse affirmative action programs and clearly differentiate between racial goals and quotas. The pair also strongly recommended that the Justice Department seek to have the case remanded to the lower courts to determine whether the sixteen places reserved for disadvantaged students in the Davis program represented a goal or a rigid quota.[6]

The president thought that remanding the case might be "ill advised," although he did not explain why. But he agreed that the brief should be rewritten to include an unequivocal statement of support for affirmative action. Accordingly, he sent it back to the Justice Department for redrafting. When one of the lawyers involved in the revision told HEW Secretary Joseph Califano that it was impossible to write a brief defending a special admissions policy, Califano exploded. "Like hell it's impossible," he responded. Similarly, Mondale reminded the attorney general that the *Bakke* case represented an extremely important policy decision and that the president wanted any administration pronouncement to be consistent with his position of standing for affirmative action but against quotas. The chair of the Equal Employment Opportunity Commission, Eleanor Holmes Norton, and Califano also prepared legal arguments in opposition to *Bakke*, which they submitted to Bell.[7]

In accordance with the president's instructions, the new brief, which the Justice Department filed with the Supreme Court on 19 September, contained a very strong endorsement of affirmative action. "In our view," the document concluded, "only one question should be finally resolved in the present posture of this case: whether a state university admissions program may take race into account to remedy the effects of social discrimination."[8]

The Supreme Court did not decide the *Bakke* case until the following June. In a five to four decision, it sanctioned affirmative action programs but found that the Davis medical school had employed an unconstitutional quota system in denying Bakke a place. It therefore ordered that Bakke be admitted to the school's next class. By this time, the case had ceased to be a political problem for the White House. Blacks and other civil rights activists were generally pleased with the position the administration had taken on *Bakke*. Indeed, black leaders pointed to the Justice Department's brief as one of the administration's major contributions to the cause of civil rights.

On the negative side, *Bakke* had revealed divisions within the administration. Both Bell and Califano, who held substantially different views on affirmative action, later complained about the hurdles they had encountered—Bell attributing them to the liberal elements within the administration, Califano to the Georgia clique supposedly running the White House. In a sense, both men were right. Certainly the two persons who most influenced the president in the *Bakke* case were Eizenstat and

Lipshutz, two moderately conservative Georgians, but they were balanced by Mondale, a liberal outsider. According to Bell, in fact, Mondale was his greatest irritant in civil rights cases (a statement that directly contradicted claims about the vice president's diminished status within the administration).

Throughout most of the discussion on *Bakke*, the president had remained surprisingly disengaged. Califano saw him as determined "to walk the tightrope between affirmative action and reverse discrimination," while Bell believed that he was attempting "to gloss over [the] fundamental differences" in political philosophy between Carter and Mondale. According to the attorney general, this detachment "helped produce the unclear, all-things-to-all-people voice that the public heard so often from the administration."[9] In fact, because much of the internal bickering over *Bakke* was leaked to the press, it contributed to the perception of an administration incapable of commanding the loyalty of its own people. Even Jordan criticized the White House's conduct of the case. "I would like to share with you my serious concern about the manner in which we are handling . . . the Bakke case," he wrote to the president. "If you knew and were aware of the approach that is being taken on your behalf, I don't think you would be either happy or satisfied." Indeed, Chief Justice Warren Burger and Associate Justice Harry Blackmun told Solicitor General Wade H. McCree Jr. that the entire Court was offended and displeased by the news leaks that had taken place.[10]

Bakke was a sensational case that elicited vocal opinions from all sides on the affirmative action issue. Far more mundane were the daily reports of a shrinking economy, yet it was this issue that solidified the administration's increasingly unfavorable public image. Like the administration itself, the economy seemed more and more chaotic and lacking in direction. The administration also sent out conflicting signals, which created confusion and uncertainty within business and financial circles and among the American people.

After a year in office, there was still no single person to whom the president routinely deferred for economic advice or who spoke for him on economic issues. Eizenstat and Charles Schultze came closest to serving Carter in these capacities, but neither of them set policy. Eizenstat was not a trained economist, and Schultze was not part of Carter's inner circle. Although Treasury Secretary Michael Blumenthal headed the administration's Economic Policy Group, he had already clashed with the White House over tax reform and had been largely ignored in the development of the administration's welfare and energy programs. Nor did the new director of the OMB, James McIntyre—or, for that matter, anyone else—enjoy as much influence with the president as had McIntyre's predecessor, Bert Lance.

As a result, when one of these officials took a public position, business leaders were never certain whether they were speaking for themselves or for the president. This was particularly unsettling because Eizentat and Schultze tended to be more moderate on spending issues than Blumenthal and McIntyre were. The business community remained uneasy over what the news media described as "stagflation," or an economy suffering simultaneously from low growth and high inflation. Although capital spending at the beginning of November was about 8 percent above that for 1976, the economy was still slack, and the unemployment rate continued to hover around 7 percent. To stimulate the economy, some analysts recommended a substantial increase in federal spending, but others believed that the 6 percent inflation rate had to be addressed first.

Finally, businesses were concerned about the economic impact of pending legislation for refinancing the ailing Social Security system and reforming the nation's tax structure, both of which were high-priority items for the administration. Soon after taking office, Califano had discovered that Social Security was drowning in a sea of red ink. Driven by inflation, benefits were increasing, but revenues were diminishing. Moreover, the population was aging, and the resultant strains on the system were projected to continue well into the next century. To keep the system solvent, Califano estimated that $83 billion more would be needed over the next five years, which he proposed to obtain through modest increases in Social Security taxes, supplemented in times of high unemployment by general revenue funds. Satisfied to follow HEW's lead on Social Security, Carter presented this plan to Congress on 9 May.

In the Senate the proposal was attacked as a raid on the federal treasury, but lawmakers in the House voted overwhelmingly for a large increase in both taxes and the wage ceiling on which Social Security taxes were paid. With these changes, the maximum tax would rise from $965 in 1977 to $2,854 in 1986, a threefold increase in ten years. Even though the legislation flew in the face of the president's campaign promise not to raise payroll taxes, he decided to support the bill, hoping that the Senate would trim it before sending it to the Oval Office for his signature. Failing that, he would try to compensate for the hike with cuts in the income tax as part of his tax reform proposal. Regardless of the reasoning behind it, the administration's support for a measure that promised to be the largest ever peacetime tax increase fueled business pessimism about the economy.

So did speculation about Carter's plans for tax reform. Because the administration had been divided over what changes to recommend in the existing system, and because it was not even certain that Congress would pass any reform bill, the White House had decided in October not to send its recommendation to Capitol Hill until near the end of the session. In the interim, the president's economic advisers, including Blumenthal, Mondale, Schultze, McIntyre, and Eizenstat, reached a consensus on a tax package. This proposal significantly slimmed down the one presented by the treasury secretary in September but included greater incentives for capital formation and more tax breaks for lower-income groups. But until the specifics of the program were finally worked out and then made public, the business community did not know whether the White House would emphasize economic incentives for business, as Blumenthal wanted, or assault tax write-offs and business profits, as some business leaders feared.

Together with the administration's energy package, therefore, the proposal to increase Social Security taxes and the unknown direction of tax reform suggested to the business community the possibility of an alarming scenario of higher taxes, higher interest rates, runaway inflation, huge budget deficits, and subsequent recession. The lack of business confidence in the economy was reflected in the stock market, as the Dow-Jones average dropped to just over 800 by early November, its lowest level in two years and 195 points less than its closing numbers on the previous New Year's Eve. Apprehension about the economy also extended to the general public. According to a Harris poll taken about the same time that the stock market was skidding toward its two-year low, only 26 percent of the public approved of the president's conduct of economic affairs, down from 46 percent in May. Moreover, of the people polled, 54 percent believed that the country was in a recession, a view generally not held by most economists.

The surveys also revealed the extent to which Carter had antagonized many of the key voting groups that had helped get him elected in 1976. Blacks expressed dismay that he had not paid more attention to their problems. Labor remained miffed at his failure to endorse a larger increase in the minimum wage. Farmers did not forget that he had proposed lower price supports than those finally approved by Congress. These groups looked to Carter's budget for fiscal year 1979 to discover the course he would follow in his second year as president. Since he had inherited Ford's budget for 1978, this proposal would be the first spending plan that carried Carter's imprint alone. Describing the budget as "tight and lean" but "compassionate" enough to meet the nation's social needs, the president announced in his budget message that this would be the year of the economy. "Our main task at home," he said, "is the nation's economy." The economic recovery of 1977 must continue in 1978 "to provide new jobs and better income, which our people need."

Anyone hoping for expanded government assistance or more innovative programs in the year of the economy was greatly disappointed. To was standing next to him, and remarked, "Bert, I'm proud of you." Later, Hamilton Jordan commented that although the controversy over Lance would not end "tomorrow or next week . . . it won't go on much longer." As for Lance, he made it clear that he intended to stay in office.[15]

The president had badly misinterpreted the comptroller's report, however, and the normally prescient Jordan had likewise missed its political implications. Although Carter believed that the report had cleared Lance of wrongdoing, it actually revealed that the former banker had skirted the edge of probity and ethical behavior—for example, his custom, as chairman of the Calhoun bank, of permitting sizable overdrafts on the personal accounts of its officers and their relatives. More generally, the report accused Lance of "unsafe and unsound banking practices."[16]

Instead of vanishing, the Lance affair mushroomed over the next two weeks as new charges were leveled against the OMB director. One involved his private use of the NBG's two airplanes, including unreported free trips by Carter while he was campaigning for president. It was also alleged that an investigation had been under way into the Calhoun bank's handling of overdrafts on accounts maintained by Lance's campaign organization during his run for governor in 1974, but that the probe had been squashed by the U.S. Attorney's Office in Atlanta the day before Carter announced Lance's appointment as OMB director. The Internal Revenue Service (IRS) undertook its own investigation to determine the validity of these claims. The *New York Times* charged that Lance was not making the same financial disclosures that the White House required of other high administration officials and that he still had business associations that were conflicts of interest.

By the beginning of September the White House was in a near state of siege over the Lance affair. On 3 September Senators Ribicoff and Charles Percy of Illinois, the ranking Republican on the Governmental Affairs Committee, sent the president a memorandum outlining a number of matters concerning Lance that had not been covered in the comptroller's report. "Information has been brought to our attention," they told Carter, "which would appear to substantiate allegations that the Justice Department acted improperly in failing to fully investigate potential criminal violations of Federal banking law growing out of the Lance for Governor campaign and Mr. Lance's personal affairs during that time."[17] Pressure mounted for a special prosecutor to be named to examine Lance's tangled affairs and for the OMB director to resign. On 6 September the White House received a second report from Heimann that showed "a pattern" of borrowing by Lance from other correspondent banks "similar to that established in the other report." Heimann also informed the White House that his office was referring the issue of the private use of the NBG airplane to the Justice Department and the IRS for investigation.

offset higher Social Security taxes and to build on the economic expansion of the previous year, the president proposed a $25 billion tax cut. But the theme that resounded in his budget request was the scarcity of the government's resources and its limited ability to correct society's woes. "Government cannot eliminate poverty or provide a bountiful economy or reduce inflation or save our cities or cure illiteracy or provide energy," Carter stated when he presented his budget to Congress. His priorities for fiscal 1979 would be to lower unemployment, fight inflation, and control federal spending.[11]

Hurt the most by the president's wielding of the budget ax were new funding proposals to aid urban areas. As far back as June 1976, two weeks before he won the Democratic nomination, Carter had told the U.S. Conference of Mayors that if he were elected president, they would "have a friend, an ally, and a partner in the White House." In January, one day before he was inaugurated, he sent eight cabinet-level members of his new administration to meet with a group of mayors gathered in Washington to assure them that he would give precedence to urban problems.

Over the next nine months, the president signed into law several of the mayors' recommendations, including an increase in the number of public-service jobs and a $12.5 billion urban aid bill targeted at the nation's most distressed cities. He also established an Urban Regional Policy Group (URPG), headed by Secretary of Housing and Urban Development (HUD) Patricia Harris, whose mandate was to develop a national urban policy. To demonstrate his personal concern about the plight of the cities, he traveled at the beginning of October to the South Bronx and, with dozens of reporters in tow, viewed the wreckage of that ravaged area. Obviously moved by what he saw, Carter returned to Washington and instructed the URPG to prepare a plan of action for the South Bronx that would "serve as a prototype for other blighted urban areas."[12]

Despite Carter's commitment to a national urban policy, however, he never intended any major additional spending for the cities. Rather, he was interested in improving the targeting, coordination, and efficiency of existing programs—supplying some (but not much) supplemental funding for economic development, encouraging more local and neighborhood planning, eliminating redlining in home purchases, and increasing private-sector involvement in urban development projects.

The administration therefore rejected the URPG's 150-page draft report, which called for an additional $8 billion to $12 billion in aid to cities and towns, to supplement the $50 billion already received. Instead, Eizenstat recommended to the president a much more restrained and less costly role for Washington. Unlike the Harris task force, which still believed that well-conceived federal programs could bring about urban revitalization, Eizenstat argued that Washington could be most useful serving as a catalyst, promoting "public-private partnerships at the local level" and facilitating "greater involvement by neighborhood and citizen's groups."[13] Carter agreed with his chief domestic adviser. "Don't tell me we'll spend more money all around and then we'll call it an urban policy," he said at a meeting with the URPG in December. "Give me something worth funding if you want more money." The next day he instructed McIntyre not to include any urban initiatives in the 1979 budget.[14]

Aside from the price tag, the president had good reason to reject the URPG's report and to order the task force back to the drawing board. Many of its recommendations were conceptually flawed. Its much-touted proposal for an urban development bank, for example, assumed that the low cost of credit, which the bank would presumably make available to investors, would spur economic development in distressed areas. But the URPG did not analyze carefully the other critical factors affecting investment, such as operating costs, availability of land and a skilled labor force, governmental regulation, and crime rates.

In deciding not to include any additional funding for cities in his budget, the president displayed considerable political courage, for, as he anticipated, this action angered urban interests, whose support was so essential to his presidency. A spokesman for the U.S. Conference of Mayors stated that if the president failed to provide more aid to the cities, his administration would "be viewed as a traitor to urban America." Rather than being intimidated by such warnings, Carter stood his ground, intending for his urban policy to stress the role of state and local governments and of neighborhood and voluntary groups, not an infusion of federal dollars.[15]

The president lost a chance, however, to turn the urban policy issue to his own advantage, to make it a centerpiece of his appeal to a new American center with programs that included federal-local and public-private partnerships. Such a policy also might have emphasized his commitment to curbing inflation while underscoring his image as an alternative to conventional Democrats, as someone who was not an advocate of past programs or an apologist for past failures. During the election and in his first year as president, he had told the American people that more was not necessarily better; although Washington had economic and social responsibilities, especially for the poor and the underrepresented, there were limits to what the federal government could do. Voters had responded by electing him and giving him high marks in the polls. The issue of aid to the cities offered an excellent opportunity to build on these themes and to benefit from the swelling suspicion of big government that existed even within his own party. In this way, he might have regained some of his dwindling support in the polls and compensated for the losses he had suffered among traditional Democrats as a result of his willingness to challenge standard liberal and Democratic dogma about the interventionist responsibilities of the federal government.

Yet Carter never seized the moment. Instead of making the case for a "new liberalism" or a "new federalism" based on a healthy skepticism about Washington and the need for better rather than more government, for citizen participation, and for grassroots activism—all of which, the polls said, had great appeal among the nation's urban residents—he resorted to timeworn conservative arguments about fiscal economy and budgetary frugality. In the process, he neglected to articulate strongly enough his own view that the nation's cities required not new money but new approaches. The impression left in the minds of the public was not of a president prepared to challenge convention, lead the nation in fresh directions, and help the cities in innovative ways, but of a fiscal conservative at the head of a divided administration.

In fact, there was such a lack of originality in Carter's economic proposals that journalists commented that his economic agenda could have been put together just as easily by former president Ford. Carter was not even able to win the confidence of the business community. In February the Dow-Jones reached a thirty-four-month low of 753, as business and financial leaders continued to bet against the long-term prospects for economic growth under Carter. Inflation, which was still running at around 6 percent, remained an insistent problem. Interest rates had also jumped sharply over the previous twelve months, with the prime rate on business loans climbing from 6.25 percent to 8 percent during this time. Developments such as these led many businesspeople to anticipate slow economic improvement at best and recession at worst.

Another area of concern to the business and financial communities—and one that weighed heavily on the economy—was the growing uncertainty about the dollar in world currency markets because of the United States' mounting trade deficits. At the beginning of 1978 Americans were still consuming a huge quantity of foreign oil and other imports. At the same time, foreign demand for more expensive U.S. products remained weak, thereby driving down the need for—and the price of—dollars. The first two trading days of January witnessed the largest sell-off of dollars since the early 1970s.

To prop up the demand for and the price of dollars, the Federal Reserve Board (FRB) and the Treasury Department responded by making available up to $25 billion in foreign currencies to buy dollars. Two days later the FRB, in cooperation with the president, raised its discount rate (the rate it charged member banks for its funds) from 6 percent to 6.5 percent, a move intended to attract foreign capital. News that the administration had intervened to support the dollar had the desired effect. At a cabinet meeting on 16 January Blumenthal reported that the dollar had "held its own" against other currencies during the previous week and was continuing to do well in European markets. Nevertheless, business and financial leaders were unconvinced that the administration's action was enough to stop the dollar's protracted decline. "Intervention can change things for a day or a week," observed Henry C. Wallich, a Federal Reserve governor, "but it cannot make any permanent change."[16]

The president's economic program, therefore, came under attack by such disparate groups as representatives of urban interests, who accused Carter of not doing enough for urban areas and poor people, and the business and financial communities, which were worried about Carter's ability to sustain long-term economic growth. To make matters worse, the president decided not to reappoint Arthur Burns to a third term as chairman of the FRB, nominating instead G. William Miller, the chairman of Textron Inc. and a director of the Federal Reserve Bank of Boston. Although Miller was well qualified for the position, he lacked Burns's credentials as an inflation fighter. Most business leaders simply did not know him and so did not know what to expect once he took over the helm of the FRB.

In truth, Carter faced an economic riddle as he began his second year in office. He needed to deal with a catalog of competing and seemingly contradictory claims on government and his administration: to promote employment while halting inflation, to reduce taxes while meeting pressing social needs, to maintain business confidence without completely alienating his Democratic base, to stabilize the dollar abroad without undercutting his economic program at home. That the president understood the situation was evident at a January press conference, when he acknowledged that the success of his economic plan depended "on a very careful balance between different interests, between sometimes conflicting national needs, between doing too much, on the one hand, [and] doing too little on the other." He was also aware that his ability to carry out this delicate task was hampered by the fact that his credibility as a leader, even among the Democratic faithful, was already badly tarnished. "In no case that I can think of do we have the kind of relationship that will be needed to command their enthusiastic support in 1980, and that includes many of the original Carter supporters," Hamilton Jordan told him in December.[17]

In an effort to win back the groups he had alienated, Carter had already begun to polish his presidential persona. For example, his decision to stress unemployment over inflation in his budget message to Congress, despite his own misgiving about doing so, was intended to help heal the administration's growing rift with organized labor. But because he was never able to articulate a program that resonated with the American people, his standing in the polls continued to drop. A nationwide survey taken in mid-February by NBC and the Associated Press reported that only 34 percent of Americans thought that he was doing an excellent or good job—a 21 percent decline in six months. Statewide polls taken by Peter D. Hart, a Democratic pollster, revealed a similar drop in Carter's popularity ratings. Projecting toward the 1980 election, Hart found the results extremely disappointing. "One can only hope," he concluded, "that Shakespeare's line from *Measure to Measure*, 'The Best men are molded out of faults, and for the most, become the better for being a little bad,' applies to President Carter."[18]

Some of Carter's efforts at bridge building were undermined by events over which he had little or no control. A case in point was the coal strike of early 1978, which for a time threatened to paralyze the eastern half of the nation. The episode actually began on 6 December 1977 when 165,000 members of the United Mine Workers (UMW) walked off the job after failing to reach an agreement on a new contract with the coal operators, represented by the Bituminous Coal Operators Association (BCOA). At issue was the miners' right to engage in wildcat strikes to protect infractions of their contract or violations of safety standards. Although most observers anticipated a short walkout, by February it had surpassed the fifty-nine-day record set by UMW strikers in 1949. Meanwhile, coal production slipped from almost 15 million tons a week in January to less than 6 million tons by the middle of February. As coal stocks dwindled to emergency levels, power companies in the Midwest and in the Atlantic states asked their biggest customers to curtail their use of electricity. Diminishing supplies of coal also brought scattered layoffs, school closings, and shortened workweeks in the affected regions.

At first, the administration did not take much official notice of the strike, but as the walkout continued, pressure intensified for the White House to do something about it. According to Frank Moore, Carter's liaison on Capitol Hill, lawmakers were "in a panic" over the strike. In February Carter finally responded by bringing the negotiators to the White House. By the end of the month he had even decided to seek a Taft-Hartley injunction, forcing the strikers back to work, and legislation that would authorize him to seize the mines. Just as he was about to announce these moves, the BCOA and UMW reached a tentative agreement on a new contract. The truce was broken a few weeks later when the rank and file rejected the contract by a two-to-one margin and sent the negotiators back to the bargaining table. Frustrated, the president declared on 9 March that he was invoking the Taft-Hartley Act but would delay any attempt to take over the mines. Not until 24 March was another agreement reached and then ratified by the miners, who had been off the job for 109 days.[19]

During the strike, Tom Wicker of the *New York Times* and several other journalists had observed that Carter's response to the walkout would have a significant influence on the way the American people viewed him. Even after it was over, Peter Hart noted that a "coal strike settlement could have been the catalyst to improve the President's standing with the American public." But as Hart's comments indicated, and as an NBC–Associated Press poll showed, the strike had just the opposite effect: two-thirds of the people surveyed believed that Carter had performed poorly during the walkout.[20]

Actually, there was probably little Carter could have done to shorten the strike or to mitigate its impact. Certainly it would have been imprudent not to allow collective bargaining to run its course before resorting to more drastic measures. Once arbitration was under way, he tried to use his office as a "bully pulpit," moving the negotiations to the White House and then applying considerable pressure on the BCOA to come to terms. At one point, Carter even told executives of big steel corporations with mining subsidiaries that he would not assist the industry with its trade problems unless they were more forthcoming in their negotiations with the UMW. After it became clear that collective bargaining was not working, he employed the Taft-Hartley Act.

Nevertheless, Carter antagonized both sides in the strike by waiting almost four months before seeking an injunction against the miners and then by being the first president in more than twenty years to invoke Taft-Hartley. Indeed, the fact that he chose that measure, which was aimed primarily at labor, instead of seizing the mines, which would have chiefly affected the coal operators, made him seem antilabor to many union leaders. At the same time, his hard-line approach to the mine owners, demanding that they settle with the UMW, also made him appear antibusiness to many business leaders. Depending on one's perspective, therefore, Carter had done too little or too much, too late or too soon.

During the strike the president also became entangled in the so-called Marston affair. David Marston had been working on the staff of Pennsylvania senator Richard Schweiker when President Ford appointed him U.S. attorney for Philadelphia. After Marston refused to resign from what was normally a patronage post, Attorney General Griffin Bell fired him. Although Bell's action was in line with demands from Democrats on Capitol Hill and from the president himself that patronage positions be filled by Democrats, the attorney general—and later the president—tried to justify Marston's dismissal on the grounds that he had come to the job straight from a senatorial staff without any trial experience. But it was hard to fault the thirty-five-year-old Republican for his lack of ability when his office had vigorously and successfully prosecuted a number of powerful state legislators.

More important, the circumstances of Marston's firing were suspect. Bell had waited until November 1977 before asking him for his resignation and had acted only after receiving a telephone call from the president, telling him to expedite Marston's ouster. Also, both he and Carter had been urged to dismiss Marston by Democratic congressman Joshua Eilberg of Philadelphia, whose law firm was being investigated by Marston's office. In fact, the president had telephoned the attorney general immediately after talking to Eilberg. As it happened, neither Bell nor Carter knew about Marston's probe of Eilberg's law firm at the time they decided to dismiss the U.S. attorney. Even so, what made the Marston affair such an embarrassment to the administration was the *appearance* of impropriety. The president also performed poorly in his public comments about the controversy, at one point even denying that he had discussed the Eilberg case with Bell. He then erroneously told a group of Democratic congressmen that the Justice Department could not confirm that Marston was investigating Eilberg. He also refused to acknowledge that, with the benefit of hindsight, he might have handled matters differently. As a result, new doubts were expressed about his commitment to high moral and ethical standards in government.

To the American people, however, the president's greatest problem remained the economy, and increasingly, this meant inflation. Throughout the autumn of 1977 the administration had considered a number of proposals for dealing with inflation, including an innovative concept recommended by Arthur Okun of the Brookings Institution to use tax cuts as an alternative to wage and price increases. But after much discussion, the administration rejected the idea because of its complexity and the difficulty of integrating it into the general tax cut the president was already seeking.

Instead, in his January 1978 State of the Union message, Carter called for a voluntary system of wage and price guidelines. Although he made every effort to underscore the fact that the program was not mandatory, most business and labor leaders were convinced that guidelines were a prelude to controls, which they strongly opposed. The ambiguity of the proposal contributed to their fears. "It's like commanding the tides to stop moving," said Beryl Sprinkel, vice president of the Harris Trust and Savings Bank of Chicago. Labor leaders were also concerned that wages would bear the brunt of governmental intervention. AFL-CIO chief George Meany termed the whole concept of voluntary wage and price guidelines as "wishboning."[21]

Over the next four months, inflation worsened. Rising food prices, larger than anticipated increases in energy prices, higher than expected labor costs, an accelerated depreciation of the dollar on world currency markets, and a jump in the wholesale price index of 1.1 percent in February, the highest in thirty-nine months, all contributed to the problem and dampened hopes of recovery. "The price outlook is deteriorating," Blumenthal and Schultze advised the president on 15 March. Instead of the 6 percent inflation rate the CEA had forecast at the beginning of the year, it now estimated that inflation for 1978 would be 7 to 7.25 percent.[22]

Carter's advisers split over how to contend with inflation. Blumenthal and Schultze suggested a number of anti-inflation initiatives, including holding pay raises for federal workers to 5 percent rather than the 6 percent provided for in Carter's 1979 budget and asking state and local governments to check their own pay increases while reducing sales and property taxes. But Eizenstat, Powell, and Jordan were worried about the political damage that implementation of the Blumenthal-Schultze proposals might cause. Well aware that Ford had tampered with federal pay raises just before the 1976 election, they warned that the White House was playing with "political dynamite" and urged the president to make no decision on the proposals until he returned on 3 April from a trip to Africa and South America.[23]

Carter agreed to defer action on the inflation front, but once he was back in the United States, he adopted most of Blumenthal and Schultze's recommendations. In a speech on 11 April before the American Society of Newspaper Editors he stated that he would "take the lead in breaking the wage and price spiral" by limiting pay raises for federal workers to 5.5 percent and freezing the salaries of 2,300 political appointees. He also asked all the governors and the mayors of major cities to hold down the wage increases of state and city employees and to consider lowering sales taxes. In addition, he renewed his plea to labor and industry to keep wage and price hikes below the average of the previous two years, and he announced that he was appointing his special trade representative Robert Strauss as special counselor on inflation.

Knowing that its inflation program lacked vital support inside and outside the administration, the White House had stressed the importance of that speech. Its "whole purpose," Schultze told the president, "is to establish your own commitment to inflation-fighting. . . . This is absolutely necessary as a prelude to getting cooperation out of the stubborn and reluctant business and labor communities."[24] Yet the response was tepid, even skeptical. Business leaders expressed disappointment that the president had failed to address convincingly what they regarded as the prime causes of inflation—the ballooning federal budget deficit and the growth of the nation's money supply. Organized labor was angry that the White House was concentrating its efforts on fighting inflation rather than on stimulating the economy, and labor leaders were unwilling to practice wage deceleration without evidence of a slowdown in price increases.

By April inflation was exacting a heavy toll on the administration. According to a *New York Times*–CBS poll conducted during the first two weeks in April, 63 percent of the people surveyed cited inflation as their greatest concern, and only 32 percent approved of Carter's record on the economy. By this time, too, Carter's domestic agenda for 1978 was in shambles. In both his budget and his State of the Union messages in January, the president had pledged to revitalize the cities of the Snowbelt region, bring down the unemployment rate, reform the nation's tax structure, cut taxes by $25 billion, tame the inflation rate, and sign into law his energy program. He had also tried to regain some of his support among urban leaders and organized labor while at the same time winning back the confidence of the business community.

Except for a drop in the unemployment rate, the president's efforts were largely unsuccessful. His administration still lacked an urban policy. His tax and energy programs were on hold. On Capitol Hill there was growing sentiment for a scale-back of the recent increase in Social Security taxes and a reduction in the size of the tax cut as a means of coping with inflation. Instead of mollifying organized labor, Carter had exacerbated existing tensions as a result of his anti-inflation program and his use of the Taft-Hartley Act to end the coal strike. Among the business community, many corporate heads still doubted the president's competency to deal with the hard economic times they thought lay ahead. It was not surprising, therefore, that an NBC–Associated Press poll taken in late April gave the president only a 29 percent positive rating (his lowest yet) or that a Gallup survey, taken about the same time, showed Carter trailing Massachusetts senator Edward Kennedy by a margin of 53 percent to 40 percent for the 1980 Democratic presidential nomination.

6

★ ★ ★ ★ ★

THE YEAR OF NEGOTIATIONS

Paralleling the disenchantment with President Jimmy Carter's handling of domestic policy was widespread dissatisfaction with his conduct of foreign policy. According to a Harris poll published at the end of 1977, only 38 percent of Americans approved of the way the president managed foreign affairs, while 51 percent disapproved. Events over the next six months did little to change this low opinion of Carter as a world leader or to remove the sense of gloom and doom that now pervaded the White House. The president did achieve a major victory when the Senate, in the spring of 1978, ratified the Panama Canal treaties. However, even as late as the summer of that year, most of Carter's other foreign policy initiatives were still in limbo, and the president's ratings in the polls stayed abysmally low.

From June 1977 to June 1978 the president continued to devote much of his time to the Middle East crisis. Carter had denounced Israeli prime minister Menachem Begin's decision in July 1977 to build additional settlements on the West Bank, declaring them illegal and obstacles to peace. But he did not allow Begin's action to interfere with his goal of reconvening the Geneva conference on the Middle East, which had been dormant since 1973. On 19 September Israeli foreign minister Moshe Dayan met with President Carter and Secretary of State Cyrus Vance in the Oval Office and promised that Israel would delay settlements in the occupied territories for at least a year. Dayan even indicated that Israel might accept Palestinians at Geneva as part of a pan-Arab delegation. When he left the White House after the meeting, Dayan said that a Geneva meeting could be set up by year's end.

On 1 October, however, the administration took a step that even the secretary of state later acknowledged was counterproductive. It issued a joint communiqué with the Soviet Union formally calling for a new Geneva conference. The joint statement produced a storm of protest in Israel and the United States. From his hospital bed, where he was being treated for a heart condition, Begin accused Washington of trying to force a settlement on Israel. In the United States, Jewish groups and other supporters of Israel picketed the White House.

Critics of the communiqué objected to it on three grounds. Most important, they protested against a reference in the statement to "the legitimate rights of the Palestinian people." Since these were code words used by the Palestine Liberation Organization to justify its struggle against Israel, Washington had always referred to Palestinian "interests" rather than "rights" in the past. Second, the communiqué made no reference to United Nations Resolution 242, which had been approved after the Six Days' War in 1967 and recognized Israel's right to exist in secure borders. Finally, it seemed to invite the Soviet Union, which had been thrown out of the Middle East in 1973, back into the region, something that most Americans, as well as Israelis, were anxious to prevent.

The opposition from Israel and from American Jews put the conference on life support. On 21 October, therefore, Carter asked Egyptian president Anwar Sadat for his help. Sadat, who had been skeptical of the idea of a Geneva conference, had actually been talking secretly with Begin since July—apparently with the United States' knowledge—and had let him know through Secretary Vance that he was eager to meet with the Israeli leader. Begin responded by inviting Sadat to come to Jerusalem. Distressed by the lengthy and tedious negotiations over calling for a Geneva conference, the Egyptian leader accepted, hoping that this might break the stalemate.

Sadat's three-day trip to Jerusalem and his address to the Knesset (the Israeli parliament) drew worldwide attention. Thousands of Israelis, many waving Egyptian flags, turned out to welcome him. In an hour-long speech to the Knesset, Sadat captured the poignancy of the moment when he said that he had come to Israel not to sign a peace but to break down "the barriers of suspicion, fear, illusion, and misrepresentation" that for so many years had kept his country and Israel from even talking about peace. However, the Egyptian leader's actions incurred the wrath of much of the Arab world. As Carter and Vance had feared, his visit to Israel undermined whatever chance remained of holding a Geneva conference. Returning home, the Egyptian president invited "all parties to the [Middle East] conflict" to come to Cairo "to prepare for a Geneva conference." But not one Arab leader—not even those from such moderate states as Tunisia, Morocco, the Sudan, or Saudi Arabia—went to Cairo. Instead, representatives from anti-Sadat nations such as Iraq, Algeria, and Libya gathered in Tripoli, where they formed a "rejectionist" front and condemned the Egyptian leader.

Determined to rally Arab support behind him, Sadat sent Begin an urgent message asking him to make some positive statement on the Palestinian question and the occupied territories. Begin's response, which he conveyed to the Carter administration during a visit to Washington rather than directly to Sadat, was disappointing. While agreeing to withdraw Israeli forces from the Sinai in three to five years, the prime minister refused to guarantee Palestinian home rule in the West Bank and Gaza. As if to underscore the gap separating the two nations, talks between Begin and Sadat that began on Christmas Day proved unproductive; most of their time was spent arguing over Sadat's demands that Israel leave the occupied territories and grant Palestinian self-determination.

Matters went from bad to worse. Although Carter had hoped to involve Jordan's King Hussein in the peace process begun by Sadat, the king made it clear that he would not participate in the negotiations until Israel withdrew from the occupied lands and agreed to Palestinian autonomy. The Saudis basically concurred. Israel also pursued a hard line. In an interview, the Israeli prime minister revealed how distant a Middle East accord truly was. When asked if there were any conditions under which Israel could accept Palestinian self-determination, Begin replied that there were not. When questioned about new Israeli settlements on the West Bank and the Sinai peninsula, he answered by referring to the "rights of the Jews to acquire land and settle in Judea, Samaria and Gaza."[1]

The administration now concluded that the United States needed to become more involved in the negotiating process if Sadat's peace initiative was to succeed. Consequently, the president decided to invite the Egyptian and Israeli leaders to Washington. Sadat would come first so that Carter could reaffirm his support for the former's overtures and develop a common strategy for dealing with Israel's intransigence. This would give the appearance that the administration was siding with Egypt against Israel, but as National Security Adviser Zbigniew Brzezinski later commented, "the bilateral Egyptian-Israeli talks were leading nowhere. Sadat now needed American help desperately in order to obtain an accommodation."[2]

The Egyptian president arrived on 3 February. He called Begin's position regarding Israeli settlements in the Sinai and Palestinian self-determination "ridiculous" and urged the United States to play a more instrumental role as mediator. Carter agreed, but little progress was made over the next three months in obtaining an agreement between Israel and Egypt, much less in arriving at a comprehensive settlement. Indeed, as the weeks passed Carter became less interested in a broad accord and more interested in a separate peace between Egypt and Israel. However, even that more limited objective seemed to be beyond reach because of worsening relations between Jerusalem and Washington. On 8 February, the day Sadat left the United States, Carter told American Jewish leaders that Israel was the biggest obstacle to a Middle East peace because of its position on the settlements issue. That same day Vance also attacked the settlements and said that they should be dismantled. Begin lashed out at the administration, accusing it of "taking sides" against Israel. When he later learned that the White House had decided to sell fighter planes to Saudi Arabia and Egypt (part of a deal that also included the sale of jet fighters to Israel), he blasted the proposal as a threat to Israel's national security.

Concerned by this deterioration in Israeli-American relations, Dayan traveled to Washington and, on 16 February, met separately with Secretary Vance and President Carter. Neither discussion went well. Both Vance and Carter told Dayan that Sadat wanted Jordan's King Hussein brought into the peace process, but the Jordanian leader would not participate until Israel agreed to withdraw from the West Bank and the Sinai. Dayan responded that Israel would welcome Hussein's involvement, but not on the basis of advance commitments. Carter, disheartened, later wrote that "Dayan, in his highly critical mood, had not helped much to prepare us for the upcoming Begin visit."[3]

The Israeli leader arrived in the United States on 20 March. Brzezinski described the president's two days of talks with the Israeli prime minister as "generally unpleasant." Carter was clearly in a fighting mood. Although he had been appalled by a PLO attack along the Israeli coast on 11 March in which 35 people were killed, he told Begin that Israel had overreacted by invading southern Lebanon—an invasion that left more than 1,000 dead and 100,000 homeless. He also insisted that, under UN Resolution 242, Israel would have to remove its forces from all the occupied lands, including the West Bank. After five years, during which neither Israel nor Jordan would lay claim to the West Bank, the Palestinians living in that occupied territory would have the right to decide for themselves whether to affiliate with Israel or with Jordan or to continue under the so-called interim government.[4] The prime minister, however, refused to show any flexibility. Carter was so frustrated and angered by his talks with Begin that he did not even walk the Israeli leader to his waiting limousine when the meeting was over. He then told congressional leaders that Begin was to blame for the impasse in the negotiations.

Meanwhile, Carter had angered American Jews. His plan to sell jet fighters to Saudi Arabia and Egypt, combined with the PLO's attack on Israeli citizens, had united the American Jewish community against the administration. Its clout was felt on Capitol Hill, where the proposed sale of sixty F-15 long-range bombers to Saudi Arabia set off a fierce legislative battle. To win the support of pro-Israeli lawmakers, Carter offered twenty F-15s to Israel. Following ten hours of emotional, sometimes nasty, debate, and despite an intense lobbying effort against the transaction by Israel's backers, the Senate rejected a resolution that would have killed the sale, thereby handing the American Jewish lobby its most serious legislative defeat ever.

The president's surprising victory on the sale of the bombers occurred on the heels of another success—final Senate ratification of the Panama Canal treaties. In a campaign successfully orchestrated by Hamilton Jordan and having all the trappings of a bid for public office, the White House labored tirelessly throughout the fall of 1977 and the early winter of 1977–1978 to win the necessary two-thirds vote in the Senate. At first, it seemed that the president's quest was hopeless. A poll conducted in October by Pat Caddell found that sentiment was running against the treaties by a nearly two-to-one margin. But White House lobbying efforts helped turn opinion around. According to a Gallup poll released on 1 February, 45 percent of the American people now favored the amended treaties, with 42 percent opposed—the first time a plurality of Americans had supported the agreements. On 16 March the Senate ratified the neutrality treaty (the first of the two canal accords) after turning back a series of "killer amendments" that, if implemented, would have required the treaties to be renegotiated and resubmitted to the Panamanians for another referendum. The administration, however, gained approval of the neutrality pact with only two votes to spare (sixty-eight to thirty-two).

The close vote in favor of the first treaty meant that passage of the second agreement—which would transfer the canal to Panama in the year 2000—would likely prove difficult as well. Panamanian leader Omar Torrijos became angry when he learned that the Senate had added a "reservation" to the neutrality treaty, proposed by Democratic senator Dennis DeConcini of Arizona, giving the United States the right to intervene militarily to reopen the canal if it ever proved necessary. However, when the Senate agreed to another stipulation in the second treaty prohibiting the United States from interfering in Panama's internal affairs, this seemed to satisfy Torrijos. On 18 April the Senate ratified the second agreement by the same sixty-eight to thirty-two margin.

Approval of the Panama Canal treaties was a major triumph for the president, in many ways his most important one since taking office. Over the months of debate on Capitol Hill, he had contacted every senator at least once, and some as many as eight times. He had also met privately with all but a few lawmakers and encouraged ambivalent senators to visit Panama to talk with military leaders and meet with Torrijos. In addition, he had Vance, Vice President Walter Mondale, Defense Secretary Harold Brown, and the Joint Chiefs of Staff spend much of their time on Capitol Hill lobbying for the agreement. Finally, he had won over undecided lawmakers by putting the prestige of the presidency on the line and by making support of the treaties a test of Democratic loyalty to his administration and of Republican support for a bipartisan foreign policy.

Political observers took note of Carter's achievements on Capitol Hill. Many commentators who had been highly critical of the president just weeks earlier now wondered whether they had jumped to a premature judgment. There was even talk in the news media of a "new Carter"—tougher and more in command of his administration, more flexible and pragmatic, more deferential to Congress, and more prepared to compromise on major issues than the "old Carter."[5]

Nevertheless, a Gallup poll published in May 1978 showed that registered voters preferred Senator Edward Kennedy over Carter as their 1980 presidential candidate by a margin of 53 percent to 40 percent. According to the latest Harris poll, the president's approval rating with voters had sunk to 30 percent, a drop of 17 percent over the past four months. Even Carter's victories on the canal treaties and the sale of F-15s to Saudi Arabia did not improve his prestige among American voters. "Ordinarily a president grows stronger by winning a hard political fight," historian Gaddis Smith noted. "But Carter's narrow triumph gained him no credit at home." Instead, ratification merely spurred public attacks and a more concerted political effort against the administration and against pro-treaty senators seeking reelection by the conservative Right, which had led the fight to defeat the agreements. The sale of the F-15s to the Saudis simply aggravated the White House's already tenuous standing among American Jews.[6]

Other foreign policy issues that caused the president much consternation both at home and abroad included rapidly changing developments in Africa, relations with the Soviet Union, a growing controversy with NATO allies over a radiation-emitting neutron bomb, and the state of the international economy. Together, these concerns placed a huge burden on the president's schedule and strained the circuits of decision making in the Oval Office.

African problems centered on two regions: southern Africa and the Horn (the central eastern coast). In the former, the difficulty was how to assist a transition from white minority to black majority rule while avoiding a bloody civil war. No previous administration had championed the cause of black nationalism as much as the Carter administration had, and cases in point were its policies on South Africa and Rhodesia. This effort led to criticism from right-wing Republicans such as Jesse Helms of North Carolina, who argued (as he had with regard to Carter's sanctions against Argentina) that the United States needed to support friendly governments. In contrast, most black Africans showered the administration with praise. According to Zambian president Kenneth Kaunda, Carter had "brought a breath of fresh air to our troubled world."[7]

The administration found that its ability to influence events in southern Africa was limited, however, particularly in the case of South Africa. Criticism of South Africa's system of apartheid had been growing since the 1960s as a result of the U.S. civil rights movement, independence movements in Africa, and Pretoria's use of repression against those protesting white minority rule. President Carter made clear his support for black majority rule in South Africa and had Mondale deliver a message to Prime Minister John Vorster denouncing apartheid. Meanwhile, UN Ambassador Andrew Young chastised Pretoria for its racist policies. Vorster responded by cracking down even harder on opponents of his government. The White House turned up the pressure by banning the shipment of spare parts for military items already delivered to South Africa, as well as any civilian goods that had potential military use. These measures did little good, as Pretoria was already getting substantial military aid from France, Israel, and other sources. Indeed, Vorster used the anger generated by U.S. pressure to win reelection in 1977.

Achieving change in Rhodesia was also proving difficult. As in South Africa, Carter supported black majority rule, but the situation in Rhodesia was even more unstable than that in South Africa. In 1965 the United Nations had imposed economic sanctions against Rhodesia after its white-supremacist government declared its independence from Britain. The United States had complied with the UN action until 1971, when lawmakers on Capitol Hill lifted the ban on Rhodesian chrome. But in 1977 Carter had persuaded Congress to restore the sanctions.

Opposing the Rhodesian white minority government was the militant black Patriotic Front. The Patriotic Front wanted immediate majority rule, but Prime Minister Ian Smith insisted on a guarantee of white seats in parliament. In early 1978 Vance attempted, but failed, to broker a compromise between the two sides. Smith then announced an "internal settlement" that would establish a new government and include black moderates; however, Smith would remain prime minister, and whites would be assured enough seats in parliament to prevent any constitutional changes. Predictably, the Patriotic Front denounced the plan and intensified its five-year guerrilla war against the Rhodesian government.

Smith's proposal for an internal settlement exposed the growing estrangement between Vance and Brzezinski. Differences between the two men had already appeared elsewhere, such as over U.S. policy toward China. Brzezinski, who had played a key role in the rapprochement between Beijing and Washington, hoped to achieve a rapid normalization of relations with China. He also advocated the formation of a Sino-American front against the Soviet Union, which, he felt, would increase the pressure on Moscow to reach agreement on SALT. Vance strongly opposed rapid normalization, believing that it would anger the Kremlin and undermine the SALT talks. Carter, though favoring normalization, sided with Vance.

The split between the president's secretary of state and his national security adviser was reflected in their reaction to Smith's proposal for settling the years of strife in Rhodesia. Vance believed that Smith's plan was a subterfuge designed to keep whites in power; Brzezinski believed that it offered a reasonable means of "let[ting] moderate Africans take over from Smith." This time Carter sided with his national security adviser. Hoping that Smith's strategy would eventually lead to majority rule, and under strong pressure from congressional conservatives to lift sanctions against Rhodesia, he ordered the American delegation at the United Nations to abstain on a resolution condemning the plan.[8] Liberal lawmakers on Capitol Hill and black leaders at home and abroad were angered by what they considered the White House's tacit endorsement of Smith's internal settlement. Conservative senators were not much happier; led by Helms, they accused the president of lending implicit support to the Patriotic Front by opposing their efforts to lift sanctions against Rhodesia before a final settlement was reached.

Another, more serious international problem in Africa was the presence of Cuban troops in the Horn of Africa, which included the countries of Somalia and Ethiopia. Bordering on the Red Sea and Gulf of Aden and jutting out into the Arabian Sea, the Horn was one of the most desolate and economically destitute regions of the world. But because of its location on the flank of the Middle East, it was also one of the most important strategically. Not surprisingly, the Horn attracted the attention of the Soviet Union. In 1974 Moscow signed a treaty of friendship with Somali president Mohammed Siad Barre. Three years later Mengistu Haile Mariam seized power in Ethiopia, established a Marxist government, and also sought close ties with the Kremlin.

The problem for Moscow was irredentist claims by Somalia to the Ogaden desert in southern Ethiopia, which was inhabited by Somali nomads. In 1977 Somalia invaded Ethiopia in an attempt to take over the Ogaden. The Soviets, not wanting to see two of its client states at war, attempted to work out a negotiated settlement, but Siad Barre, who had been receiving military assistance under the Soviet-Somali friendship treaty, refused. Angry with the Somali leader, Moscow began to send military aid to Mengistu, prompting Somalia to abrogate its treaty with the Kremlin and to turn to the United States for help. Fearing the internationalization of the conflict, the Kremlin in late 1977 airlifted 12,000 Cuban soldiers and 1,500 Soviet advisers to Ethiopia in the hope of pushing the Somalis out of the Ogaden and achieving a peace as quickly as possible. The crisis in the Horn once again brought the Vance-Brzezinski differences to the fore. The secretary, fearing that a hard line toward the Soviets in the Horn could upset the SALT discussions, favored a negotiated settlement that would include the Soviet Union. Although he was willing to provide defensive weapons to Mogadishu, Vance would agree to provide such weapons only if the Somalis withdrew from the Ogaden. The National Security Council saw things differently. Paul Henze, who was responsible for intelligence coordination, agreed with Vance about not providing military aid to Siad Barre, declaring that doing so would give the Soviets and the Cubans justification to continue their activities in the region. Negotiations involving the Soviets was another matter, however. "I have grave doubts," he wrote to Brzezinski in January 1978, "about . . . getting the Soviets involved in negotiations on the assumption that they would have some common interest in negotiating seriously." Vance's willingness to involve the Kremlin was "a remarkable testimonial to the poverty of real thinking in State on this problem," Henze added in a separate communiqué to his superior. Rather than trying to work with Moscow to achieve peace in the Horn, Henze believed that Washington should work on its own to bring Somalia and Ethiopia to the negotiating table "and let the Russians take the onus for playing one nation against the other."[9]

Brzezinski went even further than Henze. Believing that Soviet actions in the Horn were part of a larger global effort by the Kremlin to spread communism in the Middle East, he proposed to the president that an aircraft carrier be sent to the region. Additionally, he promoted the idea of using U.S. air support to defend Somalia should Ethiopia, which had begun a successful counterattack with Cuban and Soviet assistance, press its advantage and invade its neighbor. Finally, he publicly announced that Soviet actions in the Horn jeopardized the SALT talks.

Faced with this division between his two top foreign policy advisers, Carter chose to split the difference. He rejected sending an aircraft carrier to the region and opposed any form of arms assistance to the Somalis unless they withdrew from the Ogaden. But he approved increased public criticism of Soviet and Cuban activities in the Horn. This paper-clipping of the policies favored by Brzezinski and Vance only served to confuse onlookers about who was speaking for the administration. Soviet ambassador to the United States Anatoly Dobrynin told Averell Harriman (who, at Carter's request, had been holding talks with Soviet officials since the 1976 election) that Moscow was not sure "what the President's position really was." Henze agreed: "The countries of the Horn, of the rest of Africa and the Middle East, the world at large and, last but not least, the

111

U.S. public all seem confused about some aspects of U.S. policy toward the Horn." In his view, there was a "need to explain our policy more comprehensively than we have done."[10]

By early spring, Ethiopian and Cuban troops had driven the Somalis from the Ogaden and returned the territory to Ethiopian control. The Ethiopians, who had promised not to cross into Somalia, kept their word and stopped at the Somali border. As a result, the war wound down, and the crisis ebbed. But Cuban forces, backed by the Soviet Union, remained in force on the African Horn.

The Cuban presence there and elsewhere on the continent was shaping Carter's African policy. On 11 May a detachment of Cuban-trained exiles from Zaire's mineral-rich province of Shaba (formerly known as Katanga) crossed into Zaire from Angola. A year earlier a similar force of Katangese exiles trained in Angola had invaded Shaba, but the administration had treated the attack as a local matter rather than an issue in Soviet-American relations. This time Carter took a more global view of the Angolan invasion by blaming it on the Soviets' Cuban proxies.

In a major foreign policy address at Wake Forest University on 17 March 1978, the president warned about an "ominous inclination on the part of the Soviet Union to use its military power . . . with full logistical support and encouragement for mercenaries from other Communist countries." By this time Carter had come to share Brzezinski's bipolar perception of world politics, which pitted the United States in global conflict against the Soviet Union. His hardened stance toward the Soviet Union came about despite considerable progress over the last six months on the SALT II negotiations. As early as the spring of 1977, Washington had agreed to accept the Vladivostok ceiling on missiles as a basis for arms reduction, and Moscow had indicated that it would consider a modest reduction in the cap of 2,400 missiles. At the end of September the Soviets agreed to reduce the Vladivostok ceiling to 2,250 and made several other concessions, such as accepting the U.S. position on the number of its submarine- and land-launched MIRVs. Differences still remained, including those concerning the cruise missile, the Backfire bomber, and the introduction of new ICBMs, but the two nations had, in effect, reached agreement on the broad outlines of a SALT II compromise. Privately, the White House began to plan for a meeting with the Soviet leader.

In no way, however, did this mean that the United States and the Soviet Union had entered into a new era of détente. The White House continued to flay Moscow for its repression of Soviet dissidents (although in less strident terms), while the Kremlin continued to complain about President Carter's obstinacy on human rights. Other issues also bedeviled Washington's relations with Moscow. Angered that the United States was apparently backing away from a Geneva conference, the Soviets also suspected that Washington was trying to push them out of the Middle East. The United States' direct involvement in the Egyptian-Israeli negotiations confirmed that impression. But no issue was more ominous from the Soviet perspective than the new attitude the White House was adopting toward the People's Republic of China.

Relations between the Beijing government and the Kremlin had been deteriorating since the 1950s; by 1977 war threatened to break out over a disputed border along the Amur River. The White House was again divided on how to respond to this mounting crisis between the two communist powers. At issue was whether to move forward with the normalization of relations with China. Although both Vance and Brzezinski wanted to normalize relations with Beijing, they differed over the timing. Still emphasizing the need to reach a SALT II agreement with the Soviets, Vance opposed the open courting of China. In contrast, Brzezinski, who chose to link a SALT II agreement to Soviet behavior in the African Horn and elsewhere, sought to pressure the Kremlin by playing the "China card"—that is, by making well-publicized overtures to Beijing, much as former President Richard Nixon had done in 1972. Indicative of Brzezinski's growing influence over Carter and of the president's own tougher policy toward the Kremlin, the president agreed to send his national security adviser to China in May 1978 for talks with Beijing officials, even though Vance opposed the trip.

Apparently, Brzezinski's visit to China did not have the anticipated effect; that is, it did not hinder the SALT process, but it did not hasten it either. Certainly the national security adviser tried to play the China card, referring suggestively to "the polar bear to the north" and accusing the Soviets of supporting "international marauders" in Africa. According to Soviet ambassador Dobrynin, however, the Kremlin refused to allow these tactics to undermine its efforts at achieving a SALT agreement. Rather, what prevented forward movement were Carter's denunciations of Soviet violations of human rights and of Soviet and Cuban involvement in Africa, as well as continued differences over SALT itself, such as the Backfire bomber and the testing and deployment of new ICBMs.[11] Recently declassified memorandums of Foreign Minister Andrei Gromyko's conversations in late May with Carter and Vance appear to reinforce Dobrynin's analysis, since there was no discussion of China; rather, the focus was on SALT, Africa, and human rights matters.[12]

Brzezinski's trip did, however, add to what was an increasingly tense relationship between the two superpowers. Recognizing that the timing of the journey to China had been designed to increase pressure on Moscow, Brezhnev referred to the ploy as "a short-sighted and dangerous policy." What remained uncertain to Moscow was how far the Carter administration planned to go in using the China card.[13]

The continued standoff in the SALT negotiations and the polemics between Washington and Moscow led some journalists to talk of a "new cold war." Carter set the tone for his side of the superpower dialogue in a key address to the graduating class at Annapolis in June. Advocating détente and continuation of the SALT process, he also accused the Soviets of waging "an aggressive struggle for political advantage" that could "escalate into graver tensions. . . . The Soviet Union can choose either confrontation or cooperation," he added. "The United States is adequately prepared for both."

The president saw no inconsistency between censuring the Kremlin on the one hand and pursuing the SALT negotiations on the other. He also denied any linkage between the SALT process and what he considered Soviet misconduct. But his repeated attacks on Moscow created an atmosphere in which linkage was certain to be made. Democratic senator Robert Byrd of West Virginia commented that he saw no chance for ratification of a SALT agreement until the Soviets got out of Africa and improved their record on human rights.

The president had wanted a reasoned and measured policy toward the Soviet Union, one that balanced outrage at Soviet misconduct with the imperatives of ending the cold war. What he achieved, however, was a policy strewn with contradictions and inconsistencies and a jumbled message that neither the Kremlin nor the American public knew how to interpret or respond to. As Dobrynin informed the Kremlin in July 1978, "Soviet-American relations during the Carter administration have been characterized by instability, major swings." He concluded that "the immediate future . . . will be an extremely complex period in Soviet-American relations, and it will be difficult to count on any sort of noticeable positive shifts."[14]

Relations between the United States and its European allies had also grown more tense. Although Carter and German chancellor Helmut Schmidt had settled their differences over West Germany's plan to sell nuclear equipment to Brazil, Schmidt remained upset with Carter over his human rights policy and his failure to consult with his NATO partners in negotiating with Moscow. Schmidt's differences with Carter reached crisis proportions after the president decided not to go forward with the development of an enriched-radiation weapon (ERW) commonly known as the neutron bomb. Designed to deter a Soviet attack in Europe by enabling Western forces to destroy enemy tank concentrations without ravaging nearby population centers, the ERW was actually a nuclear warhead propelled by an artillery shell or a short-range missile. The warhead produced a surge of radiation that would kill enemy forces without the blast, heat, and damage caused by other weapons emitting the same amount of radiation. Although a similar program had been canceled in

1973, military planners had recommended full-scale production of ERWs in 1977.

Carter faced a difficult decision. On the one hand, the neutron bomb offered a means to redress the military balance between NATO and the Warsaw Bloc without a long and costly buildup of NATO forces. Yet many Americans and Europeans regarded a weapon that killed people but preserved property as morally repugnant. Critics also maintained that the deployment of ERWs would increase the chance of war, since it implied an ability to wage, win, and recover from a nuclear attack. On 20 March, the eve of an important meeting of the NATO ambassadors, Carter spoke out for the first time against the weapon. On 7 April he announced that he was deferring production of the bomb.

The president's decision created a political tempest in the United States and throughout western Europe. Americans and Europeans alike accused him of vacillation. When word leaked out that Carter's advisers, including Brzezinski, Vance, and Defense Secretary Brown, had urged him to go forward with the production and deployment of ERWs, the furor grew louder. Angry telegrams flooded Capitol Hill from proponents of the bomb. Democratic senator Sam Nunn of Georgia warned that cancellation of the ERW program would "place in the minds of the Soviets the image of a timid and hesitant America which lacks the courage to confront the difficult choices ahead." Republican Howard Baker of Tennessee, the Senate's minority leader, told reporters that cancellation would be "another in a long line of national defense mistakes" by the president. "First we gave away the B-1 bomber and now we are going to give away the neutron bomb." In Europe, Schmidt charged the president with betrayal, while other NATO leaders quietly began to question U.S. leadership.[15]

Much of the European uproar smacked of sanctimony. The president told his advisers that one reason he had put off a decision on the bomb was that none of the European leaders had agreed to deploy the weapon on their own soil. Faced with strong left-wing opposition, European leaders sought to cut their political losses by making their support contingent on the failure of arms control. Schmidt, in fact, favored deployment of the bomb but faced a storm of objection from Germans who did not want the weapon in their country. Thus, when the German chancellor declared that production of the ERW was "solely an American decision," he was not being completely straightforward. Nevertheless, the president's action represented a significant setback in alliance relations that was not quickly resolved.

Questions regarding uranium processing also caused problems in the United States' relations with Japan. During the summer of 1977 the two nations wrestled with the question of whether to permit the nuclear reprocessing plant at Tokai Mura to begin operation. In September Washington and Tokyo finally reached an agreement: the United States would provide uranium to the Tokai Mura facility, and in return, Japan would not build a plant to convert the plutonium produced there into reactor fuel. This represented a major Japanese concession, since it would keep any plutonium produced at Tokai Mura from being used for a nuclear weapon. The administration could therefore argue that it had not violated its own nuclear nonproliferation program. But the intensity of the dispute over Tokai Mura left the Japanese frustrated.

A final matter that took its toll on global amity was the fragile state of the international economy. Following a brief recovery in late spring, the worldwide economic picture began to darken once more. An ongoing problem was the imbalance in world trade, particularly among the United States, Japan, and West Germany. Carter had urged Japan's prime minister, Takeo Fukuda, to increase U.S. imports to offset growing protectionist sentiments among Americans. In December the Japanese agreed to stimulate their economy to promote import buying, but with an annual economic growth rate of 7 percent, they questioned whether there was much more they could do in this regard. Besides, they believed that the United States' trade deficit was due primarily to the instability of the dollar and an inflation-driven demand for imports. Because Germany also blamed the United States' unfavorable balance of trade on its voracious consumption of oil, it refused to expand its economy.

As the U.S. trade imbalance worsened, the free fall of the dollar in foreign exchange markets resumed. When it became apparent that the trade deficit for 1978 would be larger than that for the previous year, a wild scramble to unload dollars began. By the end of the year the Japanese yen, the German mark, the French franc, and the British pound had all made substantial gains against the dollar, which forced those countries to intervene in foreign exchange markets to buy dollars and stabilize exchange rates.

The White House's primary strategy for dealing with the nation's trade and currency problems (aside from reducing oil imports) was to persuade its trading partners to do more to stimulate their domestic economies. That was the message the president took with him as he traveled to Bonn, West Germany, in July for another economic summit with world leaders. Since Carter's competence to handle domestic and global economic problems was under renewed attack at home and abroad, the administration attached great importance to the two-day conference.

The results of the summit were mixed. Schmidt agreed to recommend a tax cut to energize Germany's economy. The Japanese were also more forthcoming than the White House had expected. Just before the summit Tokyo announced a $1 billion "emergency import" program to curb its massive export surplus. Yet no growth targets were set for the "locomotive economies" of the United States, Germany, or Japan (to use the metaphor Carter had employed at the London summit a year earlier). Nor were any solutions offered for redressing the world's trade imbalances or ending the turbulence in foreign exchange markets. The problems of sluggish economic growth, inflation, a weak dollar, excessive oil consumption, and trade protectionism continued to perplex and confound world leaders.

By the end of the summer there was another run on the dollar. Some of the reasons for this latest attack on the U.S. currency, such as the continuing trade imbalance and the deadlock on an energy bill, were depressingly familiar. New ones included the perception that the Bonn summit had not come up with any dollar-strengthening proposals and persistent rumors that the petroleum-exporting nations were planning to stop pricing their oil in dollars, using instead a basket of strong currencies. More generally, the depreciating dollar was symptomatic of a continuing loss of confidence, even among the United States' closest allies, in its economic leadership. In terms of inflation, labor productivity, energy consumption, investment, and economic growth, Washington seemed incapable of managing its own economy, much less that of the world. As such, foreign investors were reluctant to gamble on the U.S. dollar, causing it to drop and thereby undermining Carter politically at home.

By September Carter faced mounting grievances internationally as well as domestically. Critics of the president took issue not only with his domestic policies and programs but also with a foreign policy that appeared to be inconsistent, directionless, and even contradictory. Neither the president nor his advisers as a group seemed to know what their foreign policy goals were. The division of authority between the State Department and the NSC was muddled; foreign policy issues were compartmentalized (for example, into arms control, human rights, détente, and Soviet policy in Africa) rather than integrated; and, in a change from Carter's first days in office, there was little sense of priorities. What applied, therefore, to Carter's domestic policy—lack of a coherent agenda tied to a series of clearly defined objectives—seemed to apply with equal force to the president's foreign policy.

7

★ ★ ★ ★ ★

WAR ON INFLATION

Domestically, inflation remained "public enemy number one" for the Carter administration as spring gave way to summer in 1978. All other endeavors were subordinated to winning the war against inflation, which surged by early summer to an annual rate of over 10 percent. Yet the results of the administration's efforts were not victory over inflation but the further alienation of Democratic constituencies that had voted for the president in 1976 and a continued deterioration of his ranking in the polls.

Overall, the economy grew nicely in the second quarter of 1978. Rebounding strongly from slow first-quarter growth, the GNP increased at an annual rate of 7 percent, industrial production at 15 percent, and retail sales at 25 percent. At the same time, unemployment held steady at about 6 percent, which was under the 6.2 percent rate projected by the CEA at the beginning of the year. Yet the White House and business and financial leaders were increasingly pessimistic about the economy. Although the administration and most private forecasters believed that an outright recession (defined as two quarters of negative growth) was unlikely, many economists predicted a "growth recession," in which business would continue to expand, but so slowly (1 or 2 percent annually) that the unemployment rate would begin to rise.

By the end of the quarter, economic growth was already slowing down. Although the government's index of ten leading indicators, a major gauge of economic activity, still pointed upward, its performance was increasingly sporadic. Business and financial leaders were also disturbed by the cost of home mortgages, which had been advancing steadily and threatened the housing industry, and by a sharp jump in short-term borrowing costs when the Federal Reserve Board increased its discount rate from 6.5 percent to 7 percent.

No problem was more worrisome to the business community and the White House, however, than inflation. Even excluding higher mortgage rates and food prices, which had been climbing by more than 1 percent a month since the beginning of the year, inflation was still close to 7 percent and rising. In January the administration had forecast an overall inflation rate of 6.2 percent for 1978 and 6 percent for 1979; it now refigured that rate at 7.25 percent and 7.5 percent, respectively. By stepping on the monetary brakes, the Federal Reserve sought to curb inflation. But many economists, including the administration's own forecasters, feared that a too restrictive monetary policy coupled with a tight fiscal policy could turn a mild slowdown into a full-fledged recession.

For that reason, the president was opposed at first to a growing movement on Capitol Hill to roll back his proposal for tax cuts and reforms amounting to $25 billion. But there was such strong resistance to his tax proposals, even among Democrats, that he agreed to scale back his tax cut to $19.4 billion and to delay its effective date from 1 October to 1 January. In fact, he came to share the view on Capitol Hill that the tax cut should be trimmed to fight inflation, and in June 1978 he indicated that he would not object too strenuously if it were rolled back to $15 billion.

The White House remained convinced that the best way to deal with inflation was through voluntary controls to keep wages and prices below the average of the previous two years. Responsibility for monitoring the program lay with the Council on Wage and Price Stability (COWPS), directed by Barry Bosworth, a thirty-five-year-old economist from the Brookings Institution. In a tactic known as "jawboning," COWPS and the White House applied public pressure on business and labor leaders to restrain price hikes and wage demands. A particular target of their campaign was hospital costs, which were rising at an annual rate of 15 to 16 percent, or about 5 percent more than the consumer price index. In April the president proposed legislation to cap increases in hospital costs at about 11 to 12 percent, effective 1 October.

Almost immediately the measure was attacked by the American Hospital Association, the American Medical Association, and other lobbyists for the health care and medical professions, who contended that the bill would lead to a decline in the quality of medical care. Even organized labor, which wanted to contain soaring health costs, feared that containment would come at the expense of hospital workers' wages. In July a House committee gutted the legislation, endorsing instead a voluntary cost-cutting program suggested by the hospital industry itself. Defeated in the House, the president decided to carry the fight to the Senate, where the Human Resources Subcommittee had already reported out a bill drafted by its chairman, Senator Edward Kennedy, that was almost identical to the administration's proposal. But few political observers gave it much chance of reaching the Oval Office for Carter's signature.

The administration's drive for voluntary wage and price controls did not fare much better outside of Congress. Throughout the spring and summer, Carter, Bosworth, and other administration officials met regularly with leaders of business and labor in an effort to win support for wage and price restraint. But both prices and wages continued to rise. Business leaders accused the unions of making inflationary wage demands, while leaders of organized labor insisted that there had to be progress in holding down prices before they would agree to smaller increases in wages.

In August Carter banished AFL-CIO president George Meany from the White House after Meany denounced a newly negotiated agreement with the postal unions that kept wages within the guidelines established by COWPS. Meany's attack on the contract guaranteed that the rank and file would turn it down when they voted on it the following week. The president was furious. "I don't want anybody else coming in here and telling me [Meany is] senile and didn't really mean what he said. He knows exactly what he is doing," Carter told aides after hearing of the labor leader's remarks.[1]

Some good news arrived from Capitol Hill at the end of July when Congress approved a measure that the president strongly favored: $1.65 billion in federal loan guarantees for New York City so that the bankrupt metropolis could reenter public credit markets. Moreover, despite the opposition of labor unions representing government workers, the House and Senate also passed separate civil-service reform bills incorporating Carter's proposals for a new merit system and more leeway for managers to fire incompetent employees. The president had pressed his cabinet hard to line up behind the bill. "Your help on Civil Service Reform has put us in a good position in both houses of the Congress," he told each member of the cabinet toward the end of August. "Please give Frank Moore and his staff your complete and enthusiastic help and cooperation."[2] Lawmakers also failed to override the president's veto of a military procurement bill that included $2 billion for a nuclear aircraft carrier, which Carter maintained was not needed. That vote was particularly noteworthy because it was the first time the House and Senate had sustained a veto of a major defense authorization bill.

Carter's veto of the defense measure came at a heavy cost, however, as he incurred the wrath of Democratic and Republican hard-liners in Congress. "The burden of your message is that Congress does not have a place in defense policy-making except insofar as it is prepared to 'rubber stamp' recommendations of the Executive Branch," the powerful chairman of the House Armed Services Committee, Melvin Price, wrote to the president. "I reject that philosophy."[3]

On taxes and other pieces of his legislative agenda, the president fought a losing battle with Congress. In August the House approved a $16 billion tax cut that had been vigorously opposed by the administration. Stu Eizenstat referred to it as "the most regressive tax change ever proposed in Congress" because it catered to higher-income taxpayers by reducing the capital gains tax (the tax paid on such assets as stocks, bonds, and real estate) from 49 percent to 35 percent.[4] The House also rejected most of the reforms contained in the tax program that Carter had first sent to Congress in January. Gone were his proposals for eliminating tax deductions, except for the disallowance of state and local gasoline taxes. Gone also was the president's recommendation for replacing the $750 personal exemption with a tax credit of $240. Instead, the House increased the personal exemption from $750 to $1,000, which, because of the progressive nature of the income tax, favored higher-bracket taxpayers.

Lawmakers also rejected what remained of Carter's proposals about welfare. Stonewalled on Capitol Hill, the president laid aside his plans for comprehensive reform. Instead, he signaled his support for a proposal that would make changes in existing welfare programs without overhauling the entire system. In June the administration reached agreement with the House leadership on the broad outlines of legislation incorporating the principle of welfare reform within the existing welfare framework. But even this proposal failed to make it onto the House floor. Realizing that there were insufficient votes to pass the measure, House Speaker Tip O'Neill announced that he was putting off consideration of welfare reform for the remainder of the session.

In the midst of these struggles with Congress, Carter found himself drawn into a bitter battle with Kennedy in the summer of 1978 over the explosive issue of national health insurance (NHI). Although most Americans were covered by Medicare and Medicaid programs or some form of private health insurance, an estimated 10 percent of the population—mostly the working poor and the unemployed—still had little or no medical coverage when Carter took office. As a result, many Democrats, particularly organized labor, sought legislation that would provide insurance for all Americans. Seeking labor's support in his quest for the party's presidential nomination in 1976, and genuinely concerned about the inadequate health care of millions of Americans, Carter had called in April 1976 for a comprehensive and mandatory system of NHI. Left unanswered, however, were such questions as how comprehensive the coverage should be, how it should be financed, and how it should be implemented.

Following his election, Carter's transition team identified two options for an NHI plan. The first provided for universal, federally financed health insurance; the second mandated private health insurance supplemented by federally financed coverage for catastrophic illness. Accompanying both plans were measures for curbing spiraling medical costs. Both options would also be phased in over three years—and that was the rub. Although the new president was committed to a comprehensive program, he wanted gradual implementation beginning in 1978, and then only as the budget would allow. But organized labor and liberal Democrats—especially Senator Kennedy, who for more than a decade had led the fight for NHI on Capitol Hill—wanted legislation enacted early in the new administration. In a major address in May before the annual convention of the United Auto Workers (UAW), Kennedy made clear his exasperation at Carter's decision not to introduce an NHI measure in 1978. "The American people," he said, "should not tolerate any delay on national health insurance."[5]

The president was caught between a rock and a hard place. He was scheduled to address the UAW the next day, and he was not eager to be upstaged by the Massachusetts senator or appear to be reneging on his campaign promises. Moreover, he still needed and valued the support of Kennedy and other Democrats who had made NHI part of their liberal oath. Indeed, in the few months that he had been president, Carter had gone out of his way to consult with the senator, and Kennedy had responded by generally backing the president on such matters as tax reform and hospital cost containment.

Yet Carter's advisers distrusted Kennedy's liberal slant and his political ambitions. "Kennedy is likely to represent the labor-liberal coalition on the ongoing NHI debate and to preserve differences with the Administration until late in the game," Hamilton Jordan warned the president. Besides being unprepared to submit a proposal to Congress at this stage, the president was increasingly concerned about the inflationary impact of a comprehensive plan.[6]

In his speech to the UAW, Carter therefore promised "legislative proposals early next year," but he warned that any NHI program would be disastrous unless health care costs were tamed first. By the fall Carter was contemplating not even introducing NHI legislation in the next session of Congress. His administration had made little progress in developing an insurance plan, and CEA chairman Charles Schultze had advised the president that, because of rising inflation and a sluggish economy, he should give NHI low priority when the House and Senate reconvened in January. The president reached the same conclusion. After discussing the details of a no-cost NHI program with HEW Secretary Joseph Califano Jr., who was responsible for designing the proposal, Carter suggested that they might be able to satisfy advocates of NHI by pledging to have a bill ready by 1979.

That was wishful thinking. Kennedy, the UAW, and other proponents of NHI would not wait another year; moreover, they disagreed with the White House over some fundamental issues. Carter called Kennedy to the White House to discuss their differences. Although he promised that he would send an NHI measure to Congress late in 1978, the president stated plainly that he could not support the legislation favored by the senator and labor leaders, which provided for mandatory health benefits for all Americans paid for by payroll taxes and general revenues.

Over the next seven months Kennedy met regularly with Carter, Califano, Eizenstat, and their staffs in an ongoing effort to resolve their differences. The president also met with UAW president Douglas Fraser and other union officials to discuss NHI options. But none of the principals involved were willing to compromise very much—certainly not the president, who had been told by congressional leaders that Congress would never agree to a substantial increase in federal spending or in the size of the federal bureaucracy to administer a national health plan.

Relations between Carter and Kennedy had always been amicable, but as the deadlock in the negotiations continued, they became more critical of each other. According to Califano, at a meeting with Carter on 6 April, the Massachusetts senator "spoke in a tone so insistent that it was almost disdainful of the President." For his part, Carter rejected as "premature" Kennedy's proposal to establish a working group of administration officials, labor representatives, and members of his own staff to hammer out a bill.[7] The president recognized that he had to take some action on NHI during the fiscal year because, as Eizenstat reminded him, he could not back down from the pledge he had made to Kennedy and organized labor. But Eizenstat also warned him that proceeding with an NHI plan would be viewed on Capitol Hill as evidence of the administration's inconsistency—"talking about inflation and budget restraint one day and proposing what will be seen as an inflationary budget-busting scheme the next." Accordingly, he recommended that Carter state the principles on which national health care should be based but defer actual legislation until the next session. "It is one thing to honor a commitment," he said. "It is quite another to have the UAW and Kennedy dictate the date on which you send this proposal to us."[8]

Following Eizenstat's advice, Carter met with Kennedy in July in a final attempt to come to terms. The meeting was a disaster. In a concession to Carter, the senator indicated a willingness to accept a phasing in of NHI *provided* the president agree to a schedule for implementing a comprehensive plan regardless of economic or budgetary circumstances. Carter declined the offer. Meeting later with reporters, Kennedy accused the president of a "failure of leadership" that would cripple any national health care program from the start. The open split between Carter and Kennedy meant that there would be no NHI legislation anytime soon. Given the state of the economy and the opposition to NHI on Capitol Hill, a consensus had already been building within the administration not to go forward with even a phased-in plan. The break with Kennedy and organized labor over the issue left the White House without any incentive to lobby for an idea whose time, it appeared, had passed.

The president's position on NHI was reasonable. Estimates for the comprehensive Kennedy-labor plan varied considerably, but even a modest version had a projected cost of at least $30 billion, which would have made a sham of Carter's endeavors to fight inflation. And even with the White House's backing, it was far from clear that the House and Senate would have approved any plan in light of the concern over inflation.

Yet from a policy and political point of view, it might have been worth a fight for an NHI plan that included (1) health insurance for those Americans not already protected by private plans or through public assistance, (2) protection against catastrophic illness for all Americans, (3) hospital cost containment measures, and (4) measures to make the delivery of health services more equitable and efficient. Schultze and OMB director James McIntyre had outlined the principles of such a plan to the president in June. In developing these principles they strove to balance improving the nation's health care with cutting spiraling costs. They made it clear that the expense of a plan based on these principles would have to be shared by the private sector, state and local government, and individuals. Although they singled out organized labor as the interest group certain to oppose the concept of cost sharing, they had no illusions about the opposition that such a plan would generate. However, they believed that a phased-in NHI program, beginning with medical coverage for those without any protection or with catastrophic medical needs, would meet Carter's campaign commitment to a national health plan. "We can move toward expanded benefits for all Americans through later legislation," they concluded.

By emphasizing hospital cost containment as part of a broader national health plan that included coverage for the uninsured, protection in case of catastrophic illness, and a more accessible and efficient health care system, the president might have been able, once again, to make the case for a "new federalism" or "new liberalism." This concept could have been predicated on a compassionate, responsive, and efficient government tackling difficult social problems in innovative ways, taking into account the economic reality of limited resources and a festering inflation, and working in partnership with state and local government and the private sector. "No American should face the threat of financial ruin due to a catastrophic illness, and no American should be denied access to essential health care because of insufficient income," Schultze and McIntyre stated as one of the principles of a national health plan.[9] If pursued vigorously as part of a coherent domestic policy, this principle of social justice might have resonated well with the American public, allowing Carter to counter the challenge from the Democratic Left while building a new American center within the Democratic Party.

The odds of success were long, but the alternative of giving up the fight for a national health plan beyond hospital cost containment, which by itself enjoyed no strong constituency, was a lost opportunity for Carter and the Democratic Party. As matters stood, the Carter-Kennedy breach merely further divided an already fractured party and increased the likelihood of a Kennedy challenge for the party's nomination in 1980.

In other ways as well, the summer of 1978 appeared very much like the summer of 1977, when nothing seemed to go right for the White House. Dissatisfaction was rampant among traditional Democrats, and the president had to contend with two political brush fires involving members of his administration. First, UN Ambassador Andrew Young came under renewed attack for remarks he had made during a newspaper interview. Referring to the trial of Soviet human rights dissident Anatoly Shcharansky, Young had said that there were "hundreds—perhaps even thousands—of people [in American prisons] whom I would call political prisoners." Barely a week later, Dr. Peter Bourne, Carter's chief health adviser and a close personal friend, was discovered to have prescribed Quaaludes, a powerful sedative, to one of his assistants, who had tried to fill the prescription using a fictitious name.

The White House did not allow storms to develop over these blunders—as it had in the past—but sought to quell the public clamor immediately. Instead of rushing to Young's defense, as before, Carter was persuaded by his staff to issue a release saying that statements on U.S. foreign policy "came from the President and the Secretary of State" and that Young's remarks did "not reflect the policies of this administration." Rather than stand by Bourne, as he had stood by Lance, the president accepted Bourne's resignation at once.

Nevertheless, for those observers recalling the summer of 1977, there was a lingering sense of déjà vu. A year earlier, however, Carter had still been a popular president with an approval rating of between 60 and 70 percent. By 1978 only the South remained solidly behind him. In an ABC-Harris poll in August, 69 percent of the people surveyed did not approve of the job Carter was doing. Inflation remained the most compelling issue for the majority of Americans. Although the inflation rate declined from 11 percent in June to 6 percent in July as a result of a drop in food prices, the administration's own economists presented him with a dour economic forecast. The United States had recovered well from the recession of 1974–1975, CEA chairman Schultze and Treasury Secretary Blumenthal told him at the end of July. "But having come this far, we now face a number of difficult and protracted economic problems, and a lack of a coherent long range strategy for dealing with them." Luck and a "careful policy along traditional lines" might avoid a major catastrophe, they continued. "But the risks are on the downside, and even with good luck—the outlook points to results which range from very mediocre to poor on the economic and political scorecard."

Although escalating inflation was their major concern, it was not the only one. One development that had been ignored by many economists but that Schultze and Blumenthal emphasized was the declining level of productivity in the United States, which was growing by less than 1 percent a year. "The lower productivity growth contributes to inflation, slows the advance in living standards, and erodes the competitiveness of the United States in the world economy," they remarked. Other concerns they pointed to included persistent levels of structural unemployment, chronic external accounts deficits, and government regulations.

Schultze and Blumenthal's memorandum may have been the grimmest and most cheerless report on the economy that Carter had received since becoming president. But although they pointed out the lack of a coherent economic policy and emphasized the need for one, they failed to offer the president one of their own. Instead, they suggested a Camp David meeting of the president's major advisers just to figure out the nature of the economic and social problems plaguing the country. "We think this ought to be a mind stretching exercise, *not* a meeting of government officials to lay out specific programs."[10]

For many Americans, however, the most serious problem facing the country was not inflation or any of the other problems described by Schultze and Blumenthal; it was high taxes. In fact, a taxpayers' revolt was taking place throughout the United States as largely white middle-class home owners called for cuts in property taxes and local government spending, both of which had burgeoned over the last decade. The taxpayers' revolt first attracted national attention in California when Howard Jarvis, a seventy-five-year-old businessman, collected more than a million signatures to force a referendum on Proposition 13, a proposal to slash property taxes by $7 billion and place tight lids on the power of local government to raise revenues by other means. On 6 June California voters stunned the nation by approving Proposition 13 by almost a two-to-one margin.

Movements began in other states to get similar proposals on the ballot. Potential presidential candidates, such as Republican congressmen Jack F. Kemp of New York and Philip M. Crane of Illinois, tried to tap the tax revolt sentiment by mapping a national strategy that was firmly rooted in lower taxes. Meanwhile, the administration pointed to taxpayers' anger to validate its own commitment to budget cuts and tax reform. Ironically, by compelling Congress to pay greater attention to the tax-cutting demands of the middle class, Proposition 13 sealed the fate of the administration's tax reform and tax reduction proposals, which were aimed toward low-income families.

Unquestionably, then, Carter faced a discouraging situation midway through his second year in office. Inflation had replaced economic recovery as the nation's major economic problem, but the standard ways of handling inflation (higher taxes, higher interest rates, reduced federal spending, wage and price guidelines or controls) offended old-line Democrats. At the same time, the taxpayers' revolt—ostensibly a grassroots movement directed against local government—had national ramifications that made a more liberal fiscal policy politically untenable, even if the president had been so inclined.

Increasingly concerned about his declining political fortunes and his dwindling popular support, Carter took several steps over the summer to boost his public image. In July he appointed Gerald Rafshoon, the successful Atlanta advertising executive who had directed his media campaign for governor and president, as his assistant for communications. Press secretary Jody Powell remained responsible for daily briefings and other day-to-day communications issues, and he continued to be one of the president's closest advisers. But Rafshoon was responsible for changing the public's perception of the president.

Rafshoon proved ideal for the task. Believing that the American people did not know Carter well enough, Rafshoon put together a tight schedule of highly visible public appearances. He even arranged a televised "town meeting" from Berlin during Carter's visit to Germany in July. He also got the president to invite various editors and publishers to the White House for dinner. Denying that he was emphasizing image and style over substance, he coached the president on what he should say and how he should say it. "You should be serious, methodical, purposeful—working hard and *successfully*, on a *few* of the most important problems facing our country," he instructed the president soon after joining the administration.[11] As another part of his responsibilities, Rafshoon took control of the speechwriting staff. This arrangement was far from perfect. Carter liked to write his own speeches whenever possible and rarely gave the staff a sense of his own priorities or long-term vision for his presidency. The media, at first impressed by Rafshoon's effectiveness in projecting a new image of the president—even using terms such as *Rafshooning* and *Rafshoonery* to describe his techniques—eventually became irked at what they regarded as his efforts to manipulate them. Nevertheless, the president stayed on message most of the time (as also pre-scribed by Rafshoon), and his approval ratings began to climb. Rafshoon quickly established himself as one of Carter's top advisers along with Jordan, Powell, Eizenstat, and Moore.

Rafshoon's arrival was part of the most extensive shake-up of the White House since Carter took office. In addition, the president's appointments secretary, Tim Kraft, was moved to the senior staff and given the task of liaison to the Democratic Party, a recognition by the administration that its relations with the party regulars needed to be improved. In a similar and ongoing effort to repair relations with Congress, Frank Moore was assigned additional staff and authority. Finally, Midge Costanza, the administration's outspoken and often controversial special assistant for public liaison, resigned after losing most of her staff. Carter named Ann Wexler as her replacement; Wexler had been one of George McGovern's top advisers in his 1972 presidential campaign, and she was serving as deputy undersecretary of commerce at the time of her appointment.[12]

By September the White House reorganization and Rafshoon's public-relations campaign appeared to be having some effect. Lawmakers returning from an August recess reported continued goodwill for Carter among their constituents, despite lingering doubts about his competency. There was even some concern that criticism of the president had gotten out of hand. After visiting New England and the Rocky Mountain states, Haynes Johnson of the *Washington Post* relayed "an underlying sense of sympathy for the president." As a result of reports like these, the mood at the White House turned noticeably upbeat. "This month will be remembered as a critical one for your Presidency," Rafshoon told Carter. "In my earlier memos to you I talked of this period as a 'turning point.' I am even more convinced that this can be the case. The all-encompassing theme is GETTING CONTROL."[13]

Attitudes at the White House changed from upbeat to downright euphoric when, just two weeks later, President Carter appeared before Congress to announce the successful conclusion of the historic Camp David accords between Egyptian president Anwar Sadat and Israeli prime minister Menachem Begin (see chapter 8). In the first weeks after Camp David, it seemed as if the administration had been born again. The president's new popularity was evident in the polls, which leaped by as much as 5 percent in less than a month, and in his junkets on behalf of Democratic candidates seeking election in November. Traveling to New Jersey, the Carolinas, and the Midwest, an exuberant and exhilarated Carter was greeted by huge crowds wherever he went.

On Capitol Hill the Senate finally passed the president's watered-down energy legislation, which he had submitted to Congress eighteen months earlier. The measure had been held up since the spring over the issue of natural gas deregulation. Although a conference committee had reached a compromise on deregulation in May, it took until the end of July for congressional staffers to translate the agreement into legislative language. It then took another month to sway enough votes in the conference committee to send the beleaguered gas bill to the full House and Senate.

The battle that followed was intense. Kennedy, joined by such unlikely bedfellows as Republicans John Tower of Texas and Clifford P. Hansen of Wyoming, opposed the conference committee report but could not prevent its approval by the Senate. In the House, Speaker Tip O'Neill fought off an attempt to separate gas deregulation from the rest of the energy package. A filibuster by retiring Democratic senator James Abourezk of South Dakota came to an end when he realized that he was only angering his colleagues, who were anxious to return home to campaign. With the filibuster ended, lawmakers sent the five-part energy program to the president on 15 October, thereby ending its long odyssey through the halls of Congress.

The legislation that Carter signed into law was hardly "the moral equivalent of war" he had described in April 1977. Nor was the Senate's last vote on gas deregulation "the most important decision" it would make in the 95th Congress, as Carter had predicted when lobbying on behalf of deregulation. Most of the original proposals, which had been based on the principle of conservation through taxation rather than through deregulation and tax credits, had been either scaled back or, like the crude oil equalization tax, eliminated entirely.[14] Still, the final package was a momentous accomplishment. By deregulating natural gas and establishing a single price for intra- and interstate gas, Congress made important strides toward conserving gas and distributing it more rationally. It also encouraged energy conservation and the expanded use of nonfossil fuels through various tax credits. Most significant, it attempted to grapple with a problem that only promised to worsen if left unattended.

Carter had been instrumental in maneuvering his energy program through Congress. To get the gas deregulation measure out of the conference committee, he had brokered a deal with Senator James B. McClure of Idaho. In exchange for McClure's vote, the president agreed to soften his position on so-called breeder reactors. Because these nuclear reactors produced plutonium that remained radioactive for thousands of years, Carter had vetoed an authorization bill in 1977 providing $150 million in start-up costs for the construction of a demonstration breeder plant on the Clinch River near Oak Ridge, Tennessee. Over the next six months he continued to fight with Congress over the Clinch River project. But to obtain McClure's assent on gas deregulation, he agreed to withhold his opposition until a feasibility study was completed on a more modern breeder reactor using a fuel other than plutonium.

In lobbying for the energy legislation, Carter was ably assisted by the Democratic leadership on Capitol Hill. But in the end, what made the difference were the president's telephone calls and personal messages, his meetings and his staff's sessions with lawmakers and influential business, labor, and community leaders. Almost all observers agreed that the conferees' crucial compromise on deregulation would not have been possible without this patient but persistent intervention by the president and his staff.

The energy bill was only one of a rash of measures that Congress approved just before adjourning in the middle of October. Another was an $18.7 billion tax cut. Like the energy bill, the tax legislation signed into law by Carter bore little resemblance to the tax reform proposals he had recommended at the beginning of the year; the House had rejected most of those in August. In September the Senate Finance Committee added insult to injury by approving cuts in capital gains taxes broader than those passed by the House and increasing the total tax reduction (by providing relief for virtually every taxpayer) to an estimated $22.6 billion—or about $3 billion more than the administration was now willing to accept. Nevertheless, by going head-to-head with Senate Finance Committee chairman Russell Long and House Ways and Means Committee chairman Al Ullman, the president was able to fashion a bill that provided greater relief for lower- and middle-income taxpayers than the measure approved by the House, and it still cost well under $20 billion.

Going into the 1978 elections, few could doubt Carter's political momentum. He was having considerable success on Capitol Hill, and his public image seemed to be synchronized with the message the American people were sending to Washington—distrust of big and wasteful government, hostility to special-interest groups, opposition to more and higher taxes, insistence on economic frugality and greater local responsibility, and an emphasis on personal values. The White House felt confident, therefore, that the November elections would be a triumphant referendum on Carter's presidency.

Clearly the president had learned important lessons in his first twenty months in office. He had become more savvy in his dealings with Congress and had made important changes in the White House, both of which were paying off in legislative accomplishments. The Office of Public Liaison under Anne Wexler became especially effective in promoting the president's agenda. Concentrating her attention almost exclusively on those policy issues before Congress that the president considered of highest priority, Wexler established "outreach programs" involving citizens at the grassroots level. Seeking not only to activate key constituents but also to convert or neutralize opponents of the administration, she practiced two basic maxims of politics: (1) deputize your supporters, and (2) give citizens access.

Instead of objecting to her interference on their turf, lawmakers generally welcomed Wexler's intercessions because, among other things, she involved them in her operations. For example, she asked them for the names of individuals from their districts to invite to her outreach programs, thereby allowing them to demonstrate their access to the White House and to reward their constituents. Because federal law prohibited the use of federal funds for lobbying purposes, the outreach programs were always presented as educational in purpose, adding a cloak of legitimacy to what might otherwise be regarded as simple advocacy. Still, Wexler made certain to involve administration officials who could make the strongest arguments in support of the White House's position.

In numerous ways, Carter also honored his commitment to an open and caring administration that was protective of what he regarded as the people's interests, as opposed to special interests. Having decided, for example, that he could not win the battle in Congress to establish a Consumer Protection Agency, he did by executive order what he could not do by legislative fiat. He made his special assistant for consumer affairs, Esther Peterson, head of a newly created Consumer Affairs Council and gave her authority to oversee new consumer advocacy programs with forty-three federal agencies. She also had input into all administration proposals that affected consumers. With this mandate, Peterson worked in specific and practical ways to protect and enhance the rights of consumers and to make government at all levels more responsive to consumers' needs. She provided consumers with information on a wide range of matters, from how to save on food and energy bills to how to form neighborhood co-ops. She represented consumer interests at public utility hearings, and she appealed to grocery stores not to raise prices during times of inflation. She also convinced Carter to sign an executive order, later repealed by Ronald Reagan, banning the export of products that were considered unsafe in the United States.

A similar commitment to safeguarding the people's interests was reflected in Carter's dedication to protecting the environment and conserving the nation's natural resources. These were lifelong interests going back to his boyhood, when he had hunted and fished with his father and friends.[15] He was also the first successful presidential candidate to campaign on environmental issues. Soon after taking office he sent Congress a sweeping message on the environment in which he emphasized shifting the responsibility for environmental protection to the executive branch. But, calling the widespread existence of toxic chemicals "one of the grimmest discoveries in the industrial era," he also asked for, and won, congressional approval of legislation to prevent these chemicals from entering the environment in the first place, including reauthorization of the clean air and clean water acts and surface mining control legislation that had been vetoed during previous congressional sessions. In addition, he instructed Charles Warren of the Council on Environmental Quality (CEQ) to develop a plan to ensure the control of toxic wastes.[16] Over the next eighteen months the CEQ worked assiduously with other federal agencies, including the Department of Interior, which was headed by Cecil D. Andrus. As governor of Idaho, Andrus had won the respect of the environmental community for his efforts to protect the environment, including saving peregrine falcons; as secretary of the interior he had championed the protection of wild and scenic rivers.

One can only wonder whether Carter might have succeeded as a transitional president if his early actions in the White House had been conducted with the same astuteness he exhibited well into the second year of his presidency. Certainly his earlier mistakes continued to cloud the remainder of his presidency. For one thing, key liberal Democratic blocs remained alienated from him. In October leaders from more than 100 of these groups assembled in Detroit to hold Carter to his 1976 campaign promises. Although UAW president Fraser, who had been responsible for arranging the meeting, tried to reassure the White House that the gathering was not the birth of a "Dump Carter" movement, the labor leader had to work hard to squelch talk among the attendees of bolting from the Democratic Party or courting Kennedy for the Democratic nomination in 1980.

Carter's relations with one of the groups represented at the meeting, the Congressional Black Caucus, had become especially nasty. Black leaders had been critical of the president from the outset, complaining that he had abandoned blacks even though they had been responsible for his election in 1976. In fact, Carter had done nothing of the sort. During his presidential campaign he had pledged to increase the number of black and other minority candidates for federal judgeships, and this he had done. By the time he left office in 1981, Carter had appointed more blacks (twenty-eight) and Hispanics (fourteen) to the federal judiciary than any other president before him, raising the percentage of black federal judges from 4 percent in 1977 to 9 percent in 1981. His administration also channeled more government contracts to minority firms, boosted substantially the amount of federal deposits in minority-owned banks, strengthened the Justice Department's enforcement of the voting rights statutes, and increased the effectiveness of the Equal Employment Opportunity Commission in settling job discrimination cases. But most of the president's efforts to assist blacks and other minority groups were undertaken through executive and agency action rather than through legislative initiatives, and their greatest impact was on middle- and upper-income minorities, not the poor.[17]

Consequently, the Congressional Black Caucus accused the administration of being unresponsive to the fundamental needs of most blacks and even attacked Carter's record on civil rights and federal appointments. In a lengthy document sent to the president at the end of September, the caucus listed some of its grievances against the administration. The lawmakers charged that there was less federal funding for housing and economic development programs under Carter than there had been under Nixon and Ford, that the administration had not done enough to create new jobs, that Carter had never given a major speech on civil rights, and that he had made only "limited Black appointments to top positions, [noting] particularly the absence of Blacks in top economic positions."[18]

In September 1978 leaders of the Congressional Black Caucus met with the president to discuss these issues and to chastise him for not throwing his weight behind the Humphrey-Hawkins full employment bill, under which the government would provide "last resort" jobs, if necessary, to guarantee full employment. Carter had supported this bill when it had been before Congress in the fall of 1977, but only after considerable prodding from black leaders and organized labor. He had also insisted on provisions that took into account the need to deal with inflation. In effect, the president had sidestepped a frontal attack on unemployment through specific job-creating measures by the government.

Nevertheless, the black caucus made administration support for Humphrey-Hawkins, which had passed the House in March 1978 but was now tied up in the Senate, the test of its commitment to a black agenda. Carter and Vice President Mondale told the group that the president had always regarded full employment as a "top priority," but there were other urgent matters to deal with, such as producing an energy bill and curbing inflation. The caucus members warned that the White House would be blamed if Congress failed to pass Humphrey-Hawkins. When Carter and Mondale heatedly challenged that assertion, Congressman John Conyers of Michigan stalked out in anger. After Conyers left, Parren J. Mitchell of Maryland (chairman of the caucus) and Ron Dellums of California took up the argument. According to Mitchell, he and Mondale engaged in a shouting match.

Surprised by what had taken place, both Mitchell and the White House tried to patch up their differences. Mitchell set up another meeting between black lawmakers and the president at which Carter agreed to work harder for the Humphrey-Hawkins bill. In keeping with this promise, the president pressured Senate leaders to complete action on the legislation. At the same time, Hamilton Jordan arranged a White House conference with lobbyists from a number of black organizations to "demonstrate Administration activity" on behalf of the measure.[19]

On 15 October the Senate approved the Humphrey-Hawkins legislation, but the final product was a bitter disappointment to its original proponents. Although the goal of reducing unemployment was intact, the Senate had added another goal of lowering the inflation rate to 3 percent by 1983 and eliminating it entirely by 1988. Backers of the bill feared that the inflation objective would undermine the measure's primary purpose of stemming unemployment. Many black leaders were grateful for the White House's assistance in forcing senatorial action on the bill, but there was also resentment that the administration had not worked earlier and harder on behalf of the legislation.

Likewise, feminist leaders were disappointed with the administration, even though Carter's record on most women's issues—as on many of the issues raised by black leaders—was actually good. As a presidential candidate he had campaigned for the equal rights amendment (ERA), which Congress had passed in 1972 but still needed to be ratified by four more states. As president he supported legislation providing funding for a National Women's Conference in Texas in 1977 and then gave his firm endorsement to its agenda for achieving women's rights. In addition, he established an Interagency Task Force on Women and a National Advisory Council for Women and strongly backed an extension of the seven-year limit for passage of the ERA when it became apparent that not enough states would approve it by that deadline. Keeping his campaign pledge to appoint women to top positions in his administration, he not only selected Patricia Harris and Juanita Kreps for his cabinet but also named significantly more women to high-level posts, including federal judgeships, than any previous president had.

Moreover, Rosalynn Carter blazed new trails in assuming a major role in the administration. She frequently substituted for Carter at ceremonial affairs, advised him on important policy matters, and helped plan political strategy. In June 1977 she visited seven Latin American countries as an official envoy of the United States and conducted high-level negotiations with foreign leaders on such issues as the arms buildup in Peru, human rights violations in Brazil, and drug trafficking in Colombia. She often participated in NSC briefings on foreign affairs. Domestically, she pushed aggressively for the ERA, making dozens of calls to lawmakers in states where it was under consideration and traveling throughout the country to drum up support on its behalf. According to the president, both his staff and the news media understood that she could speak for him "with authority."[20]

Nevertheless, many of the women who had worked for Carter's election in 1976 accused the president of relying too much on his wife and daughter-in-law to secure ERA passage instead of doing his own campaigning. They were also angry at Carter's opposition to federal funding of abortion except in cases of rape, incest, or when a woman's life was in danger—a stance he had maintained even as a candidate. And, like many black leaders, they were concerned that the president was sacrificing economic and social programs that benefited the poor, including working mothers and single parents, to fight inflation.

By every economic indicator, however, inflation was getting worse, not better. From August to September, producer prices, which often set the stage for consumer prices, shot up at an annual rate of 11.4 percent. Additional price hikes were announced by manufacturers of tractors and automobiles, as well as producers of copper, lead, aluminum, and stainless steel goods. Given the rate of inflation by October, and the fact that even the administration's own economists did not anticipate much improvement in the coming months, the White House realized that it had to reevaluate its system of voluntary wage and price controls, which were simply not working. Unwilling to abandon the program entirely, the administration switched to explicit numerical standards for wage and price increases and to specific government actions that would be triggered when the standards were exceeded.

On 24 October the president went on national television to announce "phase two" of his anti-inflation program. Increases in wages and fringe benefits, he told the American people, would be limited to 7 percent, and prices would go no higher than 0.5 percent below a firm's average annual rate of increase for 1976–1977. The budget deficit for 1979 would be held to $30 billion "or less." COWPS would announce specific price targets for the nation's major industries and would scrutinize the prices, wages, and profits of the nation's 400 largest corporations. In what Carter described as "real wage insurance," workers whose wage increases were kept below the 7 percent limit in a given year would get a tax rebate if inflation exceeded 7 percent during the year. Through these and other measures, the White House hoped to cut the inflation rate to 6.5 percent in 1979.

Following his televised address, Carter appointed Alfred Kahn chairman of COWPS and his chief inflation fighter. Kahn was a sixty-one-year-old former professor of economics at Cornell who, as chairman of the Civil Aeronautics Board, had made his mark on Washington by deregulating many airline operations and making the industry more competitive. Carter had been attracted to Kahn because of his own populist-progressive conviction that deregulation was a way to simplify government and unleash the efficiencies of the marketplace.

The administration arrived at its new anti-inflation strategy only after considerable debate among its top economic advisers over the size of the budget reduction required by the plan. That there had to be a major cut in the deficit was never in question. However, Blumenthal wanted the president to state publicly that he intended to reduce the 1980 budget deficit to the $30 billion range. Eizenstat and Schultze feared that if the budget was cut too drastically (to around $30 billion) it could lead to a recession, which would actually increase the deficit. In the end, Blumenthal's fiscal conservatism prevailed.

In announcing his new assault on inflation, the president knew that there would be an intense struggle among congressional Democrats over the size of the budget deficit and the programs that would be cut. But the reaction was worse than he expected, and it came not only from Democrats on Capitol Hill but also from business and financial leaders in the United States and abroad, who thought the program was still too weak and argued that the basic cause of inflation was not rising wages or prices but excessive demand for goods and services. Reflecting this displeasure, Wall Street was hit with a wild selling spree immediately after the president's speech, driving the Dow-Jones average down by almost 10 percent. Even more serious, the dollar plunged against gold and other currencies, with gold shooting up $17 an ounce, to $243, in five days. The continued slide of the dollar, Blumenthal warned in a news interview, would undermine any chance that phase two might succeed.

Taken aback by the dollar's fall, Carter summoned reporters to the White House press room on 1 November and announced that the cascading dollar threatened the world economy and that additional steps were being taken to prevent its collapse. Blumenthal then outlined the new measures, which included raising the discount rate by a full percentage point to 9.5 percent (the sharpest jump in forty-five years), reducing the funds available to banks for loans by $3 billion, increasing foreign currency reserves by $30 billion, and stepping up monthly gold sales. By tightening credit, the White House hoped to convince investors that it was determined to stop inflation, even at the risk of recession. By stockpiling foreign reserves and selling gold, it also intended to demonstrate its resolve to protect the dollar against unwarranted speculation.

In contrast to the president's address on 24 October, the initial response to this plan was highly favorable. The stock market soared a record thirty-five points in a single day, while the dollar appreciated 7 to 10 percent against all major currencies. But the elation was short-lived. Although the dollar was still gaining ground, by week's end stock and bond prices had retreated. Within a few weeks the dollar also began to come under heavy selling pressure. By the end of December it had lost about half its November gains, and the administration had begun to cut into its $30 billion support fund.

Meanwhile, Carter was losing the fight against inflation. The year ended with an overall inflation rate of 9 percent. Food prices finished 10 percent higher than the year before, with the cost of meat up more than 18 percent. Although many economists expected inflation to slow by 1979, few believed that it would dip below 7 percent. Moreover, any drop would be the result of tighter credit and a slowdown in the growth of the money supply, not a result of the administration's guidelines. Accordingly, there was a consensus among business leaders that the economy would either be sluggish or actually drift into recession. Although the White House was generally more optimistic, the CEA raised its forecast for inflation in 1979 from 6.5 to 7 percent.

It was still far too early to evaluate the effectiveness of the administration's wage and price standards, which by year-end were only beginning to be implemented. But there were signs of trouble there as well, since some guidelines were already being bent. In December COWPS modified the 7 percent cap on wages to exclude automatic increases in health and pension benefits. Although COWPS hoped that this action would make the rules more acceptable to organized labor, its decision threatened to open a Pandora's box of additional exclusions.

Even with the concession, many labor leaders remained adamant in their opposition to the guidelines, particularly AFL-CIO president Meany. In November Meany had written to Kahn requesting a public hearing on the new wage and price standards, but he had been turned down. Then Meany let the White House know that he wanted to discuss the wage and price restrictions with the president. He indicated that he might support the program if the wage level exempted from the cap was raised from $4 an hour to $5 an hour. Kahn, Eizenstat, and Schultze urged the president to meet with Meany, but the president first wanted assurances that the labor leader would support his anti-inflation measures. "Right now Meany looks like shit," he remarked, "and we look good and he knows it." Rebuffed, Meany became even more obstreperous in his opposition to the wage and price standards.[21]

By year's end, Democratic liberals were also preparing to do battle with the administration over the budget. Even though Carter had pledged to hold the deficit for fiscal year 1980 to $30 billion or less, he had also promised NATO allies in May that he would increase defense spending by 3 percent over inflation. This meant that most of the $15 billion in budget cuts would have to come from domestic programs. Reductions of that size could push the economy into recession. To liberals, therefore, the administration was offering an economic prescription that might well have been written by the Republican Party. Not only could it lead to economic disaster, but it would also mean a renunciation of the Democratic Party's commitment to minorities, the poor, and the underprivileged. Even the president's advocacy of deregulation as part of his anti-inflation strategy appeared to many Democrats to be a convenient excuse for relaxing protections against job hazards, toxic emissions, and pollution of the land and waterways.

Despite the disaffection of traditional Democrats, the most serious political question for Carter in the late fall of 1978 was how blue-collar workers, professionals, businesspeople, consumers, and farmers—the millions who had voted for him in 1976 precisely because he was not tied to traditional politics—viewed his administration. Election results from November 1978 offered little solace for him or for liberals on Capitol Hill. Although Democrats remained in firm control of both houses of Congress and the majority of gubernatorial offices, five Democratic liberals in the Senate—Dick Clark of Iowa, Floyd Haskell of Colorado, Wendell Anderson of Minnesota, Thomas McIntyre of New Hampshire, and William Hathaway of Maine—and one moderate Republican—Edward Brooke of Massachusetts—were defeated in their bids for reelection. Yet such right-wing Republicans as Strom Thurmond of South Carolina, Jesse Helms of North Carolina, and James McClure of Idaho were returned to office. Joining them were newly elected conservatives Roger Jepsen of Iowa, Gordon Humphrey of New Hampshire, William Armstrong of Colorado, and Thad Cochran of Mississippi. Off-year elections are rarely a referendum on a presidency, and the results of the 1978 elections appeared to be more a rejection of liberalism in traditionally Republican or swing states than a movement away from Carter. But they made it clear that the president was not winning new cohorts to the Democratic Party and that his potential for success as a transitional president was diminishing.

Although the rightward shift by voters was likely to signal greater support on Capitol Hill for the fiscal restraint Carter wanted, it did not mean the end of his strife with Congress. The defeated Democratic senators had generally supported the administration, and they were being replaced by some of the staunchest foes of the president's policies. In the previous Congress Carter had been able to count on the occasional endorsement of minority leader Howard Baker, who had been indispensable to his victories on the Panama Canal treaties. Now Baker would find it politically more hazardous to come to the president's aid. "It's a new ball-game," one moderate Republican commented after the election. "It doesn't take much to change things around."[22]

As 1978 came to a close, the president's position was increasingly precarious. Attacked by Democratic liberals for being too conservative, he faced a new Congress that was more conservative and more partisan than the 95th Congress had been. Although his political future depended largely on his success in curbing federal spending, he could hardly do so without further embittering major Democratic constituencies. Even within the administration, there was considerable grumbling about the impending budget cuts. Labor Secretary Ray Marshall cautioned that the cuts should not fall too heavily on jobs programs, because the administration would "have to prove that putting people on unemployment and welfare [was] less inflationary than giving them jobs." Stu Eizenstat's Domestic Policy Staff concurred, adding that it was "crucial to the Administration's credibility that youth funding not be cut in this year of rising unemployment." In a similar vein, HUD Secretary Harris sent a sharply worded memo to OMB stating that she could not live with proposed reductions in her department.[23]

It was no wonder, then, that many political analysts predicted a divisive contest over the president's budget when the 96th Congress convened in January and that others speculated openly about Carter's vulnerability to a Democratic challenger in 1980.

Jimmy and Rosalynn Carter with Admiral Hyman Rickover and his wife, Eleonore. Rickover was an influential person in the president's life. (Courtesy Jimmy Carter Library)

The Carters at the inauguration. (Courtesy Jimmy Carter Library)

Carter meeting with his cabinet. Around the table, starting on the left, are James Schlesinger, Jay Janis, John C. White, Michael Blumenthal, Walter Mondale, Griffin Bell, uncertain (either Robert J. Brown or Richard Moe), Andrew Young, Joseph Califano, Cecil Andrus, Cyrus Vance, Jimmy Carter, Harold Brown, Juanita Kreps, Brock Adams (?), Bert Lance, and Robert Strauss. Robert J. Lipshutz, Douglas M. Costle, Stuart Eizenstat, and Jane L. Frank are along the wall at the right. (Courtesy Jimmy Carter Library)

Carter holding a breakfast meeting with national security adviser Zbigniew Brzezinski (sitting next to the president), Vice President Walter Mondale, and Secretary of State Cyrus Vance (sitting across from Carter). Vance and Brzezinski were Carter's two main foreign policy advisers. (Courtesy Jimmy Carter Library)

Carter with Bert and LaBelle Lance. Lance, the president's close friend and director of the Office of Management and Budget, was forced to resign because of alleged financial improprieties. (Courtesy Jimmy Carter Library)

Press secretary Jody Powell (left) and Carter's chief staff aide, Hamilton Jordan. Powell and Jordan opposed the inflation-fighting proposals of Council of Economic Advisers chairman Charles Schultze. (Courtesy Jimmy Carter Library)

Carter and West German chancellor Helmut Schmidt. Schmidt was one of Carter's strongest international critics. (Courtesy Jimmy Carter Library)

Carter meeting with the Congressional Black Caucus. The caucus criticized the president for not doing more for African Americans. (Courtesy Jimmy Carter Library)

The Camp David accord, signed by the leaders of Israel and Egypt, was one of Carter's greatest successes. From left, Egyptian president Anwar Sadat, President Carter, Israeli prime minister Menachem Begin. (Courtesy Jimmy Carter Library)

Carter and the shah of Iran, Mohammad Reza Pahlavi. The administration was divided over how to handle growing opposition in Iran to the shah's rule. (Courtesy Jimmy Carter Library)

The president and Speaker of the House Thomas "Tip" O'Neill of Massachusetts. The relationship between Carter and O'Neill grew increasingly tense during the president's term in office. (Courtesy Jimmy Carter Library)

Carter and Senator Edward Kennedy of Massachusetts. Upset with Carter's policies, Kennedy ran against him for the Democratic nomination in 1980. (Courtesy Jimmy Carter Library)

Jimmy and Billy Carter. The president's younger brother's ties to Libya embarrassed the administration. (Courtesy Jimmy Carter Library)

Carter and his pollster Pat Caddell. Caddell had serious concerns about Carter's debate with Ronald Reagan because of Reagan's reputation as the "great communicator." (Courtesy Jimmy Carter Library)

8

★ ★ ★ ★ ★

CRESCENT OF CRISIS

Jimmy Carter's most significant foreign policy success in his first two years as president occurred at Camp David during early September 1978, when President Anwar Sadat of Egypt and Prime Minister Menachem Begin of Israel agreed to a framework of peace for the Middle East that promised to end thirty years of hostilities between Israel and its Arab neighbors. Even more than the signing of the Panama Canal treaties, Camp David was hailed throughout the world as a monumental diplomatic accomplishment. For Carter, who had brought Sadat and Begin together and then been instrumental in hammering out an agreement, the accords reached by the two leaders were a personal triumph and his administration's crowning achievement.

The administration's strategy for a Middle East settlement had been based on close collaboration with Sadat and separate negotiations with Begin, in the hope that Israel would soften its position on the occupied territories. The result was not compromise but impasse. Carter's efforts to restart the negotiations during the first six months of 1978 got nowhere. Begin still refused to guarantee eventual autonomy for the residents of the West Bank and the Gaza Strip; instead, he held firm to his proposal for limited home rule for the occupied territories for three to five years, after which Israel would evaluate how it was working. In July Carter sent Secretary of State Cyrus Vance to Egypt and Israel. Both Sadat and Begin agreed to a request by Carter that they send their foreign ministers to meet with Vance later in London, but the London session produced no concrete results.

With the failure of the London meeting, Carter and Vance agreed that the latter should return to the Middle East once more. Despite a vitriolic public exchange between Sadat and Begin, the Egyptian president still seemed anxious to bring the United States back into the negotiating process. Begin, whose cabinet was divided over the occupied territories, also seemed to welcome a new initiative. Hopeful, Carter decided to take the bold move of inviting Begin and Sadat to Camp David. The president had concluded that the only way to reach an agreement between Israel and Egypt was to bring the principals together for as long as it took to work out their differences. Once that was achieved, the door would be open to a general Middle East settlement.

Camp David was a gamble for the president. Although Begin and Sadat accepted Carter's invitation almost immediately, there was a good chance that they would not see eye to eye on anything. William Quandt, the NSC's Middle East expert, later recalled thinking at the time, "'We're here for group therapy. What are we doing?' My impression was, from everything I had read, that Begin and Sadat could not stand one another, and that this was going to turn out to be a disaster."[1] Failure at the Camp David talks would only add to the public perception of an ineffectual president. In addition, Camp David violated a cardinal rule of summitry: heads of state did not come together until agreements had been worked out at lower levels of government, so that summits were merely ceremonial.

For Carter, however, the risk was worth it. His missionary zeal and longtime interest in the Middle East convinced him that he had to take this step to bring about peace in that part of the world. He prepared for the Camp David meeting with the same diligence and thoroughness with which he approached any major undertaking. Vance and national security adviser Zbigniew Brzezinski thought that the president's main task should be to persuade Begin to make concessions on the Palestinian question, but Carter believed that he should concentrate on achieving an Egyptian-Israeli accord without linking it to progress on this perennial stumbling block. Consequently, he directed the American team accompanying him to Camp David to "assume [that] our immediate ambition" was a peace agreement between Egypt and Israel.[2]

Sadat and Begin both arrived at Camp David on 5 September. The talks got off to an inauspicious start. There was little chemistry between Carter and Begin, whom the president described as rigid, unimaginative, and more concerned with particulars than with the larger picture of a Middle East settlement. Even Carter's first session with his good friend Sadat did not go well. Carter was disappointed by Sadat's insistence that no agreement was possible until Israel withdrew from all the occupied lands.[3]

In coming to Camp David, the Egyptian leader was at a disadvantage. Although Begin could leave the summit at any time without penalty, Sadat had incurred the wrath of the other Arab nations and risked his own political future by undertaking this peace initiative; he could not return home empty-handed. His hope was that Carter could force Begin into a crucial easing of Israeli demands. But Sadat had underestimated the Israeli leader's ability to resist pressure, even in face-to-face talks with the American president. Because Begin was a stickler for detail, he was far less willing to compromise on specific issues than was Sadat, who became bored by details and preferred to deal in more general terms.

At first, Carter met with Sadat and Begin together, but because the two leaders did not get along, he soon began conferring with them separately, thinking that he might be able to break down the mistrust and animosity that had developed between them. But no progress was made until12 September, when Carter presented Sadat with a proposal for an Egyptian-Israeli peace treaty, the key sentence of which would restore "full Egyptian sovereignty . . . in the Sinai." Sadat found the draft largely acceptable, but the next day Begin flatly rejected it and stated that he would never agree to the removal of Israeli settlements from the Sinai.

The critical moment of the Camp David summit had arrived. Carter had brought Begin and Sadat to the pastoral setting of Camp David with the idea that the two leaders would come to trust and work with each other. Instead, they were not even on speaking terms. Furious with Begin's intransigence, Sadat announced on 15 September that he was preparing to return to Egypt immediately. Informed that the Egyptian delegation had already packed its bags, Carter rushed to Sadat's cottage and warned him that the American people would hold the Egyptian president responsible for the failure of the Camp David summit. Relations between the United States and Egypt would deteriorate, peacekeeping efforts would end, and his own administration would be discredited. Shaken by the force of Carter's argument, Sadat agreed to continue the negotiations.

Events then moved quickly. Israeli defense minister Ezer Weizman raised the possibility that Israel might give up its airfields in the Sinai if the United States would help build new ones in the Negev desert. The president indicated that he would go along with such a deal, provided Israel relinquished its settlements in the Sinai. Under tremendous pressure, even from his own cabinet, Begin relented. On 17 September, the twelfth day of negotiations, he told Carter that within two weeks he would have the Knesset vote on whether the settlements should be removed and that he would abide by its decision. Carter persuaded Sadat to accept this arrangement. The major obstacle to a Sinai agreement had now been removed.

Less successful were concurrent negotiations on other disputed issues, most notably the Palestinian problem and the Israeli occupation of the West Bank and Gaza. Egypt wanted a commitment from Israel to withdraw from the territories by a specific date and to grant the Palestinians in the West Bank and Gaza autonomy, but Begin refused. Instead, he and Sadat finessed the matter by agreeing to an ambiguous "framework for peace," which Carter had prepared a week earlier when the summit seemed about to collapse. This second accord provided for a transitional period of no more than five years, during which Egypt, Israel, and Jordan would determine the final status of the territories based on "full autonomy" and a "self-governing authority" for the inhabitants of the two nations. Their negotiation would also be predicated on the principles of UN Resolution 242—although the pact did not spell out what that actually meant.[4]

After thirteen days, then, Carter was able to announce publicly that a consensus had been reached at Camp David, calling for the signing of a peace treaty between Egypt and Israel and providing the basis for a Middle East settlement—a prize that had eluded peacemakers for more than thirty years. The signing of the Camp David accords, at a White House ceremony carried by all the major television networks, represented the high point of the Carter presidency. The summit was widely hailed as a shining triumph, and Carter was singled out for plaudits. Begin, Sadat, the news media covering the summit, and the American public all acknowledged what the president had accomplished.

But even as Carter was being acclaimed, some observers expressed reservations about the pacts. Several commentators noted that the "framework for peace" said nothing about the building of new Israeli settlements on the West Bank and Gaza. Moreover, the accords assumed that Jordan and the Palestinians living in the occupied lands would participate in the negotiations over the West Bank and Gaza. Yet King Hussein had said several times that he would not enter into the peace process unless Israel returned East Jerusalem, a condition that the Israelis would never accept. In addition, the two accords were replete with ambiguous terms and provisions that would make future talks extremely difficult. For example, the negotiators were expected to consider the "resolution of the Palestinian problem in all its aspects," as well as "other outstanding issues" concerning the West Bank and Gaza. But the documents did not specify what these other "aspects" or "outstanding issues" were. The president himself realized the difficulties he faced down the road, writing in the margin of a memo Vance sent him in October, "Israel will try to obstruct progress on W Bk/Gaza."[5]

In fairness to Carter, he had clearly accomplished his primary purpose at Camp David: to establish a basis for future negotiations. The

Egyptian-Israeli accord was possible precisely because it glossed over many of the most acrimonious issues blocking peace in the Middle East. Once these two enemies had agreed to a conciliatory framework, Carter hoped that the other moderate Arab nations, particularly Saudi Arabia, would join the peace process. When that happened, he believed, the remaining obstacles to a Middle East settlement could be resolved. Perhaps the president was naïve to think that peace was attainable in that troubled region, but what better alternative was there?

The fact remains, though, that the Camp David agreements were dangerously vague, that they were based almost as much on faith as on a hard assessment of Middle Eastern politics, and that, by papering over key differences between Egypt and Israel, they set up a diplomatic minefield that could very well explode in Carter's face. Amity required that the Arabs and Israelis proceed with more care and goodwill than they had previously displayed, and beyond the jubilation of the moment, there was little reason to expect such a change in behavior. Despite their public professions, Sadat and his chief aides were keenly disappointed by the results of Camp David. Egypt had obtained an Israeli commitment to withdraw from the Sinai and its rich oil fields, but Israel remained silent about the other occupied territories and the Palestinians. Sadat returned to Egypt, therefore, with little that would entice any of the other Arab leaders to a conference table with Israel.

By December the fragility of the Camp David accords became apparent. Because of Israel's announcement of new construction in the West Bank, there would be no peace agreement between Israel and Egypt by the 17 December deadline set by the negotiators of the two nations. By early 1979 the peace process had broken down completely. In a lengthy memorandum to Carter, Hamilton Jordan attributed the depression again enveloping the White House to the Middle East stalemate. "Not only have the Israeli-Egyptian negotiations taken much of our time, energy, and resources," he told the president, but "the recent growing concern that all that has been accomplished might somehow be lost has had a very negative effect on the attitude and morale of our foreign policy team."[6]

Yet Carter realized that Egypt and Israel were still anxious to come to terms. Both Begin and Sadat understood that failure to sign a peace treaty would strengthen the hand of the hard-line Arab states (Syria, Iraq, and Libya) that had denounced the Camp David agreements. The problem was how to get both sides talking again. Carter and Vance made an attempt via discussions with Egyptian foreign minister Mustapha Khalil and Israeli foreign minister Moshe Dayan at Camp David, but the effort proved unproductive. Carter then invited Begin to the United States for further negotiations.

What followed were some of the most trying sessions ever held between the two leaders. Begin announced upon his arrival at Andrews Air Force Base on 1 March that he would not be pressured "into signing a sham document." Carter was hardly more diplomatic, stating at a dinner for the nation's governors on the eve of Begin's arrival that the inability of Egypt and Israel to reach a peace agreement was "disgusting."[7] But by the second day of talks, the atmosphere had improved considerably. Perhaps chastened by the hasty impasse, the Israeli leader became less confrontational and more flexible on several key points. One issue was whether an Egyptian-Israeli peace treaty would take precedence over some defense agreements Egypt had with other Arab nations. The Israelis held that it would, but Egypt maintained that it would not. Carter resolved the problem by stipulating in the draft treaty that the agreement would not supersede Egypt's other treaties, nor would those agreements supersede the Egyptian-Israeli pact. Begin seemed amenable to language proposed by Carter that *implied* a linkage between the treaty and Palestinian autonomy, stating that the treaty was part of the "framework for a comprehensive peace treaty signed at Camp David." And Begin indicated a willingness to go along with ambiguous phrasing recommended by the president calling for a "goal" rather than a "timetable" of twelve months for arriving at an agreement on Palestinian autonomy but leaving unanswered what would happen if the "goal" was not achieved. After consulting with his cabinet, Begin informed Carter that his proposals were acceptable to Israel. Now the president had to sell them to Sadat.[8]

To finalize a pact, Carter decided to visit Egypt and Israel at the end of March 1979. After further discussions with Sadat and Begin, Carter was able to announce the conclusion of an Egyptian-Israeli peace treaty. Both sides had compromised. Egypt dropped its insistence on stationing personnel in the Gaza Strip preliminary to agreement on the fate of Palestine and also accepted the Israeli wording on a timetable for Palestinian autonomy. For its part, Israel gave up Begin's demand that Cairo guarantee to sell Jerusalem oil from the Sinai fields being returned to Egypt. Israel also promised to remove its forces from the western half of the Sinai within nine months, as Sadat had requested. In return, Cairo would exchange ambassadors with Jerusalem one month after that phase of the withdrawal was completed.

Carter had achieved another diplomatic coup to match the Camp David accords. Once more, he was greeted with a tremendous outpouring of public acclaim for his achievement—hailed as a statesman who had gone the extra mile and grasped the impossible. At Andrews Air Force Base, several thousand invited spectators maintained a midnight vigil to welcome him home.

Like the Camp David accords, however, the Egyptian-Israeli agreement had been reached only by avoiding the two crucial obstructions to a meaningful peace in the Middle East: Palestinian autonomy and Israeli withdrawal from the occupied territories. Arab reaction to the treaty was swift and negative. Jordan's King Hussein, whose support was essential to any settlement involving the West Bank, held an emergency meeting of his cabinet and then called for implementation of economic measures against Egypt. Saudi Arabia, which could have attempted to topple Sadat by denying Egypt crucial financial support, maintained a cryptic silence. Sadat had become so totally isolated in the Arab world, and his political future had become so mortgaged to a comprehensive Middle East settlement, that any further diplomatic tremors could unravel the Egyptian-Israeli agreement.

That tremor took place elsewhere in the Middle East, in Iran. By 1978 a revolution had broken out in Iran against the shah, Mohammad Reza Pahlavi. The reasons for the revolution, led by Islamic fundamentalists, were complex and long-standing, but they included the repressive nature of his regime—particularly the activities of his notorious secret police, SAVAK—and his efforts at modernization, which the Islamic Right found much too liberal. In August of that year, a fire at a cinema in Abadan left 377 people dead. Although the perpetrator was unknown, Iranians held the shah responsible. Riots and protests, some involving more than 100,000 people, took place throughout the country. The shah declared martial law and banned demonstrations. When a group of protesters tried to defy the ban by assembling in Tehran's Jaleh Square, government troops fired on them, killing as many as 700. For the first time, multitudes clamored for the shah's ouster and even his death, and they appealed to the army for assistance.

During the next four months the situation went from bad to worse. Huge demonstrations became routine and more violent. Although the shah was able to stall the revolution with the army's support, a new wave of bloody protests swept the nation in December. Iranians defied the military government in scattered clashes that left hundreds dead. On Ashura, Iran's holiest day, more than 1 million anti-shah demonstrators marched through Tehran. From Paris, seventy-eight-year-old Ayatollah Ruhollah Khomeini, spiritual head of Iran's 32 million Shiite Muslims and the emerging leader of the rebels, called for a general strike and the overthrow of the shah. Iranians responded by shutting down the oil fields for the second time in little more than a month. Increasingly, Americans became the target of the protesters.

Still trying to hold on to his throne, the shah freed 122 political prisoners, relaxed an evening curfew, and did not try to block the traditional street processions that marked the holy days. As strikes continued to paralyze the country and oil production fell to a trickle, he named Shahpour Bakhtiar, an outspoken critic of the shah's regime and a leader of the opposition National Front, to head a new government. He also agreed to leave Iran for "rest and recuperation"; when he returned, he would become a constitutional monarch who would reign, not rule.

On 16 January 1979 the shah boarded a jet for Egypt. Although he claimed that his absence would be temporary, most believed that the Iranian monarch would never return. As news spread of the shah's exit, Iranians took to the streets, celebrating in joyous abandon. Within hours, virtually every public square and boulevard once named for the shah had been renamed for Khomeini. On 1 February Khomeini arrived in Iran and received a tumultuous welcome from crowds so huge that the route of his motorcade became impassable, and he had to take a helicopter into Tehran.

To consolidate his power, however, the Ayatollah had to secure the loyalty of the military, whose leaders were generally pro-monarchist. At first there was real fear of a civil war between Khomeini's millions of supporters and the military establishment backing the Bakhtiar government. Although some fighting did take place, the military quickly declared its neutrality in the country's political battles. Stranded, Bakhtiar resigned, leaving the civilian government to his replacement, Mehdi Bazargan. Although Bazargan, an adviser to Khomeini, had broad political experience, the country's power shifted to Khomeini.

The Carter administration had been slow to respond to the mounting crisis in Iran, sometimes even seeming oblivious to what was happening there. Despite the growing evidence of SAVAK's brutality, including the use of torture, and despite his own commitment to human rights, the president had continued to permit the sale of huge amounts of military equipment to Iran. Over the objections of Assistant Secretary of State for Human Rights Patricia Derian, the administration had even sent the shah tear gas and other weapons for crowd control.

Carter, Brzezinski, and Vance accepted the thesis formulated during Richard Nixon's administration that the shah merited U.S. support because, under his rule, Iran had become the bulwark of American interests in the Middle East. Vance later wrote, "Iran was seen as the major force for stability in the oil-rich Persian Gulf. Its military strength ensured western access to gulf oil and served as a barrier to Soviet expansion. Its influence in [the Organization of Petroleum Exporting Countries (OPEC)] made it important to the American economy." Brzezinski echoed these views, as did Carter, who also pointed out Iran's important role as oil supplier to Israel.[9]

Although the shah had been a "friend" of the United States in the Middle East, it was not clear whether his enemies would be. In fact, the administration had trouble developing an accurate profile of his opposition, and as a result, the White House did not grasp the full extent of Khomeini's support until sometime in November 1978. Yet even then it was not clear where he stood with regard to the United States. The CIA wrote in January 1979, "Reports on Khomeini's foreign policy views and contacts give little insight into his specific plans." The agency concluded that "we can have confidence only in generalizations about the Ayatollah's foreign policy attitudes."[10] The White House also lacked accurate information about the military—the factions within the army and the degree to which the military leadership would remain loyal to the shah.

Those individuals at the State Department with expertise on Iran doubted that the shah's regime could survive. Both Ambassador William Sullivan and State's desk officer for Iran, Henry Precht, argued that the administration had to prepare for the likelihood of a post-shah government. Sullivan, who had established a good rapport with the shah, realized by the autumn of 1978 that Pahlavi was in trouble. In November he warned the State Department, "We need to think the unthinkable at this time in order to give our thoughts some precision should the unthinkable contingency arise." It was vital, he wrote, to prepare for the transfer of power from the shah to a coalition government of Khomeini's followers and the military.[11] But Vance was so preoccupied with the Camp David process that he never became a principal actor in the unfolding drama in Iran.

Sullivan's recommendation, meanwhile, elicited a critical reaction from the NSC. Brzezinski and his staff asserted that the United States should support the shah even if he used violent military measures to put down the opposition. They dismissed as appeasement the idea of a coalition government. Believing that the Bakhtiar regime would not survive, Brzezinski favored a military coup as its successor—and he continued to advocate a coup right up to the military's declaration of neutrality following Khomeini's return to Iran.

The loudest critic of Sullivan, though, was not Brzezinski but Gary Sick, the NSC staffer responsible for Iranian affairs. Sick accused Sullivan of undermining the shah's will to resist when he should have been encouraging the monarch to take a firm stand against the militants. He also charged the ambassador with misleading the White House by his optimistic reporting on the country's situation and then with abandoning the shah by establishing contact with the Islamic zealots seeking to overthrow him.[12] Sick was basically correct in his accusations. Instead of conducting diplomacy in accordance with administration policy—that is, to support the shah against the Islamic fundamentalists—Sullivan pressured the shah to leave the country, exaggerated the moderation of Khomeini's followers, and urged them to become part of a coalition government. As a result, the Iranian monarch and his military commanders were confused about what the U.S. response would be if they suppressed the opposition with military force. In the process, the ambassador diminished the prospects for an alternative to Khomeini, including a civilian government with strong military backing.

By December 1978 President Carter had lost confidence in Sullivan, whose recommendation "to think the unthinkable" he found totally unacceptable. Instead, he sent to Tehran General Robert Huyser, deputy commander of U.S. forces in Europe, who knew many of Iran's military leaders. Huyser's assignment was to bolster the military and convince it to stay in Iran should the shah beat his retreat, but this task put him at cross-purposes with Sullivan. While the general was trying to rally the military behind the Bakhtiar government, the ambassador denigrated the government's chances of survival and continued his overtures to Khomeini's followers. Sullivan even sent an angry telegram to Vance in which he charged that Carter had made a "gross and perhaps irretrievable mistake by failing to send [an] emissary" to meet with Khomeini—an accusation that no doubt played a part in the president's comment years later that he should have fired the ambassador for insubordination.[13] Not sure whether the United States would support military action, and holding Sullivan personally responsible for the shah's decision to leave Iran, the military allowed the Bakhtiar government to fall.

It is far from clear, however, that military intervention was ever a viable option. Uncertainty about the U.S. position was only one reason why the military did not launch a coup or otherwise seek to stop Khomeini. Before his departure, the shah had advised against a military overthrow because it would lead to further bloodshed. The generals also feared that draftees, who composed half the army, would not cooperate in military action against the Ayatollah. In addition, there was the risk that an unsuccessful coup might unleash economic and political chaos, which could then be exploited by the Soviet Union—the real enemy, in the generals' view.

In retrospect, it seems likely that by the time the United States became fully aware of the seriousness of the situation in Iran, it was probably too late to change the course of events. The real failure of Washington's Iran policy was the unequivocal support previously given to the shah. The decision in 1972 to rely on the Iranian monarch for the security of U.S. interests in the Middle East and the virtual blank check he received to buy U.S. military hardware fed the shah's inflated vision of his own importance and blinded him (and the United States) to the growing opposition to his rule among all strata of Iranian society. The dearth of intelligence about Iran compounded the errors.

Finally, the manner in which President Carter responded to the crisis pointed to one of the fundamental problems of his entire administration: a lack of clear leadership. One reason for this was the internecine warfare occurring within the administration. Vance's preoccupation with the Egyptian-Israeli talks allowed the NSC to take charge of relations with Iran. But this did not mean that Vance was uninterested in developments there or that the administration spoke with one voice. Precht and a number of his colleagues at the State Department had, like Sullivan, urged the White House to establish contact with Khomeini's followers and seek the formation of a coalition government. Believing, however, that these individuals were motivated by personal animus toward the shah, Brzezinski and his staff gradually cut them out of the decision-making process. Rather than choosing one side or the other, Carter chose to waffle. "We were not willing to make the shah's decision for him but he was told in unequivocal terms that we would back him in whatever action he found necessary," the White House later explained. But except for the Huyser mission, the president did little to demonstrate the substance of his administration's backing.[14]

The United States' troubles in Iran and other parts of the Muslim world seemed to multiply in the first few months after the overthrow of the shah. On 14 February Iranians stormed the U.S. embassy in Tehran and temporarily detained Sullivan and his staff. The siege lasted a few hours and was lifted by followers of the Ayatollah Khomeini. Afterward, Khomeini sent a personal emissary to Sullivan to apologize, but the incident amounted to a violation of American sovereignty.

On 15 February the U.S. ambassador to Afghanistan, Adolph Dubs, was killed; he had been kidnapped the day before by unidentified gunmen. At the time, Afghanistan was governed by Marxists who had taken power less than a year earlier after a bloody coup. The White House pleaded for restraint in the handling of the situation, but the Afghan police staged a "rescue mission" during which Dubs was killed. The administration suspected—but could not prove—that Moscow had either conspired in or knew beforehand about Dubs's kidnap and murder.

Developments such as these made the first few months of 1979 seem like an especially dangerous time to many Americans. Indeed, Brzezinski coined the phrase "crescent of crisis" to describe the area stretching along the Soviet Union's southern flank from the Indian subcontinent to Turkey and then southward along the Persian Gulf to the Horn of Africa. Calling the region of "vital importance" to the United States, the NSC adviser warned that its fragile social and political structures had already led to power vacuums that "could well be filled by elements hostile to our values and sympathetic to our adversaries."[15]

As Brzezinski's comment suggested, the regional turmoil was part of a broad clash of interests between Moscow and Washington and a general deterioration in Soviet-American relations. The tension was exacerbated when President Carter decided to grant full diplomatic status to the People's Republic of China. The American public first learned of Carter's decision during a hastily arranged television speech on 15 December 1978, in which he also announced the forthcoming visit of China's deputy prime minister Deng Xiaoping. The news even surprised lawmakers on Capitol Hill. The Chinese had insisted that before full diplomatic relations could be restored, the United States had to terminate its defense pact with Taiwan and agree not to sell Taiwan any more arms. The administration responded that it could not abrogate the pact without a year's notice and that it would continue some military sales to the Taiwanese after the treaty expired. Anxious to attract U.S. capital to help modernize China's economy, and seeking additional security in a period of growing estrangement between Beijing and Moscow, Chinese leaders accepted Carter's terms.

Although normalization of relations with the Beijing government was applauded in the United States as a major diplomatic breakthrough, the president still faced the difficult task of convincing skeptics that he had not sold out Taiwan and that his gambit had not been a mistake. He was not entirely successful. In the Senate, Barry Goldwater of Arizona termed the president's decision on China "one of the most cowardly acts ever performed by a President of the United States." In both the House and Senate, bills and amendments were introduced incorporating language that would have been unacceptable to Beijing—including a formal U.S. commitment to protect Taiwan in case of an attack by mainland China. Although the administration defeated most of these measures in committee, the final legislation that Congress approved at the end of March provided for stronger guarantees of Taiwan's independence than the White House had wanted.[16]

At the end of February, China's invasion of Vietnam confirmed the worst fears of everyone who had denounced diplomatic recognition of the Communist Chinese government. Six weeks earlier, Vietnam had attacked Cambodia, driving Pol Pot and his Khmer Rouge forces into the mountains and then renaming the country Kampuchea. China was determined to punish Vietnam for its invasion of Cambodia. Carter, who had been told of the planned offensive by Deng, tried to dissuade the Chinese, arguing that it would undermine one of the administration's best arguments for normalization—its contribution to peace and stability in Asia.

But Deng rejected this advice; Vietnam had to learn that it could not attack one of its neighbors with impunity.

The Chinese offensive held to its retaliatory purpose. The forces drove twenty-five miles across the border and withdrew after only seventeen days. But Republican senator Charles Mathias of Maryland expressed the sentiments of many Americans when he condemned the administration for "misplaying the China card." To such critics, China's attack across the border was no different from Vietnam's aggression against Cambodia, and it proved that the Chinese leopard had not changed its spots.[17]

With its turnabout in China, the White House provoked the Soviet Union. Although President Carter tried to reassure the Soviets that normalization was not directed against Moscow, Kremlin leaders were disturbed by Carter's willingness to allow Deng to speak out against the Soviet Union while in the United States. Moreover, in a final communiqué, the president joined the Chinese leader in denouncing "hegemony," a Chinese code word for Soviet expansion.

These events prompted Vance to observe later that "the sudden surge of Soviet inflexibility [on SALT] in the winter of 1978–79 was due primarily to developments relating to China."[18] There is some question as to the accuracy of this assertion, however. Certainly the rapprochement between Washington and Beijing raised visceral Soviet fears of a Sino-American alliance that would tilt the strategic balance in favor of the United States. But Soviet ambassador Anatoly Dobrynin has stated that Foreign Minister Andrei Gromyko had instructions from Moscow "to make an announcement [on SALT] in Geneva by the end of the year," despite news that Deng Xiaoping would be coming to the United States. "He was prepared," added Dobrynin, "a week later to sign SALT."

What seems to have prevented the signing of SALT in late 1978 or early 1979 was simply the complexity of the issues holding up a final pact. The two nations could not agree, for example, on a definition of new types of ICBMs. Without such a definition, existing missiles could be modified without violating the SALT I restriction that allowed each side one new ICBM system. Even more important, they could not resolve the highly technical problem of telemetry encryption, which involved the Soviets' encoding of electronic signals from their missile sites to keep information about the missiles secret. The White House feared that failure to achieve an agreement banning encryption would lead to questions in the Senate about the United States' ability to verify Soviet compliance with SALT and endanger the treaty's ratification. According to Dobrynin, it was this demand about encryption, rather than U.S. relations with China, that caused the Soviets to fail to agree to SALT by the end of the year, an assessment with which Leslie Gelb, assistant secretary of state for political and military affairs, agreed.[19]

Carter and his advisers, in other words, had underestimated the intricacies of the unresolved points and overestimated Moscow's readiness to sign a treaty. In the spring Brzezinski had gone to the People's Republic of China in an attempt to pressure the Soviets to reach a new SALT agreement. If anything, playing the "China card" in this way had the opposite effect. In an interview with reporters from *Time* magazine in January, Soviet leader Brezhnev warned that there were "some in the U.S. and in other western countries who have found the hostile course toward the Soviet Union followed by the Chinese leadership so much to their liking that they are tempted to turn Peking into an instrument of pressure on the world of Socialism." Under these circumstances, he was not inclined to be flexible in the final stages of the SALT talks.[20]

Indeed, it appears that Deng's purpose in coming to Washington may have been, at least in part, to undermine the SALT negotiations. Just before leaving for home, he belittled the SALT talks, remarking that such agreements "are neither as significant nor as useful as the normalization of relations between China and the U.S." Rather than the United States playing its "China card," as Brzezinski had intended, perhaps China had successfully played its "American card."[21]

By early spring 1979 the United States appeared to many observers to be a hapless giant in an increasingly unfriendly world. Moreover, the "crescent of crisis" delineated by Brzezinski now seemed to include South Korea and the small Central American country of Nicaragua. President Carter's call for withdrawing U.S. troops from South Korea had agitated Congress, and the Tongsun Park case had only complicated matters. In 1978 Park finally appeared before Congress to testify about the efforts of the South Korean Central Intelligence Agency to influence the U.S. political system, but this did not calm congressional concerns over the withdrawal plan.

Pressure from Congress, the U.S. military, and the Japanese forced the administration to revise its withdrawal plan in 1978; specifically, the withdrawal process would occur more slowly than originally called for. However, a report leaked to the *Army Times* in January 1979 put the White House into a full-scale retreat. According to the report, North Korea's military forces were significantly larger than originally estimated. Lawmakers thus insisted that the administration shelve further talk of removing U.S. ground troops from South Korea. "Ever since the Congress became aware of our upgraded intelligence estimates of the North Korean order of battle," Brzezinski wrote to Carter in January, "pressure has been building for a review of our policy of withdrawing U.S. combat forces from the Republic of Korea." He continued that he, Vance, and Defense

Secretary Harold Brown "agreed that the revised estimates . . . warrant a thorough review . . . of the withdrawal policy." The following month Carter publicly announced that the United States was "holding in abeyance any further reductions," pending a reevaluation of North Korea's capabilities.[22]

For Carter's critics, the new information on North Korea's order of battle only confirmed their belief that withdrawing U.S. troops from South Korea was foolhardy. Not only had the president sought to remove American forces from a U.S. ally that faced a persistent threat from its neighbor, but he had done so without taking a full account of the capabilities of that neighbor. Although Carter's critics could be pleased with his decision to suspend indefinitely the withdrawal initiative, they still remained concerned about his willingness or ability to respond to threats to the United States or its allies. Nicaragua became a case in point.

In Nicaragua a civil war had been raging for two years between the forces of the country's dictator, Anastasio Somoza, and leftist guerrillas known as the Sandinistas. Throughout the fighting in Nicaragua, the administration followed a zigzag course—criticizing Somoza's human rights violations, deploring even more the Sandinistas' Marxist leanings and Cuban support, but advocating a mediated end to the war. At the same time, the president's inconsistency alienated both the Nicaraguan dictator and his opposition.

As the Sandinistas grew stronger militarily and gained popular support, the White House applied more pressure on Somoza to give up the reins of power. Believing that Somoza's continued presence increased the chance of a radical takeover, the White House finally terminated military aid and most economic assistance and reduced the size of the U.S. embassy in Managua. Still, Carter continued to vacillate; there was even a report in the *Washington Post* that the administration was considering the resumption of some aid to Nicaragua. Although this did not happen, it seemed to demonstrate that Carter was incapable of a resolute response to a deteriorating situation even in the United States' own backyard.

As a result, Carter came under attack by many of the same people who just a few months earlier had praised his statesmanship and diplomatic skills. The president's high marks for getting Egypt and Israel to sign a peace treaty were overshadowed by the growing perception of national impotence, which was attributed to Carter's inexperience, his indecisiveness, and his inability to define and achieve his foreign policy goals. According to an NBC–Associated Press poll taken in late March, immediately after the president's successful trip to the Middle East, only 29 percent of those surveyed approved of the conduct of his presidency. Although the low figure had more to do with Carter's handling of the economy than with any other issue, less than half the respondents (44 percent) applauded the direction of his foreign policy. The president's role as peacemaker, though widely praised, had done little to improve his overall approval rating with the American people, which was up only 1 percentage point from February.

In the realm of domestic policy, however, the paralysis of leadership seemed to be most pronounced, and it was there that the president was most vulnerable. Consequently, the strongest attacks against the Carter administration were focused on that area.

9

★ ★ ★ ★ ★

A GROWING SENSE OF CRISIS

Each year the proposed federal budget sets forth the administration's assumptions and priorities for the next fiscal year. Once approved by Congress and signed into law, it determines who will be that year's principal beneficiaries of the government's largesse. The budget is predicated on economic assumptions about the state of the economy; therefore, it is a political document as much as an economic one, with substantial winners and losers that no administration can ignore, except at grave political risk.

President Carter understood this elemental fact about the budgetary process. To his credit—and against the recommendations of some of his closest advisers—he nevertheless tried to subordinate political considerations to his war against inflation in preparing the budget for fiscal year 1980. His primary weapon in this fight was budgetary austerity, but the politics of austerity encroached on his economic program and further eroded his support among traditional Democrats. More important, it added to a growing sense of crisis and to the image of a president incapable of keeping his own house in order, much less managing the affairs of state.

The battle lines between the president and his more liberal foes within the Democratic Party were drawn at the party's second midterm conference held in Memphis in early December 1978. At the gathering Carter's forces clashed with opponents over the size and priorities of the budget for 1980. In his October speech on inflation the president had stated his intention to present Congress with a lean budget that limited the deficit to around $30 billion; he repeated this pledge in Memphis. But because of automatic adjustments for inflation in certain programs and the president's previous commitment to NATO to increase defense spending 3 percent over the rate of inflation, there would be only a small pool left for projects dear to the hearts of many Democrats—health, education, housing, jobs, and aid to the cities.

Led by UAW president Douglas Fraser, liberal delegates attacked Carter's appeal for frugality. Although the administration was able to beat back this challenge, the three-day meeting in Memphis underscored the depth of the fissures within the Democratic Party. Indeed, the warmest reception was given not to the president but to Senator Edward Kennedy, who, in contrast to Carter's bland defense of his administration, stirred the emotions of the attendees with his evocation of historic Democratic values.

During the conference Hamilton Jordan and the president made clear their intention to run the 1980 campaign much as they had the one in 1976—as outsiders appealing to the broad mainstream of American voters rather than to Democratic loyalists. This was demonstrated by their reaction to the vote on the administration's budget resolution, which had been subjected to a floor fight by the liberal contingent. But Jordan made light of the 40 percent who voted against it, remarking that the "makeup" of the meeting was not representative of the Democratic Party. Carter shared this view, telling his cabinet later that delegates at such gatherings typically came from the most liberal wing of the party and that he had never been their man.[1]

Other members of the administration were less sanguine. Stu Eizenstat, Vice President Walter Mondale, Labor Secretary Ray Marshall, HUD Secretary Pat Harris, and a number of White House aides were deeply worried about the divisive impact of the administration's budget on the Democratic Party. They were also concerned that the proposed budget was a retreat from the president's commitment to social justice. Carter responded to their fears by restoring about $2 billion in budget cuts in the areas of education, health, jobs, and urban aid. But he still remained firmly wedded to economic austerity. In his budget message to Congress on 22 January 1979 he called for total expenditures of $532 billion, which included a projected deficit of $29 billion, or $12 billion less than the 1979 deficit. Although total spending was about 8 percent greater than that for the current fiscal year, the bulk of the increase was due to the 3 percent growth in defense spending and the automatic hikes previously legislated by Congress.

Reaction to the president's budget proposals was predictable. Reporters dubbed the anticipated struggle the "battle of guns vs. butter." Organized labor closed ranks to fight the president's plan. House Speaker Tip O'Neill indicated to the president that he would fight the administration on a number of the social programs targeted for cuts.[2] Inevitably, speculation mounted about a Kennedy challenge to the president in 1980. At the Memphis conference Kennedy had accused the White House of ignoring traditional Democratic constituents—the needy, the elderly, workers, and minorities—and had called Carter's austerity plan "seriously defective." But his strongest disagreement with the president continued to be over national health insurance. Carter postponed the unveiling of his own health insurance plan; instead, he limited his budget recommendations to modest increases in Medicare and Medicaid coverage for low-income children and pregnant women. He also urged lawmakers to pass legislation (defeated last year) that would contain hospital costs, which he believed to be the largest contributor to inflation. Kennedy condemned the president's health funding as unacceptable.[3]

Although Kennedy stated on numerous occasions that he would support Carter in a bid for reelection, political pundits continued to predict, and Democratic liberals continued to hope, that the senator would oppose Carter in 1980. In such a contest Kennedy remained the odds-on favorite. A *Los Angeles Times* poll in January 1979 showed the president trailing the Massachusetts lawmaker by 23 points in a national election and by 51 points in a New Hampshire primary, the site of the first scheduled primary contest in 1980.

If there was no recession in 1979 and inflation abated without increased joblessness, Carter's political advisers were confident that they could defeat a Kennedy challenge. Pointing to the conservative mood of the country, they maintained that budget austerity was not only good economics but also good politics. However, a number of leading economists were already questioning whether Carter could hold the budget deficit to under $30 billion without bringing on a recession and more unemployment. Alan Greenspan, who had headed President Gerald Ford's CEA, thought that a recession was indeed likely and that it would probably cause a deficit of $40 billion to $50 billion.

Figures for the first three months of 1979 seemed to justify these pessimistic forecasts and to expose the fallacy of the White House's predictions, particularly on inflation. The White House had estimated that its endeavors would push the inflation rate down to 7.4 percent in 1979 and 6.6 percent in 1980. But by the end of March it was clear that inflation was defying the administration's projections. Over the last six months the consumer price index (CPI) had increased at a 10.4 percent annual rate, compared with 9.4 percent during the previous six-month period.

The upturn in fuel costs was especially sharp. Because of the revolution in Iran, oil production in that country had nearly stopped, ending a worldwide glut of oil that had kept oil prices stable for more than a year. The oil-exporting countries responded by raising the price of their oil by as much as 17 percent, causing oil prices to skyrocket. The cost of food, up

suggest that if my earlier diagnosis of the unhealthy condition of the anti-inflation program is at all close to accurate, your political and economic advisors had better bestir themselves to think of some dramatic actions [that could have an immediate impact on prices]."[5]

Even as Kahn warned the president that his anti-inflation program was unraveling, discontent spread on Capitol Hill over the president's strategy of curbing inflation by means of a tight budget. Black lawmakers and other black officials were particularly strident in their criticism of the White House. Statistics for February revealed that unemployment among black teenagers had increased during the month from 32.7 percent to 35.5 percent. The administration argued that its jobs programs were being targeted to the hard-core unemployed. But in Washington, stores were broken into and looted after hundreds of black teenagers reported for snow-shoveling work only to be told that the jobs had already been filled. Similar disturbances occurred in Baltimore. Many local leaders, including black elected officials, blamed the unrest on the president's austerity program. "They do not buy the linkage between the battle on inflation and the need to cut job programs," Louis Martin, Carter's assistant for minority affairs, told the president.[6]

Although the economy was the administration's principal domestic concern in the winter of 1979, the White House also had to contend with a scandal involving the Libyan connections of the president's brother. Billy Carter's personality was very different from that of his older brother, and he was commonly lampooned as a redneck with a beer belly. But his good-natured humor and his willingness to laugh at himself were so well received by the American public that he became a popular guest on talk shows and was in great demand on the lecture circuit. The situation changed dramatically after Billy returned to Georgia in September 1978 from a trip to Libya, where he had been the guest of the Libyan government. In January he helped host a lavish reception in Atlanta for a "friendship delegation" from Libya. When asked the reason for his involvement, he replied, "The only thing I can say is there is a hell of a lot more Arabians than there is Jews." He also remarked that the "Jewish media [tore] up the Arab countries full-time," and he defended Libya against charges of state-sponsored terrorism, noting that a "heap of governments support[ed] terrorists and [Libya] at least admitted it."[7]

The public outcry was immediate and loud. President Carter tried to disassociate himself from his brother's statements. In an interview with NBC News, he expressed the hope that the American people would "realize that I don't have any control over what my brother says [and] he has no control over me." Billy later apologized for his comments, claiming that they "were not intended to be anti-Semitic." But the incident publicly embarrassed the president and touched some raw nerves, particularly among American Jews, whose relations with the president were already troubled. "If [Billy's] not working for the Republican Party, he should be," quipped the *Atlanta Constitution* in summarizing the political damage done to the administration.[8]

The formal signing of the Egyptian-Israeli agreement at the end of March provided some political relief for Carter, but not for long. Oil shortages hit the West Coast especially hard, and by mid-May long lines of cars were waiting an hour or more to reach the gas pumps. Fights broke out at numerous gas stations, and weapons ranged from fists to guns, knives, and broken beer bottles. Across the nation, gas stations were closing on Sunday or shortening their weekday hours to have enough gas on hand until their next deliveries.

As president, Carter had repeatedly warned of impending energy shortages and had proposed a comprehensive energy plan whose fundamental premise was energy conservation through both a wellhead tax on domestic production and a tax on industrial users of oil and gas. Instead, Congress had approved legislation with no provisions for oil pricing. As a result, efforts to conserve fuel were hampered because fuel prices remained substantially below world prices. The cost of domestic production, which in March 1979 still accounted for 52 percent of American consumption, was determined not by the international market but by the Energy Policy and Conservation Act of 1975 (EPCA)—a complex piece of legislation that set different prices for old and newly discovered oil. About 70 percent of all domestic crude oil production was subject to EPCA price ceilings. Although the world price of oil was around $15.20 per barrel, price ceilings ranged from about $5.50 a barrel for old oil to $12.65 for new.

As oil shortages became more serious and OPEC started to raise prices, the White House struggled to find new ways to conserve oil. As required by the EPCA, the administration submitted a standby gasoline rationing plan to Congress. But the administration had little enthusiasm for rationing, which would be cumbersome to execute and politically unpopular. Another idea was to unleash gasoline prices by removing EPCA controls on domestic oil. Under current legislation, all price controls on oil were to be lifted in October 1981, but the president could phase in decontrol at an earlier date. This would have the desired effect of raising prices, but the oil producers would reap higher profits. Even though the oil companies argued that such revenues were needed for exploration and discovery of new petroleum deposits, considerable opposition arose on Capitol Hill, with many lawmakers asserting that decontrolling prices would be inflationary and would benefit only the oil industry.

After reviewing various alternatives for dealing with the energy predicament, including immediate decontrol, the president decided at the end of March to implement a phased elimination of oil price controls. On 5 April Carter outlined his "phase two" energy plan in an address from the Oval Office, telling the American people that they would have to use less oil and spend more for it, and announcing that he was phasing out all controls on oil by 1 October 1981. Since the oil companies stood to gain some $13 billion when domestic prices rose to world levels, the president also called for a "windfall profits" tax, which would return about half those profits to the government. The tax would be used to fund the development of alternative fuel sources, help poor families pay for the rising cost of fuel, and stimulate the construction of energy-efficient mass-transit systems.

Carter could not have chosen a more opportune time to address the American people on the importance of energy conservation. Just one week earlier, the worst accident in the history of nuclear power had occurred at a plant on Three Mile Island near Harrisburg, Pennsylvania. For six days Americans contemplated the horror of a nuclear meltdown or an explosion that would send lethal radioactive gases into the atmosphere. Although that did not happen, the accident undermined claims about the safety of nuclear energy and led to a lengthy investigation and report (the Kemeny Commission Report) on the future of nuclear reactors as an energy source for the nation. Without eliminating the nuclear option entirely, Carter made it clear that he regarded nuclear energy as a source of last resort.[9] During the same week as the Three Mile Island accident, OPEC ministers meeting in Geneva agreed to raise oil prices for the second time in a little more than three months—this time by 9 percent. By dramatizing the limited options for the United States, these events should have generated support for Carter's new energy program. That they failed to do so was in part the president's own fault. Assuring the American people that the energy crisis was "real," he nevertheless delivered a harsh indictment of the oil industry, which seemed to assign sole responsibility for higher oil prices to it , thus diluting the urgency of the situation. "Just as surely as the sun will rise," he stated, "the oil companies can be expected to fight to keep the profits they have not earned."

Moreover, there was a basic miscalculation in Carter's energy plan. At a time when the greatest concern of the American public was inflation, the president proposed to handle energy shortages by allowing prices to rise even higher. From a conservation viewpoint, this made sense, but politically, it was a disaster. Democratic lawmakers reacted forcefully against the president's decision to decontrol, and they maintained that the windfall profits tax was still too generous to the oil companies. Calling Carter's program "seriously flawed," Kennedy claimed that the oil lobby had intimidated the president "into throwing in the towel" on decontrol without even "entering the ring." He urged the president to continue controls at least until a windfall profits tax had been passed. But, having tried and failed with that approach over the wellhead tax, Carter was determined to decontrol first and make Congress responsible for the tax. Democrats were so angered by the president's actions that they began a legislative drive to take away his power to lift controls.[10]

Amid the storm over decontrol and windfall profits, the White House was also battered by other dour economic news. Figures released in May revealed that inflation was growing at an annual rate of about 14 percent and that the economy had entered a slump. Meanwhile, the administration's wage and price standards now faced a judicial challenge. At the end of May a federal district court judge ruled that the president had exceeded his authority in promulgating guidelines and then threatening to withhold federal contracts from companies that violated them.

There were assaults on other fronts as well. In the May *Atlantic Monthly*, former presidential speechwriter Jim Fallows, who had become disenchanted with Carter's policies and left the White House, delivered a scathing attack against the president in which he accused him of being "ignorant" of how power could or should be exercised. A few weeks later a grand jury in Atlanta indicted Bert Lance for his loan practices as president of the National Bank of Georgia. The charges came after a lengthy investigation, and there had been allegations that part of a loan to the Carter family peanut business had been illegally diverted to the 1976 presidential campaign. Although the president and his brother Billy, who ran the company, were exonerated, the indictment reopened an old scandal that the White House would just as soon have forgotten.[11]

By this time, a crisis of confidence in the White House had developed in American society that extended well beyond traditional Democratic constituencies. A Yankelovich poll found that only 23 percent of the people questioned believed that things were going well in the country. In contrast, 64 percent believed that the nation was "in deep and serious trouble," up from 41 percent a year earlier. Although the main concern of the interviewees was still inflation, a more general feeling of pessimism seemed to be spreading throughout the country. In a lengthy memorandum titled "Of Crisis and Opportunity," Pat Caddell warned the president that if he could not effectively deal with inflation and restore the confidence of the American people, he would lose the election in 1980.[12] As public disenchantment with Carter grew, Democrats intensified their pressure on Kennedy to oppose him in 1980. The Massachusetts senator continued to deny any plans to seek the Democratic nomination in 1980. His office even tried to halt a pro-Kennedy meeting in Iowa that drew more than 100 labor leaders who were disgruntled with the administration. Despite his disavowal of presidential ambitions, Kennedy remained at odds with Carter on a number of issues, and their most serious dispute continued to be over national health insurance.

In March the White House unveiled a proposal for national health insurance that attempted to stake out a middle ground between Kennedy and Russell Long of Louisiana, whose plan provided only for catastrophic insurance. As Eizenstat described it, "We offer Kennedy our opposition to a catastrophic-only bill and our commitment in principle, to a comprehensive plan. We offer Long our support of first-phase legislation [Medicare and Medicaid reform and catastrophic coverage] . . . which has a credible chance of passing." But Kennedy rejected the White House compromise. Instead, he announced in May his own comprehensive national health plan and called on the president to support it, warning that he would do everything he could to defeat the president's scheme.[13]

The White House was annoyed by the senator's threats and personal barbs, but it also fretted over the prospect of Kennedy in the 1980 race. The latest Gallup poll in May showed Kennedy beating the president among Democrats 54 percent to 31 percent. And a *New York Times*–CBS survey published in June placed the president's personal rating (as opposed to his job rating) in the negative for the first time—that is, only 33 percent of the people interviewed rated him favorably, while 45 percent rated him unfavorably. Caddell termed this result "staggering." "Almost no candidate whose personal rating has been negative has survived reelection," he told the president. As the economy unraveled and Carter's slide in the polls continued, the president's cool restraint foundered. He became increasingly agitated and short-tempered. At a White House dinner with a small group of lawmakers in June, he boasted that if Kennedy challenged him in 1980 he would "whip his ass."[14]

However, during the spring most of the president's malice was directed at Congress, which was busy mauling his legislative agenda. By this time, the fractures and fissions that had existed between Carter and congressional Democrats since he entered the White House had grown wide and deep. Lawmakers who gained and held office more by building personal organizations than by being loyal Democrats became even more protective of their own interests. In early April Congress killed Carter's wage insurance plan by slashing $2.5 billion slated for the program from the budget. The next month it defeated Carter's standby gasoline rationing plan. At the end of May Democrats sent a message to Carter by voting in caucus, 139 to 69, to reinstate controls on oil. All this left Carter utterly frustrated. "What do you suggest I do?" he asked Democratic congressman James Hanley of New York. "Ignore the [energy] problem and hope it will go away? Find a scapegoat?"[15]

In response, the president devoted a great deal of attention to building coalitions on specific issues, but he did not provide the vision or spirit of comity necessary to cement those coalitions. In fact, he often appeared to be running with the fox while chasing with the hounds—appealing to traditional Democrats in language that seemed more appropriate for conservative Republicans, without satisfying either of these constituencies or creating a coalition that would be loyal to him.

Part of the problem was that the White House—which just a few months earlier seemed to have honed its message—once again appeared to be incapable of being consistent. Was there a gas shortage? The president said there was, and most economists agreed that supplies in the spring were short by 5 to 20 percent. Yet Carter seemed to downplay the crisis when he emerged from a meeting with California governor Jerry Brown and suggested that federal assistance was not needed to solve that state's gasoline shortage. At Carter's side, Secretary of Energy James Schlesinger declared that "it would be safe to say that we hope the worst is over." During a speech in Iowa the president also indicated that he would not veto a bill extending controls if it were passed by Congress. His statement came as a shock even to his own staff. "This gives the impression of an absence of leadership," Eizenstat told Carter. "This gives the impression of waffling on a critical issue."[16]

Likewise, administration officials and White House aides complained that although Carter had identified inflation as the nation's most serious domestic problem, he had not developed a coherent strategy for dealing with it. "We have not shown a clear direction to our policy," Treasury Secretary Michael Blumenthal told the president in March. "We have spent too much time debating options, when action was more important than substance"—a rather startling statement for a treasury secretary to make.[17]

Carter himself was dissatisfied with the quality of the economic advice he was receiving and with the chorus of voices claiming to speak for the administration. However, the situation could largely be traced to the president's own refusal to focus on one economic counsel and to the internal quarrels among his advisers. Alfred Kahn, whose loose tongue on such topics as decontrol (which he first publicly opposed and then supported) was becoming an irritant to the White House, did not get along with his own director of COWPS, Barry Bosworth. Eizenstat and Schultze were often at odds with Blumenthal; politically more liberal than Blumenthal, they were generally more reluctant than he to cut social programs or raise interest rates.

By the summer of 1979 the Carter administration confronted a widespread sense that the nation had come to a critical pass—and nothing that happened over the summer and fall alleviated that feeling. Indeed, the economy seemed out of control. For June the CPI went up 1 percent, less than the 1.1 percent increase in April and May, but still a disturbing annual rate of 12.5 percent. Although this slowing of prices gave Carter's economic advisers some hope that inflation might be easing, that optimism was shattered by the announcement that wholesale prices had jumped in July at an alarming annual rate of 13.7 percent.

As inflation raged, pressure on the dollar again mounted in international monetary markets. In a rescue effort, Carter named Paul Volcker chairman of the Federal Reserve Board. Volcker would replace William Miller, whom the president had appointed treasury secretary following Blumenthal's resignation (discussed later in this chapter). The lanky and rumpled new FRB chairman had served as undersecretary of the treasury under Richard Nixon and was president of the Federal Reserve Bank of New York at the time of his appointment. In these positions he had gained an international reputation as a brilliant monetary technician and diplomat. His selection was widely praised on Capitol Hill and in international financial and banking circles.

Volcker proved to be a nightmare for the administration. His solution for inflation was to allow money markets to determine interest rates by drastically tightening the money supply through open-market sales of treasury securities instead of manipulating the rates themselves through periodic increases (or decreases) in the discount rate (the rate at which banks could borrow from the Federal Reserve). This meant drastically higher interest rates and lower economic growth in an already sluggish economy. By allowing the market instead of the FRB to set rates, even as he pushed rates higher by tightening the money supply, Volcker also shielded the FRB from political pressure; in effect, the administration's future became mortgaged to the will of the FRB. The nation's major banks responded by raising their prime rates, first to 13 percent and then to 14.5 percent. Many analysts predicted that the prime rate would go even higher by year's end, possibly throwing the economy into recession.

While the FRB sought to counter the economy's woes through monetary policy, the administration's approach was to tinker with its program of wage and price controls and renew its struggle with Congress for hospital cost containment legislation. Its wage and price guidelines did have some mitigating effect. Overall wage increases in major union contracts declined from 8.2 percent in 1978 to 7.5 percent through June 1979, but the moderation in salaries was not uniform. Such powerful unions as the Teamsters and the UAW won raises of more than 30 percent over three years, while the 1979 salaries of top business executives increased by nearly 15 percent. As for the president's proposal to restrain hospital costs, it was again rejected emphatically by the House (234 to 166) after Carter ignored warnings by House leaders that he did not have the votes to win. Instead, the House approved a motion creating a national commission to study hospital expenses, a measure that Jody Powell called a "joke" because it merely delayed legislative action on the issue.[18]

Meanwhile, inflation marched on. Wholesale prices for August jumped 1.2 percent, much higher than most economists had predicted. Conditions were worsened by further increases in the cost of oil and growing uncertainty about future oil prices. In September Nigeria imposed a $3 to $5 per barrel surcharge, and Venezuela announced that it was cutting its oil exports by 7 percent, thereby putting additional upward pressure on oil prices. Although OPEC was not expected to discuss another general rate increase until its December meeting, Saudi Arabian oil minister Ahmad Zaki Yamani warned that the OPEC nations would not tolerate a continuing erosion of their purchasing power.

On commodities markets, international traders and speculators again drove up the price of gold. In September gold reached a record $340 an ounce. In one day alone it soared $37; two days later it jumped another $16. Tighter money, rising inflation, and concern about oil prices also led to pandemonium on Wall Street as stocks, which had been climbing most of the year, nose-dived. In just five days in October the Dow-Jones average plunged 58.62 points, the second steepest one-week decline ever, ending the week at 838.99.

Clearly, then, much of the American public's discontent with the Carter administration in the fall of 1979 was the result of a deteriorating economy, particularly rising inflation and the energy crisis. But what distressed Americans almost as much as the economy was their perception of presidential ineptitude. This malaise intensified in July following a sequence of unusual events—a presidential speech on energy was postponed without explanation, leaders from a broad cross section of American society trekked to Camp David for discussions with the president, and five members of Carter's cabinet resigned.

The catalyst for these events was OPEC's June announcement (while the president was attending the Tokyo summit) of its fourth and largest price surge in five months. Even before this latest development, American drivers had been expressing their frustration and anger. In Levittown, Pennsylvania, truckers barricaded expressways and set off the nation's first energy riot, resulting in two nights of violence that left 100 injured and led to more than 170 arrests. In North Carolina, Governor James Hunt mobilized 900 National Guardsmen to avert a blockade of fuel deliveries in Greensboro and Charlotte.

The latest OPEC increase only exacerbated Americans' rage. Following the advice of his top aides, Carter hurried back from Tokyo, skipping a planned vacation in Hawaii, to address the nation on energy. Work on the speech began in flight, and the White House asked the television networks for time on 5 July for a major presidential address. But just thirty hours before Carter was scheduled to go on the air, the White House canceled the speech without offering any explanation.

For the next eleven days the president remained at Camp David conferring with prominent people from business, government, labor, and the academic and religious communities. He also made secret helicopter flights to the homes of two "average, middle-class" families in Pennsylvania and West Virginia. Again, no explanation was given for these meetings other than a statement by Jody Powell that the president was consulting people in and out of government on "major domestic issues ... which include, but go beyond, the question of energy."[19]

In truth, Carter was dissatisfied with the various drafts of the speech he had received; each reflected the opinion of one clique of advisers concerning the proper content and tone of the message. Eizenstat wanted the president to identify OPEC as the chief culprit of the energy crisis and to emphasize his commitment to a synthetic fuels program. He and Schlesinger also pushed for a more optimistic tone, while media coordinator Gerald Rafshoon thought that the president should make a more realistic (and pessimistic) assessment of the situation. Jordan argued for a message stating concrete solutions for the nation's problems; Caddell believed that the president needed to embrace a broader theme than energy. As a result of these differences among his own people and his personal conviction that Caddell was right, Carter decided to delay his speech and undertake a complete reevaluation of his administration.

The president's overhaul covered a wide range of topics, from the energy crisis to presidential style. In a meeting with a small group of influential public figures, including Clark Clifford, Lane Kirkland, Jesse Jackson, and John Gardner of the consumer group Common Cause, the president was sharply criticized for his lack of leadership. In discussions with his own advisers, Caddell again made the point that the president had to address the crisis of spirit, which he maintained was the most serious problem affecting the nation.

Mondale strongly disagreed, stating that what bothered most Americans had little to do with a crisis of spirit but a lot to do with energy problems, inflation, and economic stagnation. The president's other advisers supported this pragmatic view. Carter needed to display leadership, Rafshoon argued, not sermonize on the failings of the American people. But the president ignored this counsel. When he finally came down from Camp David and gave his long-delayed speech on 15 July, he subordinated the energy crisis and the nation's other economic ills to the "crisis of spirit"—the country's most pressing problem, according to the president. Carter never defined exactly what he meant by this phrase, but it was interpreted by the news media to denote a pervasive mood of despair about the nation's future. Although the president did not use the term *malaise*, it rapidly became the catchword for his message.[20]

As he presented additional recommendations for dealing with the energy situation, the president continued to emphasize this intangible undercurrent plaguing the American people. Carter called for limits on oil imports, cutting them by one-half, or 4.5 million barrels per day, by 1990. He also proposed the establishment of an Energy Security Corporation to help finance the development of synthetic fuels and an Energy Mobilization Board to cut through the red tape that often strangled nascent projects. Resolving the energy crisis, he said, was crucial to the health of the U.S. economy, but it also involved a test of American will—a test the American people had to pass if the United States was to remain a vibrant nation. "We are at a turning point in our history," he declared. "All the legislation in the world can't fix what's wrong with America. What is lacking is confidence and a sense of community. . . . Energy will be the immediate test of our ability to unite this nation."

The president's speech was well received. After eleven days in seclusion, rumors abounded about his physical and mental health, ensuring a large audience for his address. Most Americans were impressed by his presentation. Following Rafshoon's advice, he used short, crisp sentences; spoke with passion and eloquence; appeared candid and sincere; and inflected his voice for dramatic effect better than he had at any time before. Finally, and most important, he appeared strong, decisive, and ready to take on the enemies of the consumer—even the oil giants and the OPEC cartel.

Yet a few days later Carter undermined his improved standing with the American people by accepting the resignations of five members of his cabinet: Treasury Secretary Michael Blumenthal, Attorney General Griffin Bell, HEW Secretary Joseph Califano, Energy Secretary James Schlesinger, and Secretary of Transportation Brock Adams. The president had been considering a purge of his cabinet since returning from Tokyo. A group of his top advisers, including Mondale, Powell, and Jordan, told him that if he was going to reassess his administration, he should be prepared to make changes in his cabinet. In particular, the White House staff recommended that Schlesinger, Califano, and Blumenthal be replaced because they did not work well with the staff or with Congress. At first, Carter argued against the idea, but the senior Democratic leaders he consulted at Camp David gave him much the same advice. He had also been disturbed for some time by embarrassing leaks and by what he regarded as disloyalty among top administration officials. He concluded, therefore, that a shake-up of his administration was warranted.

At a cabinet meeting on 17 July he asked all his cabinet secretaries and the senior members of his staff to submit "pro forma resignations"; he would then decide which ones to accept. "I have one and one-half years left as President," he said, "and I don't deserve to be re-elected if I can't do a better job." The next day he announced that he had accepted the resignations of Schlesinger, Blumenthal, and Califano; a day later he accepted those of Bell and Adams. Of the five cabinet secretaries, only Bell had intended to resign (although Schlesinger had offered to leave earlier).[21]

Certainly the president had just cause for taking this action. As he had been told at Camp David, Schlesinger, Califano, and Blumenthal had long-standing difficulties with Congress and the White House staff. Schlesinger's arrogance had infuriated lawmakers on Capitol Hill, and they also held him responsible for the country's energy mess. Although Califano was highly regarded in Washington for his intelligence and management of the government's most complex agency, he could also be insufferable, and White House staffers, including Hamilton Jordan, suspected that he was the source of a number of leaks on such issues as welfare reform and national health insurance. Because of his more conservative economic views, Blumenthal frequently clashed with Eizenstat and Schultze on fiscal policy; like Califano, he was not regarded by the White House as a "team player." As for Adams, he was forced out mainly because of his unbridled tongue and his refusal to follow a directive from the White House to fire his top assistant.

Even so, many lawmakers on Capitol Hill were incensed by both the suddenness and the sweeping nature of the cabinet dismissals. In particular, liberal Democrats were outraged by the firing of Califano, who claimed that he had been removed at the insistence of the Georgia coterie influencing the president. Carter admitted later that he handled the cabinet changes poorly. "I . . . should have announced immediately," he wrote, "that Treasury Secretary Mike Blumenthal and HEW Secretary Joe Califano had resigned, and that I had accepted the resignation, which I had been offered many months ago by Jim Schlesinger." Instead, his gambit of asking for mass resignations made it appear that the government was falling apart.[22]

The mass resignations also aroused controversy over the First Lady's influence on her husband. Since her trip to Latin America in 1977, Mrs. Carter had continued to play an ever-increasing role in the administration. In February 1979 she became only the second First lady to testify before Congress, calling for greater funding for the mentally ill. She also helped write some of the president's speeches—among them the July energy speech. Her activities in the administration and her apparent influence even led some in the media to refer to her as the "second most powerful person in the United States" and "Mrs. President." The president himself later wrote that "aside from a few highly secret and sensitive security matters, she knew all that was going on."[23]

Mrs. Carter came under increasing criticism because many Americans believed that she had crossed the line of the proper role of a First Lady. The criticism became even greater after it was learned that she had participated in discussions on the purge of the cabinet. Although she opposed the mass resignations her husband favored, she wanted Califano fired because she believed that he was responsible for leaking information to the press and because he had opposed the creation of a Department of Education, which she favored. When asked about the cabinet shake-up, she commented, "I just . . . uh . . . I . . . uh, Jimmy thought, and I agreed with him that it was better to do it fast." The confusion of her pronouns led many observers to conclude that she had gone too far. Rosalynn had her defenders, however. Columnist Carl Rowan declared, "I'll be damned if I ever want my country run by a President who is too dumb to consult with his wife!" But the image perceived by many Americans was of a chief executive who needed his spouse's help to make key decisions.[24]

As part of his shake-up, Carter named Hamilton Jordan as chief of staff and instructed the rest of the White House staff to obey Jordan's orders "as if they were the President's own." Critics of the administration had long maintained that Carter needed someone to run the White House's day-to-day operations, ride herd over the cabinet, and limit intrusions on his time, but the president's appointment of his young and controversial aide—a sometime target of the gossip columns—was unsettling. Then, as one of his first acts as chief of staff, Jordan distributed a questionnaire to every senior member of the administration asking them to grade their own senior subordinates on their work habits, interpersonal relations, and loyalty to the White House. The questionnaire not only was insulting in tone but also made it seem that another bloodletting—this time reaching into middle management—was imminent and that allegiance to the administration would be at least as important as competence in deciding who was fired.

Carter was able to undo some of the damage from the purge by selecting highly qualified people to fill the vacant slots. To head the Department of Energy he named Charles Duncan, a Pentagon official and former executive with Coca-Cola who was respected for his managerial expertise. To replace Blumenthal he appointed FRB chairman William Miller. For HEW secretary he moved Patricia Harris over from HUD. As Harris's successor he named Moon Landrieu, a former mayor of New Orleans and past president of the U.S. Conference of Mayors. For transportation secretary he appointed Neil Goldschmidt, mayor of Portland,

Oregon; at age thirty-nine, Goldschmidt had already made a name for himself based on his knowledge of urban affairs and his focus on mass transit. Finally, Carter replaced Bell with the attorney general's trusted lieutenant, Benjamin Civiletti, who had been assistant attorney general in charge of the criminal division.

In the weeks that followed, Carter and his new chief of staff also undertook a major reorganization of White House personnel to calm the "semi-hysteria" that Jody Powell claimed had been caused by the cabinet changes. In particular, they named Alonzo L. McDonald, an expert on administrative management and managing director of the international consulting firm McKinsey and Co., as assistant to the president and White House staff director serving directly under Jordan.

In six weeks McDonald changed the layout and operation of the West Wing. Walls and doorways were shifted. Seventy-five people had their offices moved, in some cases out of the West Wing and into the nearby Executive Office Building. The rationale for changing the layout of the White House offices was not only to better coordinate operations; it was also intended as a psychological tool. By positioning his own office between those of the president and Jordan, McDonald wanted to let the staff know who was in charge; the hierarchically oriented staff was also reminded that their purpose was to serve the president, not to enhance their own position. In addition, McDonald regularized daily meetings of the senior staff and their deputies, introduced agendas, established a system of monitoring to make sure that assignments were carried out, and took charge of the speechwriting operation following Rafshoon's departure from the White House to join the campaign staff.

Although McDonald did not resolve all the management problems that had plagued the Carter White House, he established a degree of centralized control and administrative order that had not existed prior to 1979. Although some egos were bruised, most White House aides seemed pleased with the new efficiency and hard-nosed management he brought to the administration. Hedley Donovan, the recently retired editor in chief of Time Inc., joined the administration as senior adviser to the president at about the same time that McDonald was hired. He later remarked, "McDonald was a first-class administrator, which his boss Hamilton Jordan . . . was not."[25]

In announcing McDonald's appointment as his deputy, Jordan had told the White House staff that it would give him "more time to think and plan."[26] Aware that he was not popular on Capitol Hill—indeed, that House Speaker O'Neill regarded him with open contempt—Jordan also tried to improve his relations with lawmakers by visiting them in their offices and soliciting their views. In a meeting with O'Neill, he apologized for his past indiscretions. "You have really opened the door for me on the

Hill," he wrote to the Speaker afterward, "and I realize the great mistake I made in not establishing some relations there the past two years."[27]

Nevertheless, the cabinet shake-up was a disaster for the president. By summarily firing four members of his cabinet and accepting the resignation of a fifth, the president destroyed both the progress made in restoring his image as a forceful leader and the goodwill created by his 15 July address. An NBC–Associated Press poll taken after the dismissals gave Carter a "good-to-excellent rating" of only 23 percent, which was two points lower than his rating at the time of his address to the nation.

Carter was also unwise to choose the energy crisis as the tinder on which to rekindle the American spirit, for there was no more divisive issue in 1979 than energy. Notwithstanding the proposals Carter outlined to the American people in July, a windfall profits tax remained the core of his program. In June the House had approved a measure providing for a 60 percent tax on decontrolled oil, which was expected to generate revenues of $277 billion before being phased out by 1990. Capitulating to public outcry after reports of record earnings by the oil industry, the Senate passed its own tax measure; weaker than the House bill, it was supposed to raise $178 billion in taxes by 1990. In committee the House and Senate conferees agreed to a compromise $227 billion target but had not yet worked out other differences by year's end. Regardless, a final bill, passed by both houses and ready for the president's signature, seemed assured soon after Congress reconvened in January.

In addition to the windfall profits tax, lawmakers approved a standby gas rationing bill. They also seemed ready to concur on the establishment of an Energy Mobilization Board, to speed up the construction of energy-related facilities, and an Energy Security Corporation, to spearhead the development of synthetic fuels (synfuels) such as liquids and gas from coal, oil from shale, and alcohol from grain.

By the close of 1979, therefore, the president was on the verge of gaining congressional approval for the most comprehensive energy legislation in the nation's history. But, as in any bruising fight, especially one with such important stakes, the costs of victory were high. Instead of winning broad support for his energy plan, the president alienated even groups whose support might have seemed beyond question. Environmentalists usually found themselves on the same side as Carter on legislative issues, such as the protection of millions of acres of Alaskan land from commercial development (see chapter 13). However, they vigorously opposed the creation of a powerful Energy Mobilization Board, which they feared would ignore laws protecting the environment if it sought to facilitate the licensing and building of new energy plants. Similarly, they fought the administration's proposal for an Energy Security

Corporation, concerned that synfuel production would pollute the air and create heavy demands on scarce water supplies.

Representatives of low-income Americans, who, as Eizenstat reminded the president, spoke for "substantial segments of the Democratic party's basic constituency," also condemned the administration's energy program. Looking at the energy situation in terms of higher prices rather than as a test of American will, they did not like what they saw. Aware of the opposition to the president's energy plan even within the Democratic ranks, Eizenstat warned Carter that Americans could be persuaded to pay the price of his energy program only on the basis of clear economic and political arguments—such as Iran's cutoff of oil—not by obscure references to American angst.[28]

In other words, Eizenstat told Carter in November what Mondale had contended in July—that Americans were not suffering from emotional collapse and in need of catharsis; they were suffering from real and tangible conditions. It was not so much a crisis of spirit as the president's apparent inability to do anything about inflation, the energy problem, and rising unemployment that made his administration seem so ineffective. This perception was reflected in a Yankelovich-*Time* magazine poll conducted in October 1979 that used a leadership scale to rank potential presidential candidates. In contrast to Kennedy, who received the highest rating, Carter received the lowest in a field that also included such Republicans as former treasury secretary John Connally, former California governor Ronald Reagan, former CIA director George Bush, and Tennessee senator Howard Baker. In commenting on the survey, Caddell explained to the president that "the [American public] see too much of what has troubled them the last two years—*that events dominate us, that we react to, not lead events.*"[29]

The last half of 1979, then, was an extremely difficult period for the Carter presidency. To many political observers, the president was on the ropes and about to go down for the final count. Even some notable victories on Capitol Hill—such as passage of a $5.7 billion welfare reform program, approval of a $3.5 billion aid package for financially strapped Chrysler Corporation, and adoption of a measure establishing a new Department of Education (which candidate Carter had promised to the National Education Association in 1976)—were unable to improve his standing with either the American people or traditional Democratic constituencies. Liberals continued to criticize him for his "first-phase only" national health insurance strategy. Urban leaders persisted in their complaints about inadequate help for the cities. Black leaders remained unhappy with the administration's efforts on behalf of the poor and the unemployed.

The black community was also deeply upset by the forced resignation in August of UN Ambassador Andrew Young after it was revealed that Young had held an unauthorized meeting with a representative of the PLO, Zehdi Labib Terzi. Two hundred black leaders assembled at a meeting called by the National Association for the Advancement of Colored People (NAACP) to vent their anger. Since American Jewish leaders had led the call for Young's dismissal, the session was punctuated by anti-Semitic outbursts. Eventually cooler heads prevailed, and both Jewish and black leaders attempted to heal the rift that had developed between them. But even Carter's appointment of another black, Donald McHenry, to replace Young at the United Nations failed to lessen the bitterness that many blacks felt toward the administration.

The president was also hurt in August by charges that Hamilton Jordan had used cocaine while visiting a fashionable discotheque in New York and might have used cocaine at other times as well. A special prosecutor was appointed by the Justice Department to investigate the charges leveled against Jordan. The department decided that the case was without merit, but the accusations themselves were enough to taint the administration with scandal.

Ready to replace the president at the head of the Democratic ticket in 1980 was Ted Kennedy, who ended months of speculation by announcing in November that he would challenge Carter for the Democratic nomination. All the opinion polls showed that Kennedy was the first choice among Democrats, leading Carter decisively in every region of the country except the South, where the president maintained a slim lead. Yet the White House and some perceptive observers sensed that Kennedy's support was wide but not deep and that he was vulnerable on a number of counts. In fact, the administration entered the primary season confident that the president would best Kennedy. What it could not have anticipated, however, was how developments in Iran and in the little-known country of Afghanistan would boost Carter's chances.

10

★ ★ ★ ★ ★

FOREIGN POLICY, PATRIOTISM, AND POLITICS

In contrast to such domestic concerns as inflation, budget austerity, and oil and energy policy, there was no burning foreign policy issue before 1980 that aroused the American people against the White House. In fact, on most foreign policy matters, Americans agreed with the president. Jimmy Carter had, after all, won their approbation for his efforts in the Middle East that resulted in the signing of the Egyptian-Israeli peace treaty. Also, by a margin of better than two to one, both Democratic and Republican voters viewed the SALT talks favorably; even a substantial number of conservatives approved of SALT. Similarly, a clear plurality (46 percent) of Americans surveyed supported the president's decision to increase military spending, even at the expense of domestic programs. Sixty percent agreed with Carter's diplomatic recognition of the People's Republic of China.

The paradox was that although most people did not fault Carter on any specific issue, their overall assessment was negative. Moreover, many Americans in the spring and early summer of 1979 had serious concerns about the implications of the president's conduct of foreign policy. Fifty-four percent of the people polled by Pat Caddell thought that the United States' position in the world was only "fair" or "poor," while 44 percent believed that it was "excellent" or "good." More important, only 13 percent of the interviewees thought that the nation's position in the world was "growing stronger"; 62 percent believed that it was "becoming weaker."[1]

a staggering 18 percent from a year ago and 4.5 percent in February alone, also drove the CPI higher. Even excluding fuel and food, the CPI was still growing at an annual rate of 9 percent.

Not surprisingly, all the polls indicated that Americans considered inflation to be the most urgent national problem, and many people felt that the president was not doing enough to address rising prices. The White House's program of wage and price standards was singled out for criticism. Despite price controls, corporate profits had soared by as much as 25 percent between the first quarters of 1978 and 1979. This led labor leaders to demand higher wage hikes than were permitted under the administration's guidelines. Even Alfred Kahn, the president's chief inflation fighter, recognized that the system of wage and price controls was coming unglued. After learning of the jump in business profits, Kahn declared the program "a catastrophe."[4]

Something of a curmudgeon, Kahn had a colorful personality and a sharp, analytical mind. As chairman of the Civil Aeronautics Board, he had led the administration's fight to deregulate the nation's airline industry. With considerable gusto and flair and a wry sense of humor, he was able to raise and respond to complex issues in an understandable and commonsense fashion that turned him into something of a Washington celebrity and made what he did and said newsworthy. He also developed a public reputation as being irreverent and fiercely independent. Even among the most-well known figures of the Carter administration, Kahn stood out in the public mind, usually in a highly favorable way, although the White House staff became increasingly annoyed with his brashness.

In a lengthy and typically candid memorandum written at the end of February, Kahn warned the president that his anti-inflation program was falling apart. "Surely you have discovered by now," he told Carter, "that neither your economic nor your political advisors are ever going to present you with *the* solution to the problem of inflation, ready made." His most immediate concern was the likelihood of pressure to increase wages. "I simply do not know how long we can expect labor to be willing to come in with settlements at the 7% level or even close to it, when the [consumer price index] shows every sign of double-digit range." In an effort at self-effacement, he acknowledged that he had only his own "half-baked" ideas to offer but stated, "in some circumstances one does [a president] a disservice by holding off, for fear of criticism, until the baking is complete." Although he mentioned a number of proposals, the one he stressed was the need to press harder for real wage insurance—a guarantee to reimburse workers if the CPI rose higher than 7 percent, the amount of their wage increases. But even with real wage insurance and other anti-inflation measures such as better monitoring of voluntary wage and price increases, Kahn remained gloomy about the future. "I

There were a number of factors that supported this feeling of national weakness. The country's growing dependence on oil imports and the declining value of the dollar left it more exposed to the whiplashes of the international economy. Despite the SALT negotiations, the cold war remained as frigid as when Carter first took office thirty months earlier. Indeed, some Soviet specialists forecast a period of great instability in Soviet-American relations when the visibly ailing Soviet leader, Leonid Brezhnev, stepped down or died. Considerable uncertainty also surrounded developments in Rhodesia, where the election of a black prime minister failed to stop the escalation of guerrilla forces, and in Nicaragua, where the dictatorship of Anastasio Somoza was about to be toppled by leftist Sandinistas. But the most serious situation facing the president was occurring in Iran, where anti-American sentiment, encouraged by the Khomeini regime, was reaching dangerous proportions.

Both the energy crisis and the weakened dollar had already revealed the nation's vulnerability in the world economy, as did its unfavorable balance of trade. Economic relations between Washington and its trading partners became increasingly strained as protectionist sentiment spread in the United States. But protectionism was only the tip of the iceberg of world economic problems. As the Joint Economic Committee of Congress warned the president in June 1979, inflation, unemployment, and excess industrial capacity were increasing worldwide; productivity was languishing; and the "energy picture [was] becoming more troubling."[2]

At the end of the month Carter attended the Tokyo economic summit, hoping that the United States and its trading partners would stand together against OPEC—perhaps even establish an international corporation to fund the development of alternative fuels. Instead, the meeting underscored significant differences among the world's strongest industrial powers and OPEC's largest customers. Although the seven leaders in Tokyo ratified an American proposal to set specific country-by-country ceilings on oil imports, they did so only after an acerbic exchange between Carter and West German chancellor Helmut Schmidt. Moreover, the agreement reached on oil imports was not impressive. Carter announced that the United States would restrict its imports of petroleum to 8 million barrels a day, but this was slightly more than current levels and considerably more than those of a year earlier. As if to accent the danger of such energy dependence, OPEC, meeting at the same time in Geneva, jacked up the world price of oil to between $20 and $21 a barrel—up 15 percent from the previous week, 50 percent since the first of the year, and 1,000 percent from the price ($1.80) at the beginning of the 1970s. More and more it seemed that Carter was becoming a prisoner of events he could not control.

Even the signing of a SALT agreement in June furnished few political benefits to the beleaguered president. Although Moscow and Washington had been close to an accord since the end of 1978, disagreement on technical issues, particularly encryption, had delayed final action on a pact. Months of secret negotiations resolved the remaining points. The Soviets agreed to ban encryption in cases in which it would affect verification of compliance with the treaty; they issued a statement declaring that the Backfire would not be given intercontinental capability; and they accepted the American definition of new ICBMs—any missile type differing from an existing missile by more than 5 percent in length, width, total weight, or throw weight.

Concluding a SALT agreement, however, was only half the fight; winning Senate approval of the treaty promised to be just as arduous. The battle lines over SALT had been forming for two years. Opponents, led by the Committee on the Present Danger, claimed that it would give the Soviets significant military advantages over the United States; that it would foster a false sense of security among the American people; and that, with the loss of important "listening posts" as a result of the Iranian revolution, Soviet adherence to its provisions could not be monitored. The administration responded that the treaty should be considered on its own merits, not on the basis of ongoing U.S.-Soviet differences; that it would place important limits on the strategic arms race; and that there was enough intelligence overlap to verify Soviet compliance without the Iranian listening posts.

At the end of June 1979 the White House began an extensive public-relations campaign to mobilize public support for the SALT agreement, just as it had for the Panama Canal treaties a year earlier. But the foes of SALT II were equally vigorous in their efforts to defeat the treaty. Their most effective tactic was to link the pact to other issues touching on Soviet-American relations, such as the Cuban presence in Africa and Soviet violations of human rights. Senate majority leader Howard Baker, whose backing was essential if a SALT agreement was to be approved, stated that the administration and the Soviets should recognize that "linkage is a fact of life."[3]

Republicans were not alone in opposing the agreement. In the Senate, defense hard-liner Henry Jackson kept up an unrelenting drumfire against SALT. Although he had promoted deep cuts in the U.S. and Soviet nuclear arsenals, he felt that SALT as it stood weakened the United States' defense posture. In contrast, Democrats William Proxmire of Wisconsin and George McGovern of South Dakota, who normally supported arms control measures, informed the president that they might vote against SALT II because it did not go far enough in restricting the strategic arsenals of the two superpowers. Proxmire, McGovern, and a number of other lawmakers also thought that the president was making too many concessions to win over the opposition. In particular, they objected to Carter's decision to develop the MX mobile missile system. Intended to give the United States the same capability to launch a first strike against the Soviet ICBMs as the Soviets were believed to possess against the United States, the MX would be the one new missile system permitted to the United States under the terms of the SALT treaty. The president had chosen this course with great reluctance. "It was a nauseating prospect to confront, with the gross waste of money going into nuclear weapons of all kinds," he recorded in his diary on 4 June. But national security adviser Zbigniew Brzezinski persuaded him that without the MX trade-off, a SALT agreement had no chance in Congress.[4]

A few days after making his decision on the MX, Carter traveled to Vienna to meet with Brezhnev for the signing of the SALT II accord. Within two hours of his return from the summit, he was on Capitol Hill urging the Senate to ratify the SALT treaty he had just signed. Hard-liners remained unpersuaded. Republican Jake Garn of Utah told the president that the upper chamber was not likely to approve the SALT pact in its present form. Senator Baker, whose vote the White House had counted on, shocked the administration by announcing that he too would reject the agreement unless significant changes were made, including a requirement that the Soviets dismantle all their huge SS-9 and SS-18 missile launchers.

In testimony before the Foreign Relations and Armed Services committees, administration officials proved highly adept at defending the treaty against critics who charged that it gave the Soviets an advantage because they were not required to scrap their heaviest land-based missiles, which had far greater destructive capability (throw weight) than American MIRV launchers. Turning that argument on its head, Vance pointed out to the Armed Services Committee that the heaviest Soviet missiles could be armed with as many as 30 warheads—in contrast to the maximum of 10 warheads allowed under SALT II. What mattered, asserted Brown and Vance, was the total number of warheads permitted to each side. Under the SALT treaty, the Soviets would have between 10,000 and 12,000 warheads, or about the same as the United States.

As the hearings on the treaty continued into August, the debate over SALT turned from the details of the accord to the size of the military budget. At the end of July, Georgia senator Sam Nunn, widely respected on Capitol Hill as an expert on arms control, declared that he would not vote for the SALT treaty without a commitment by the president to increase the defense budget by 5 percent after inflation. A week later Nunn, Jackson, and Republican John Tower of Texas sent the president a letter asking him to "make public" his administration's plan for defense for the next five years. Former secretary of state Henry Kissinger made a similar request, asserting that the United States could achieve an enduring peace only by having the world's strongest military force. By shifting the debate over SALT to broad questions of the military balance of power and the size of Carter's defense budget, Nunn and Kissinger effectively tied approval of the treaty to the type of arms race that liberal Democrats such as McGovern and Proxmire opposed—an arms race that was also bound to have an adverse impact on Carter's efforts to slash the deficit. The president would have to accede to a larger budget or cut domestic spending.

As the administration fought to win ratification of the SALT treaty, Senate Foreign Relations Committee chairman Frank Church of Idaho announced at the end of August that a Soviet combat brigade had been discovered stationed in Cuba. The issue had first surfaced in July when the magazine *Aviation Week* published a CIA report about Soviet military exercises in Cuba. Confronted with this report, senior administration officials conceded that they had received intelligence that the Soviet Union was setting up a high-ranking command structure in Cuba that would be able to handle a brigade-sized unit. Stepped-up reconnaissance over the next month confirmed that the Soviets had a force of between 2,000 and 3,000 men who appeared to have been in Cuba since at least 1975 or 1976 and who had recently participated in combat field maneuvers. The force was small and did not violate any agreement between Washington and Moscow. In fact, a Soviet brigade had been in Cuba since before the Cuban missile crisis of 1962. During that incident, President John F. Kennedy had asked Moscow to remove the troops; receiving no response, the subject had been dropped.

Fighting to keep his seat against a formidable right-wing challenge, Church attacked the White House for allowing Soviet troops in Cuba. Church's assault put the administration on the defensive regarding SALT and added another element to the ongoing dispute between Vance and Brzezinski. Robert Pastor, the NSC's Latin American expert—who had to cut short his honeymoon to deal with the brigade crisis—commented that the NSC adviser and secretary of state differed on how to respond to the situation and save SALT. Vance felt that it was best to "play down the brigade issue." Brzezinski argued that the administration should make clear that it "recognized this increasing threat of Soviet-Cuban military collaboration" and should "demonstrate that SALT was one element of a larger strategy of responding to this threat."[5] He also charged that the State Department had mishandled the crisis by being overly "acquiescent" to the presence of the brigade.[6]

The result was once again a paper-clipping of policy. On 5 September Vance held a news briefing in which he tried to minimize the significance of the Soviet brigade by noting that the Soviet troops had been in Cuba for many years—perhaps even since the 1960s. But he also stated that he would "not be satisfied with the maintenance of the status quo," and his remarks were echoed by the president two days later. Carter and Vance later acknowledged that their statements were harsher than they had intended and that what they really wanted were changes in the function and structure of the brigade so that it would not constitute a combat force.

The fact was that the president and secretary of state had taken an inconsistent stance. While asserting that the Soviet troops were not a new phenomenon and so posed no military threat,[7] they simultaneously demanded changes in the status quo. What were the Kremlin, members of Congress, and the American public to make of this contradiction? In particular, how were the Soviets supposed to react to what seemed to be an artificially created crisis over the presence of a Soviet brigade that had been there for years? Clearly, the Kremlin was suspicious and angered by the whole situation; indeed, it refused to alter the composition of the brigade or to discontinue its field operations. Veteran foreign policy makers also were critical of the administration's conduct. Believing that the administration was being indecisive, White House counsel Lloyd Cutler and senior adviser Hedley Donovan persuaded the president to invite sixteen senior statesmen to offer their views on the issue of the Soviet brigade. Dubbed the "Wise Men," the diverse group included such well-known Washington figures as George W. Ball, McGeorge Bundy, Henry Kissinger, John J. McCloy, W. Averell Harriman, Dean Rusk, and Clark Clifford. Their overall conclusion was that the brigade had been in Cuba since the 1960s, that it was not a threat to the United States, and that the administration had mishandled the affair.[8]

Meanwhile, opponents of the SALT treaty used the issue to attack and delay ratification of the SALT agreement, claiming that the presence of the troops demonstrated the Soviets' untrustworthiness and threw into question the quality of U.S. intelligence. Senator Tower stated categorically that the agreement would not be approved so long as combat troops remained on the island. Even Church—a backer of the treaty, despite his instigation of the controversy—believed that there was "no likelihood whatever that the Senate would ratify the SALT treaty" until the Soviet forces left Cuba.[9]

On 1 October Carter delivered a speech from the Oval Office in which he tried to put the controversy behind him. He called the brigade "a political challenge to the United States" and announced that he was increasing surveillance over Cuba and strengthening the U.S. presence in the Caribbean. At the same time, he conceded that "the greatest danger to American security [was] not the two or three thousand troops in Cuba

[but] the breakdown of a common effort to preserve the peace and the ultimate threat of nuclear war."

Carter succeeded in defusing a potential explosion in Soviet-American relations, but his message failed to disarm critics of the SALT treaty. Not until the end of October was the Democratic leadership able to refocus the debate over SALT by asking the president to inform Congress of his defense spending plans for the next five years. The following month the Foreign Relations Committee gave a nod to SALT, but prospects for its ratification by the full Senate were not good. The vote in committee had been nine to six, less than the two-thirds that would be needed for final passage.

Aside from the debate on the SALT treaty, the president had to deal with problems in three different parts of the world—Rhodesia, Nicaragua, and Iran—that vied for media attention during 1979 and tested his ability as a crisis manager. In Rhodesia the issue facing the president was whether to lift sanctions against the country following the April election of its first black prime minister, Bishop Abel T. Muzorewa. Although the voting appeared to have been conducted fairly, the Patriotic Front and most African countries denounced it as a sham. In the United States black leaders showed their support for the Patriotic Front by arguing against lifting the sanctions.

Carter agreed. On 7 June he stated that he would continue to impose sanctions indefinitely. Although the elections had been "reasonably free," Carter noted that they still fell short because blacks were not allowed to vote on the new constitution and because whites continued to occupy too many top government positions. On Capitol Hill congressional supporters of Rhodesia lashed out at the president. The Senate even attached an amendment to a Defense Department authorization bill requiring the immediate removal of sanctions. Lobbying hard against the provision, the administration was able to work out an acceptable compromise whereby the president would lift sanctions against Rhodesia by 15 November unless he determined that it was not in the interests of the United States to do so.

Meanwhile, after promising genuine black majority rule in Rhodesia, the British succeeded in getting the Patriotic Front to sit down in London with Muzorewa. In September the two sides agreed to a new constitution, general elections, and a cease-fire. On 15 December Carter responded to this development by withdrawing sanctions against Rhodesia (renamed Zimbabwe Rhodesia). Although no longer a foreign policy concern, the question of sanctions had left its contentious mark on relations between the White House and Capitol Hill.

Also dividing Congress and leading to harsh attacks on the White House was the administration's policy toward Nicaragua. At the beginning of 1979 the president had imposed sanctions against that country after Somoza refused to hold elections supervised by the Organization of American States (OAS). By late spring it had become apparent that Somoza's days as Nicaragua's strongman were numbered. At the end of May the Sandinistas launched their final offensive by seizing León, the country's second-largest city, and capturing a string of towns both north and south of the capital. The Sandinistas also established a five-man junta to serve as head of a provisional government.

In the United States the president came under conflicting pressures from foes and friends of the Somoza regime. Opposition to the dictator mounted after a correspondent for ABC News, Bill Stewart, was forced to lie down on the ground and then was shot in the back of the head by a member of Somoza's National Guard. The execution, shown on national television, shocked and infuriated the American public. Thousands of letters and telegrams poured into the White House demanding immediate reprisals of some sort. But Somoza had his own backers in Congress who argued that the Sandinistas were Marxists and that their victory would create another Cuba in the Western Hemisphere. On 13 June more than 120 members of the House signed a letter urging the president to stop the reported flow of arms from Cuba and Panama to the Sandinistas.

Worried about the leftist leanings of the Sandinistas and their ties to Cuba, the White House sought a middle road that would permit a more moderate government to take power, rather than allowing the Sandinistas to assume control after toppling Somoza. The State Department therefore proposed to establish an OAS peacekeeping force and an interim government of national reconciliation. But this plan, which Vance outlined to the OAS on 21 June, was doomed from the start. Neither the Sandinistas nor the other members of the OAS would support a proposal that did not recognize the right of the Sandinistas to install a temporary government pending elections.

In truth, the administration's policy toward the Nicaraguan revolution was shortsighted. The State Department had anticipated that its plan would be rejected, yet it had no acceptable alternative. As a result, the White House had little diplomatic leverage when Somoza fled the country in July and the Sandinistas assumed control. To the president's credit, he tried to work with the new government—establishing formal relations on 24 July, sending emergency food and medical assistance, and asking Congress for $75 million in economic aid. But even though the junta agreed to a cabinet dominated by moderates, the Sandinistas had their own agenda, which involved accepting Cuban military aid and moving the country politically to the left.

The outcome of the revolution trapped the administration between two sets of critics. The Sandinistas objected to Washington's earlier assistance to Somoza and its later efforts to direct the course of the revolution, as did a number of lawmakers on Capitol Hill. At the same time, the president incurred the wrath of Somoza supporters by not doing more to save him and by allowing the Sandinistas to take over. As reports circulated in Washington that the Sandinistas were lending their support to leftist elements in El Salvador, Guatemala, and Honduras, the censure of Carter became more strident.

Of the foreign policy problems that Carter faced as president, however, none absorbed more of his time or had a greater impact on his administration than the ongoing upheaval in Iran. In the months after the February storming of the U.S. embassy in Tehran, relations between the United States and Iran had actually returned to a semblance of normalcy. Despite the bitter anti-Americanism of the Ayatollah Khomeini, the administration reasoned that once the religious leader had won his revolution, he would quickly recede into the political background. Washington would then be able to maintain diplomatic relations with the Tehran government through Mehdi Bazargan, a loyal follower of Khomeini but also a leader of the major moderate political group in Iran, the Liberation Movement.

What the White House and most Middle East experts failed to realize was that Khomeini was bent on founding an Islamic theocracy in Iran; that to achieve this, he had to discredit the moderates; and that he would use their contacts, whom he referred to as the "Great Satan," for this purpose. Nor did the administration fully apprehend the religiosity of the vast majority of Iranians and their devotion to Khomeini as their spiritual *and* temporal leader.

Not until a group of Iranian militants seized the U.S. embassy in Tehran on 4 November, taking sixty American hostages, was the fallacy of U.S. policy starkly revealed. The storming of the embassy was precipitated by the president's decision at the end of October to allow the shah to enter the United States to receive treatment for cancer. Carter was aware that this action would place the embassy in jeopardy. Following the first attack on the embassy in February, he had rescinded an invitation to the deposed Iranian leader, who was then living in Morocco, to reside in the United States. Vance had warned him then that if the shah was allowed into the country, American lives in Iran would be endangered. Instead, the administration arranged for Mexico to grant him asylum.

By October, however, the shah's health had begun to deteriorate. Two of his loyal and influential friends, Henry Kissinger and New York banker David Rockefeller, informed the White House that the shah might die if he was not allowed to come to the United States for medical treatment. Both Vance and Carter were still reluctant because of the reaction it might cause in Iran. Nevertheless, the president decided to permit the shah entry after the Tehran government indicated that it would take no retaliatory action if he came only for medical treatment.

For several days nothing happened, and it seemed that the deposed monarch might be able to complete his treatment without incident. But then militant Iranians claiming to be students seized the embassy, took hostages in the name of Khomeini, and demanded that Washington send the exiled shah home to face "revolutionary justice." Apparently they acted without Khomeini's knowledge and never expected to retain the embassy and the surrounding compound for any length of time. But the Ayatollah sensed an opportunity to get rid of Bazargan and other moderates and to solidify Islamic control over Iran. When the Iranian prime minister ordered the militants to withdraw from the embassy and release the hostages, Khomeini refused to back him and instead encouraged the militants to hold fast. In despair, Bazargan resigned.

For Carter, the taking of the embassy was a nightmare. Reviewing his options, he ordered preparations for military action but quickly ruled out an immediate strike as impractical; the United States simply lacked the military capability to rescue the hostages. He also considered the possibilities of breaking diplomatic relations with Iran and mining Iran's harbors if the militants put the hostages on trial.[10] His immediate response, however, involved using diplomatic channels to obtain the hostages' release, including asking the international community for assistance. He followed up this decision on 12 November by stopping all oil purchases from Iran. Two days later he froze Iran's assets in the United States. The president hoped that this pressure, as well as pressure from Iran's middle class, would persuade Khomeini and the militants to yield.

The American public gave Carter high marks for the calm and deliberate manner in which his administration reacted to the crisis. As Americans watched Iranian crowds taunt the United States, the president's prestige soared. According to a Gallup poll, in the four weeks since the hostages' seizure, public approval of Carter's presidency jumped from 30 percent to 61 percent, the sharpest gain ever in a Gallup survey of presidential popularity. Seventy-seven percent of the people questioned specifically approved of Carter's handling of the crisis.

Carter's resurgence in the polls was reflected in his bid for reelection. Presidential preference polls conducted in October showed the president trailing badly behind Senator Edward Kennedy of Massachusetts, who did not even formally announce his candidacy until 7 November. The hostage crisis changed matters. In one of the most remarkable turnabouts in U.S. political history, in December the president found himself with a commanding lead over his Democratic challenger.

According to most polls, moreover, Carter led Kennedy in every section of the country, among all age groups, and even among those who called themselves liberal Democrats. In trial heats against the leading Republicans candidates, Carter also enjoyed comfortable leads, including a fourteen-point edge over former governor Ronald Reagan. The administration realized that the hostage crisis could help Carter's reelection bid. "Don't forget," Hamilton Jordan told Phil Wise, the president's appointments secretary, "the press will be looking at this in the context of the campaign. It'll be over in a few hours, but it could provide a nice contrast between Carter and our friend from Massachusetts on how to handle a crisis."[11]

Irrespective of the hostage crisis, Carter had always believed that Kennedy was vulnerable on several fronts, including his liberal voting record, the traditional stigma of challenging an incumbent president from one's own party, and widespread doubts about his character because of the Chappaquiddick incident ten years earlier.[12] Once Kennedy officially entered the race, the president's advisers were confident that the senator's huge lead in the polls would evaporate. A matchup in Florida on 13 October gave an early indication that their instincts were correct, as a referendum to select county representatives to the state Democratic convention presaged the relative strength of the candidates. Unwisely, leaders of a draft-Kennedy movement in the state declared that they would win at least 35 percent of the delegates. Instead, the Carter organization outspent and outblitzed the Kennedy camp, sending in such heavy artillery as Rosalynn and Lillian Carter, Vice President Mondale, and former ambassador Young. When the votes were counted, Carter's supporters had beaten the Kennedy slate by two to one.

Over the next few weeks the campaign between Kennedy and Carter intensified. The president continued to take advantage of his incumbency to dispense patronage, announce federal grants, and respond to local concerns wherever he traveled. By the end of October the polls showed the president gaining on the senator. Then on 4 November—the day the White House received word that demonstrators had overrun the U.S. embassy in Tehran—CBS aired an interview that Kennedy had taped with correspondent Roger Mudd. In what might have been the worst public appearance of his political career, Kennedy seemed unable to give a direct answer to any of the questions Mudd asked him, such as why he was running for president or how his administration would differ from Carter's if he was elected. Halting and rambling, Kennedy also faltered when questioned about Chappaquiddick.

For Kennedy, things seemed to go from bad to worse when, in response to a reporter's question about the possibility of the shah living permanently in the United States, he stated that the former Iranian leader had headed "one of the most violent regimes in the history of mankind." How could the United States justify taking in the shah, he asked, "with his umpteen billions of dollars he'd stolen from Iran?" Kennedy instantly came under criticism by the administration and the press for his remarks. Furious, Carter told a bipartisan congressional delegation, "I don't give a damn whether you like or do not like the shah. The issue is that American hostages, fifty of them, are being held by kidnappers—radical and irresponsible kidnappers."

Thus, the president could announce his candidacy on 4 December with an aura of confidence. In a brief televised statement he addressed the leadership issue, since the Kennedy forces were trying to make it the campaign's theme, and described his own style as calm, strong, and effective. But then he surprised listeners by stating that he was postponing any stumping. "While the crisis continues," he remarked, "I must be present to define and lead our response to an ever-changing situation of the greatest security, sensitivity, and importance." Two weeks later Carter also decided that, because of the hostage crisis and the recent invasion of Afghanistan by Soviet forces, he would cancel a planned debate in Iowa with Kennedy and California governor Jerry Brown (who was not regarded as a major factor in the race).

The Soviet Union's decision in December to send 85,000 troops into Afghanistan caught the president off guard, even though he had been warned by Brzezinski that the Soviets might invade the country. The situation in Iran had a direct impact on the Soviets' decision. The Kremlin had already been concerned about the Afghan revolution against the Marxist government of Nur Mohammad Taraki and had sent between 5,000 and 10,000 military advisers to Afghanistan and provided other military aid. After Taraki's second in command, Hafizullah Amin, murdered the Afghan leader in October 1979, the Soviets began to consider a full-scale invasion. Believing that Amin might do what Egyptian president Anwar Sadat had done—turn away from Moscow and toward Washington—the KGB warned that if Amin joined the American camp, the United States could put its "control and intelligence centers close to our most sensitive borders."[13]

If the Soviet Union was going to intervene, however, Premier Leonid Brezhnev would have to give the go-ahead. Defense Minister Dmitri Ustinov and KGB chief Yuri Andropov began a campaign to convince the Politburo and the Soviet leader of the importance of quick action. On 8 December Brezhnev agreed that intervention was necessary, and four days later the Politburo followed suit. With the acquiescence of the Politburo, the stage was set for the attack just over two weeks later.[14]

At the time the Soviet Union invaded Afghanistan, much of the Islamic world, including the vital Persian Gulf, was in turmoil. The fervor of the Islamic revolution in Iran appeared to be spreading throughout the region. In Saudi Arabia a small but fanatic Muslim sect seized the Grand

Mosque in Mecca, Islam's holiest shrine, and held hundreds of pilgrims hostage. After two weeks of bloodshed in which as many as 200 pilgrims and 300 guerrillas may have died, Saudi forces were finally able to regain control of the shrine. In Pakistan 20,000 Muslim rioters stormed and burned the U.S. embassy in Islamabad, shouting, "Kill the American dogs." They murdered two Americans after rumors circulated that the United States and Israel had been responsible for the raid on the Grand Mosque.

With so much of the Middle East in upheaval, the president feared that unless he took a firm stand against the Afghan invasion, the entire region would be vulnerable to Soviet attack. "A successful takeover of Afghanistan," he later wrote, "would . . . pose a threat to the rich oil fields of the Persian Gulf area and to the crucial waterways through which so much of the world's energy supplies had to pass." On 3 January 1980, therefore, he asked the Senate to table indefinitely its consideration of the SALT II agreement. Speaking to the American people the next day, he announced that the Soviet Union would be barred access to high-technology and other strategic items and that he was placing an embargo on U.S. grain sales to the Soviets. He also raised the possibility that the United States might boycott the 1980 Summer Olympics in Moscow. "We will deter aggression, we will protect our nation's security and we will preserve the peace," he declared to the nation.[15]

Imposition of the grain embargo on the Soviet Union had been the most contentious issue within the administration. Mondale and Eizenstat strongly opposed the ban on the grounds that it would cause great injury to American farmers. "Food is not, in my opinion, an appropriate weapon to use in the international political arena," Eisenstat told the president. With the Iowa caucuses only a few weeks away, there was also real concern at the White House about the embargo's political impact on that heavily agricultural state. Although sensitive to these arguments, Carter believed that a stoppage of grain, coincident with an agreement by other nations not to replace the supplies withheld by the United States, was the most powerful leverage Washington could use against Moscow. He was also prepared to compensate farmers for the losses they might suffer as a result of the embargo.[16]

The response to the president's speech was generally favorable. According to Hamilton Jordan, telephone calls to the White House ran two to one in support of the president. Moreover, in the Iowa caucuses on 21 January, Carter beat Kennedy decisively, carrying ninety-eight of ninety-nine counties and even defeating the senator in blue-collar and Catholic areas, where he was supposedly popular. At least as important as Kennedy's own failings as a candidate was the fact that patriotism prevailed over politics for Iowan Democrats. Farmers did not like the grain embargo, but they decided to back the president in a time of international emergency.

Buoyed by the results in Iowa, Carter delivered his State of the Union address two days later. In his toughest attack on the Soviet Union since taking office, he enunciated what became known as the "Carter Doctrine." "Let our position be absolutely clear," he told a joint session of Congress. "An attempt by any outside force to gain control of the Persian Gulf region will be regarded as an assault on the vital interests of the United States of America, and such an assault will be repelled by any means necessary, including military force."

The president followed up his State of the Union address with a fundamental shift in U.S. policy toward the strategically important Horn of Africa. In 1977 Carter had refused a request for weapons by the Somali government of Mohammed Siad Barre because of Somalia's invasion of Ethiopia's Ogaden region. Even after the Ethiopians, with Cuban and Soviet support, had pushed the Somalis out of the Ogaden in 1978, the president had stuck to his no-arms policy even though Brzezinski wanted to provide military support to Somalia. In 1980, however, Brzezinski got his way. Carter now regarded good relations with Somalia, and access to its naval facilities at Berbera, as vital to U.S. security interests in the region. Notwithstanding concerns among some members of Congress that Somalia might again attack the Ogaden, the administration provided Somalia with $20 million in defensive weaponry.

The White House also began to court countries in Latin America that it had once condemned for human rights violations. When Buenos Aires refused to join the U.S.-led grain embargo on the Soviet Union, the administration sent the superintendent of the U.S. Military Academy, General Andrew J. Goodpaster, on an ultimately unsuccessful mission to get the Argentine junta to change its mind. When Brazil also refused to participate in the embargo, Carter asked the State Department to review Soviet policy toward Argentina, Brazil, Chile, Peru, and Uruguay. Undersecretary of State Warren Christopher replied that although the anticommunist sentiment in those countries was likely to prevent the Soviet Union from making "significant" gains in the region, the United States' "overriding objective will be to reinforce" that sentiment. He added, "We will continue to pursue our human rights policy but remain conscious of the need to execute it in a way that minimizes adverse effects on our other interests."[17]

The president's policy on nuclear nonproliferation also underwent a shift in his last year in office. Despite Carter's willingness to allow the Tokai Mura plant to begin operations in Japan and his decision to back down on West Germany's proposed sale of nuclear technology to Brazil, the president had sought to maintain control over the spread of nuclear information. Congress shared this desire, passing in 1978 the Nuclear Non-Proliferation Act (NNPA), which required any nation receiving nuclear materials from the United States to open all its atomic facilities to international inspection.

Pakistan became a testing ground for the NNPA. In April 1979 the United States cut military and economic aid to Pakistan because of that nation's effort to acquire a nuclear fuel enrichment plant from France. But after the Soviet invasion of Afghanistan, the White House reconsidered its position. On 28 December Michael Oksenberg, an NSC specialist on China, wrote to Brzezinski: "I consider the Soviet invasion of Afghanistan a major watershed event. . . . In strategic importance, it outweighs the hostage problem in Iran. . . . The president's nuclear non-proliferation and arms restraint policies must take second place to a concerted effort to teach Moscow that aggression does not pay."[18] The president agreed. Instead of linking the sale of conventional arms to Pakistan's efforts to acquire nuclear technology, the administration offered Pakistan $400 million in economic and military aid.[19]

While attempting to court Pakistan—and India[20]—the White House also determined to draw militarily and politically closer to China. Ever since the United States had instituted diplomatic relations with the People's Republic of China at the beginning of the year, Brzezinski had been pushing for closer military ties with Beijing irrespective of—indeed, precisely because of—the ramifications for U.S.-Soviet relations. Until the invasion of Afghanistan, Vance, who wanted a more balanced relationship between the United States and the two communist powers, had been able to persuade the president not to sell arms to the Chinese or to allow military linkages with China.

That changed, however, as a result of the Soviet aggression in Afghanistan. With the support of Defense Secretary Brown, Brzezinski quickly proposed the establishment of a "U.S.-Chinese defense relationship." The Chinese, not wishing to be a pawn in the geopolitical rivalry between Washington and Moscow, balked at the idea, but they were allowed to purchase military hardware and high-technology items whose export to the Soviet Union was now prohibited. In addition, they were granted most-favored-nation trade status, which was also denied to the Soviets.

Pique more than prudence dictated Carter's response to the Afghan invasion. Indeed, he may have acted as much out of frustration over other differences with Moscow and despair over the Iran hostage crisis as out of foreign policy considerations. If his purpose was to force the Soviets out of Afghanistan, he and Vance used a questionable strategy. In the first place, there was no intelligence to indicate that a grain embargo, a boycott of the Olympics, or any other action the president proposed would deter the Soviets from their aggressive course. Moreover, rather than narrowing down a list of options, the president fired a volley of measures at the Soviets that were meant to punish them as much as convince them to leave the country they had just invaded.

The president also proposed initiatives without fully understanding the difficulties in implementing them. The Olympic boycott was a case in point. The administration assumed that it could convince American athletes and those of other countries to join in the boycott and persuade them to compete in alternative games. The White House failed to grasp that the International Olympic Committee, national Olympic committees, and many athletes would renounce what they considered to be an attempt by the United States to politicize the games. It also overlooked the fact that there were specific rules governing amateur sports that would ultimately prevent any chance of establishing alternative games. Even getting American athletes to endorse the boycott proved to be a long fight that the White House won only after threatening legal action against them and the U.S. Olympic Committee.

Even Brzezinski, who had seized the opportunity to convert the president to his view of the Soviet Union as a global menace, questioned Carter's tactics. Although he regarded the invasion as part of Moscow's hegemonic foreign policy, he recognized the need for a more temperate response—one that would be punitive but also allow for dialogue and take into account future relationships with the Soviet Union.

The president was not insensitive to such arguments, but because he was bent on punishing the Soviets, he adopted virtually every punitive measure suggested to him, regardless of its immediate or long-term consequences or the difficulty of actually putting it into effect. "I was sobered . . . by our strained relations with the Soviets," he later acknowledged, "but I was determined to make them pay for their unwarranted aggression without yielding to political pressure at home."[21] As a result, U.S.-Soviet relations became mortgaged to the Soviets' withdrawal from Afghanistan; dealings between Moscow and Washington became even more strained; and ratification of the SALT II agreement, which had been one of Carter's highest priorities since taking office, was postponed indefinitely.

In Europe, NATO allies were deeply troubled by the U.S. response to the Soviet invasion. Although they condemned the Soviet action, they refused to become involved, arguing that the attack did not necessarily mean aggressive designs on other nations outside the Soviet orbit. Of Europe's leaders, only Britain's new prime minister, Margaret Thatcher, fully backed Carter's tough line toward Moscow. In contrast, Schmidt of Germany was harshly critical of the president, complaining again that Carter conducted foreign policy without considering its impact on western Europe.

For the moment, then, Carter was able to capitalize politically on the developments in Iran and Afghanistan, but his own advisers were already wondering how long this would continue. If the hostage crisis dragged on, the American public might begin to blame the president. Moreover, it was difficult to gauge the depth of the people's concern about distant and alien Afghanistan—or whether they would hold the president responsible if the Soviets refused to withdraw. At some point, Americans might even wonder if these developments could have been avoided—if the president bore the brunt for a nation incapable of responding to violators of international law. Should that happen, it would be campaign fodder for the president's political opponents.

11

★ ★ ★ ★ ★

ECONOMIC PAIN AND POLITICS

In response to the hostage crisis in Iran and the invasion of Afghanistan by the Soviet Union, the American people had rallied behind President Carter. As a result, the president was able to run an effective Rose Garden campaign for renomination against Senator Kennedy. Ultimately, however, the outcome of the 1980 election—which, in April, was more than seven months away—would be determined by public perceptions of Carter's overall performance. Large elements of the Democratic Party, and even larger segments of the American public, still were not satisfied with his presidency. Lengthening unemployment lines, prime interest and inflation rates nearing 20 percent, and skyrocketing prices for gold and other precious metals troubled Americans. As the economy seemed to be spinning out of control and the hostage situation reached an impasse, Carter's ability to lead the nation came into question once more.

Inflation remained the White House's most serious domestic problem. In November 1979 Alfred E. Kahn, who rarely minced words, had written the president a lengthy memorandum in which he stated, the "time has come for [the administration] to admit to ourselves that our present anti-inflation program has failed." Pointing out that some of Carter's other economic advisers were recommending putting off additional anti-inflationary measures until the State of the Union address in January, he warned that such a course would spell disaster. "Two more months of unabated inflationary experience unaccompanied by any visible basis for anticipating deceleration," he remarked, "could so intensify inflationary expectations as to make the tendencies even more difficult to root out than they are now."[1]

Kahn's memorandum was significant for several reasons. First, it represented an acknowledgment by the administration's chief inflation fighter of just how unsuccessful the White House's efforts against inflation had been. Second, it underscored the lack of agreement, even among the president's chief economic advisers, about which new measures should be implemented to help fight inflation. CEA chairman Charles Schultze continued to emphasize that one of the major problems causing inflation was low industrial productivity, and he proposed a small $6 billion to $8 billion "productivity package" for new technologies, increased capital investments, and streamlining of regulations. But he acknowledged that his proposal was merely a start that might provide "some hope that beating inflation does not condemn us to a long-term grind of tight money and slow growth." Still, Carter turned his request down.[2]

Finally, Kahn's November memorandum made clear his own lack of qualifications to serve as the nation's anti-inflation czar. As he was the first to acknowledge, his considerable expertise was as a deregulator, not an inflation fighter—a position he had never wanted. In his typically offhand manner, his overarching recommendation to the president was surprising, given his previous admission: "First, we have to decide that we must go somewhere—provided, of course, there is somewhere we can responsibly go. . . . Second, however, we must remain true to our principles. This means we must pursue our present policies of restraint with even more dedication and imagination."

Beyond greater economic restraints, Kahn's only substantive proposals were to impose selective credit controls and to attack the problem of energy more vigorously by decontrolling oil completely, "accompanied by even more drastic windfall profits taxes; or heavy additional taxes on gasoline." Carter dismissed both tax proposals as "not feasible in Congress." He did not comment on the proposal for credit controls, which Kahn had been arguing for since April.[3]

A few weeks later Kahn added another proposal: a White House conference on state and local regulatory reform. "One of the main foci of our continuing effort to involve state and local governments in our anti-inflation program has been regulatory reform," Kahn pointed out. Although the president approved this recommendation, he warned that "there must be a positive result" from the conference, something that Jack Watson, Carter's special assistant for intergovernmental affairs, doubted would happen. Shortly thereafter, Secretary of Energy Charles Duncan announced a print and radio campaign in sixty cities "to promote awareness of the shortages caused by dependence on foreign oil and . . . simple conservation measures."[4]

Taken together, the proposals set forth by Kahn, Schultze, and Duncan represented at best a scattering, at worst a bankruptcy, of ideas rather than a concerted program for dealing with a problem that threatened to consume the administration unless it was addressed immediately and meaningfully. Stu Eizenstat, Alonzo McDonald, and Hedley Donovan made a similar point in other memorandums they sent to the president in response to the Economic Policy Group's call for policy options on an economic and energy program for 1980. "Our people are reasonable and realistic," McDonald told Carter. "They know we must begin changing our lifestyle, but they want guidance and help to do this over time with a minimum of disruption and no unnecessary sacrifices." Donovan added, "Nothing is more *destabilizing* to the national psyche than the present rate of inflation. I think it is imperative for you to have ideas—and be seen to have ideas—as to how significant growth in real income can be resumed."[5]

In the wake of the warnings he was receiving about both the economy at home and his handling of the Soviet invasion of Afghanistan, Carter's mood seemed to darken, and he became especially short and testy with his staff. If anything, he also appeared more determined to stay the course rather than make the corrections being suggested by his advisers. "Who sent a letter from me endorsing a dam in Oklahoma? Why?" he asked Eizenstat on 17 January. "Tell State and others (and you) to get out of the Olympics business. Let [White House counsel] Lloyd [Cutler] and me handle it," he wrote to Jody Powell the same day. "I am tired of fooling around. This is business as usual. Give me the long-awaited estimate (by agency) and sharpen this up. Return this memo early tomorrow at latest," he responded to a memorandum that Jack Watson and OMB director Jim McIntyre were preparing about energy conservation by federal agencies.[6]

Kahn's November prediction that inflation would get completely out of control if left unaddressed for two more months came true. During January 1980 the CPI rose 1.4 percent, for an annual rate of about 18.2 percent—the highest in six years. Wholesale prices for January climbed at an annual rate of 21 percent; prices for finished goods, which had actually declined the previous month, began to escalate once more. Wage increases failed to keep up with the inflation rate, so that the purchasing power of the average urban employee declined 1.4 percent for February alone. Most unnerving of all, some private economists predicted that double-digit inflation would persist throughout the 1980s.

While the White House tried to grapple with inflation through voluntary wage and price controls, fiscal restraint, and tighter credit, unemployment and interest rates rose dramatically. The Labor Department reported that during April the nation's jobless rate had ballooned to 7 percent and the number of unemployed workers had jumped to 7.3 million, the largest increase in overall unemployment since January 1975. The prime rate by the beginning of March 1980 had increased to 16.75 percent; by the end of April it stood at about 18.5 percent, and some business leaders predicted that it might hit 20 percent or more. As both the inflation rate and interest rates climbed, housing starts fell, dropping 6 percent in January to 1.4 million, the lowest level since July 1976. The freefall in housing, which continued throughout the first quarter of 1980, had a ripple effect, causing related businesses to close down or lay off workers.

Responding to the worsening economy, the nation's financial and commodities markets began to slip. Anticipation that the Carter administration would increase defense spending as it responded to the invasion of Afghanistan had led the Dow-Jones average to rise to 904 by 13 February. But as fear grew within the business community that inflation was getting out of hand, stocks began to spiral downward, closing in the third week of March at 785—its lowest level since April 1978.

Seeking a safe haven for their money, investors speculated in precious metals, so that the price of gold zoomed to more than $850 an ounce. When billionaire Nelson Bunker Hunt attempted to corner the silver market, the price of silver jumped from $6 an ounce in early 1979 to $50 an ounce by February 1980. But this level could not be sustained, and by April, silver prices had fallen to around $10 an ounce. The price of gold also dropped to around $450 an ounce.

Meanwhile, in a February *Newsweek*-Gallup poll, almost half the people interviewed (48 percent) identified inflation as their primary worry (up from 39 percent a month earlier). This anxiety—which encouraged consumers to spend now in anticipation of higher prices later—was also evident at the White House. "I believe we are truly on the verge of an economic crisis which is as severe for the country as the foreign policy crises you have been dealing with over the last several months," Stu Eizenstat told the president on 26 March.[7] In the same February *Newsweek*-Gallup poll, 52 percent of the respondents supported government limits on wage and price increases as a way to cope with inflation. Ted Kennedy attacked Carter relentlessly for not imposing controls or freezing oil prices. Even politicians and economists opposed to controls insisted that the president needed to take new steps to deal with the nation's economic problems.

Although still reluctant to deviate from the program of fiscal and monetary restraint that he and Paul Volcker were pursuing, Carter recognized that he would have to address some of the economic and social concerns of traditional Democratic constituencies to keep Kennedy at bay and win reelection in November. Therefore, in his 1980 budget proposal he called for substantial expansions in such highly visible areas as housing and jobs, including a new $2 billion youth employment program. Revenues for this spending would come from the additional income tax receipts resulting from inflation, the windfall profits tax, and increased Social Security taxes.

The proposed budget was received with skepticism, even cynicism. Because of inflation and the economic slowdown, the projected $29 billion deficit for fiscal 1980 would have to be revised upward to $40 billion, and few economists or financial leaders believed that the prediction of a $15.8 billion deficit for 1981 would remain constant. In fact, only a few weeks after Carter had sent his budget to Capitol Hill, the White House realized that it would have to reconsider the economic assumptions on which it was based. The recession proved to be much more tenacious than most economists had foreseen. The nation's two most important industries, housing and automobiles, virtually collapsed. Housing starts in March were down 42 percent from a year earlier after suffering the sharpest monthly decline in twenty years. Car sales were also off 24 percent from the previous year. Unemployment in Detroit reached a staggering 24 percent. Either because of or in spite of the administration's economic policy, the nightmare of "stagflation"—higher prices, severe unemployment, and a stagnant or declining economy—had come true.

The president responded to this economic crisis by conducting a scaled-down version of the previous summer's Camp David domestic summit. Seeking a national consensus around what he hoped would be a bipartisan economic plan, he held a weeklong series of meetings in March with more than 300 Democratic and Republican members of Congress, business and financial leaders, and representatives from various farm, labor, and civic groups. The upshot of the sessions was a call to balance the budget as a first, visible step toward fighting inflation. Working closely with the congressional leadership, the White House then molded a new economic program predicated on balancing the budget through another round of cuts. As did lawmakers on Capitol Hill, the president's advisers agreed that for the program to be credible, the reductions had to be across the board, even though this meant curtailing programs for the elderly and the poor.

On 14 March the president announced his new economic plan to the American people. Asserting that inflation threatened the nation's security, he stated that his major goal would be to balance the $612 billion budget for 1981. He would also curb credit-financed spending, which "fed" inflation; expand the monitoring activities of COWPS; impose a "gasoline-conservation fee" on imported oil of about ten cents per gallon; and develop specific recommendations for revitalizing the U.S. economy. These actions would not produce a "quick victory" over inflation, he warned. But they would bring inflation under control by year's end and "put an end to the fear about the future that afflicts so many of our own people and so many of our institutions."

Yet the program Carter unveiled to the nation fell short of delivering the shock treatment that many economists thought was necessary to break the whirling inflationary cycle. In the first place, total federal spending for 1981—even if Congress approved the president's recommendations—would still be about $43 billion more than current levels. Furthermore, the reductions by themselves would not balance the budget; that would require the approval of other revenue-raising measures, including the fee on imported oil. Again, passage of such legislation was far from certain. Although Carter did not itemize the specific budget cuts he would make, it was widely—and correctly—reported that he would not touch such entitlement programs as Social Security, veterans' benefits, and unemployment relief, even though these were the fastest growing portions of the budget.

Even Eizenstat was surprised by the indifferent response to the president's inflation-bashing endeavor. "Despite the effort which went into your anti-inflation announcement," he told the president, a recent survey indicated that "a significant majority of Americans are unaware of it." Referring to the "growing national sense that things are out of control," he urged the president to leave the White House and travel the length and breadth of the country, meeting the American people and explaining his economic program to them. "You need not debate Kennedy or even 'campaign,'" he said. "The key is to get out and let the people know you are the general in charge."[8]

The president refused, however, to alter his political strategy—even though Democratic voters indicated their frustration with the administration by giving Kennedy a clear primary sweep in New York and a victory in Connecticut on 25 March. Carter's defeat in New York was a serious setback for his campaign. Heretofore, the contest for the Democratic presidential nomination had seemed to be a mismatch. The president, stubbornly ensconced in the White House, had beaten the Massachusetts senator in his own backyard of New Hampshire. The polls also showed Kennedy losing support in the rest of the country, particularly in the South and Midwest. On 11 February Pat Caddell reported to the president that Kennedy's negative rating in Illinois had climbed to 60 percent—higher than in any southern state. According to his analysis, "Unless the mid-Atlantic is surprisingly better—New York and Pennsylvania—it is hard to see where Kennedy goes without a major shift in fundamentals."[9]

Some even began to speculate about how much longer Kennedy would stay in the race. With contributions starting to dry up and money running out, it was clear that he had to score a substantial victory soon and that the upcoming primaries in Illinois and New York were his last chance to do so. All the polls predicted that he would lose in Illinois, and even in New York he appeared to be in trouble.

In March, however, the administration made a colossal diplomatic blunder when the United States voted in favor of a UN resolution calling on Israel to dismantle civilian settlements in occupied Arab territories, including Jerusalem. Twice before in 1979 the United States had abstained on similar votes, but Carter and Vance decided that they had to register their displeasure with the continued building of Israeli settlements on the West Bank. On 1 March the secretary of state informed the president that reference to Jerusalem had been omitted from the UN resolution, and he asked that the United States be allowed to vote in favor of it. The president agreed, and the resolution carried unanimously.

The Israeli government and American Jewish leaders were infuriated by the vote and by the fact that, due to an error, references to Jerusalem had not been removed. When the president learned of the mistake he issued a statement saying that he had approved the resolution "with the understanding that all references to Jerusalem would be deleted." In other words, Carter reaffirmed his administration's support for the resolution, which most of the American Jewish community regarded as anti-Israeli, whether Jerusalem was included or not. New York's large Jewish population reacted by voting in overwhelming numbers for Kennedy, who defeated Carter by 16 percent.

But the Jewish vote was not the sole reason for Kennedy's margin of victory in New York or for his win in Connecticut. By all indications, Democratic voters were casting their ballots as much against the administration as in support of Kennedy. For the first time, according to a *New York Times*–CBS survey, more voters trusted Kennedy than Carter (49 percent versus 46 percent). More than half the people questioned believed that the president was being "too soft" with Iran, and only 17 percent thought that his handling of the Afghan crisis had improved the United States' global image. "The East wind that chilled the Carter candidacy this week was made up of four I's—Inflation, Iran, Israel, and Ineptitude," commented *New York Times* columnist William Safire after the New York primary.[10]

Kennedy's chances of beating the president at the Democratic convention remained slight, since the senator would need to win 62 percent of the remaining delegates. That prospect was unlikely, because the contest now shifted to the South, Midwest, and West, where Kennedy had little popularity, organization, or money. Nevertheless, the president's political advisers were shocked by what his defeats in New York and Connecticut exposed: the size of the anti-Carter protest vote. A Yankelovich poll taken a week later confirmed their worst fears. The survey found that 70 percent of the people questioned thought that it was time for a change in the Oval Office. Eighty-one percent of the respondents thought that the United States was in serious trouble. For the first time, Republican front-runner Ronald Reagan moved ahead of Carter in the polls, 44 percent to 43 percent. Only 18 percent of those surveyed rated the president "a very strong leader," compared with 38 percent who characterized Reagan that way and 27 percent for Kennedy.[11]

Despite Carter's growing political vulnerability, he beat Kennedy convincingly in the Wisconsin primary and Kansas caucuses on 1 April and drove Jerry Brown out of the race entirely. But in Wisconsin, which permitted crossover balloting (that is, Democrats voting for Republicans and vice versa), thousands of Democrats voted in the GOP primary. Consequently, Republicans outdrew Democrats for the first time in twenty-five years, and Ronald Reagan, the Republican winner over George Bush, received a larger total than the president did.

By this time the president also had to contend with the possibility of a third-party challenge from Republican congressman John Anderson of Illinois. Anderson had entered the presidential race as a liberal alternative to the other Republican candidates. Although few observers took his campaign very seriously, he began to attract support because of his willingness to take politically unpopular positions, such as advocating a fifty-cents-a-gallon tax on gasoline as a conservation measure. Although no one could be certain whether Anderson would hurt Carter or Reagan more if he appeared on the ballot in November, it seemed more likely that he would woo liberals away from the president than capture moderate Republicans.

What Carter apparently expected was for Kennedy to acknowledge that he could not win the nomination, withdraw from the race, and endorse the president. Only then could the healing process among the factious Democrats begin, which was vital if they expected to win in November. "Fritz [Mondale] and I needed several months to pull together our badly divided party to prepare for the general election," Carter later commented. But instead of withdrawing, the Massachusetts senator announced his intention to say in the contest all the way to the convention.[12]

As of the first week in April, then, Carter's campaign advisers were more confident than ever that the president would be renominated in August, but they also remained greatly concerned about the obstacles posed by Kennedy, Reagan, and Anderson. Even though Kennedy could not win the nomination, he could keep the party divided and undermine Carter's chances in November. Former governor Reagan was proving to be a much more formidable candidate than the president's staff had anticipated, while Anderson's candidacy inserted a discomfiting wild card into the race. Any adverse change in affairs at home or abroad could be fatal to Carter's reelection drive.

Three weeks after the Wisconsin primary, Kennedy narrowly defeated Carter in Pennsylvania and in the Michigan caucuses. The president's figures indicated that he had 1,507 of the 1,666 first-ballot votes needed for the nomination, compared with Kennedy's 707, but these two most recent victories, combined with those in New York and Connecticut, gave Kennedy enough staying power to carry his uphill campaign into the 3 June primaries. His assaults on the president were also becoming increasingly effective, thereby whittling away at Carter's prospects in November. At the very least, Carter's strategists anticipated a loud and divisive brawl with Kennedy forces over the party platform.

The major news story during the week of 25 April, however, was not the campaign but the failed attempt to rescue the hostages. Preparation for some form of military action against Iran had been under way at the White House since 6 November 1979, when Carter asked national security adviser Brzezinski to look into a rescue mission. However, the president intended this only as a contingency measure; he opposed using military action, declaring that "the problem with military options is that we could use them and feel good for a few hours—until we found that they had killed our people. And once we started killing people in Iran, where does it end?"[13]

But by the second week of April the president had changed his mind. Diplomatic efforts to free the hostages (or even transfer them to the Tehran government) had foundered. In February a political moderate, Abolhassen Bani-Sadr, had been elected Iran's first president, leading the White House to hope for an early resolution of the crisis. In an interview with ABC News, Bani-Sadr expressed his own expectation that the situation would soon be sorted out. Secret negotiations between Hamilton Jordan and two men with close ties to Iran's Revolutionary Council—one a French lawyer and the other an Argentine businessman living in Paris— fed these hopes. Through the two intermediaries, Bani-Sadr agreed to a plan by which a UN fact-finding mission would go to Iran to hear Tehran's grievances and then obtain the release of the hostages. But Khomeini subverted the plan by instructing the militants holding the hostages not to hand them over to the new government.

As the possibility of a quick release faded, interest shifted at the White House from unofficial negotiations to some type of military rescue action. The fact that a small plane had successfully penetrated Iranian airspace and examined a potential rescue staging site without being detected convinced Carter that such a mission was feasible. On 7 April, therefore, the president informed the NSC of his decision to break diplomatic relations with Tehran and impose new sanctions, including an embargo on all U.S. goods except for food and medicine. Four days later, at another meeting of the NSC, he announced his decision to go forward with the rescue mission. In his opinion, nothing less than the nation's honor was at stake in freeing the hostages.[14]

Of the NSC members, only Secretary of State Vance, who had been vacationing in Florida and was not even present at the hastily called 11 April meeting, opposed the president's decision. Vance had previously advised against cutting relations with Iran, arguing that it was much easier to sever ties with a country than to restore them. Moreover, by isolating Iran, the United States would be handing the Soviets a target of opportunity in the Middle East. Believing that a rescue mission could not succeed without many hostages being killed or wounded, Vance asked for another attempt at diplomacy. He failed to budge Carter, however.

According to the intricate Joint Chiefs of Staff scheme for rescuing the hostages, eight helicopters would fly from the aircraft carrier *Nimitz* in the Gulf of Oman to a site south of Tehran designated Desert One. There they would be joined by six C-130s carrying ninety members of a rescue team plus fuel and supplies. Having delivered their cargo, the transport planes would leave Iran. The helicopters would then take the rescue team to cover in the mountains 100 miles outside of Tehran. The next night, trucks purchased in Tehran by American agents would carry the rescue team into the city. The highly trained force would attack both the foreign ministry building and the U.S. embassy compound, overpower the guards at the two locations, and free the hostages. The team and the hostages would then be retrieved by the helicopters (still hidden outside Tehran) and flown to an abandoned airstrip near the city, where two C-141s would be waiting to take them across the desert to safety in Saudi Arabia.

Military experts and scholars continue to debate the feasibility of the rescue mission. Some argue that more helicopters should have been used, others that the plan was too complex and dependent on too many variables to succeed. But three points are clear. First, the president did not issue the order to begin the operation until he was confident that it would work. Second, the ill-fated mission was the victim of circumstances that doomed it almost from the outset. Third, its failure was a devastating political and personal blow to Carter from which he and his administration never fully recovered.

The details of the mission have become fairly well known. It began to fall apart within hours after it commenced on 24 April. The plan provided for two spare aircraft in addition to the six helicopters required for the mission. Soon after entering Iranian airspace, one of the choppers developed mechanical problems and had to be abandoned. A second got lost in a sandstorm and had to return to the *Nimitz*, taking with it the margin of safety built into the plan. After the remaining six aircraft landed, one of them developed a hydraulic problem after refueling and could not take off. Down to five choppers, the mission was aborted.

As the force was boarding the C-130s and preparing to evacuate, one of the five operational helicopters rose fifteen to twenty feet into the air and then banked sharply to the left, slashing the fuselage of one of the transports. Eight servicemen were killed and four others badly burned.

The survivors abandoned the scene, leaving the four remaining helicopters and the dead behind in the flaming wreckage. A few hours later, in the early morning, a visibly shaken Carter went on national television to report the disaster to the American people.

Although initial reaction to the hapless mission was supportive of the president, the failure of the rescue attempt probably did more to undercut the Carter presidency than any other event. Even before this incident, the hostage crisis had become a political liability for the president. A *Newsweek*-Gallup poll taken on 9 and 10 April showed that the number who approved of the president's handling of the crisis had fallen to just 40 percent. As details of the botched plan were revealed, it became another entry on a long list of failures that many Americans attributed to the president. On Capitol Hill some lawmakers expressed indignation that Congress had not been consulted before the venture. American allies were also distressed that they had not been briefed in advance. Indeed, they were disturbed by the president's entire approach to the situation, including the imposition of new sanctions on Iran, which they believed would be ineffective, and a trade embargo, which they feared might be the first step on the road to war with Iran.[15]

As the primary season entered its final month, the president's whole foreign policy seemed to be in disarray, and this perception was further strengthened by Secretary of State Vance's resignation. Vance had been increasingly upset with the direction of the administration's foreign policy and the erosion of his own influence with the president, particularly since the Soviet invasion of Afghanistan. As Carter turned more and more to Brzezinski for counsel, the secretary appeared increasingly tired, drained, and withdrawn. Carter's decision to go ahead with the rescue mission in Iran was the final straw. Deputy Secretary of State Warren Christopher recalled that when Vance learned on 14 April that the president had given the green light to the mission, the secretary's "reaction was volcanic—the angriest I'd ever seen him. Not only did the idea of a rescue mission infuriate him, but also that a matter of such moment had been raised and decided in his absence." When the secretary failed to persuade the president to change his mind, he decided to resign.[16]

The news media seized on Vance's resignation as evidence that the president's foreign policy was in a quagmire. "As things now stand," *Newsweek* reported, "the President's uncertain diplomatic strategy has left allies perplexed, enemies unimpressed and the nation as vulnerable as ever in an increasingly dangerous world." Because of his high profile and combative cold war views, Brzezinski came under particular attack, prompting Jody Powell to urge Carter to curb the NSC adviser's public appearances. "To put it bluntly," Powell stated, "Zbig needs to almost drop from public view for the next few months at least."[17]

In response to his mounting political problems, Carter decided to abandon his Rose Garden campaign in favor of a more public candidacy. Up to this point, the president had relied primarily on the First Lady to act as his stand-in on the stump. Although she received praise for her campaigning ability, controversy continued to swirl around her influence in the administration, with a columnist for *McCall's* magazine asking, "Is Rosalynn really running the country?"[18]

The president's staff had been urging him to change course since at least the New York primary, noting that his standing with the American people and his fund-raising were being hurt by his stay-at-home strategy. His argument that he needed to remain at the White House to deal with fast-breaking developments in the hostage crisis was being met with increasing skepticism. Critics charged that he was hiding behind the hostages to avoid debating Kennedy. The debacle of the rescue mission provided a convenient moment to break out from his six-month hermitage in the White House. As Carter returned to the campaign trail, his ascendancy over Kennedy seemed assured. Victories in Indiana, Tennessee, and North Carolina gave the president at least 1,500 of the 1,666 votes needed for nomination.

Carter became an active candidate again just as he received some encouraging economic news. After growing at an annual rate of 18 percent during the first quarter of 1980, in May the annual increase in the CPI slowed to only 10.9 percent—the slowest rise in nearly a year and a half. Interest rates began to tumble almost as fast as they had escalated at the beginning of the year. Some economists even predicted that the annual rate might dip as low as 5 or 6 percent before the end of the year. Major banks dropped their prime interest rate to 13 percent, well below the peak of 20 percent reached in April.

On Capitol Hill the president scored two political victories when Congress passed a $227 billion windfall profits tax and the Energy Security Act, which established a Synthetic Fuels Corporation with the authority to spend up to $88 billion over the next ten years to develop alternative energy sources. Both laws were key parts of the energy program Carter had sent to Congress almost a year earlier. These measures, along with previous legislation deregulating natural gas prices and gradually decontrolling domestic oil, represented the most sweeping energy legislation in the nation's history and a great personal achievement for the president.

Yet the president's struggle for reelection was far from over. The Democratic Party remained divided and clearly unenthusiastic about either Carter or Kennedy. Strident environmentalists, for example, were angry at a host of decisions Carter had made, including his proposal for an Energy Mobilization Board to speed up the development of new power plants by exempting them from environmental regulations; his decision to allow completion of the Tellico Dam on the Little Tennessee River south of Knoxville, even though it threatened the endangered snail darter; and his decision not to kill the Clinch River breeder reactor in order to win passage of his energy legislation, even though he personally regarded the reactor as "a complete waste of dollars."[19] The irony was that Carter had already compiled one of the best environmental records of any president since Theodore Roosevelt, including sweeping protection for the outer continental shelf and a vast expansion of national park and wilderness areas. In addition, one of his highest priorities in 1980 was passage of the Alaska Lands Act, which would set aside about one-third of Alaska as a wilderness area. Lamenting the failure of environmentalists to line up solidly behind the president, Eizenstat later commented, "the president's environmental record was unimpeachable, except as it seemed to the organized environmentalists."[20]

Aware of Democratic disaffection with both Carter and Kennedy, Governor Hugh Carey of New York urged both candidates to throw the Democratic convention totally open by releasing their delegates. The *Des Moines Register* called on Carter to stand down in favor of Vice President Walter Mondale. Meanwhile, the Republican Party was uniting behind Ronald Reagan, who took a commanding 9 percent lead over Carter in the latest Harris poll.

Compounding Carter's political troubles was a still mutinous Congress. Except for energy legislation, the president's scorecard on Capitol Hill was nearly blank during the first half of 1980. For example, lawmakers never acted on his only new domestic initiative—a youth employment program aimed primarily at minority teenagers. They also neglected other measures the White House supported, such as the president's three-year-old plan to upgrade health benefits for poor children and his proposal to expand the Commerce Department's Economic Development Association and place more federal development programs under its jurisdiction.

However, these setbacks paled beside two crushing defeats for the White House: Congress's rejection of the president's proposal for an Energy Mobilization Board, because lawmakers feared that it would trample on states' rights and environmental laws; and the peremptory override of his veto of a joint resolution that would have prevented him from imposing a ten-cents-a -gallon surcharge on imported oil. The surcharge, which Carter had implemented as part of his 14 March anti-inflation program, and which was supposed to take effect on 15 May, had run into trouble on Capitol Hill because lawmakers were concerned about imposing a new tax during an election year. Under provisions of the newly enacted windfall profits tax, Congress could block enactment of the surcharge by passage of a joint resolution subject to a presidential veto, which it could still override by a two-thirds vote in both houses. On 4 June both the House and Senate overwhelmingly passed a resolution killing the surcharge.

Why the president insisted on challenging Congress on such an unpopular measure when relations with Capitol Hill were already so strained is something of a mystery. Clearly Carter thought that the tax was necessary to balance the budget, and he was angry with the Democratic leadership in both the House and the Senate, which had actually encouraged him to impose the fee. "This is a new low in performance for the Congress since I've been in office," he recorded in his diary on 13 May. He also regarded the willingness of Congress to uphold his right to impose the tax a test of his ability to work with legislators. Nevertheless, the override of his veto represented a humiliation that had not been inflicted by the House or Senate on a president of its own party since the Truman administration in the 1950s—an embarrassment that Carter could have easily avoided.[21]

Relations with Congress, then, continued to undermine the administration's political viability—just as they had throughout much of Carter's presidency. Economic developments had a similar impact. Despite some favorable statistics on inflation and interest rates, the economy was still in trouble. Inflation was down, but most economists, including the administration's top analyst, Alfred Kahn, believed that the underlying rate of inflation would hold at a disturbing 8 percent. Interest rates were falling, but they were still higher than at any time before 1979.

Although inflation and interest rates appeared to be dropping, the same could not be said of unemployment rates. As the recession spread from housing and automobiles to other industries, unemployment shot up to 7.8 percent in May. Meanwhile, sales of American-made cars and the number of new housing starts continued to decline. New orders received by U.S. factories in April also fell 5.6 percent from the month before, the sharpest drop in more than five years. These and other economic indicators, including a slump in industrial and commercial construction, prompted *Time*'s Board of Economists to conclude that the 1980 recession would be longer, deeper, and more painful than it had forecast jut a few weeks earlier.[22]

In order to stimulate the economy, Reagan called in May for an across-the-board 10 percent cut in personal income taxes, and Republican lawmakers on Capitol Hill seconded the idea. The proposal was so popular that Democratic leaders in the Senate offered a preemptive bill of their own, despite Carter's plea for fiscal austerity and his opposition to a tax cut, which would forestall any chance of achieving the balanced budget he had promised for fiscal year 1981.

Mindful of the coming election, however, the White House became less concerned about balancing the budget and more concerned about winning in November. Eizenstat told the president in May that his economic policy was widely "viewed solely as austerity, pain, and sacrifice"; moreover, he knew "of no President who had been re-elected during a serious recession for which he could be blamed." For that reason, Eizenstat joined CEA chairman Schultze, OMB director McIntyre, Vice President Mondale, and the president's other economic advisers in urging a moderate spending program and a tax-cut pledge as a way to satisfy Kennedy, preempt the Republicans, and prod the economy. "I feel strongly that time is running out to unify the Party," Eizenstat told Carter on 26 May. "Unless we take actions now, we will simply not get Anderson or Kennedy supporters to return to the fold and vote in November."[23]

Carter rejected both increased spending and reduced taxes, considering such measures fiscally imprudent. He also lobbied against a Senate budget resolution that would have offset an increase in defense spending with cuts in domestic programs; instead, the president endorsed a House budget resolution more in line with his own spending recommendations. Notwithstanding vigorous efforts by the White House, the joint budget agreement approved in conference committee was much closer to the Senate version and authorized $6.8 billion more for defense and $4.3 billion less for domestic programs than what the White House considered acceptable. After weeks of bedlam on Capitol Hill, during which Senate Democrats rebelled against the president for denouncing the budget compromise, Congress approved the plan with only minor modifications— another slap in the administration's face.

As the primary campaign neared its close in June, President Carter could look forward with confidence to his renomination. But in his bid for reelection, he was clearly at a disadvantage. His domestic and foreign policies were largely in ruin; the nation's economic problems seemed incurable; the hostage crisis was dragging on, with no end in sight; major differences had surfaced between the United States and its allies over Iran and Afghanistan; a Congress controlled by his own party had rebuked him; not even Democratic loyalists were enthusiastic about his candidacy; and he had the lowest approval rating of any president ever—lower even than Richard Nixon's during the height of the Watergate affair. Given these factors, what now seems surprising is not the outcome of the November election but how close the presidential race was up to the last days of the campaign.

12

★ ★ ★ ★ ★

GLOOM AND DOOM

In some respects, the period from June through early September 1980 was the worst for the Carter presidency. The president suffered major defeats on Capitol Hill concerning the oil import surcharge and the budget resolution. Voters in five of the eight states casting ballots on 3 June—"Super Tuesday," as the final day of the primaries was dubbed—rejected his administration by voting for Ted Kennedy. The economy shuffled along in recession, which contributed to a flare-up of racial unrest in the nation's urban ghettos. Allies in Europe openly impugned Carter's leadership of the Western alliance. In the Middle East a deadline for settling the Palestinian question passed without any progress, and relations between Israel and Egypt sputtered to their lowest point since the Camp David accords. Ronald Reagan received the Republican nomination for president on 16 July and jumped into a twenty-eight-point lead over Carter in public opinion polls. Potentially damaging congressional hearings on Billy Carter's relations with the Libyan government began. No headway was made toward freeing the Iranian hostages. In a convention whose most memorable moment was Kennedy stepping up to the podium, Democrats nominated Carter for a second term without much excitement and with real doubts about whether he could beat Reagan in November.

According to most delegate counts, including the president's, Carter was less than twenty-five votes shy of securing the nomination before Super Tuesday. Thus, the 321 delegates he won that day were more than enough to fend off any challenge at the convention in August from Ted Kennedy. But the results of the final primaries represented another repudiation of the president by Democratic voters. Of the three biggest states holding elections that day, Kennedy took California and New Jersey, and the president carried Ohio. Kennedy also won in Rhode Island, South Dakota, and New Mexico, while Carter prevailed in Montana and West Virginia.

A month earlier, confident of his party's nod, Carter had ordered his staff to stop attacking Kennedy. He also took other conciliatory steps to turn his political rival into an ally against Reagan. In a television interview on the eve of Super Tuesday, the president described his relationship with the Massachusetts senator as "one of respect, one of personal friendship, one of admiration." But the senator did not reciprocate. Buoyed by his victories over the president, Kennedy told a cheering throng on primary night that he was unwilling to concede the nomination to Carter. Later, when the president phoned to congratulate Kennedy and invite him to the White House for a discussion on the campaign, an aide told him that the senator was resting and could not be disturbed. When he finally did return the president's call four hours later, Kennedy proposed that they confer the next day.

The meeting in the Oval Office did not heal the breach between the two men. The president again tried to appease Kennedy. Instead of asking him to get out of the race now that the primaries were over, he stressed the importance of a unified party, offered to help Kennedy pay off his campaign debts, and pledged that the senator would be treated properly at the convention. But with his own nomination practically assured, Carter rejected any major concessions—for instance, allowing Kennedy to write the party platform to include comprehensive health insurance or wage and price controls. More than any other issue, national health insurance had contributed to the falling-out between Kennedy and Carter. Now Kennedy wanted the Democratic Party on record as supporting a comprehensive insurance program; Carter was determined to prevent that from happening.

As the meeting proceeded, its tone became increasingly acerbic. "It took him about an hour to fumble around and say we had issues dividing us, and we needed to have a personal debate in front of the TV cameras in order to resolve those differences," the president wrote about Kennedy after the session. "However, he would not agree to support me and Fritz [Mondale] even if we had such a debate." For his part, the senator, looking grim, told reporters as he left the White House only that the meeting had been a step toward party unity.[1]

Following his talk with Carter, Kennedy pressed to have an "open convention." Current party rules required delegates to vote on the first ballot for the candidates they had pledged their support to in the primaries and caucuses; the senator claimed that this made delegates little more than automatons. The Kennedy campaign assumed that if the rules were changed, many of the delegates obligated to Carter would switch to the senator because of the president's dismal showing in the polls. The proposal enraged Carter. After the senator's "overwhelming defeat in the primaries," he later wrote, "having disproved Kennedy's major premise for running—that he could win and I could not—there was no logical reason for him to persist in the debilitating campaign which so weakened his party's chances for success in November."[2]

With Carter's comfortable lead in the delegate count, it was highly unlikely that Kennedy could persuade the Democratic convention to change the rules. But because the senator refused to bow out, the overarching political reality facing Carter after the primaries was a potentially explosive convention showdown with Kennedy and a badly splintered party that seemed to be hoping for an alternative to both Democratic contenders.

More recession and continued high unemployment added to the sense of gloom at the White House and of doom among the Democratic faithful. Although inflation appeared to be under control and interest rates were dropping, the recession continued. Despite a 1.4 percent increase in retail sales and a significant pickup of housing starts in June, consumer demand remained anemic, resulting in a drastic decline in corporate profits. Although the automobile industry was the hardest hit, the bottom line for other basic industries, such as steel, rubber, and chemicals, withered. Between April and June corporate profits plunged by more than 18 percent, the third biggest drop since World War II.

As the recession persisted into July, unemployment replaced inflation as the nation's most serious economic problem. The Department of Labor set the number of jobless in July at 8.2 million, up a startling 1.9 million since February. Even Carter's own economists predicted that the unemployment rate of 7.8 percent would reach 8.5 percent by the end of the year and hover between 8.5 and 9 percent through most of 1981. Other analysts broached the idea of impending double-digit unemployment. "On the basis of both our own and private forecasts, economic recovery will be very sluggish in 1981,"CEA chairman Charles Schultze concluded at the end of July.[3]

Economic hard times helped spark the worst summer of racial violence in more than a decade. There had been earlier incidents in Boston and Wichita, Kansas, but the most serious outbreak occurred at the end of May in the Liberty City section of Miami. After an all-white jury in Tampa acquitted four white policemen charged with the beating death of a black insurance salesman, three days of looting, shooting, overturning cars, and burning property ensued, leaving 16 dead, more than 400 injured, and an estimated $100 million in property damage. "Black folks ain't worth a damn in this country," Benjamin Hooks of the NAACP commented afterward. Sporadic violence erupted in the Miami area throughout the summer. In Chattanooga, Tennessee, a demonstration turned into a riot when another all-white jury acquitted whites accused of murdering blacks.[4]

President Carter responded to the twin problems of recession and unemployment in several ways, though none offered any immediate relief for impoverished minorities. First, he ordered restrictions removed on consumer credit, which the Federal Reserve Board had imposed in March. Second, he encouraged the FRB to increase the money supply, which chairman Paul Volcker had earlier tightened to fight inflation. To help the battered automobile industry, he also announced a $1 billion government assistance program that included a relaxation of some emissions standards, up to $400 million in loans to car dealers, and $50 million in aid to local communities to rebuild old auto plants. In addition, he promised a faster review of a UAW request for restrictions on imports of Japanese cars.

The president also reconsidered his position on taxes. Republican candidate Ronald Reagan had made a $36 billion tax cut—including a 10 percent blanket reduction in personal income taxes and faster write-offs for business investment—the centerpiece of his plan for overcoming the recession. Reagan's call for a tax cut put the White House on the defensive. Carter had long resisted the idea, identifying inflation as the nation's chief economic culprit and believing that a balanced budget was essential to winning the inflation battle. As inflation receded and the recession worsened, however, the president began to look more favorably on a tax cut. Although he was firmly opposed to a reduction as large as the one suggested by the Republicans, Stu Eizenstat and other economic advisers persuaded Carter to present a more modest proposal—one that encouraged business investment through accelerated appreciation rather than a reduction in personal income taxes. Such a plan could be economically stimulating, helping to improve the nation's industrial productivity, which had been a matter of considerable concern to Schultze, and still be noninflationary.

In July Carter announced his third economic recovery program for the year at Detroit's Metro Airport—deliberate timing, since the Republicans were simultaneously holding their convention in that city and nominating Reagan as their candidate for president. Reaction to the president's plan was mixed. On Capitol Hill the response largely followed party lines—Democrats defending the program as "statesmanlike," Republicans charging that it was "too little, too late, too political." Within the business and financial community the reaction was described by Carter's own staff as "ho-hum." Although business leaders generally approved of the thrust of the program, some commented that it had been put together too hastily and lacked a comprehensive economic strategy. Likewise, other commentators described the plan as an "economic smorgasbord," with some morsels for business, some for individual taxpayers, and even some for government (by increasing its involvement in the economy).

Considering the poor state of the economy and the uneven response to his newest economic proposals, Carter was well aware of his vulnerability on domestic issues in the upcoming campaign. In contrast, Reagan was widely believed to be weakest on foreign policy because of his inexperience and his often simplistic views and because of the president's own achievements in that area—most notably the Panama Canal treaties and the Camp David accords. It behooved the president, then, to stress his mastery of world politics in contrast to his Republican opponent's ignorance. But even here, Carter's credibility was tarnished by several serious problems concerning the Atlantic alliance, the unresolved Arab-Israeli dispute, U.S.-Soviet relations, and Iran's holding of the American hostages.

When Carter took office in 1977, Zbigniew Brzezinski had said that "wider cooperation" with the United States' key allies would be the first priority of the new administration's foreign policy. However, by the spring of 1980, Washington's relations with its allies had slipped into alarming disorder. A former top aide to Henry Kissinger, Helmut Sonnefeldt, told an influential European audience that the Atlantic alliance was "undergoing its deepest tensions in thirty years." No one challenged that assertion.

Part of the friction was attributable to the barely concealed disdain that West German chancellor Helmut Schmidt had for Carter, as well as the president's view of Schmidt as unstable, unreliable, and egotistical. The latest problem between the two leaders occurred when Schmidt gave a speech in April 1980 calling for "both sides"—NATO and the Soviet Union—to forgo deploying new missiles in Europe. To Schmidt, such deployment would undermine efforts to start a new round of arms control talks. To Carter, the chancellor's speech appeared to contradict an allied decision in December 1979 to go forward with the deployment of Pershing 2 and ground-launched cruise missiles; indeed, at the time, Bonn had agreed to accept some of the cruise missiles and 108 of the Pershing 2s.[5] In a telephone call to the president, Schmidt said that he had been misquoted, although he acknowledged his support of talks with the Soviets on arms limitation. Soon, however, new stories began circulating that the German chancellor favored a suspension of new missiles. Carter then sent Schmidt a communiqué expressing concern about the confusion his statements were causing. The message became public, and Schmidt became furious, convinced that the president was trying to undermine efforts at arms control.

French president Valéry Giscard d'Estaing also harbored a low opinion of Carter, whom he accused of being inconsistent, ineffective, and unnecessarily provocative in his dealings with the Soviet Union. He also criticized the American president for allegedly expecting Europe to follow every twist and turn of U.S. foreign policy. Like other European leaders, d'Estaing sought a more balanced U.S. approach to the Middle East, one that took into account Europe's heavy dependence on Persian Gulf oil. Similarly, he urged a more reasoned response to the Soviet invasion of Afghanistan, which reflected western Europe's close proximity to the Soviet Union.

In May the French president met privately in Warsaw with Soviet president Leonid Brezhnev; plans for the five-hour session had been kept secret from the United States. About the same time, rumors were spreading around Washington that the annual economic summit of the Western industrial powers and Japan, scheduled to be held in Venice on 22–23 June, would be the occasion of a European demand that the Palestine Liberation Organization be allowed to participate in all future negotiations in the Middle East and that UN Resolution 242, the heart of most long-range peace formulas for the Middle East, be revised to remove its reference to the Palestinians as mere "refugees."

President Carter's new secretary of state, former senator Edmund Muskie of Maine, turned livid when he heard of the Brezhnev-d'Estaing summit and the plans afoot to pressure the United States and Israel into an accommodation on the Palestinian question. Strong-willed and known to have a fiery temper, Muskie was nevertheless highly respected in Washington, and his appointment as Cyrus Vance's replacement had generally been well-received, even though he had no particular expertise in foreign affairs. Although Muskie had initially been one of the president's most outspoken critics, he was also one of the few lawmakers on Capitol Hill with whom the president had cultivated a warm personal relationship. Carter had selected Vance for his management and negotiating talents, but he intended Muskie to serve as the administration's spokesman on foreign policy, leaving other matters to his able deputy secretary of state, Warren Christopher, whom many at the State Department—including Christopher himself—had expected to succeed Vance.[6]

While in Venice to attend a foreign ministers' meeting, Muskie had been scolded by French foreign minister Jean Francois-Poncet on the United States' failure to consult its allies. But the minister had neglected to mention d'Estaing's forthcoming meeting with Brezhnev. When Muskie finally learned of the Soviet-French conference, the secretary of state did not mince words about French hypocrisy: "I'm concerned that when I was being given a lecture on consultation, the lecturer was not inclined to practice what he was preaching," he commented caustically to reporters. In a thinly veiled reference to the allies, he also attacked what he referred to as the meddling in the Middle East "from the sidelines."[7]

By the time Carter left for the Venice summit in June, so much distrust had emerged among the Western powers, and so much scorn had been heaped on the president, that many political observers feared the meeting would be a disaster. Instead of a diplomatic fiasco, however, the Venice summit proved to be a personal success for Carter. Before the start of the gathering, the president met with Schmidt to try to settle their conflicts. In a stormy session, Schmidt claimed that he had been insulted by Carter's last message to him and that Germany was not the United States' fifty-first state. But after Carter agreed to make a public statement expressing confidence in Schmidt and noting their concurrence on theater nuclear forces, matters quieted down, and the surface cordiality between the two men reappeared.

Once the summit began Carter was determined to use it to restore his own standing as a leader. Using skillful negotiation and sheer doggedness, Carter convinced Schmidt and the other leaders at Vienna to condemn the Soviets for endangering world peace by invading Afghanistan; in return, the president agreed to shelve his demand for further punitive measures against the Kremlin and to consider the possibility of negotiations with Moscow at some later date. On the economic front, Carter achieved most of the goals he had set for himself at Venice, including an agreement to limit oil imports to levels lower than those agreed to at Tokyo the previous year and a commitment to double the use of coal by the end of the decade.

Yet, as most political observers recognized, the heads of state at Venice had papered over their differences rather than resolved them. The president cautioned the Japanese about the growth of protectionist sentiment in the United States because of Japanese imports and barriers to U.S. exports. He feared that Schmidt would break ranks with the allies and make concessions to Moscow on arms control. For their part, Europe's leaders remained suspicious of Carter and wondered whether the Atlantic alliance was still sustainable or even desirable.

Disharmony also reigned between the United States and its friends in the Middle East. Despite repeated affirmations by both Israel and Egypt of their solid commitment to the Camp David peace process, they made little progress in resolving their dispute. The immediate problem remained Palestinian autonomy in the West Bank and Gaza Strip. Although the 1979 Camp David accords called for an agreement on self-rule by 26 May 1980, Israeli prime minister Menachem Begin held steadfastly to a definition of Palestinian autonomy that was limited largely to municipal affairs. Under no circumstances would he permit Palestinian self-determination, which was what Egyptian president Anwar Sadat eventually intended for the Palestinians. President Carter tilted toward the Egyptian position, believing that the Palestinians were entitled to "full autonomy."

At the end of March Carter sent Sol Linowitz, who had helped negotiate the Panama Canal treaties, to the Middle East to develop a set of proposals acceptable to both Israel and Egypt. His mission failed because of Israel's unwillingness to suspend the building of new settlements on the West Bank until after 26 May and Egypt's refusal to hold additional talks on the autonomy issue until Israel halted the new construction. The president himself attempted to achieve a breakthrough by inviting both Begin and Sadat to Washington for separate talks, but he had no better luck than Linowitz. Sadat agreed to ignore the May cutoff and even said that if Israel assented to a formula for Palestinian autonomy, he would be willing to state publicly that there should be no separate Palestinian state. But Begin would not budge from his positions on either Palestinian independence or the building of Israeli settlements in the occupied territories. All that Carter achieved was Begin's acquiescence to nonstop talks between Egypt and Israel during the forty days before 26 May.

Carter had recognized at the time of the Camp David accords that achieving progress on the occupied territories would be difficult, but he may not have understood until these latest meetings that the terms contained in the documents—such as "autonomy," "security," "Palestinian rights," and even "West Bank"—had different connotations for each of the parties involved. At issue, moreover, was not semantics but the foundation of a final agreement. For Israel, that meant security; for the Palestinians, their legitimate rights as a people; for Egypt, its credibility and influence in the Arab world. Under these circumstances, there was scant room for compromise. As a result, weeks of talks between Egyptian and Israeli negotiators bore no fruit.

Two weeks before the 26 May target date, Sadat broke off the sessions after Begin stated that security in the West Bank and Gaza "must remain exclusively in Israel's hand." During this two-month interval, Begin lost considerable public support, even in Israel, for his hard-line approach to the Palestinian problem and the occupied territories. There was also vocal criticism of Begin's policies from the American Jewish community. In July 56 prominent American Jews signed a statement already endorsed by 250 influential Israelis censuring "extremists" within the Israeli government who "distort Zionism and threaten its realization."[8]

Nevertheless, the Israeli prime minister and his Likud coalition remained defiant. At the beginning of August the Knesset passed a measure making an undivided Jerusalem the capital of Israel, even though U.S. ambassador Samuel Lewis had already warned Begin that the United States might not be able to conduct face-to-face meetings with him if he moved his offices to East Jerusalem. With Begin resistant to outside pressures, there was little hope of further progress in the bilateral talks between Egypt and Israel. Carter was increasingly distracted by his campaign for reelection, and European leaders were anxious to undertake their own Middle East initiative. Thus, the peace process begun at Camp David a year earlier had simply run out of time.

The Arab-Israeli controversy compounded Carter's political problems at home. Although American Jews were now more apt to criticize Begin, this did not translate into praise for the president. As Stu Eizenstat and Al Moses, the White House's liaison with the Jewish community, told the president in early October, American Jews simply did not trust the administration. They believed that if Carter were reelected, he would "recognize the PLO or put an untenable amount of pressure on the state of Israel to make concessions to the Arabs that would run counter to their national interest and security."[9]

Carter's policy toward Cuba was also having an impact on his political problems. When he first took office, the president had hoped to improve relations with the government of Fidel Castro, but those efforts had been undermined by Cuban military involvement in Africa, the Soviet "brigade" in Cuba, reports that the Sandinistas had been receiving aid from Havana, and general distrust of Cuba within the United States. Meanwhile, thousands of Cubans sought to leave their country, whether to reunite with family members who had fled to the United States or to escape the Castro regime. This worsening of relations, combined with Cubans' desire to leave, led Castro to warn that he might permit a boatlift similar to the one in 1965, during which nearly 150,000 Cubans had fled to the United States.

In April 1980 matters reached a head when six Cubans smashed a bus through the gate of the Peruvian embassy and demanded asylum. When the Peruvians refused to return the six individuals, Castro declared that any Cubans wanting to leave the country could go to the embassy. Within three days, more than 10,000 people had assembled on the embassy grounds. Embarrassed by the sheer number of individuals seeking to leave Cuba, but seeing it as an opportunity to get rid of people who might cause him problems later, Castro announced that he would open the port of Mariel to any Cubans, including those at the Peruvian embassy, who wished to leave; he would also allow, he said, relatives from the United States to come to Mariel to claim their loved ones. Carter, believing that it would be wrong to deny entry to those seeking asylum, declared that the United States would "provide an open heart and open arms for the tens of thousands of refugees seeking freedom from Communist domination."[10]

The president may have believed that he was doing little more than expressing the sentiment felt by many Americans during the course of the cold war, but Cuban Americans took his statement as a green light to proceed with the boatlift. Hundreds of boats streamed to Mariel harbor, bringing 6,000 Cubans to Key West during the first week and a daily average of 3,000 during the month of May. The Refugee Act, passed in March 1980, had imposed a yearly immigration cap of 19,500 Cubans, with each person required to go through a review process before receiving refugee status. Not only were many more Cubans entering the United States than were permitted under the Refugee Act, but the administration, caught off guard, had made no provision for housing or documenting them. Tent cities went up in Florida, some of the new arrivals were transported to military bases as far away as Arkansas and Wisconsin, and still others were incarcerated for crimes they had committed in Cuba.

The flood of so many individuals—125,000 by the time the boatlift ended in September—caused an uproar among Americans. Reports of confrontations between National Guard troops and Cubans and the destruction of federal property by some of the immigrants only added to the furor. A Gallup poll taken in May found that nearly 60 percent of Americans opposed the Cuban influx, versus only 19 percent in support. Floridians were especially enraged, since their state bore the brunt of it. White House assistants Gene Eidenberg and John White informed Carter in September that despite steps taken by the administration to process the immigrants, "the perception, aided by a negative Miami press, that we have 'dumped' this problem on the taxpayers of Florida is widespread." Carter, knowing the importance of Florida in any reelection bid, could only write in the margin, "Do something about this."[11] Although the end of the boatlift reduced some of the pressure on the administration, the political damage had been done.

Foreign policy spilled over into domestic politics even more dramatically during the summer of 1980. In July the press reported that President Carter's brother Billy was being investigated by the Senate and the Justice Department. At issue was whether Billy had violated federal law by accepting $220,000 as the first installment of what he called a "loan" from the Libyan government without registering as its agent. Even more serious were suggestions by the media that the White House might have interceded improperly in Billy's affairs and in the probes into them.

Billy's fortunes had declined dramatically since his 1978 trip to Libya. His "good ol' boy" image no longer seemed charming or amusing, and the celebrity circuit shunned him. The loss of fees he had once received for public appearances left him in debt, and he began to drink so heavily that he admitted himself into an alcoholic treatment center in California, where he spent seven weeks. A recovering alcoholic with outstanding obligations, he turned to his Libyan friends for help, and they were more than happy to oblige the brother of the U.S. president. Between January and April 1979 they advanced him $220,000 of a $500,000 "loan." Although this business deal eventually fell through because of a cutback in Libyan oil production, Billy could have made as much as $5 million annually by helping to procure an additional 100,000 barrels per day of high-grade Libyan oil for a Florida business concern, the Charter Oil Company.

Because of his close association with Libya, the Justice Department had asked Billy in 1979 to register as a foreign agent under a 1933 law requiring all persons who did political or public relations for a foreign government to disclose their activities and pay. Billy ignored the request on the grounds that he had never acted as an agent for Libya. Lacking sufficient evidence to take action against him, the department began an investigation into his affairs. In May it discovered the $220,000 "loan." Two weeks later Billy agreed to be interviewed by Justice Department officials. On 14 July he registered as a foreign agent and filed a report showing the $220,000 he had received as compensation.

News of what some Republicans called "Billygate" produced a political storm. Legitimate questions were raised as to what Billy had done to earn Libyan largesse and why he had agreed to register as a foreign agent after insisting for nearly eighteen months that he was just a friend of the Libyans. More specifically, reporters and lawmakers wanted to know if the White House had any role in Billy's activities or in the Justice Department's investigation. On 22 July the White House issued a statement disclosing what it knew about the matter and flatly asserting that there had never been any connection between the White House and the Justice Department's investigation into Billy's finances. But admissions made in this disclaimer only made a bad situation worse. The White House acknowledged that, at Brzezinski's request, Billy and a Libyan official had met with the national security adviser in November to explore the possibility of getting the Libyans to help free the Iranian hostages. In addition, the White House conceded that Carter had learned in March of Billy's effort to get more Libyan petroleum for Charter Oil and had done nothing about it.

Questions continued to be raised over the next several weeks as apparent errors and omissions were discovered in the White House's initial release. None was serious enough to suggest a Watergate-style cover-up, but they kept the political cauldron boiling. Carter revealed that, after checking his records, he found that Attorney General Benjamin Civiletti had in fact told him earlier that Billy needed to register as a foreign agent. Lawmakers then learned that in early 1980 Billy had traveled to Libya for a second time and that he had been given some confidential cables from the State Department. As it turned out, the cables were routine ones that the State Department often made available to individuals and companies doing business abroad. But the fact that the White House had not mentioned the documents in its earlier statement caused many political observers to wonder about their contents and whether they had enhanced Billy's standing with the Libyans. Many people were also dismayed to learn that First Lady Rosalynn Carter had raised the idea of using Billy's Libyan connection to help free the Iranian hostages. Was the president trying to conceal this evidence of amateur diplomacy?

In truth, the White House concealed nothing. To avoid even the semblance of wrongdoing, as soon as news of Billy's "loan" broke, it adopted a policy of openness and candor—of letting the chips fall where they may. On Capitol Hill the Senate Judiciary and Foreign Relations committees appointed an ad hoc committee to conduct an investigation of Billy's activities. In response, the president announced that he would be available for interviews. But because the White House had to keep amending its 22 July account, doubt was cast on Carter's forthrightness.

It was again Carter's presidential timber rather than his integrity, however, that hung in the balance. Few Americans believed that the president was guilty of misconduct that he was now attempting to hide, just as few Americans ever contested his moral character. But on the eve of the Democratic convention, the Billy Carter affair added new misgivings about Carter's competence to serve a second term. "The damn Billy Carter stuff is killing us," Hamilton Jordan told Pat Caddell.[12]

The release of the hostages almost certainly would have improved Carter's drive for reelection. Although the death of the shah on 27 July led to some speculation that the Iranians might free the captives in return for some face-saving concessions—such as a UN inquiry into Iran's grievances, as had been proposed earlier in the year—absolutely no progress was made toward their release.

Washington's relations with Moscow also remained stalemated, primarily because of the Soviet occupation of Afghanistan. The invasion had prompted NATO in December 1979 to agree to place intermediate-range nuclear weapons in Europe to counter Soviet SS-20 rockets aimed at the West. It also led to Carter's decision in July to sign Presidential Directive 59 (PD-59), authorizing the largest arms procurement program in thirty years. Conceived by Brzezinski and Defense Secretary Harold Brown, PD-59 was intended to break away from the doctrine of mutual assured destruction (MAD), which provided the rationale for much of the nation's strategic planning. MAD presumed that the ability of the Soviet Union and the United States to devastate each other's civilian population centers would deter both superpowers from beginning a nuclear war. Brzezinski and Brown concluded, however, that the buildup of Soviet strategic forces and the improved accuracy of their nuclear warheads gave the Soviets the means to engage in a more limited war against military targets. Therefore, a nuclear strategy based on the existence of a countervailing force left Washington in the untenable position of either responding with a massive strike against civilian population centers, resulting in the full-scale Soviet retaliation projected in the MAD scenario, or giving in to nuclear blackmail. PD-59 proposed to address this strategic deficiency by requiring defense planners to target military installations as well as population centers. If it could respond in kind to a Soviet attack, the United States would achieve a credible nuclear deterrent.

In reality, PD-59 was not so much a new doctrine as a modification of an existing doctrine. Defense planners had been moving toward a more flexible nuclear strategy since at least 1962, when Defense Secretary Robert McNamara had considered the idea of a counterforce but rejected it because of the cost. Nevertheless, the disclosure that Carter had signed PD-59 led to a new round of complaints against the administration. Some critics said that Brzezinski had purposely leaked the story to embarrass Muskie—who did not even know the details of PD-59 until he read them in the newspaper. Other commentators suspected a political motive—perhaps to blunt the charge of the Republican Party platform that the administration's nuclear and strategic policy provided "a Hobson's choice between mass mutual suicide and surrender."[13]

Advocates of arms reduction asserted that PD-59 actually increased the chances of a nuclear war because the president would be more tempted to resort to war during a crisis. Others maintained that the Soviets might launch a preemptive first strike of their own. Former CIA deputy director Herbert Scoville Jr. observed that anything that made it easier to fight a nuclear war was "a step in the wrong direction." Lawrence Korb of the American Enterprise Institute, a conservative think tank, added that the "irony" of the doctrine was that "it could make war either more or less probable. . . . It is stoppable, but because it is, it is also more startable."[14]

Moscow also blasted the White House's revised strategy. *Tass* referred to it as "madness"; *Pravda* called it "nuclear blackmail" and warned of an accelerated arms race. Considering PD-59 in the same context as the planned deployment of Pershing missiles in Europe, the White House's decision to construct the MX missile system, and the indefinite shelving of the SALT II treaty, Soviet analysts became convinced that Washington was seeking a strategic advantage over the Soviet Union. Despite administration claims to the contrary, they also concluded that Washington's long-standing acceptance of strategic parity with Moscow—the very basis of détente—was now a thing of the past, and the United States and the Soviet Union were entering a new period of confrontation.[15]

As Democrats prepared to hold their nominating convention in New York, the president was being battered by domestic and foreign problems. Inflation, recession, and unemployment; racial unrest; the Mariel boatlift;

Billygate and the Libyan connection; the Middle East situation, including the hostage crisis; and the Afghan crisis—all these were working against Carter. A Gallup poll in August showed the president with a 21 percent approval rating, three points lower than that of Richard Nixon during the depths of Watergate and the worst rating of any American president in the history of polling. A survey in California placed Carter third in the state, behind Reagan and John Anderson. An ABC-Harris poll also revealed major shifts throughout the country in favor of Republicans in races for Congress, governorships, and state legislatures.

The convention itself did little to instill confidence about the president's chances for reelection in November. On the first day Carter's forces were able to defeat Kennedy's motion to eliminate the rule binding delegates to the candidates they had supported in the primaries and caucuses. Although Kennedy subsequently announced that he was withdrawing his candidacy, he fully intended to have his views reflected in the party platform. At issue were four economic planks favored by Kennedy but opposed by Carter: wage and price controls, a $12 billion program to create 800,000 new jobs, opposition to any action that would cause "a significant increase in unemployment," and a pledge not to fight inflation with high interest rates and unemployment. The president's position on wage and price controls was fairly well established, and he believed that passage of these planks would leave him vulnerable to Republican charges that he favored big government and was unwilling to take the steps needed to revive the economy.

Speaking for his platform proposals the next night, Kennedy delivered a powerful address in which he excoriated Reagan for such idiocies as attributing 80 percent of air pollution to trees and calling unemployment insurance "a prepaid vacation plan for freeloaders." But the heart of his message was an emotional appeal to the convention not to abandon traditional Democratic values. Do not let "the great purposes of the Democratic Party become the bygone passages of history," he told the delegates. "For all those whose cares have been our concern the work goes on, the cause endures, the hope still lives, and the dream shall never die."

Kennedy's speech moved even Carter delegates in the convention hall, who joined the Kennedy people in a demonstration lasting almost forty minutes. Meanwhile, a deal was being struck below the podium between the Carter and Kennedy forces. Kennedy consented to withdraw the plank on wage and price controls; in return, Carter agreed not to contest the other economic proposals. After a voice vote from the floor, Tip O'Neill ruled the three planks approved. Rather than endorsing the articles outright, the president simply promised to "accept and support the intent" of the jobs plank and "pursue policies that will implement [its] spirit and aims."

The main business of the convention, nominating the Carter-Mondale ticket for a second term, took place on 13 August, but it was anticlimactic. The major battles were over, and all that remained was for the candidates to give their acceptance speeches. Mondale's remarks consisted mainly of humorous barbs directed against Reagan. Calling out a list of Democratic programs, he asked in each case who had supported them and then responded by shouting, "Not Ronald Reagan!" The delegates soon joined in the refrain.

In contrast, there was little humor in the president's speech, but it was carefully crafted and well presented. Carter gave clear notice that he intended to make Reagan rather than his own presidential record the key issue of the campaign. The election, he said, was a "choice between two futures." His was one of "security, justice, and peace," and his opponent's one of "despair" and "surrender." Carter's future would strive toward world peace, while Reagan's would court "risk—the risk of international confrontation, the risk of an uncontrollable, unaffordable, and unwinnable nuclear war."

Of more immediate interest to most of the delegates in the convention hall was whether Kennedy would join the president after his speech in a final show of party unity. Almost deferentially Carter reached out for the senator's support and spoke directly to him through the medium of television. "Ted, your party needs—and I need—you," he said. "And I need your idealism and your dedication working for us." Kennedy's response was a keen disappointment to Carter and to other Democratic leaders. The senator arrived late to the convention hall, found himself in the midst of a milling crowd that had also been called to the podium, and was clearly uncomfortable making even a brief appearance next to Carter. As soon as possible, he left the hall and returned to his hotel. "If that's the best they can do in unity," observed Reagan, who was watching the convention on television, "they have a long way to go."[16]

As the convention adjourned, Carter clearly faced a herculean task in the coming campaign. In the weeks following his nomination, the president's fortunes actually improved, so that the two major candidates ran virtually neck and neck in all the polls. But Carter's turnaround was not enough to stave off defeat. For the next twelve weeks Reagan asked the American people if they wanted four more years of Carter. In November they answered no.

13

★ ★ ★ ★ ★

DEFEAT

Despite his instability in the polls, the president returned to the White House after the Democratic convention confident of victory in November. His campaign staff was in place, the Democratic Party had survived intact, and the news media could be expected to turn its attention from his intraparty battle with Kennedy to the presidential contest with Reagan. That, the president was convinced, would work in his favor. Other circumstances gave additional cause for optimism. "Billygate," which had dogged him for months, proved to be a puff of wind without much political impact. The threat to his campaign posed by independent candidate John Anderson diminished, and signs also pointed to an economic improvement in the fourth quarter of 1980, which could have a substantial impact on the election.

However, these developments did not add up to victory. Had he not tried to make Reagan the central issue of the campaign, or had economic recovery occurred faster, or had he secured the release of the Iranian hostages, perhaps Carter would have succeeded in his drive for a second term. As it was, he made a remarkable comeback in the polls and, until the last week of the campaign, seemed close to winning. But Reagan was a more adept campaigner than the president had anticipated; indeed, the president's competency, not Reagan's, became the recurring theme of the campaign. In the end, Carter became the first elected president since Herbert Hoover in 1932 to fail in his bid for reelection.

Well before the Democratic convention, Hamilton Jordan had decided to focus the campaign on Reagan. In June, Pat Caddell and Jerry Rafshoon had persuaded Jordan to give up his position as White House chief of staff and join the campaign full-time. Jordan was delighted to es-cape the straitjacket of his White House duties. By agreement with the chairman of the campaign, Robert Strauss, Jordan would be responsible for the overall strategy while Strauss would handle the nuts and bolts.

On 25 June Jordan prepared a memorandum for Carter laying out the obstacles the president would have to overcome to win in November and proposing a blueprint for victory. It was a sobering report. Two weeks earlier Jordan had met with a group of prominent California Democrats to learn more about Carter's likely opponent in the fall. State treasurer Jesse Unruh had warned Jordan not to "make the mistake that every per-son in this room has made at one time or another and underestimate Ronald Reagan." Jordan took this advice seriously, but his main concern was the damaging impact of Kennedy's challenge to Carter. "The most costly consequence is that support for you based on your being a likable, well-intentioned, compassionate and at times atypical politician has eroded badly," he told Carter.

A growing number of Americans had come to believe that it really did not matter who was elected president—that there was not much dif-ference between Carter and Reagan. To win the election, therefore, Carter had to turn the campaign away from the controversial issues that alien-ated voters (particularly liberal Democrats). At the same time, he had to convince the American people that this was indeed a critical election with two very distinct candidates. Jordan's idea was that Carter should ham-mer away at Reagan's fitness to be president. "I was troubled by the in-sinuation of my own analysis that we couldn't just run on our record," he later acknowledged.[1]

Carter had anticipated as early as October 1979 that he would be running against Reagan, and he agreed that Reagan's qualifications, rather than his own position on the major issues, should dominate Dem-ocratic campaign strategy in 1980. By no means were current affairs ig-nored entirely, since that would have been politically impossible. However, both Jordan and pollster Pat Caddell believed that the presi-dent could not win reelection without offering the American public his conception of the country's future. "You must tell us what your vision, your plans and hopes are for our people and nation," Jordan told the president. "I know that you have such a vision, but it must be communi-cated to us."[2]

Repeating a mistake of his presidency, however, Carter did not offer his campaign staff, much less the American voters, a clear sense of where he intended to lead the country over the next four years. Accordingly, he was unable to define himself in a way that might have affected the elec-tion's outcome. By attacking Reagan's presidential fitness, moreover, he opened himself up to counterattacks about his own competency as president.

For most of the campaign, though, it appeared that the president's strategy might work. Carter kicked off his bid for reelection on 1 September with a huge rally at Tuscumbia, Alabama. At the event were about twenty robed members of the Ku Klux Klan, whom the president denounced as cowards who "counsel[ed] fear and hatred." Nevertheless, Reagan insinuated the next day that Carter was seeking the support of racists. Reagan realized immediately that the comment was a mistake: "I shouldn't have said it because the minute after I said it, I knew that this was what would be remembered." The Republican candidate's remark was only the latest of a series of gaffes on his part. Earlier he had called the Vietnam War a "noble cause," expressed personal doubts about the theory of evolution, remarked that the New Deal was patterned after Benito Mussolini's state socialism, proposed making Social Security voluntary, and voiced pro-Taiwan views that threatened relations with the Beijing government. "If Reagan keeps putting his foot in his mouth for another week or so we can close down campaign headquarters," Caddell gloated after one of Reagan's blunders.[3]

Other political developments also seemed to break in Carter's favor. First, Billygate was successfully defused as a campaign issue. A week before the Democratic convention, Carter prudently held a televised news conference devoted mostly to answering questions about his role in his brother's dealings with Libya. The president admitted that Billy's case gave the appearance of favoritism, but he denied any effort at a cover-up. Carter informed reporters that his White House counsel, Lloyd Cutler, was drafting an order prohibiting any executive branch employee from associating with a member of the president's family under circumstances that might suggest improper influence. He also stressed that Billy had no say in U.S. foreign policy.

The president's earnest, nothing-to-hide manner, buttressed by a lengthy White House report and thousands of official documents and excerpts from his personal diary, sapped the sensationalism of Billygate. But it was Billy Carter's nine hours of testimony on 21 and 22 August before the Senate committee looking into his activities that finally put the controversy to rest. Denying that he was a "buffoon, a boob, or a wacko," he described himself as "a common citizen with uncommon financial and family problems." He also disputed charges that he had been an influence peddler for Libya. "I have not asked anything of Jimmy Carter or of any U.S. Government representative on behalf of the Libyan government," he said. Rather than profiting from being the brother of the president, Billy maintained that he had suffered financially from the connection. Ten separate investigations into his affairs, including several by the Internal Revenue Service, had meant enormous legal fees, and negative publicity about his ties with Libya had cost him as much as $500,000 a year in public appearances.

Instead of the beer-guzzling clown often depicted by the news media, Billy proved to be an articulate, courteous, even sympathetic witness. His testimony, moreover, supported the president's claims that he had known nothing about his brother's $220,000 loan and that the White House had extended no special treatment to Billy. On 2 October the Senate investigation concluded with a report criticizing the president for trying to involve his brother in attempts to free the Iranian hostages but acquitting him of any other charge.[4]

Even the economy seemed to be smiling on the president's endeavors. The economic signals had been mixed and indicated a slow recovery at best, but by the beginning of October there were a number of signs that the recession was bottoming out. Housing starts were up, businesses were borrowing more to expand production and increase inventories, and the Department of Commerce was estimating that the GNP, which had been falling since the first quarter, would rise in the fourth quarter and continue to grow slowly through the second quarter of 1981.

As a result of these occurrences, the president managed to close the gap separating him from his Republican opponent. A *Newsweek* poll taken at the end of September showed Reagan leading Carter by a margin of only 4 percent, with 12 percent of the voters surveyed still undecided. According to the president's own polls, in states such as Connecticut, where Carter had been trailing Reagan by a more than two-to-one margin in the middle of July, or in Iowa, where he had been behind by almost three to one, he had pulled even or close to even by the middle of September. In other states such as Maryland and North Carolina, where he was already ahead, he had enlarged his lead. A potential political blowout thus seemed to be turning into a cliff-hanger.[5]

The fall brought a tactical dilemma for the Carter campaign: whether to participate in a three-way debate sponsored by the League of Women Voters. The president's advisers were anxious to have Carter face Reagan alone, and they were opposed to a debate that included independent candidate John Anderson. Conducting a National Unity campaign with Patrick J. Lucey, the former Democratic governor of Wisconsin, as his running mate, Anderson had issued a lengthy and detailed platform in September that called for gun control, passage of an equal rights amendment, overhaul of the nation's mass transportation system, and a fifty-cents-a-gallon tax on gasoline. Besides adding to the legitimacy of his campaign, Anderson's inclusion in the debate would provide an opportunity for Reagan and him to gang up on the president. Since the polls showed support for Anderson's participation in any presidential matchup, the president's staff agreed to a three-way exchange on the condition that Carter first debate Reagan alone. But the League of Women Voters took the position that Anderson should participate in all the debates if he received at least 15 percent support in the national public opinion polls. When the polls showed that Anderson had that level of backing, the league sent out invitations to all three candidates for the first debate in Baltimore on 21 September.

Carter was in a political bind. Either he would strengthen Anderson's campaign by appearing with him, or he would be accused of refusing to debate the issues before the American public. Regardless, Reagan would come out ahead. In this no-win situation, the president's staff concluded that Carter had more to lose than gain by joining Reagan and Anderson on stage. Afterward, Hamilton Jordan, who had watched the debate on television, acknowledged that Carter had been hurt by not participating. "When it was over," he remarked, "I didn't feel very good. Reagan had not made any big mistakes and Anderson had handled himself well." Yet the damage was not lasting. Polls taken a few days after Anderson's dialogue with Reagan showed him still running a distant third behind his Republican and Democratic opponents. Reagan also seemed to have profited little from the debate. Thirty-three percent of survey respondents said that they were now more likely to vote for him, but 30 percent said that they were less likely to.[6]

Another source of consternation for the Carter campaign was the so-called meanness issue. After Reagan had accused him of seeking the votes of racist elements in the South, the president had retaliated by suggesting that Reagan himself was a racist. Carter also delivered a series of hard-hitting speeches in which he portrayed the choice between the Republican candidate and himself as one between war and peace. In a short radio address on 2 October, which the president had largely rewritten, he returned to values that he deeply believed in but had never been able to articulate in a cohesive manner. "Our commitment to freedom and justice, our shared ideals, our strong families and communities are the foundation of American strength," he wrote into the speech. He also stressed the concept of "community" in another section of the address and offered hope to the American people by substituting the word "opportunities" for "challenges" in the coming years.[7] Unwisely, however, he returned to his attack on Reagan just a few days later. In an address in Chicago on 6 October he said that Reagan's election would divide the nation, "black and white, Jew from Christian, North from South, rural from urban," and could well "lead our country toward war."

Jordan, Rafshoon, Caddell, and other campaign advisers had urged the president to tone down his denunciations of Reagan. "Mr. President, you've just got to be careful what you say," Jordan had entreated after a speech in Atlanta. Whatever most Americans thought of Carter's conduct of the presidency, his advisers realized that he was still largely perceived as a decent and honorable person. By attacking Reagan in this way, the president could damage one of his most valuable campaign assets—especially since his mudslinging was directed against an opponent who, like himself, was widely regarded as a good and fair-minded individual. Reagan played on his own "nice guy" image by responding to Carter's remarks with expressions of "sorrow" and "regret" rather than by lunging for the jugular, as the president seemed to be doing.

Other Republicans were less restrained. Carter's "intemperate and totally misleading statements demean the office of the Presidency," former president Gerald Ford retorted. "I'm appalled at the ugly, mean little remark Jimmy Carter made," added Republican vice presidential candidate George Bush. The news media also seized on the temper of Carter's speeches and peppered him with questions. "We have a major problem on our hands, and we are going to have to eat a little crow to put this 'meanness' thing behind us," Jordan finally told the president on 7 October, the day after his Chicago speech. The president got the message. In a televised interview he admitted that the campaign had "departed from the way it ought to be between two candidates for the highest office in this land" and that he had gotten "carried away" in some of his comments. In the future he would lay aside personalities and stick to the issues.[8]

In reality, the president merely repackaged his attacks on Reagan, making them less strident and more statesmanlike. He no longer claimed that Reagan would divide the United States, only that Carter would unite it. With increased effectiveness, he also put Reagan on the defensive by pounding on the theme that a Reagan presidency would be more likely to lead the nation into war than his own would. Almost overnight, "war and peace" replaced "meanness" in campaign priorities, as Carter tore into Reagan's proposals to scrap the SALT II agreement and use the threat of a new arms race to force Moscow back to the bargaining table.

The Carter campaign also had a field day with Reagan's statements on the environment. After his early bloopers, Reagan's staff assigned a top-level political adviser to travel with him to make certain that his speeches did not contain any embarrassing bombshells. He was also urged to refrain from making any impromptu remarks. Afterward, Reagan's blunders decreased, but they did not disappear entirely. Reagan commented on one occasion that although he was not a scientist, he suspected that the recent Mount St. Helen's volcano in Washington State had "probably released more sulfur dioxide into the atmosphere of the world than has been released in the last ten years of auto driving or things of that kind." The next day the Environmental Protection Agency (EPA) reported its estimate that man-made sulfur dioxide emissions amounted to 81,000 tons a day, while total emissions from the Mount St. Helen's explosion were between 500 and 2,000 tons. Another time, Reagan said that air pollution in Los Angeles had been "substantially controlled," only to have his plane diverted from Los Angeles shortly thereafter because the city was enveloped in some of the worst smog in its history.[9]

In contrast to Reagan, Carter had compiled an impressive record on environmental issues, which he carried into the 1980 campaign. Unlike his opponent—who claimed that "environmental extremists in Washington wouldn't let you build a house unless it looked like a bird's nest"— the president insisted on strict enforcement of EPA regulations, spoke out against sacrificing air or water quality for the sake of economic development, and favored new legislation to clean up chemical dumps. On Capitol Hill his administration was working hard for the passage of legislation that would protect much of the federal wilderness in Alaska. Worried about the world's rapidly growing population, its shrinking resources, and what he believed to be its worsening environment, the president even had the Council on Environmental Quality and the Department of State undertake a comprehensive study of trends in global resources and the environment outside of the United States.

By the middle of October the momentum of the campaign had shifted in Carter's favor. Reagan's own pollsters reported that, for the first time in the race, the president had moved ahead of Reagan (by 2 percentage points) and that in several key states, such as Illinois and Texas, the Republican lead was narrowing. The Reagan camp became concerned that the president might pull an "October surprise" by obtaining the release of the hostages in Iran. As the Republicans were aware, economic sanctions, dwindling financial reserves as a result of cutbacks in oil production, the freezing of Iranian assets in the United States, and Iran's inability to resupply its military were taking a toll. Border skirmishes between Iraq and Iran were also escalating into a major war. Faced with an economic and military crisis, the Tehran government might seek to cast off its image as an international pariah by freeing the hostages.

There was ample reason for Republican apprehension. On 9 September Iran, which was concerned about its growing isolation in the world, let the United States know through the German ambassador in Tehran that it was ready to discuss a resolution of the hostage issue. Having already been disappointed several times, the White House was extremely leery of these new overtures. But, confirming the sincerity of Iran's offer, the Ayatollah Khomeini announced later in September new conditions for a settlement: a pledge by the United States not to interfere in Iran's internal affairs, release of all of Iran's frozen assets, cancellation of all claims by Americans against Iran, and return of the shah's wealth to Iran. Notably absent was an earlier demand that the United States apologize for its past policies toward Iran. Although considerable negotiation was still required on all these points, their presentation offered the best hope yet that an end to the crisis was possible, even imminent.

On 13 September a five-person delegation, headed by Deputy Secretary of State Warren Christopher, left Washington for Bonn, West Germany, to hold exploratory talks with Sadegh Tabatabai, a distant relative of Khomeini's. Tabatabai took back to Iran the United States' detailed but generally positive response to the Ayatollah's recent demands. The outbreak of the Iran-Iraq war stalled negotiations for several weeks, but when Tabatabai was finally able to return to Bonn in October, he brought encouraging news: the U.S. reply to Khomeini's conditions had "fallen on fertile ground."

In mid-October Iranian prime minister Mohammed Ali Rajai came to the United States to present Iran's case against Iraq to the United Nations. Although he declined an invitation to meet with the president, he told a New York press conference that Washington now seemed "ready to cooperate" in resolving the hostage situation. Carter also received word that the hostages, who had been separated into groups following the ill-fated rescue mission in April, had been returned to the U.S. embassy in Tehran and that there seemed to be a consensus among Iranian leaders that it was time to free the American captives.

These developments led to widespread public speculation that the hostages might be released before the election. Carter fed the conjecture by promising during an Ohio campaign speech to thaw Tehran's assets and lift the trade embargo after the hostages were freed. For Reagan, who had earlier assured national security adviser Zbigniew Brzezinski that he would not criticize the administration's Iranian policy, the release of the Americans just before the election would be a political disaster. In private, Republican leaders even accused the president of playing politics with the hostages.[10]

Sensing that the campaign was slipping out of their grasp, Reagan and his advisers reconsidered their refusal to debate the president without John Anderson. All the surveys of public opinion indicated that voters were turning to Carter mainly because of the cogency of the war-and-peace argument and concerns that the Republican nominee was not very smart. There was, however, no groundswell of enthusiasm for the president; rather, many voters supported him simply as the lesser of two evils. If Reagan could dispel his image as a warmongering zealot who lacked the intellect to be president, he stood a good chance of breaking Carter's toehold. The best way to achieve this was to debate Carter one-on-one.

For these very reasons, some of the president's advisers opposed a Carter-Reagan meeting. In particular, Caddell was concerned about Reagan's well-deserved reputation as the "great communicator," a skill that he displayed once more by upstaging the president when they both appeared on 15 October at the annual Alfred E. Smith dinner in New York. "Isn't there any way we can avoid debating him?" Caddell asked Jordan when he learned that Reagan was ready to proceed without Anderson, whose ranking in the polls had fallen below the 15 percent mark required by the League of Women Voters for participation. But Jordan believed that there was no way to dodge the confrontation without doing irreparable harm to Carter's candidacy. The president had been committed to a two-man debate with Reagan for too long to reject it now. Besides, Jordan and most of the president's other advisers were confident that, in a forum pitting the president's superior intellect and mastery of the issues against Reagan's superior showmanship, Carter would prevail.[11]

They were wrong. Strategically, Reagan's decision to debate Carter was the crucial move of the campaign and probably won him the election. The debate was held in Cleveland on 28 October, just one week before election day. During his ninety-minute session with Reagan, Carter handled himself well. Having spent long hours in preparation, Carter projected himself as a deliberate and thoughtful policy maker with a firm grasp of complex issues. Much of the time he was on the attack, emphasizing the substantial differences between himself and his opponent, especially on foreign policy. His one major mistake was to relay a conversation he had had that day with his daughter, Amy; asking Amy what she regarded as today's most important issue, she had responded, "nuclear weaponry and the control of nuclear arms." By seeming to trivialize a serious problem, the president opened himself to ridicule. Some reporters quipped later that if Carter was elected, the country would be run by a teenager. But most political pundits agreed that in terms of debate points, the president had bested his opponent.

In terms of style and image, however, Reagan was the clear winner. Appearing relaxed, reasonable, and informed, and avoiding any obvious mistakes, he effectively undermined the single concern that had propelled Carter into a virtual tie with him in the polls—that he was not up to the job of chief executive. He also came across as warmer than the president and more intimate with the voters, often fending off Carter's jabs with a sorrowful shake of the head followed by "aw, shucks" or "there you go again."

But the masterful stroke of the debate came at the end when Reagan returned to the two issues—the economy and the United States' position in the world—that had surfaced in the polls more often than any others, except for Reagan's own fitness to be president. "Are you better off than you were four years ago?" he asked. "Is it easier for you to go and buy things in the stores than it was four years ago? Is there more or less unemployment in the country . . . ? Is America as respected throughout the world as it was? Do you feel that our security is safe, that we're as strong as we were four years ago?" If the voters answered no, he concluded, "Why then I think your choice is very obvious as to whom you'll vote for."

In all the polls taken after the debate, Reagan was the victor. A *Newsweek* survey of people who had watched the debate showed the Republican beating the president by a margin of 34 percent to 26 percent, with 31 percent calling the event a draw. An ABC News–Harris poll favored Reagan over Carter by an even wider margin, 44 percent to 26 percent. Even Caddell acknowledged that the debate had produced "a pause" in the president's momentum: "It seems basically a wash with maybe a slight edge for Reagan."[12] Reagan's senior adviser, James Baker, had predicted that all the Republican candidate had to do to win the debate was to stay even with the president. But he had done more than that. With seven days remaining in the campaign, he had returned the attention of the American voters back to the issues on which Carter was most vulnerable. Once more the election had become a referendum on the Carter presidency.

During the final days of the race, the Republicans also benefited from a new twist in the hostage crisis. Always anxious about an "October surprise," they had strongly implied that voters should be on guard against political manipulation of the hostage situation. The president seemed to be guilty of precisely that type of gamesmanship when, on the Sunday before election day, he broke off campaigning, returned to Washington, and announced to the American people that the Iranian parliament had set terms for the release of the hostages in what he called a "significant development." In effect, the Iranian legislature had informed the United States through intermediaries that it was now prepared to free the American captives if the United States met the four conditions stated by Khomeini in September.

Carter and his advisers were of two minds in learning of the latest Iranian communication. They understood that the hostages would not be released before the election because provisions such as canceling Iranian debts could take months of negotiations and adjudication. They were also aware that the Republicans had primed the American people so well about a last-minute ploy that publication of the latest dispatch could cause a backlash against the president. Nevertheless, Carter was optimistic that a breakthrough had been made in the hostage crisis that could ultimately bring about the liberation of the Americans. Jordan also felt that a "statesmanlike response" to the Iranians would still constitute "a political plus." On Jordan's advice, the president decided to follow this course. "We are within two days of an important national election," he told the American people. "Let me assure you that my decision on this crucial matter will not be affected by the calendar."[13] Yet the president's eleventh-hour announcement turned many undecided voters against him. They were suspicious of his motives, and his televised message only highlighted his inability to secure the hostages' release earlier. The realization that the long Iranian hostage crisis was still not over also left many Americans with a sense of futility and impotence for which they blamed Carter.

On 4 November a majority of voters expressed their displeasure by rejecting the president's bid for reelection. Reagan received 51 percent of the vote to Carter's 41 percent and Anderson's 7 percent. In terms of electoral votes, Reagan's victory was even more clear-cut: he lost in the District of Columbia but carried every state except Rhode Island, West Virginia, Georgia, Minnesota, Maryland, and Hawaii, for a total of 489 electoral votes to Carter's 49. Reagan's performance in the debate with Carter and the president's final report on the hostage crisis seem to have been decisive. According to an ABC postelection analysis, more than one out of every four voters had settled on a candidate during the last week of the campaign. Of this group, 44 percent voted for Reagan and 38 percent for Carter.[14]

Another reason for Carter's loss was that the voter turnout among several traditional Democratic groups—Catholics, Jews, blacks, union members, and urban dwellers—was significantly lower than it had been four years earlier. Among blacks Carter captured an estimated 80 to 90 percent of the vote, about the same as in 1976, but about 5 percent fewer blacks voted in 1980 than in 1976. Indeed, the voter turnout in 1980 was just over 52 percent of eligible voters—2 percentage points lower than the turnout in 1976 and the lowest since 1948. Many people expressed their disinterest in or dislike of all three candidates by not voting at all.

In thirteen states Anderson received a vote greater than Reagan's margin of victory over Carter, but he appears to have been a spoiler for Carter in only a few states—most notably Massachusetts, New York, and perhaps Connecticut. Had Anderson not run, exit polls nationwide indicated that Carter would have picked up barely half (49 percent) of his votes, while 37 percent would have switched to Reagan. This would not have been enough to change the election's outcome.

Vice President Walter Mondale and a few other members of the Carter entourage had sensed the swing in voter sentiment just before the campaign ended. "What I heard," said Mondale after the election, "was a series of negative, cynical questions suggesting a different public mood. I do not know, something sour happened. The last two days you could cut it with a knife." But only as Carter was returning to Plains after his final day of campaigning did he fully realize that he was going to lose. While on Air Force One he took a message from Caddell, who said that his last poll showed Reagan beating the president by 10 percentage points. "We're losing the undecided voters overwhelmingly," Caddell told him, "and a lot of working Democrats are going to wake up tomorrow and for the first time in their lives vote Republican."[15]

Results of the election stunned political analysts, few of whom had predicted such an unequivocal outcome. The final Gallup poll before the election had placed Reagan ahead of Carter by only 3 points, and the final ABC News–Harris poll had him leading by 5 points. A *Newsweek* poll actually gave the president an edge over the former California governor, 41 percent to 40 percent. As late as the end of October, the president's advisers thought that he had a good chance to win even in California, Reagan's home state. What the pollsters did not foresee was the shift of the undecided vote to Reagan in the closing days of the campaign and the decision of so many loyal Democrats to stay home on election day.[16]

The American electorate's repudiation of Carter and the Democratic Party was overwhelming. The Republicans not only took possession of the White House but also gained control of the Senate for the first time in twenty-eight years, as seven liberal Democrats, including the party's 1972 standard-bearer, George McGovern, went down to defeat. Republicans also picked up thirty-three seats in the House and, on the state level, finished with a net gain of four governorships.

Carter conceded defeat an hour before the polls even closed on the West Coast, even though his staff had warned him that doing so might cause late voters to skip the polls. The president's decision to yield so early in the evening angered Democratic leaders throughout the country, who accused Carter of sabotaging the reelection of several Democratic congressmen. In many ways, this one episode was illustrative of the entire Carter presidency. Throughout his nearly four years in office, Jimmy Carter had remained a political outsider in Washington who acted according to his own instincts of propriety, often irrespective of the counsel of his own advisers and frequently when it defied accepted political practices and placed him at odds with those whose political support he needed.

After his defeat Carter demonstrated that he was still the president for the next ten weeks and that he had an agenda to pursue, regardless of the election results. His most pressing priority, of course, was the release of the hostages. The news from Iran continued to be encouraging, as Khomeini gave permission for the militants holding the Americans to turn them over to the Tehran government. Prime Minister Mohammed Ali Rajai appointed a commission to work out the terms for the hostages' release, using Algeria as Iran's intermediary with Washington.

The negotiations were long and complex. The president did not have the legal power to confiscate and return the shah's wealth in the United States, as Tehran had wanted, nor could he simply sweep away all legal claims against Iran or unfreeze its assets in the United States. Diplomats, financial experts, lawyers, and bankers worked around the clock to overcome these obstacles. By 18 January, two days before Carter would leave office, they had settled on $9 billion in frozen assets as the amount to be transferred to Iran upon the return of the Americans. Having spent most of the last year of his presidency preoccupied with the hostage crisis, Carter had hoped to see their liberation during his term, but he was denied that consolation prize. The Iranians completed their deal only a few minutes after Reagan took the oath of office on 20 January.

A week after the election Congress met in an unusual session to wrap up a number of unfinished matters. In addition to bargaining for the hostages' freedom, Carter busied himself in the remaining weeks of his presidency by lobbying on Capitol Hill for several of his high-priority measures—a youth jobs bill, a superfund to clean up toxic wastes, and an Alaskan lands bill. Determined to keep Democrats in the lame-duck Congress from enacting any last-minute legislation before Reagan assumed office, Republicans in the Senate managed to keep the jobs bill tied up in committee, even though it had passed overwhelmingly in the House and had strong bipartisan support in the upper chamber.

The president had better luck persuading Congress to approve his two pieces of environmental legislation. The first of these established a $1.6 billion toxic waste superfund. A proposal for a superfund had been in the drafting stages since 1977; that year, residents of the Love Canal near Niagara Falls had been forced to abandon their homes after it was learned that they had been built on a former chemical dump and that emissions from the dump were poisoning the area. The measure that lawmakers passed was substantially weaker than the one the president and environmentalists had wanted. In particular, the superfund could not be used to clean up oil spills, only chemical contamination. A number of lawmakers in the House wanted to hold out for a tougher bill that would cover such spills, but the president believed that the Senate would not agree to a stricter and more comprehensive measure and that a watered-down version would be better than no legislation at all. Consequently, Carter made several last-ditch telephone calls to guarantee final House approval.

Passage on 12 November of the Alaskan lands bill represented a more significant victory for the president. The most sweeping proposal of its kind ever approved by Congress, the legislation more than doubled the size of the country's national parks and wildlife refuge system and almost tripled the amount of land designated wilderness. For more than two years Carter had labored to get an Alaskan lands bill through Congress, telling Frank Moore in 1978 to push the measure. But opposition from oil, gas, mineral, and timber interests, from the state government, and from Alaska's two senators, who sought to open the land for development, was strong enough to prevent the legislation from making it onto the Senate floor.[17]

In 1980, however, Carter decided to make the bill his "highest environmental priority." Working closely with Congressman Morris Udall of Arizona and other lawmakers seeking to protect the wilderness, he brought environmentalists from all over the country to the White House in July to kick off the campaign promoting the legislation. To ensure action on the measure and give its backers some leverage against pro-development forces, who hoped to force concessions through delaying tactics, Secretary of the Interior Cecil Andrus withdrew 40 million acres of Alaskan land from development, under authority given to the Interior Department in 1976. Andrus said that he would rescind this withdrawal, which provided even stricter protection of this acreage than the legislation before Congress, when an Alaskan lands bill was approved. He explained his action as an "insurance policy [against] deliberate obstructionism."[18]

The legislation that the House and Senate finally passed after a long and acrimonious struggle did not entirely satisfy the president or the environmentalists, who had never fully appreciated Carter's efforts as an environmental president. Environmental groups were unhappy with the protection afforded calving grounds for caribou and habitats for migratory birds. They disliked a provision allowing seismic exploration of certain parts of Alaska's North Slope, which was believed to hold millions of barrels of oil, and another permitting mining and logging operations in previously forbidden areas until such time as environmentalists and pro-development forces agreed over how much to preserve. But considering the legislation's sweep—it excluded from development 104 million acres, or about one-third of Alaskan lands—it is understandable why Carter termed the legislation "among the most gratifying achievements" of his administration.[19]

Resolving the Iranian hostage crisis and lobbying for his environmental legislation consumed most of Carter's last two months in office. There were also other presidential duties, such as a farewell meeting with Israeli prime minister Menachem Begin, which the president had hoped would be a prelude to another summit between Begin and Egyptian president Anwar Sadat, and the preparation of a budget for fiscal year 1982, which Reagan was almost certain to amend once he took office. Another, more serious matter arose in early December when the Soviets, concerned with the growing Solidarity movement, deployed fifteen or twenty divisions along the Polish border. Carter promptly dispatched a warning to

Soviet leader Leonid Brezhnev not to send forces into Poland, and the divisions were soon moved back.

During his last days in the White House, Carter found time to reflect on his four years in office. Although acknowledging that he had made mistakes as president, he attributed his defeat not to these errors but to his willingness to tackle difficult and politically risky issues, ranging from the Middle East crisis to the energy crisis. When asked by a group of reporters how he thought history would judge him, he answered, "I don't know yet," and then went on to list some of his achievements as president—interestingly, all of them in the international realm. "I think, in general," he told them, "that the opening of access into Africa, the normalization of relations with China, the Middle East peace effort, the maintaining of our nation's peace—in international affairs [history] will look on us well."

There can be no gainsaying the truth of what the president said about the problems he confronted and his accomplishments while in office. To his list of international achievements could be added significant domestic accomplishments in such areas as energy and environmental policy; tax, civil-service, and Social Security reform; deregulation; and the inclusion of minorities and women at the highest levels of government and on the federal bench. The empathy that Carter had for the underprivileged, the unorganized, and the underrepresented in government, and his efforts to deal with their special needs and interests, is another aspect of his administration that should not be ignored. They were the flip side of his distaste for the special interests that he always believed were too influential in the halls of Congress and elsewhere in Washington.

Carter had become president, furthermore, at the end of forty years of liberal hegemony over the nation's politics and social values—a time during which government had been viewed by Americans as an agency of reform and advancement. Even so, there had always been a significant element of Americans, including the majority of southern Democrats, who remained suspicious of control from Washington, who feared the tentacles of federal intrusion into their personal affairs, and for whom social and cultural concerns were more important than progress measured largely in economic terms. For a variety of reasons, these views were becoming ascendant at the time Carter was elected president, even though the Democratic Party remained largely controlled by remnants of the New Deal coalition.

It was Carter's fate to attempt to navigate the nation between the rock of traditional Democratic constituencies and the hard place of an emerging conservative movement whose emphasis was more on social and cultural values than on the economic concerns of the Democratic Party. It was also Carter's misfortune that he led the nation at a time of staggering inflation and growing unemployment, compounded by an oil shock over which he had little control. What is often forgotten is that for much of his administration the economy actually grew at a healthy rate. Carter had the bad luck, furthermore, of governing at a time when decades of ill-conceived policy in the Middle East, which had resulted in neglect of the Palestinian question and dependence on Iran as a pillar of stability, came back to haunt the United States.

Clearly, it would have taken a leader of consummate political skills and an unerring sense of direction to have led his party and his nation successfully through the dangerous shoals before him. Unfortunately, Carter was not that leader. Sadly, he might have been. As we have argued in this book, the elements of a coherent program that might have provided the outsider from Georgia with a base of support to make his a successful transitional presidency were inherent in who he was and what he said and did. He won the presidency by speaking out against the failures of Washington and promising new approaches to government. He came to Washington as a moralist who believed in humane government. As president, he was committed to and spoke out in favor of family values, social justice, smaller but smarter government, a sense of community, federal-local and public-private partnerships, fiscal responsibility, and personal responsibility. He embraced these values in his approach to programs ranging from urban reform to welfare reform and national health insurance. He was determined and even aggressive in pursuing his goals.

At the same time, it is hard to avoid the conclusion that Carter's was a mediocre presidency and that this was largely his own doing. He was smart rather than shrewd. He was not a careful political planner. He suffered from strategic myopia. He was long on good intentions but short on know-how. He had lofty ideals, such as in the area of human rights, which had symbolic and even lasting importance, but they often blinded him to political realities. He was self-righteous. He was an administrator who micromanaged, but not well. Most important, he was a president who never adequately defined a mission for his government, a purpose for the country, and a way to get there. This was not a formula for a successful presidency.

14

★ ★ ★ ★ ★

EPILOGUE

Immediately after the inauguration of Ronald Reagan as the nation's new chief executive on 20 January 1981, Carter, Rosalynn, and Amy returned to Plains. The next day, at Reagan's invitation, Carter flew to Wiesbaden, Germany, to welcome back to freedom the Iranian hostages. It was an exhilarating moment for Carter, but it was followed by a difficult period of transition from president to private citizen. Carter had not recovered fully from the shock of his defeat, particularly the dimension of Reagan's victory. He was also faced with personal financial problems. Before taking office in 1977 he had put his assets into a blind trust, only to discover as he was about to leave office that his principal asset, the Carter peanut warehouse business, was $1 million in debt. For Rosalynn, the return to Plains was even more traumatic. "There was no way I could understand our defeat," she later wrote. "It didn't seem fair that everything we had hoped for, all our plans and dreams for the country could have been gone when the votes were counted on election day."[1]

After a few months, however, the Carters settled into a new routine. They fixed up their home, which had not been occupied in ten years; sold the warehouse business, but kept about 2,000 acres of family land outside of Plains; and signed lucrative book contracts, thereby ensuring their financial security. They sent Amy, who had grown up in Atlanta and Washington, D.C., and had never really lived in Plains, to a private boarding school in Atlanta.[2]

In forced retirement, the former president defended his apolitical approach to the presidency—that is, making tough decisions regardless of their political consequences. In a 1984 interview with Tom Wicker of the

New York Times, he remarked, "No way could I [have done] it differently."³ But he spent most of his time writing his memoirs, teaching at
Emory University, and raising funds for the Jimmy Carter Library, Mu-
seum, and Presidential Center in Atlanta. Determined that the Carter
complex would be more than a monument to his presidency, Carter envi-
sioned the center as an institution performing vital public service—a
place where disputes between nations could be mediated in a nongovern-
mental and academic setting, and where experts from various walks of
life could come together to discuss and even take action on such important world issues as nuclear arms control, human rights, the environment,
world hunger, and health care. Since opening in 1986 the Carter Presidential Center has become a locus of research and social and political activism for all these problems and more. The former president has been
intimately involved with these endeavors, promoting improved agricultural methods and better health care in the world's most poverty-stricken
countries, especially in Africa.

Although the programs of the Carter Center remain a major part of
Carter's life, they have not been his only commitment. Beginning with a
bus trip in 1984 to the Lower East Side of New York to help renovate a di-
lapidated building, he and Rosalynn have been very active in Habitat for
Humanity, a charitable organization founded in 1973 to provide housing
for the poor. The former president has often been seen swinging a hammer at construction sites in New York, Philadelphia, and Chicago, and he
has raised large sums of money in support of Habitat's work.

Carter's desire to help the poor, stop the spread of disease, support
human rights, and bring about world peace led him to travel around the
world. In doing so, he demonstrated a determination—just as he did as
president—to speak out and act in support of what he believed was right,
even when it met with disapproval at home or abroad. In the early 1980s
he criticized President Ronald Reagan's administration for its military
buildup, depicting the sitting president as a warmonger. He denounced
Reagan's policy of "constructive engagement" with South Africa, by
which the administration kept close ties with that nation despite its adherence to apartheid. Such a policy was "a disaster," Carter said, "because of the general presumption of the world that [it] in effect means
approval [of apartheid]." In 1983 and again in 1987 he traveled to the
Middle East, where he held consultations with the leaders of Israel, Saudi
Arabia, and Jordan and the head of the Palestine Liberation Organization,
Yasir Arafat, to discuss regional peace. Simultaneously, he denounced the
Reagan administration, accusing it of being opposed to a mediated Middle East settlement. In 1986 he and his wife went to Central America,
where he held talks with the Sandinista leadership in Nicaragua.⁴

Despite his activities abroad and at home, Carter was generally held in low esteem during the first half of the 1980s. Reagan's success in getting his budget, tax cuts, and military spending increases through Congress seemed to highlight Carter's ineptitude as the nation's chief executive and to prove what Carter's critics had said—that the nation was governable if the right leader was at the helm. Accordingly, the media saw little reason to give him much attention. Even his own party distanced itself from him. Walter Mondale, who ran as the Democratic candidate for president in 1984, did not seek his former boss's endorsement. Although the former president was asked to speak at the Democratic National Convention, the party was not enthusiastic, believing that Carter's reputation would damage Mondale's chances. Indeed, his speech received little media coverage.[5]

Carter's reputation, however, began to show signs of rehabilitation starting in the second half of the 1980s. While he was excoriated by Reagan's supporters for challenging the president's policies, Americans praised him for his work with Habitat for Humanity and for his world health initiatives. His 1986 trip to Central America received widespread media coverage and praise from opponents of Reagan's Nicaragua policy.[6] Members of the Democratic Party began to court him. When Senator Joseph Biden of Delaware ran for the presidency in 1988, he sought the former president's endorsement.[7] Between 1989 and 1991 Carter and other Carter Center officials monitored elections in Panama, Nicaragua, the Dominican Republic, Zambia, and Haiti. Even Carter's critics conceded that he was turning into one of the nation's great —if not its greatest—ex–chief executive. The *Nation* magazine commented, "It is as if Carter had decided to take the most liberal and successful policies of his failed administration—human rights, peacemaking, and concern for the poor—and make them the centerpiece of a campaign for his own political resurrection."[8]

Even so, Carter remained a lightning rod for controversy. His belief that courting Arafat was key to achieving peace in the Middle East, his declarations that Israel was an impediment to peace in the region, and his opposition to the use of force in the Persian Gulf in 1990–1991 were widely criticized. Furthermore, many Americans had not forgotten his record as president. Among them was the victor of the 1992 election and a fellow Democrat, Bill Clinton. Clinton had held a grudge against Carter since 1980, when the latter had sent 18,000 Cuban refugees from the Mariel boatlift to Arkansas, many of them criminals or mentally ill. Arkansas governor Clinton, who was seeking reelection, and Arkansas voters were not pleased, and when Clinton learned that Carter planned to send more refugees to the state, he became furious with the White House. He later blamed Carter for his failure to win reelection.

Former president Carter presented the Clinton White House with difficult choices. Although Clinton disliked Carter personally and believed that he sometimes acted recklessly in carrying out his global agenda, the president also recognized that Carter's growing reputation as a man of peace could be used to defuse world crises. On several occasions, therefore, President Clinton sent Carter on missions abroad or gave his unofficial approval to one of Carter's undertakings overseas. In 1994, for example, Carter went to North Korea to try to reduce recently increased tensions on the peninsula caused by North Korea's efforts to develop nuclear weapons. The former president reached an agreement with North Korean president Kim Il-sung under which his country would freeze its nuclear program in return for American light-water reactors. But when Carter announced the agreement on Cable News Network (CNN), the White House became incensed, believing that Carter had undermined the possibility of using other options, such as sanctions, to get the North Koreans to continue negotiations. When Carter returned from North Korea, Clinton refused to meet with him, assigning his chief foreign policy adviser, Anthony Lake, and assistant secretary of state for political-military affairs, Robert L. Gallucci, to debrief Carter. "To put it mildly," Gallucci later stated, "it was not a pleasant exchange." There was also substantial criticism of Carter's mission to North Korea in the media, particularly from the political Right. Conservative columnist George Will commented, for example, that Carter's mission was "a reminder of how important and good the 1980 election was."[9]

Carter's missions to Haiti and the former Yugoslavia in 1994–1995 also created a storm of media controversy. In Haiti, the former president was able to restore to power President Jean-Bertrand Aristide, who had been elected in 1990 but overthrown in a military coup in 1991. Yet Carter undid much of the credit he received for that successful mission when he went on CNN and defended the leader of the outgoing junta and criticized the sanctions the Bush and Clinton administrations had imposed on the Haitian military government. White House officials accused him of "glory-hogging on CNN"; even Carter's attorney, Terrence Adamson, advised the former president to stop giving interviews, telling Carter that he "was talking away his accomplishment."[10] In the former Yugoslavia, Carter succeeded in arranging a cease-fire between warring Serbs and Muslims. But his willingness to meet with Radovan Karadzic, a Serbian warlord accused of the ethnic cleansing of Muslims, prompted the *New Republic* to declare that the former president "provides tyrants with the thing that tyranny cannot provide, which is legitimacy."[11] The Clinton administration, fearful of being accused of having Carter do its dirty work, and doubtful that Carter's cease-fire would be any more effective than nearly a dozen previous ones, kept its distance from him.

Carter has not allowed such criticisms or brush-offs to stop him from promoting his agenda. In 1995 he traveled to Rwanda to try to end a tribal

conflict between Tutsi and Hutu tribesmen. The following year he jour-
neyed to Jerusalem to monitor the Palestinian elections. In 2002 he went
to Cuba and met with Fidel Castro, becoming the first U.S. president to go
to that island since Castro seized power in 1959. That same year he won
the Nobel Peace Prize for his activities in support of world peace.

In 2003 the former president condemned President George W. Bush's
decision to launch a war against Iraq, declaring that that nation posed no
threat to the United States and that invading Iraq would destabilize the
Middle East. In 2005 he called on the Bush administration to close down
the prison at Guantanamo Bay, Cuba, contending that charges of prisoner
abuse at the facility were damaging the United States' reputation. Later
that year he published *Our Endangered Values: America's Moral Crisis,* an
attack on the fundamentalist Christian Right for abandoning the humane
values of Christianity in order to advance its own narrow political and
fundamentalist agenda.[12]

Carter's critics continue to assail him, stating that he is too willing to
cozy up to dictators and too unwilling to use force when necessary. In a
critical review of *Our Endangered Values,* Bret Stephens of the *Wall Street
Journal* remarked, "Bill Clinton may have the heart of the Democratic
Party, but Mr. Carter captures the Zeitgeist of the global left."[13] Yet his
reputation has continued to grow. *Our Endangered Values* reached number
one on the *New York Times'* best-seller list. An NBC–*Wall Street Journal* poll
ranked Carter "as having the highest moral character of any president,
with 67 percent [of the respondents] giving him 'very high' marks."[14]

The fact that Carter continues to gain the attention and respect of the
American public, despite his sometimes controversial views, may speak
to what Americans have come to value about, and even expect from, their
former presidents. If this is so—if future presidents will be evaluated not
only in terms of what they did in office but also in terms of how they used
their position as former presidents after leaving the White House—then
Carter's own career as an ex-president may well be his greatest legacy to
the nation.

NOTES

This study follows the practice of other volumes in the American Presidency Series of limiting citations mainly to quotations. Undocumented remarks by President Jimmy Carter come from *Public Papers of the Presidents of the United States: Jimmy Carter*, 9 vols. (Washington, D.C.: Government Printing Office, 1977–1982). Polls and surveys are from the news media, mainly *Time, Newsweek, U.S. News and World Report*, and the *New York Times*. The primary and secondary literature on which this work is based can be found in the bibliographical essay.

PREFACE TO THE SECOND EDITION

1. See, for example, Joseph J. Ellis, *His Excellency: George Washington* (New York: Knopf, 2004); David Hackett Fischer, *Washington's Crossing* (New York: Oxford University Press, 2004); David McCullough, *John Adams* (New York: Simon and Schuster, 2002); Gore Vidal, *Inventing a Nation: Washington, Adams, Jefferson* (New Haven, CT: Yale University Press, 2003); Joshua Wolf Shank, *Lincoln's Melancholy: How Depression Challenged a President and Fueled His Greatness* (New York: Houghton Mifflin, 2005); Doris Kearns Goodwin, *Team of Rivals: The Political Genius of Abraham Lincoln* (New York: Simon and Schuster, 2005); Robert Dallek, *An Unfinished Life: John F. Kennedy, 1917–1963* (Boston: Little, Brown, 2003); Robert Dallek, *Flawed Giant: Lyndon Johnson and His Times, 1961–1973* (New York: Oxford University Press, 1998); Robert A. Caro, *Master of the Senate: The Years of Lyndon Johnson* (New York: Knopf, 2002).

2. Lewis L. Gould, *The Modern American Presidency* (Lawrence: University Press of Kansas, 2003); Robert Dallek, *Hail to the Chief: The Making and Unmaking of American Presidents* (New York: Hyperion, 1996); Fred Greenstein, *The Presidential Difference: Leadership Style from FDR to George W. Bush*, 2nd ed. (Princeton, NJ:

Princeton University Press, 2004); Stephen Graubard, *Command of Office: How War, Secrecy, and Deception Transformed the Presidency from Theodore Roosevelt to George W. Bush* (New York: Basic Books, 2004); Eric Alterman, *When Presidents Lie: A History of Official Deception and Its Consequences* (New York: Viking, 2004); Bob Woodward, *Shadow: Five Presidents and the Legacy of Watergate* (New York: Simon and Schuster, 1999); E. J. Dionne Jr., *Why Americans Hate Politics* (New York: Simon and Schuster, 1991); David Gergen, *Eyewitness to Power: The Essence of Leadership: Nixon to Clinton* (New York: Simon and Schuster, 2000); Stephen Skowronek, *The Politics Presidents Make: Leadership from John Adams to George Bush* (Boston: Harvard University Press, 1993).

3. Skowronek, *The Politics Presidents Make*, p. 381.

4. Bruce J. Schulman, *The Seventies: The Great Shift in American Culture, Society, and Politics* (Cambridge, MA: Da Capo Press, 2001).

5. Dionne, *Why Americans Hate Politics*, p. 142.

CHAPTER 1: WHAT MAKES JIMMY RUN?

1. Jimmy Carter, *An Hour before Daylight: Memories of a Rural Boyhood* (New York: Touchstone, 2001), p. 96.

2. Ibid., p. 230.

3. Jimmy Carter, *Why Not the Best?* (Nashville, TN: Broadman Press, 1975), p. 8.

4. Carter to Rickover, 11 August 1976, Box 1, Presidential Papers of Jimmy Carter, Staff Offices, Office of Staff Secretary, Handwriting File, Jimmy Carter Library, Atlanta, GA. See also Francis Duncan, *Rickover: The Struggle for Excellence* (Annapolis, MD: Naval Institute Press, 2001), pp. 257–261.

5. Carter, *Why Not the Best?* p. 57.

6. Ibid., p. 60.

7. Ibid.

8. Jimmy Carter, *Turning Point: A Candidate, a State, and a Nation Come of Age* (New York: Times Books, 1992), p. 43.

9. Ibid., p. xxiv.

10. *Time*, 31 May 1971, pp. 14–20.

11. Hugh Carter, *Cousin Beedie and Cousin Hot: My Life with the Carter Family of Plains, Georgia* (Englewood Cliffs, NJ: Prentice-Hall, 1978), p. 112.

12. Cited in Kandy Stroud, *How Jimmy Won: The Victory Campaign from Plains to the White House* (New York: William Morrow, 1977), pp. 185–187.

13. Carter, *Why Not the Best?* p. 141.

14. *Time*, 22 March 1976, pp. 8–10.

15. *Time*, 19 April 1976, pp. 14–16.

16. Cited in Stroud, *How Jimmy Won*, pp. 277–281; *Time*, 26 April 1976, p. 16.

17. "Campaign Plan—Final Copy," n.d., Box 13, Michael Raoul Duval Papers, Gerald Ford Library, Ann Arbor, MI.

18. Cited in David F. Hahn, "The Rhetoric of Jimmy Carter," *Presidential Studies Quarterly* 14 (April 1984): 273.

19. Memorandum from Bailey to Cheney and Tetter, 30 September 1976, Box 1, Special Files, Gerald Ford Papers, Gerald Ford Library.

20. "The Foreign Policy Debate," 3 October 1976, Box 2, Special Files, Ford Papers.

21. Ibid.

22. "The Public Response to Gerald Ford's Statement on Eastern Europe during the Second Debate," May 1977, Box 62, Robert Teeter Papers, Gerald Ford Library.

CHAPTER 2: TRANSITION AND HONEYMOON

1. Ernest S. Griffith, *The American Presidency: The Dilemma of Shared Power and Divided Government* (New York: New York University Press, 1976), pp. v–vii, 1–15, 221–225.

2. Thomas E. Cronin, *The State of the Presidency* (Boston: Little Brown, 1975), esp. pp. 6–10.

3. Bruce J. Schulman. *The Seventies: The Great Shift in American Culture, Society, and Politics* (Cambridge, MA: Da Capo Press), pp. xi–xvii, 4–20.

4. Lewis L. Gould, *The Modern American Presidency* (Lawrence: University Press of Kansas, 2003), pp. xiii, 173, 181.

5. *New Republic*, 27 January 1979, pp. 16–18.

6. Cronin, *State of the Presidency*, p. 25. For a similar verdict, see also Griffith, *American Presidency*, p. 208.

7. Nelson W. Polsby, *Consequences of Party Reform* (New York: Oxford University Press, 1983), p. 113.

8. Patrick Caddell, "Initial Paper on Political Strategy," November 1976, Box 4, Jody Powell Papers, Jimmy Carter Library, Atlanta, GA.

9. Memorandum from Schultze to Economic Policy Group, 18 January 1977, Box 192, Stuart Eizenstat Papers, Jimmy Carter Library.

10. Stephen Hess, "First Impressions: A Look Back at Five Transitions," *Brookings Review* 19 (July 2005): 28–31. See also Memorandum for President-elect Carter from Stephen Hess, 22 November 1976, Box 1, Presidential Papers of Jimmy Carter, Staff Offices, Office of Staff Secretary, Handwriting File, Jimmy Carter Library, Atlanta, GA (hereafter cited as PHWF).

11. Carter Presidency Project, Oral Interview with Charles Kirbo, 5 January 1983, pp. 16–17, Jimmy Carter Library.

12. Ibid., pp. 17–18.

13. Carter Presidency Project, Oral Interview with Jimmy Carter, 29 November 1982, p. 8, Jimmy Carter Library.

14. "Attorney General," n.d., Box 8, Hamilton Jordan Papers, Jimmy Carter Library.

15. Jimmy Carter, *Keeping Faith: Memoirs of a President* (New York: Bantam Books, 1982), p. 65.

16. Memorandum for President Carter from Stu Eizenstat, 24 January 1977, Box 4, PHWF.

17. Carter, *Keeping Faith*, pp. 73–74.

18. *Time*, 24 January 1977, p. 45.

19. *Newsweek*, 18 April 1977, pp. 85–86.

20. Carter's handwritten comments are in the margin of Memorandum for the President from Eizenstat, 18 June 1977, Box 42, Powell Papers.

21. Thomas P. O'Neill with William Novak, *Man of the House: The Life and Political Memoirs of Speaker Tip O'Neill* (New York: Random House, 1987), p. 302.

22. Rich Hutcheson to the President, 23 January 1977, Box 51, Jordan Papers; *Time*, 31 January 1977, pp. 20–21.

23. *Time*, 7 February 1977, p. 19.

24. Carter to Eizenstat, 15 April 1977, Box 315, Eizenstat Papers.

25. *Congressional Quarterly Almanac* 33 (1977): 95–96.

26. Memorandum for the President-elect from Fritz Mondale, n.d., Box 6, Powell Papers.

27. Memorandum for the President from Greg Schneiders, 8 March 1977, Box 12, PHWF.

28. *Time*, 24 January 1977, pp. 8–13.

29. Carter's handwritten comment is in Memorandum for the President from Stu Eizenstat, 1 February 1977, Box 5, PHWF.

30. Rickover to the President, 12 April 1977, Box 17, PHWF.

31. *Newsweek*, 2 May 1977, pp. 16–18.

32. Memorandum for the President from Hamilton Jordan, 29 March 1977, Box 55, Jordan Papers (emphasis in original).

33. *Newsweek*, 2 May 1977, p. 39.

34. Carter Presidency Project, Oral Interview with Jimmy Carter, 29 November 1982, p. 22.

35. Carter Presidency Project, Oral Interview with T. Bertram Lance with Peter Petkas, 12 May 1982, p. 12, Jimmy Carter Library.

CHAPTER 3: MORALITY AND FOREIGN POLICY

1. Zbigniew Brzezinski, *Power and Principle: Memoirs of the National Security Adviser, 1977–1981* (New York: Farrar, Straus, Giroux, 1983), p. 5; Lawrence X. Clifford, "An Examination of the Carter Administration's Selection of the Secretary of State and National Security Adviser," in *Jimmy Carter: Foreign Policy and Post-Presidential Years*, ed. Herbert D. Rosenbaum and Alexej Ugrinsky (Westport, CT: Greenwood, 1994), p. 6.

2. *The Presidential Campaign 1976*, 3 vols. (Washington, DC: Government Printing Office, 1978), 1:110, 245–246; 3:97.

3. Ibid., 1:83–84, 712–714, 1043–1044.

4. Ibid., pp. 39–42.

5. J. C. to Zbig, 14 February 1977, Box 58, Jordan Papers; J. C. to Zbig, Jack, Rick, 21 February 1977, Box FG-25, Presidential Papers of Jimmy Carter, White House Central Files, Jimmy Carter Library, Atlanta, GA (hereafter cited as WHCF).

6. *Public Papers of the Presidents of the United States, Jimmy Carter, 1977* (Washington, DC: Government Printing Office, 1977), p. 2.

7. *New York Times*, 1 February 1977, p. A1.

8. Qingshan Tan, *U.S. China Policy: From Normalization to the Post–Cold War Era* (Boulder, CO: Lynne Rienner, 1992), p. 26.

9. Lake to The Secretary, 16 January 1978, Box HU-1, WHCF.

10. Caleb Rossiter with Anne-Marie Smith, "Human Rights: The Carter Record, the Reagan Reaction," *International Policy Report*, September 1984, pp. 6–18.

11. Memorandum for the President from Jody Powell, 21 February 1977, Box 208, Stuart Eizenstat Papers, Jimmy Carter Library.

12. *Time*, 30 February 1977, p. 38.

13. Cyrus Vance, *Hard Choices: Critical Years in American Foreign Policy* (New York: Simon and Schuster, 1983), p. 51.

14. Telegram No. 127, "Record of the Conversation with A. Harriman," 1 December 1976; "Record of the Conversation with the U.S. Secretary of State," 14 February 1977, Box 117; Memorandum of Conversation, 1 February 1977, Box 116, Vertical File; Brezhnev to Carter, 25 February 1977; Carter to Brezhnev, 4 March 1977; and Brezhnev to Carter, 15 March 1977, Box 17, Plains File, Subject File, WHCF.

15. Interview with Jimmy Carter, 29 November 1982, pp. 55–56, Miller Center, University of Virginia.

16. *Presidential Campaign 1976*, 3:113.

17. Ibid.

18. Richard H. Curtiss, *A Changing Image: American Perceptions of the Arab-Israeli Dispute* (Washington, DC: American Educational Trust, 1982), pp. 105–106.

19. "Work Plan: Middle East," n.d., Box 34, Jordan Papers (emphasis in original).

20. *Time*, 30 May 1977, p. 22.

21. Jimmy Carter, *Keeping Faith: Memoirs of a President* (New York: Bantam Books, 1982), p. 288.

22. Vance, *Hard Choices*, pp. 128–130.

23. Brzezinski to the President, 21 July 1977, Box 43, National Security Affairs, Brzezinski Material, Country File, Box 43, Jimmy Carter Library.

24. "Letter from Washington," *New Yorker*, 22 July 1977, p. 58.

25. Helmut Schmidt, *Men and Powers: A Political Retrospective*, trans. Ruth Hein (New York: Random House, 1989), p. 187.

26. Brzezinski, *Power and Principle*, p. 134.

27. "Discussant: William B. Quandt," in Rosenbaum and Ugrinsky, *Jimmy Carter*, pp. 61–62.

28. *Time*, 8 August 1977, pp. 8–23.

CHAPTER 4: THE DOG DAYS OF SUMMER AND FALL

1. Memorandum for the President from Stu Eizenstat, 20 June 1977, Box 315, Stuart Eizenstat Papers, Jimmy Carter Library, Atlanta, GA.

2. Memorandum for the President from Charles Schultze, 23 June 1977, Box 194, Eizenstat Papers.

3. Quoted in Charles E. Walcott and Karen M. Hult, "White House Staff Size: Explanations and Implications," *Presidential Studies Quarterly* 29 (September 1999): 644.

4. To Schultze from JC, 30 March 1977, Box 15, Presidential Papers of Jimmy

Carter, Staff Offices, Office of Staff Secretary, Handwriting File, Jimmy Carter Library (hereafter cited as PHWF).

5. Joseph A. Califano Jr., *Governing America: An Insider's Report from the White House and the Cabinet* (New York: Simon and Schuster, 1981), pp. 329–330.

6. Memorandum for the President from Joe Califano, 11 April 1977, attached to Memorandum for the President from Jack Watson, 15 April 1977, Box 60, Hamilton Jordan Papers, Jimmy Carter Library.

7. Califano, *Governing America*, pp. 336–337.

8. Memorandum for the President from Hamilton Jordan, n.d., Box 37, Jordan Papers.

9. See Carter's marginal comments on Memorandum to the President from Jack Watson and Jim Parham, 23 May 1977, attached to Rick Hutcheson to Jim Parham et al., 25 May 1977, Box 27, PHWF.

10. Memorandum to Jimmy Carter from Hamilton Jordan, n.d., Box 34, Jordan Papers (emphasis in original).

11. Handwritten memo from Carter to Bergland, 9 September 1977, Box 48, PHWF. See also Memorandum for the President from Bert Lance, Charles Schultze, and Stu Eizenstat, 7 September 1977, Jordan Papers.

12. Thomas P. O'Neill with William Novak, *Man of the House: The Life and Political Memoirs of Speaker Tip O'Neill* (New York: Random House, 1987), pp. 320–323.

13. Memorandum for the President from Stu Eizenstat and Bob Ginsburg, 16 May 1977 (emphasis in original); Memorandum for the President from Jim Fallows, 6 June 1977, Box 287, Eizenstat Papers.

14. Memorandum for the President from Charles Schultze, 15 October 1977, Box BE-4, Presidential Papers of Jimmy Carter, White House Central Files, Jimmy Carter Library.

15. Bert Lance with Bill Gilbert, *The Truth of the Matter: My Life in and out of Politics* (New York: Summit Books, 1991), pp. 130–136; Jimmy Carter, *Keeping Faith: Memoirs of a President* (New York: Bantam Books, 1982), p. 130.

16. *New Yorker*, 12 September 1977, pp. 130–136.

17. Ribicoff to the President, 3 September 1977, and enclosure attached to Memorandum for President Carter from Frank Moore, 3 September 1977, Box 31, Staff Offices, Robert J. Lipshutz, Presidential Papers of Jimmy Carter, Jimmy Carter Library (hereafter cited as Lipshutz Papers).

18. Memorandum for the President from Robert Lipshutz, 6 September 1977, Box 31, Lipshutz Papers.

19. Carter, *Keeping Faith*, p. 132.

20. Lance, *The Truth of the Matter*, pp. 139–141; *Newsweek*, 26 September 1977, pp. 20–31.

21. Carter, *Keeping Faith*, pp. 133–134.

22. Ibid., pp. 134–136; Lance, *The Truth of the Matter*, pp. 148–151.

23. Carter Presidency Project, Oral Interview with T. Bertram Lance with Peter Petkas, 12 May 1982, p. 23, Jimmy Carter Library.

24. "Summary of Issue Concerns of the American People," 12 September 1977, Box 33, Jordan Papers; *Time*, 22 August 1977, p. 28; *National Review*, 2 September 1977, p. 978.

25. Richard E. Neustadt, *Presidential Power: The Politics of Leadership with Reflections on Johnson and Nixon* (New York: Wiley, 1976), pp. 101–125.

26. Dan Glickman to President Jimmy Carter, 16 March 1977, attached to Memorandum for the President from Frank Moore, 28 March 1977, Box 14, PHWF.

27. Robert Mann, *Legacy to Power: Senator Russell Long of Louisiana* (New York: Paragon House, 1992), p. 368.

28. Memorandum for the President from Frank Moore, 26 July 1977, Box 41, PHWF.

29. Carter Presidency Project, Interview with Al McDonald (including Michael Rowny), 13–14 March 1981, p. 16, Miller Center Interviews, Jimmy Carter Library.

30. Carter to Jim Schlesinger, 29 March 1977, Box 14, PHWF.

CHAPTER 5: CAN CARTER COPE?

1. Memorandum to Robert Lipshutz and Stuart Eizenstat from Joyce R. Starr, Box 208, Stuart Eizenstat Papers, Jimmy Carter Library, Atlanta, GA; Douglas J. Bennett Jr. to Honorable E. de la Garza, 15 March 1978, and attachment, Box "Andrew Young," Name File, Presidential Papers of Jimmy Carter, White House Central Files, Jimmy Carter Library.

2. Quoted in Vicki Kemper, "A Citizen for all Seasons," *Common Cause Magazine*, Spring 1995, p. 7.

3. Exit Interview with Esther Peterson, 5 January 1981, pp. 6–10, Jimmy Carter Library.

4. Memorandum for the President, Secretary Schlesinger, and Frank Moore, 23 December 1977, Box 198, Eizenstat Papers.

5. Memorandum for Bob Lipshutz and Stu Eizenstat from Doug Huron, 2 September 1977, Box 120, Staff Offices, Counsel Margaret McKenna, Presidential Papers of Jimmy Carter, Jimmy Carter Library. See also Memorandum for the President from Stu Eizenstat and Bob Lipshutz, 6 September 1977, Box 33, Hamilton Jordan Papers, Jimmy Carter Library.

6. Memorandum for the President from Stu Eizenstat and Bob Lipshutz, 6 September 1977, Box 33, Jordan Papers; Griffin B. Bell with Ronald J. Ostrow, *Taking Care of the Law* (New York: William Morrow, 1982), pp. 29–30.

7. Joseph A. Califano Jr., *Governing America: An Insider's Report from the White House and the Cabinet* (New York: Simon and Schuster, 1981), pp. 235–238.

8. Memorandum for the President and Vice-President from Bob Lipshutz and Stu Eizenstat, 16 September 1977, Box 33, Jordan Papers.

9. Califano, *Governing America*, p. 243; Bell, *Taking Care of the Law*, p. 24.

10. Memorandum to President Carter from Hamilton Jordan, [September 1977], Box 33, Jordan Papers. See also H. J. to President, n.d., attached to Memorandum for the President from Stu Eizenstat, 9 September 1977, Box 50, Presidential Papers of Jimmy Carter, Staff Offices, Office of Staff Secretary, Handwriting File, Jimmy Carter Library.

11. Minutes of the Cabinet Meeting, 16 January 1978, Box 159, Eizenstat Papers.

12. Jimmy Carter to Pat Harris et al., 7 October 1977, Box 301, Eizenstat Papers.

13. Memorandum for the President from Stu Eizenstat, 20 January 1978, Box 309, Eizenstat Papers.

14. *New York Times*, 18 December 1977, p. 47; Memorandum for the President from James T. McIntyre Jr., 20 December 1977, Box 152, Eizenstat Papers.

15. *Time*, 12 December 1977, pp. 12–16.

16. *Business Week*, 16 January 1978, pp. 28–29. See also W. Carl Biven, *Jimmy Carter's Economy: Policy in an Age of Limits* (Chapel Hill: University of North Carolina Press, 2002), pp. 113–121.

17. Memorandum to the President from Hamilton Jordan, 14 December 1977, Box 34, Jordan Papers.

18. To the Baron Report from Peter D. Hart, n.d., attached to Memorandum for the President from the Vice-President, 20 March 1978, Box 44, Jordan Papers.

19. Memorandum to the President from Hamilton Jordan and Jack Watson, 14 February 1978, Box 9, Staff Offices, Robert J. Lipshutz, Presidential Papers of Jimmy Carter, Jimmy Carter Library.

20. *New York Times*, 7 March 1978, p. 35; *Time*, 3 April 1977, p. 26.

21. *Business Week*, 23 January 1978, pp. 90–91, and 6 February 1978, p. 39; *Newsweek*, 30 January 1978, pp. 23–25.

22. Memorandum for the President from W. Michael Blumenthal and Charlie Schultze, 15 March 1978, Box 144, Eizenstat Papers.

23. Memorandum to President Carter from Hamilton Jordan, 22 March 1978, Box 56, Jordan Papers.

24. Memorandum for the President from Charles Schultze, 8 April 1978, Box 53, Staff Offices, Council of Economic Advisers, Presidential Papers of Jimmy Carter, Jimmy Carter Library.

CHAPTER 6: THE YEAR OF NEGOTIATIONS

1. *Newsweek*, 16 January 1978, pp. 40–47.

2. Zbigniew Brzezinski, *Power and Principle: Memoirs of the National Security Adviser, 1977–1981* (New York: Farrar, Straus, Giroux, 1985), pp. 235–236.

3. Jimmy Carter, *Keeping Faith: Memoirs of a President* (New York: Bantam Books, 1982), p. 318.

4. Brzezinski, *Power and Principle*, 246; Moshe Dayan, *Breakthrough: A Personal Account of the Egyptian-Israeli Negotiations* (New York: Knopf, 1981), p. 123.

5. Memorandum for the President from Zbigniew Brzezinski, 21 October 1980; Memorandum for Jody Powell, Pat Caddell, and Jerry Rafshoon from Al McDonald, 22 October 1980; Memorandum for Al McDonald and David Rubenstein from Jody Powell, 22 October 1980, Box 8, Jody Powell Papers, Jimmy Carter Library, Atlanta, GA.

6. Gaddis Smith, *Morality, Reason, and Power: American Diplomacy in the Carter Years* (New York: Hill and Wang, 1986), p. 115.

7. See miscellaneous correspondence in Box "Andrew Young," Name File, Presidential Papers of Jimmy Carter, White House Central Files, Jimmy Carter Library (hereafter cited as WHCF); *Time*, 8 August 1977, p. 23.

8. Brzezinski, *Power and Principle*, pp. 140–141.

9. Henze to Brzezinski, 17 and 24 January 1978, Box 1, National Security Affairs, Staff Material, Horn/Special; and Henze to Brzezinski, 16 and 27 March 1978, Box 2, National Security Affairs, Staff Material, Horn/Special, Jimmy Carter Library.

10. Memorandum of Conversation, 3 March 1978, Box 117, Vertical File, WHCF; Henze to Brzezinski, 27 March 1978, Box 3, National Security Affairs, Brzezinski Material, Country File, WHCF.

11. Anatoly Dobrynin, *In Confidence: Moscow's Ambassador to America's Six Cold War Presidents (1962–1986)* (New York: Times Books, 1995), pp. 409–410; Memoranda of Conversation, 27 and 31 May 1978, Box 117, Vertical File, WHCF.

12. Memoranda of Conversation, 27 and 31 May 1978, and "Record of the Main Content of the Conversation between A. A. Gromyko and the U.S. Secretary of State C. Vance, May 31, 1978," Box 117, Vertical File, WHCF.

13. Brezhnev quoted in Dobrynin, *In Confidence*, pp. 410–411; Raymond L. Garthoff, *Détente and Confrontation: American-Soviet Relations from Nixon to Reagan*, rev. ed. (Washington, DC: Brookings Institution, 1994), pp. 779–781.

14. "Political Letter of Soviet Ambassador to the United States Anatoly F. Dobrynin, 11 July 1978," *Cold War Historical Project* 8–9 (Winter 1996–1997): 120, 122.

15. *Newsweek*, 17 April 1978, pp. 34–37; *Time*, 17 April 1978, pp.10–14.

CHAPTER 7: WAR ON INFLATION

1. *Newsweek*, 21 August 1978, pp. 56–59.

2. Memorandum to Members of the Cabinet, 18 August 1978, Box 100, Presidential Papers of Jimmy Carter, Staff Offices, Office of Staff Secretary, Handwriting File, Jimmy Carter Library, Atlanta, GA (hereafter cited as PHWF).

3. Melvin Price to the President, 31 August 1978, attached to Jimmy Carter to Price, 1 September 1978, Box 101, PHWF.

4. Memorandum for Jody Powell and Jerry Rafshoon from Stu Eizenstat and Bob Ginsburg, 21 June 1978, Box 289, Stuart Eizenstat Papers, Jimmy Carter Library.

5. Joseph A. Califano Jr., *Governing America: An Insider's Report from the White House and the Cabinet* (New York: Simon and Schuster, 1981), p. 89.

6. Memorandum to President Carter from Hamilton Jordan, 23 May 1977, Box 34, Hamilton Jordan Papers, Jimmy Carter Library; Memorandum for Peter Bourne from Hamilton Jordan, and attachment, 8 July 1977, Box 240, Eizenstat Papers.

7. Califano, *Governing America*, pp. 104–106.

8. Memorandum for the President from Stu Eizenstat, 14 June 1978, Box 242, Eizenstat Papers.

9. Memorandum for the President from James T. McIntyre and Charlie Schultze, 14 June 1978, Box 53, Staff Offices, Council of Economic Advisers, Presidential Papers of Jimmy Carter, Jimmy Carter Library (hereafter cited as CEA Papers).

10. Memorandum for the President from W. Michael Blumenthal and Charlie

Schultze, 24 July 1978, Box 53, CEA Papers. See also Memorandum for the President from W. Michael Blumenthal, n.d., attached to Mike to President, 13 September 1978, Box 145, Eizenstat Papers.

11. Memorandum for the President from Jerry Rafshoon, 18 July 1978, Box 28, Staff Offices, Gerald Rafshoon, Presidential Papers of Jimmy Carter, Jimmy Carter Library.

12. Karen M. Hult and Charles E. Walcott, *Empowering the White House: Governance under Nixon, Ford, and Carter* (Lawrence: University Press of Kansas, 2004), pp. 42, 74–77, 95–99.

13. Memorandum for the President from Jerry Rafshoon, 1 September 1978, Box 101, PHWF.

14. Carter to Donald Riegle, 31 August 1978, Box 44, Jordan Papers.

15. For Carter's love of nature and attitudes on the environment, see especially Jimmy Carter, *An Outdoor Journal: Adventures and Reflections* (New York: Bantam Books, 1988).

16. Jefffrey K. Stine, "Environmental Policy during the Carter Administration," in *The Carter Presidency: Policy Choices in the Post–New Deal Era*, ed. Gary M. Fink and Hugh Davis Graham (Lawrence: University Press of Kansas, 1998), p. 184. See also Memorandum for the President from Charles Speth et al., 8 July 1977, Box 36, PHWF.

17. M. Glenn Abernathy, "The Carter Administration and Domestic Civil Rights," in *The Carter Years: The President and Policy Making*, ed. M. Glenn Abernathy, Dilys Hill, and Phil Williams (New York: St. Martin's Press, 1984), pp. 106–122; Steven F. Lawson, *In Pursuit of Power: Southern Blacks and Electoral Politics, 1965–1982* (New York: Columbia University Press, 1985), pp. 256–262.

18. Review of the Carter Administration, 29 September 1978, and Meeting with Congressional Black Caucus, 25 September 1978, Box 22, Staff Offices, Louis Martin, Presidential Papers of Jimmy Carter, Jimmy Carter Library.

19. Memorandum to President Carter from Hamilton Jordan, 6 October 1978, Box 42, Jordan Papers.

20. Jimmy Carter, *Keeping Faith: Memoirs of a President* (New York: Bantam Books, 1982), p. 32.

21. Memorandum for the President from Stu Eizenstat, Charles Schultze, and Alfred Kahn, 6 December 1978, Box 148, Eizenstat Papers.

22. *Time*, 20 November 1978, pp. 16–19.

23. Memoranda for Stu Eizenstat and Bert Carp from Bill Spring and Kitty Higgins, 9 and 20 November 1978; Memorandum for Stu Eizenstat from Beth Abramowitz, 17 November 1978, Box 152; Memorandum for the President from Jack Watson, 20 November 1978, Box 155; Memorandum for Stu Eizenstat from Beth Abramowitz, 17 November 1978, Box 152, Eizenstat Papers.

CHAPTER 8: CRESCENT OF CRISIS

1. "Discussant, William B. Quandt," in *Jimmy Carter: Foreign Policy and Post-Presidential Years*, ed. Herbert D. Rosenbaum and Alexej Ugrinsky (Westport, CT: Greenwood, 1994), p. 162.

2. Jimmy Carter, *Keeping Faith: Memoirs of a President* (New York: Bantam Books, 1982), pp. 322–323.

3. Zbigniew Brzezinski, *Power and Principle: Memoirs of the National Security Adviser, 1977–1981* (New York: Farrar, Straus, Giroux, 1983), pp. 255–256.

4. William B. Quandt, *Camp David: Peacemaking and Politics* (Washington, DC: Brookings Institution, 1986), pp. 376–387.

5. Vance to The President, 30 October 1978, Box 39, Presidential Papers of Jimmy Carter, Plains File, Subject File, Jimmy Carter Library, Atlanta, GA.

6. Memorandum to President Carter from Hamilton Jordan, 30 November 1978, Box 49, Hamilton Jordan Papers, Jimmy Carter Library.

7. *Time*, 12 March 1979, pp. 13–16; *Newsweek*, 12 March 1979, pp. 24–27.

8. Cyrus Vance, *Hard Choices: Critical Years in America's Foreign Policy* (New York: Simon and Schuster, 1983), p. 314.

9. Ibid.; Brzezinski, *Power and Principle*, p. 354; Carter *Keeping Faith*, p. 435.

10. CIA Report, "Iran: Khomeini's Prospects and Views," 19 January 1979, National Security Archive (hereafter NSA), *Iran: The Making of U.S. Policy, 1977–1990*, microfiche.

11. Sullivan to Secretary of State, 9 November 1978, NSA, *Iran*, microfiche.

12. Gary Sick, *All Fall Down: America's Tragic Encounter with Iran* (New York: Random House, 1985), pp. 3–4, 41–48, 62–66, 69, 81–88, 119, 124.

13. Sullivan to Secretary of State, 10 January 1979, Box 23, Plains File, Subject File, Jimmy Carter Library; Charles O. Jones et al., Interview with Jimmy Carter, 29 November 1982, p. 14, Carter Presidency Project, Miller Center, University of Virginia.

14. "Talking Points on Iran," attached to memorandum for David Aaron from Tom Thornton, 17 February 1979, Box CO-5, Presidential Papers of Jimmy Carter, White House Central Files, Jimmy Carter Library.

15. *Time*, 15 January 1979, pp. 18–25; *Newsweek*, 8 January 1979, p. 14.

16. *Time*, 1 January 1979, pp. 39–40.

17. *Newsweek*, 26 February 1979, pp. 26–32.

18. Vance, *Hard Choices*, p. 112.

19. Robert M. Gates, *From the Shadows: The Ultimate Insider's Story of Five Presidents and How They Won the Cold War* (New York: Touchstone, 1996), pp. 115–116; "A Record of the Main Content of the Negotiations between Com. A. A. Gromyko and the U.S. Secretary of State C. Vance Held on 27 and 28 September 1978 in New York and on October 1, 1978 in Washington," n.d. (circa 1 October 1978), and Vance's handwritten notes from his meeting with Gromyko, 1 October 1978, Box 117, Vertical File, Jimmy Carter Library. Gates shares this assessment regarding the impact of the demand to ban telemetry encryption on the SALT talks.

20. *Time*, 8 January 1979, p. 16.

21. *Time*, 5 February 1979, p. 34.

22. Chae-Jin Lee and Hideo Sato, *U.S. Policy toward Japan and Korea: A Changing Influence Relationship* (New York: Praeger, 1982), p. 122; Dale E. Herspring, *The Pentagon and the Presidency: Civil-Military Relations from FDR to George W. Bush* (Lawrence: University Press of Kansas, 2005), pp. 244–246; Brzezinski to the President, n.d. (circa 17 January 1979), Box 66, National Security Affairs, Staff Material, Far East, Jimmy Carter Library.

CHAPTER 9: A GROWING SENSE OF CRISIS

1. Joseph A. Califano Jr., *Governing America: An Insider's Report from the White House and Cabinet* (New York: Simon and Schuster, 1981), p. 124; *Newsweek*, 18 December 1978, pp. 28–29.

2. *U.S. News and World Report*, 22 January 1979, pp. 16–18.

3. *Newsweek*, 18 December 1978, pp. 28–29.

4. Memorandum to the President from Alfred Kahn, 12 April 1979, Box BE-15, Presidential Papers of Jimmy Carter, White House Central Files, Jimmy Carter Library, Atlanta, GA (hereafter cited as WHCF).

5. Memorandum for the President from Alfred E. Kahn, 21 February 1975, Box 46, Staff Offices, Council of Economic Advisers, Presidential Papers of Jimmy Carter, Jimmy Carter Library.

6. Memorandum for the President from Louis Martin, 12 March 1979, Box 80, Staff Offices, Louis Martin, Presidential Papers of Jimmy Carter, Jimmy Carter Library.

7. *Newseek*, 22 January 1979, pp. 24–25.

8. Memorandum for Hamilton Jordan and Jerry Rafshoon from Ed Sanders, 15 January 1979, Box 1, Staff Offices, Edward Sanders, Presidential Papers of Jimmy Carter, Jimmy Carter Library; *U.S. News and World Report*, 22 January 1979, p. 6.

9. For Carter's position on nuclear energy, see his marginal handwritten comments on Memorandum for the President from Stu Eizenstat, 26 November 1979, Box 157, Presidential Papers of Jimmy Carter, Staff Offices, Office of Staff Secretary, Handwriting File, Jimmy Carter Library (hereafter cited as PHWF). On nuclear energy, the president broke from his mentor Admiral Hyman Rickover, who considered nuclear power "necessary." See Rickover to the President, 1 December 1979, Box 158, PHWF. On the various agency responses to the Kemeny Commission's recommendations, see also Memorandum to the President from Frank Press and John Deutch, 26 November 1979, and attachments, Box 157, PHWF.

10. *Time*, 16 April 1979, pp. 66–68.

11. *Atlantic Monthly*, May 1979, pp. 33–48; Bert Lance with Bill Gilbert, *The Truth of the Matter: My Life in and out of Politics* (New York: Summit Books, 1991), pp. 159–170.

12. Memorandum for President Carter from Patrick Caddell, 23 April 1979, Box 40, Jody Powell Papers, Jimmy Carter Library. See also James L. Sundquist, "The Crisis of Competence in Our National Government," *Political Science Quarterly* 95 (Summer 1980): 183–208.

13. Memorandum for the President from Stu Eizenstat and Joe Onek, 20 March 1979, Box 241, Stuart Eizenstat Papers, Jimmy Carter Library.

14. *Time*, 25 June 1979, pp. 20–21.

15. Jimmy to Jim Hanley, 23 May 1979, Box BE-3, WHCF.

16. Memorandum for the President from Stu Eizenstat, 4 May 1979, Box BE-3, WHCF.

17. "Economic Decision Making," 14 March 1979, attached to President

Carter from Hamilton Jordan, 16 March 1979, Box 34, Hamilton Jordan Papers, Jimmy Carter Library.

18. *Time*, 26 November 1979, p. 60.

19. *Time*, 23 July 1979, p. 20.

20. "Camp David Domestic Summits," n.d., Box 162, Eizenstat Papers; "Notes/Agenda Energy Meeting," ibid.; Memorandum for the President from Patrick Caddell, 12 July 1979, Box 40, Powell Papers; Memorandum to the President from Frank Moore, 8 July 1978, Box MC-16, Subject File, WHCF.

21. Memorandum to the President from Gerald Rafshoon, Copy to Hamilton Jordan, July 1979, and Powell to the President from Frank Moore, July 1979, Box 33, Jordan Papers; Califano, *Governing America*, pp. 428–431.

22. Jimmy Carter, *Keeping Faith: Memoirs of a President* (New York: Bantam Books, 1982), p. 121.

23. Hugh Sidey, "Second Most Powerful Person," *Time*, 7 May 1979, p. 22; "Mrs. President," *Newsweek*, 6 August 1979, pp. 22–23, 25; Carter, *Keeping Faith*, p. 32.

24. *Newsweek*, 6 August 1979, p. 25; Gil Troy, *Mr. & Mrs. President: From the Trumans to the Clintons* (Lawrence: University Press of Kansas, 2000), p. 265.

25. Hedley Donovan, Exit Interview, 14 August 1980, Jimmy Carter Library. See also Karen M. Hult and Charles E. Walcott, *Empowering the White House: Governance under Nixon, Ford, and Carter* (Lawrence: University Press of Kansas, 2004), pp. 42–45.

26. Memorandum for Members of the White House Staff from Hamilton Jordan, 18 July 1979, Box FG-48, Subject File, WHCF. See also Memorandum to President Carter from Hamilton Jordan, 26 July 1979, Box 37, Jordan Papers.

27. Jordan to Speaker of the House, 2 August 1979, Box 43, Jordan Papers.

28. Memorandum for the President from Stu Eizenstat, 14 November 1979, Box BE-4, WHCF.

29. Memorandum for the President from Patrick H. Caddell, 6 November 1979, Box 33, Jordan Papers (emphasis in original).

CHAPTER 10:
FOREIGN POLICY, PATRIOTISM, AND POLITICS

1. Memorandum to the Democratic National Committee from Cambridge Survey Research, 24 May 1979, Box 33, Hamilton Jordan Papers, Jimmy Carter Library, Atlanta, GA; Memorandum on Current Public Attitudes on SALT from Patrick H. Caddell [May 1979], Box 37, Jordan Papers.

2. Lloyd Bentsen et al. to the President, 14 June 1979, Box FO-46, Presidential Papers of Jimmy Carter, White House Central Files, Jimmy Carter Library (hereafter cited as WHCF).

3. Memorandum for Hamilton Jordan from Edward Sanders, 8 February 1979, Box 1, Staff Offices, Edward Sanders, Presidential Papers of Jimmy Carter, Jimmy Carter Library.

4. Jimmy Carter, *Keeping Faith: Memoirs of a President* (New York: Bantam

Books, 1982), pp. 240–241; Zbigniew Brzezinski, *Power and Principle: Memoirs of the National Security Adviser, 1977–1981* (New York: Farrar, Straus, Giroux, 1983), p. 336.

5. Svetlana Savranskaya and David A. Welch, eds., *Global Competition and the Deterioration of U.S.-Soviet Relations, 1977–1980* (Providence, RI: Center for Foreign Policy Development, 1995), pp. 306–309, in Box 117, Vertical File, WHCF.

6. Gaddis Smith, *Morality, Reason, and Power: American Diplomacy in the Carter Years* (New York: Hill and Wang, 1986), p. 215.

7. On this point, see particularly Richard E. Neustadt and Ernest R. May, *Thinking in Time: The Uses of History for Decision-Makers* (New York: Free Press, 1983), pp. 92–96.

8. Memorandum to Dr. Brzezinski from Mr. Cutler and Hedley Donovan, 27 September 1979, Box 3, Staff Offices, Hedley Donovan, Presidential Papers of Jimmy Carter, Jimmy Carter Library.

9. *Newsweek*, 17 September 1979, pp. 28–30; *Congressional Quarterly Almanac* 35 (1979): 422–423.

10. "President Carter's Notes/Instructions re Iran (Handwritten)," Box 23, Plains File, Subject File, WHCF; Minutes of National Security Meeting, 4 December 1979, Box 93, ibid.

11. Hamilton Jordan, *Crisis: The Last Year of the Carter Presidency* (New York: Berkley Publishing Company, 1982), pp. 11–12.

12. On 18 July 1969 Mary Jo Kopechne drowned when the car Kennedy was driving went off the bridge at Chappaquiddick Island. He fled the scene under circumstances that even he admitted were "incomprehensible and completely inexcusable." Cited in Richard Harwood, ed., *The Pursuit of the Presidency* (New York: Berkley Publishing Company, 1980), p. 68.

13. Odd Arne Westad, "Concerning the Situation in 'A': New Russian Evidence on the Soviet Intervention in Afghanistan," *Cold War International History Project* 8–9 (Winter 1996–1997): 129–130.

14. Ibid., pp. 130–131.

15. Carter, *Keeping Faith*, pp. 471–472.

16. Memorandum for the President from Stu Eizenstat, 3 January 1980, Box 76, Staff Offices, Lloyd Cutler, Presidential Papers of Jimmy Carter, Jimmy Carter Library.

17. Memorandum from Warren Christopher to the President, 19 June 1980, Box 27, National Security Affairs, Staff Material, North/South, Presidential Papers of Jimmy Carter, Jimmy Carter Library.

18. Oksenberg to Brzezinski, 28 December 1979, Box 1, National Security Affairs, Brzezinski Material, Country File, WHCF.

19. Shirin Tahir-Kheli, *The United States and Pakistan: The Evolution of an Influence Relationship* (New York: Praeger, 1982), pp. 98–104.

20. On the complex issue of the United States' nuclear nonproliferation policy and India during the Carter administration, see Brahma Chellaney, *Nuclear Proliferation: The U.S.-Indian Conflict* (Hyderbad: Orient Longman, 1993), esp. pp. 76, 82, 84, 90, 92. See also H. W. Brands, *India and the United States: The Cold Peace* (Boston: Twayne, 1990), p. 162.

21. Carter, *Keeping Faith*, p. 476.

CHAPTER 11: ECONOMIC PAIN AND POLITICS

1. Memorandum for the President from Alfred Kahn, 5 November 1979, Box 157, Presidential Papers of Jimmy Carter, Staff Offices, Office of Staff Secretary, Handwriting File, Jimmy Carter Library, Atlanta, GA (hereafter cited as PHWF).

2. Memorandum for the President from Charlie Schultze, 28 November and 22 December 1979, Box 157, PHWF.

3. Memorandum for the President from Alfred Kahn, 5 November 1979, Box 157, PHWF.

4. Memorandum for the President from Kahn, 17 November 1979; Memorandum for the President from Charles W. Duncan Jr., 30 November 1979, Box 157, PHWF.

5. Memorandum for the President from Al McDonald, 19 December 1979; To the President from Hedley Donovan, 17 December 1979, Boxes 159, 160, PHWF.

6. Carter to Stu, 17 January 1979; Carter to Jody, 17 January 1979; Carter's marginal notes on Memorandum for the President from Jack Watson and Jim McIntyre, 15 January 1980, attached to Memorandum for the President from McIntyre and Watson, 17 January 1980, Box 165, PHWF.

7. Memorandum for the President from Stu Eizenstat, 26 March 1980, Box BE-13, Presidential Papers of Jimmy Carter, White House Central Files, Jimmy Carter Library.

8. Ibid.

9. Memorandum for the President from Patrick H. Caddell, 11 February 1980, Box 10, Jody Powell Papers, Jimmy Carter Library.

10. *New York Times*, 27 March 1980, p. 17.

11. *Time*, 14 April 1980, p. 28.

12. Jimmy Carter, *Keeping Faith: Memoirs of a President* (New York: Bantam Books, 1982), pp. 530–531.

13. Cited in Gaddis Smith, *Morality, Reason, and Power: American Diplomacy in the Carter Years* (New York: Hill and Wang, 1986), p. 201.

14. David Patrick Houghton, *US Foreign Policy and the Iran Hostage Crisis* (New York: Cambridge University Press, 2001), pp. 125–127.

15. *Time*, 5 May 1980, pp. 26–31.

16. Warren Christopher, *Chances of a Lifetime: A Memoir* (New York: Scribner, 2001), p. 100.

17. Memorandum for the President from Jody Powell, 1 May 1980, Box 40, Powell Papers; *Newsweek*, 12 May 1980, pp. 42–53.

18. Myra McPherson, "Is Rosalynn Really Running the Country?" *McCall's*, March 1980, p. 109.

19. Handwritten marginal comment on Memorandum for the President from Charles Duncan, 15 October 1979, Box 152, PHWF.

20. Stuart E. Eizenstat, "President Carter, the Democratic Party, and the Making of Domestic Policy," in *The Presidency and Domestic Policies of Jimmy Carter*, ed. Herbert D. Rosenbaum and Alexej Ugrinsky (Westport, CT: Greenwood Press, 1994), p. 10.

21. Carter, *Keeping Faith*, p. 529.

22. *Time*, 16 June 1980, pp. 64–70.

23. Memorandum for the President from Stu Eizenstat, 26 May 1980, Box 188, PHWF.

CHAPTER 12: GLOOM AND DOOM

1. Jimmy Carter, *Keeping Faith: Memoirs of a President* (New York: Bantam Books, 1982), p. 532.

2. Ibid.

3. Memorandum for Bill from Charlie Schultze, 29 July 1980, Box 54, Staff Offices, Council of Economic Advisers, Presidential Papers of Jimmy Carter, Jimmy Carter Library, Atlanta, GA.

4. *Newsweek*, 2 June 1980, pp. 32–39.

5. Jonathan Carr, *Helmut Schmidt: Helmsman of Germany* (New York: St. Martin's, 1985), pp. 131–132, 134.

6. Warren Christopher, *Chances of a Lifetime* (New York: Scribner, 2001), pp. 105–107.

7. Carter, *Keeping Faith*, pp. 535–536; Zbigniew Brzezinski, *Power and Principle: Memoirs of the National Security Adviser, 1977–1981* (New York: Farrar, Straus, Giroux, 1985), pp. 461–463.

8. *Time*, 4 August 1980, pp. 34–35.

9. Memorandum for the President from Stu Eizenstat and Al Moses, 30 September and 3 October 1980, Box 18, Staff Offices, Al Moses, Presidential Papers of Jimmy Carter, Jimmy Carter Library.

10. Felix Roberto Masud-Piloto, *From Welcomed Exiles to Illegal Immigrants: Cuban Migration to the U.S., 1959–1995* (Lanham, MD: Rowman and Littlefield, 1996), p. 83.

11. Memorandum for the President from Gene Eidenberg and John White, 5 September 1980, Box 204, Presidential Papers of Jimmy Carter, Staff Offices, Office of Staff Secretary, Handwriting File, Jimmy Carter Library.

12. Hamilton Jordan, *Crisis: The Last Year of the Carter Presidency* (New York: Berkley Publishing Company, 1982), p. 295.

13. *New Republic*, 30 August 1980, pp. 7–9.

14. *Time*, 25 August 1980, pp. 30–31.

15. Ibid.; Raymond Garthoff, *Détente and Confrontation: American-Soviet Relations from Nixon to Reagan* (Washington, DC: Brookings Institution, 1985), pp. 796–799.

16. Jack W. Germond and Jules Witcover, *Blue Smoke and Mirrors: How Reagan Won and Why Carter Lost the Election of 1980* (New York: Viking, 1981), pp. 190–193, 207.

CHAPTER 13: DEFEAT

1. Hamilton Jordan, *Crisis: The Last Year of the Carter Presidency* (New York: Berkley Publishing Company, 1982), pp. 282–292.

2. Ibid., pp. 290–291.

3. Memorandum for the President from Stu Eizenstat, Box 12, Jody Powell Papers, Jimmy Carter Library, Atlanta, GA; Jack W. Germond and Jules Witcover, *Blue Smoke and Mirrors: How Reagan Won and Why Carter Lost the Election of 1980* (New York: Viking, 1981), pp. 209–221.

4. *U.S. News and World Report*, 1 September 1980, p. 21; *Time*, 1 September 1980, pp. 12–13.

5. Cambridge Survey Research, 23 September and 1 and 8 October 1980, Box 10, Jody Powell Papers, Jimmy Carter Library, Atlanta, GA.

6. Jordan, *Crisis*, pp. 326–327.

7. Carter's extensive handwritten changes to the draft speech can be found in "Proposed Five-Minute for October 2, 1980," Box 207, Presidential Papers of Jimmy Carter, Staff Offices, Office of Staff Secretary, Handwriting File, Jimmy Carter Library.

8. Jordan, *Crisis*, pp. 323–324, 330–331.

9. Germond and Witcover, *Blue Smoke and Mirrors*, pp. 222–223.

10. Memorandum of Telephone Call between Brzezinski and Reagan, 24 September 1980, Box 13, Powell Papers; Jimmy Carter, *Keeping Faith: Memoirs of a President* (New York: Bantam Books, 1982), pp. 557—558, 562; Warren Christopher et al., *American Hostages in Iran: The Conduct of a Crisis* (New Haven, CT: Yale University Press, 1985), pp. 289–290, 297.

11. Jordan, *Crisis*, pp. 331–334.

12. Memorandum for the President from Zbigniew Brzezinski, 21 October 1980; Memorandum for Jody Powell, Pat Caddell, and Jerry Rafshoon from Al McDonald, 22 October 1980; Memorandum for Al McDonald and Dave Rubenstein from Jody Powell, 22 October 1980, Box 8, Powell Papers.

13. Jordan, *Crisis*, pp. 342–343.

14. For a detailed analysis of the election results, see Andrew E. Busch, *Reagan's Victory: The Presidential Election of 1980 and the Rise of the Right* (Lawrence: University Press of Kansas, 2005), esp. pp. 130–144. See also *Newsweek*, 17 November 1980, pp. 31–32; *U.S. News and World Report*, 17 November 1980, pp. 26–30.

15. Germond and Witcover, *Blue Smoke and Mirrors*, pp. 288–289; Jordan, *Crisis*, pp. 348–349.

16. Memorandum for Hamilton Jordan and Bob Strauss from Al McDonald, 28 October 1980, Box 10, Powell Papers.

17. Carter's marginal notation on Memorandum for the President from Frank Moore, 30 April 1978, Box 48, Hamilton Jordan Papers, Jimmy Carter Library.

18. *Congressional Quarterly Almanac* 36 (1980): 580.

19. Memorandum for the President from Gus Speth, Jane Yarn, and Bob Harris, 18 July 1980, Box FO-58, Presidential Papers of Jimmy Carter, White House Central Files, Jimmy Carter Library; Carter, *Keeping Faith*, pp. 582–583.

CHAPTER 14: EPILOGUE

1. Jimmy Carter and Rosalynn Carter, *Everything to Gain: Making the Most of the Rest of Your Life* (New York: Random House, 1987), p. 9.

2. Douglas Brinkley, *The Unfinished Presidency: Jimmy Carter's Journey beyond the White House* (New York: Penguin, 1998), pp. 47–49.

3. Tom Wicker, "Whatever Became of Jimmy Carter?" *Esquire,* July 1984, pp. 78–84.

4. Brinkley, *Unfinished Presidency,* pp. 200–203, 232–233.

5. Ibid., pp. 129–130.

6. Ibid., p. 206.

7. Kenneth E. Morris, *Jimmy Carter: American Moralist* (Athens: University of Georgia Press, 1996), pp. 300–301.

8. Kai Bird, "The Very Model of an Ex-President," *Nation,* 12 November 1990, p. 1.

9. Brinkley, *Unfinished Presidency,* p. 409.

10. Ibid., pp. 433, 434.

11. "Merry Christmas, Mr. Karadzic," *New Republic,* 9 and 16 January 1995, p. 7.

12. Jimmy Carter, *Our Endangered Values: America's Moral Crisis* (New York: Simon and Schuster, 2005).

13. Bret Stephens, "The World According to J. C.," *Wall Street Journal,* 2 November 2005.

14. Brinkley, *Unfinished Presidency,* p. 480.

BIBLIOGRAPHICAL ESSAY

The place to begin any study of the Carter presidency is, of course, the vast holdings of the Jimmy Carter Library in Atlanta, Georgia, which houses the 26 million documents shipped from the White House after Carter left office in 1981. The White House Central File contains the bulk of Carter's presidential papers, but another important source is the 150,000-page Handwriting File. Carter made handwritten comments on just about every document he read, so this file provides a window to his thinking on major (and not so major) policy issues. Included in the presidential papers are records of members of the White House staff, most notably Lloyd Cutler, Hedley Donovan, Robert Lipshutz, Margaret McKenna, Louis Martin, Al Moses, and Edward Sanders.

There are also important collections of the papers of Carter's principal aides: Stuart Eizenstat, Hamilton Jordan, Jody Powell, Gerald Rafshoon, and Zbigniew Brzezinski. The Eizenstat Papers are a treasure trove on just about every domestic issue confronting the administration, and the Jordan and Powell Papers are rich with respect to political matters and underscore the close relationship between those men and the president; no other members of Carter's staff spoke to him with the same temerity and frankness. The Rafshoon Papers reveal the importance the White House attached to presidential image. Portions of the Brzezinski Papers are still closed, but those that are open provide vital insight into the administration's foreign policy. For matters having to do specifically with foreign economic policy, one should consult the papers of Anthony Solomon, a highly respected authority on international monetary matters and an assistant secretary of the treasury during the Carter presidency. On domestic economic matters, the papers of James McIntyre, deputy director and later director of the Office of Management and Budget, are helpful. Also at the Carter Library are a series of exit interviews with administration officials.

There are additional materials outside of the Carter Library that researchers will want to consult. The White Burkett Miller Center of Public Affairs at the University of Virginia has a Presidential Oral History collection where one can find interviews with such key individuals as Jimmy Carter, Zbigniew Brzezinski, Bert Lance, Jody Powell, and Hamilton Jordan. Copies of many of these interviews are also available at the Carter Library. The National Security Archive at George Washington University has used the Freedom of Information Act to open up previously classified materials. Scholars will find papers relating to U.S. policy toward the Soviet Union, Iran, the Philippines, Afghanistan, Argentina, and other countries. If one is studying the 1976 campaign, there are several important collections at the Gerald Ford Library in Ann Arbor, Michigan, including the Special Files, Presidential Papers of Gerald Ford; the Michael Raoul Duval Papers; and the Robert Teeter Papers. Finally, the Cold War International History Project of the Woodrow Wilson International Center for Scholars publishes translated documents primarily from the archives of the Soviet bloc and China.

A number of former officials in the Carter administration have written books and memoirs. Two essays that discuss some of these works are Edward R. Kantowicz, "Reminiscences of a Failed Presidency: Themes from the Carter Memoirs," *Presidential Studies Quarterly* 16 (Fall 1986): 655–665, and Walter LaFeber, "From Confusion to Cold War: The Memoirs of the Carter Administration," *Diplomatic History* 8 (Winter 1984): 1–12. Also important as a general introduction to the literature on the Carter presidency is Gary W. Reichard, "Early Returns: Assessing Jimmy Carter," *Presidential Studies Quarterly* 19 (Summer 1990): 603–620.

President Carter's own memoir, *Keeping Faith: Memoirs of a President* (New York: Bantam Books, 1982; reprint, Fayetteville: University of Arkansas Press, 1995), is highly selective in content, but the book provides an especially full account of the Camp David summit of 1978, as well as the events leading to Carter's recognition of the People's Republic of China and his efforts on behalf of a national energy program. This book also contains important excerpts from Carter's diary, a document that is not yet open to researchers.

Zbigniew Brzezinski's *Power and Principle: Memoirs of the National Security Adviser, 1977–1981* (New York: Farrar, Straus, Giroux, 1983) is frank and extremely rich with regard to foreign policy. Also valuable is Cyrus Vance's *Hard Choices: Critical Years in America's Foreign Policy* (New York: Simon and Schuster, 1983). Together, the Brzezinski and Vance volumes cover the full range of Carter's foreign policy and illuminate the friction that developed between the White House and the Department of State. On this score, see also Michael Charlton, "The President's Men at the NSC. Part II. The Struggle under Carter," *National Interest* 21 (Fall 1990): 100–108, which is an excerpt from an interview with Brzezinski and Vance conducted by the British Broadcasting Company in 1990. Other memoirs by former members of the Carter administration include Warren Christopher, *Chances of a Lifetime* (New York: Scribner, 2001), a candid account of the deputy secretary of state's involvement in the efforts to pass the Panama Canal treaties, achieve normalization with China, and rescue the Iranian hostages, as well as his disappointment at being passed over as secretary of state; Joseph A. Califano Jr., *Governing America: An Insider's Report from the White House and the Cabinet* (New York: Simon and Schuster, 1981), which provides details on policy matters such as

welfare, Social Security, tax reform, national health insurance, and Califano's firing as secretary of health, education, and welfare in 1979; Hedley Donovan, *Roosevelt to Reagan: A Reporter's Encounter with Nine Presidents* (New York: Harper and
Row, 1985), containing this senior adviser's brief comments on Carter's concern
with energy legislation, black-Jewish tensions, and the firing of Andrew Young;
Hamilton Jordan, *Crisis: The Last Year of the Carter Presidency* (New York: Berkley
Publishing Company, 1982), almost a day-by-day diary of Jordan's involvement
in 1980 in negotiations for the release of the Iranian hostages and in Carter's presidential campaign; Bert Lance with Bill Gilbert, *The Truth of the Matter: My Life in
and out of Politics* (New York: Summit Books, 1991), a spirited defense of Lance's
banking practices that also illustrates his continued admiration for Carter; Jody
Powell, *The Other Side of the Story* (New York: William Morrow, 1984), an attack on
the press's treatment of the Carter administration; Griffin B. Bell with Ronald J.
Ostrow, *Taking Care of the Law* (New York: William Morrow, 1982), useful only for
Bell's involvement in the *Bakke* case and as an indication of the tension that arose
between Bell and the White House; Phillip M. Klutznick with Sidney Hyman, *Angles of Vision: A Memoir of My Lives* (Chicago: Ivan Dee, 1991), an account by
Carter's second secretary of commerce that provides useful insights into the relationship between American Jewish leaders and Israel both before and during the
Carter administration; Robert Pastor, *Condemned to Repetition: The United States
and Nicaragua* (Princeton, NJ: Princeton University Press, 1987), a defense of the
administration's response to the Nicaraguan revolution by a former member of
the National Security Council (NSC) who was one of the architects of that policy;
William B. Quandt, *Camp David: Peacemaking and Politics* (Washington, DC: Brookings Institution, 1986), an excellent history of the Camp David accords by another
member of the NSC who was responsible for handling the Arab-Israeli dispute;
Gary Sick, *All Fall Down: America's Tragic Encounter with Iran* (New York: Random
House, 1985), an account by a third NSC member that describes the U.S. response
to the Iranian revolution and is highly critical of Ambassador William Sullivan's
role in the fall of the shah; William H. Sullivan, *Mission to Iran* (New York: W. W.
Norton, 1981), Sullivan's defense of his actions; Stansfield Turner, *Secrecy and De-
mocracy: The CIA in Transition* (Boston: Houghton Mifflin, 1985), an account of
Turner's efforts as director of the CIA to balance the need for secrecy in intelli-
gence gathering with the public's right to know; William H. Gleysteen Jr., *Massive
Entanglement, Marginal Influence: Carter and Korea in Crisis* (Washington, DC:
Brookings Institution Press, 1999), by the administration's ambassador to South
Korea from 1978 to 1980; William J. Jorden, *Panama Odyssey* (Austin: University of
Texas Press, 1984), by the U.S. ambassador to Panama from 1974 to 1978, who de-
tails the negotiations and debates that led to the signing and ratification of the
Panama Canal treaties; Lawrence Pezzullo and Ralph Pezzullo, *At the Fall of Somoza* (Pittsburgh: University of Pittsburgh Press, 1993), which details the U.S. ambassador to Nicaragua's negotiations with Anastasio Somoza and Somoza's
eventual downfall; Anthony Lake, *Somoza Falling: A Case Study of Washington at
Work* (Amherst: University of Massachusetts Press, 1989), in which the Carter administration's director of the Policy Planning Staff argues that the dispute between Carter's State Department appointees and career foreign service officers
hampered the White House's Nicaraguan policy; Madeleine Albright with Bill

Woodward, *Madam Secretary* (New York: Miramax, 2003), in which the former secretary of state, who was an NSC staffer during the Carter years, highlights disputes between the State Department and the NSC over policy making; Jerry J. Jasinowski, "The First Two Years of the Carter Administration: An Appraisal," *Presidential Studies Quarterly* 9 (Winter 1979): 11–15, a defense of Carter's foreign policy by a former assistant secretary of commerce; Stephen Cohen, "Conditioning U.S. Security Assistance on Human Rights Practices," *American Journal of International Law* 76 (1982): 246–279, a critical assessment of the administration's human rights policy by the deputy assistant secretary of state for human rights and security assistance; and Harrison Wellford, "Staffing the Presidency: An Insider's Comments," *Political Science Quarterly* 93 (Spring 1978): 10–12, a brief discussion by a lower-level member of the White House staff of Carter's intention to have the executive office reflect his views on major policy matters.

In addition to these works by former members of the Carter administration, the reader should consult Thomas P. O'Neill with William Novak, *Man of the House: The Life and Political Memoirs of Speaker Tip O'Neill* (New York: Random House, 1987), for a description of the strained relations that existed between Congress and the White House during the Carter administration; Kenneth W. Thompson, ed., *The Carter Presidency: Fourteen Intimate Perspectives of Jimmy Carter* (Lanham, MD: University Press of America, 1990), a series of oral interviews with President Carter, Rosalynn Carter, Vice President Walter Mondale, and members of Carter's cabinet and White House staff; Pat Anderson, *Electing Jimmy Carter: The Campaign of 1976* (Baton Rouge: Louisiana State University Press, 1994), in which Carter's chief speechwriter during the campaign presents a highly critical account of the presidential candidate; Robert M. Gates, *From the Shadows: The Ultimate Insider's Story of Five Presidents and How They Won the Cold War* (New York: Simon and Schuster, 1996), an account by a CIA agent and later CIA director who credits Carter with setting the foundation for the demise of the Soviet Union; Moshe Dayan, *Breakthrough: A Personal Account of the Egypt-Israel Peace Negotiations* (New York: Knopf, 1981); Yitzhak Rabin, *The Rabin Memoirs*, expanded ed. (Berkeley: University of California Press, 1996); Leon H. Charney, *Special Counsel* (New York: Philosophical Library, 1984), by a Jewish attorney who became an intermediary in the talks between the United States and Israel that led to the Camp David accords; Shmuel Katz, *The Hollow Peace* (Tel Aviv: Dvir and the *Jerusalem Post*, 1981), in which Menachem Begin's adviser for propaganda indicts the peace process with Egypt; Andrei Gromyko, *Memoirs* (New York: Doubleday, 1989), by the former Soviet foreign minister, who is critical of the Carter administration and charges the White House with endangering détente; Anatoly Dobrynin, *In Confidence: Moscow's Ambassador to America's Six Cold War Presidents (1962–1986)* (New York: Times Books, Random House, 1996), a far more candid account that is critical of both the Carter administration and Soviet officials in Moscow for opportunities they missed to improve superpower relations; Helmut Schmidt, *Men and Powers: A Political Retrospective*, trans. Ruth Hein (New York: Random House, 1989), in which the former leader of Germany leaves no doubt about his feelings toward President Carter.

Although not technically employed as a member of the administration, Rosalynn Carter served as one of her husband's closest advisers and was more involved in affairs of state than any presidential wife since Eleanor Roosevelt. Many of her papers—the East Wing File—are now open at the Carter Library, although researchers will find that most of the material is either routine or made up of media reports. Her memoir, *First Lady from Plains* (Boston: Houghton Mifflin, 1984), provides the reader with an insider's perspective on administration policy as well as personal information about the presidential family. In addition, scholars will want to look at the memoir of Mrs. Carter's press secretary, Mary Hoyt, *East Wing: Politics, the Press, and a First Lady: A Memoir* (Philadelphia: Xlibris, 2001). Edna Langford, a good friend of Mrs. Carter's, wrote, with Linda Maddox, *Rosalynn: Friend and First Lady* (Old Tappan, NJ: Revell, 1980). There are also several works that discuss Mrs. Carter's role in the administration and her relationship with her husband, including Gil Troy, *Mr. & Mrs. President: From the Trumans to the Clintons*, 2nd ed. (Lawrence: University Press of Kansas, 2000); Kathy B. Smith, "(Eleanor) Rosalynn (Smith) Carter," in *American First Ladies: Their Lives and Their Legacy*, ed. Lewis L. Gould (New York: Garland Press, 1996), pp. 556–582; and Diane M. Blair and Shawn J. Parry-Giles, "Rosalynn Carter: Crafting a Presidential Partnership Rhetorically," in *Leading Ladies of the White House: Communication Strategies of Notable Twentieth-Century First Ladies*, ed. Molly Meijer Wertheimer (Lanham, MD: Rowman and Littlefield, 2005), pp. 140–163. In 1990 Hofstra University held a conference, "Jimmy Carter: Keeping Faith," and Herbert D. Rosenbaum and Alexej Ugrinsky put together the papers and commentaries from that conference in two volumes. One of the volumes, *The Presidency and Domestic Policies of Jimmy Carter* (Westport, CT: Greenwood Press, 1994), has an entire section devoted to Rosalynn Carter, including comments by members of the East Wing staff.

Two Democratic elder statesmen who, at various times, were consulted by the president are Clark Clifford and George W. Ball. Clifford was also Bert Lance's lawyer during the so-called Lance affair. For their memoirs, both of which are critical of the president, see Clark Clifford with Richard Holbrooke, *Counsel to the President: A Memoir* (New York: Random House, 1991), and George W. Ball, *The Past Has Another Pattern: Memoirs* (New York: W. W. Norton, 1984). *Public Papers of the Presidents of the United States: Jimmy Carter*, 9 vols. (Washington, DC: Government Printing Office, 1977–1981), contain all of Carter's speeches and public papers.

For autobiographical material by the former president, see *Keeping Faith; Why Not the Best?* (Nashville, TN: Broadman Press, 1975), Carter's campaign biography; *An Outdoor Journal: Adventures and Reflections* (New York: Bantam Books, 1988), musings on his love for the outdoors; *An Hour before Daylight: Memories of a Rural Boyhood* (New York: Touchstone, 2001), a rich account of the life of a white boy growing up in the rural South; *Turning Point: A Candidate, a State, and a Nation Coming of Age* (New York: Times Books, 1992), the story of Carter's campaign for the state senate in 1962 that says much about county politics in Georgia; *Living Faith* (New York: Times Books, 1996), Carter's testimony of his religious beliefs; and, with Rosalynn Carter, *Everything to Gain: Making the Most of the Rest of Your Life* (New York: Random House, 1987), in which the Carters discuss their adjustment to private life after Jimmy Carter's defeat in 1980 and also offer advice on preventive health care. On the former president's continued interest in the Middle East, consult his *Blood of Abraham: Insights into the Middle East* (Boston: Houghton

Mifflin, 1985), a country-by-country historical synopsis and analysis of Middle Eastern problems. For Carter's biting criticism of the fundamentalist Right and its impact on U.S. politics, see his *Our Endangered Values: America's Moral Crisis* (New York: Simon and Schuster, 2005). For Carter's collection of his statements and speeches before becoming president, see *A Government as Good as Its People* (New York: Pocket Books, 1977). For a humorous but often biting account of the Carter family by the former president's cousin, see Hugh Carter, *Cousin Beedie and Cousin Hot: My Life with the Carter Family of Plains, Georgia* (Englewood Cliffs, NJ: Prentice-Hall, 1978).

There is no first-rate biography of Carter. The best is Betty Glad, *Jimmy Carter: In Search of the Great White House* (New York: W. W. Norton, 1980); it is long, detailed, and comprehensive, but it concludes with Carter's successful quest for the White House. For a sympathetic account of Carter, see the biography written by the Carters' longtime friend Peter Bourne: *Jimmy Carter: A Comprehensive Biography from Plains to Post-Presidency* (New York: Scribner, 1997). More critical is Kenneth E. Morris's *Jimmy Carter: American Moralist* (Athens: University of Georgia Press, 1996), which argues that Carter was a moralist who came to office at a time when the nation was not ready for one. Morris also maintains that Carter did not provide a vision for the country's domestic or foreign policies. A psychobiography that has all the faults of that genre is Bruce Mazlish and Edwin Diamond, *Jimmy Carter: A Character Portrait* (New York: Simon and Schuster, 1979). Mazlish and Diamond stress three themes of Carter's development: (1) belonging and being apart, (2) the need to measure up and win, and (3) the power of thinking and acting positively. Even less satisfactory is Peter Meyer, *James Earl Carter: The Man and the Myth* (Kansas City, MO: Sheed Andrews and McMeel, 1978), written while Carter was still in office by a person who had voted for the president and then became disillusioned with his performance. An incisive character analysis of Carter, also written while he was in office, is William Lee Miller, *Yankee from Georgia: The Emergence of Jimmy Carter* (New York: Quadrangle/New York Times Books, 1978). Miller argues that Carter was a southerner with the mind of a Yankee Puritan—logical, methodical, and punctual rather than creative and innovative.

Four books dealing with Carter's deeply held religious views are David Kucharsky, *The Man from Plains: The Mind and Spirit of Jimmy Carter* (New York: Harper and Row, 1976); Niels C. Nielsen, *The Religion of President Carter* (Nashville, TN: Thomas Nelson, 1977); Wesley G. Pippert, *The Spiritual Journal of Jimmy Carter: In His Own Words* (New York: Macmillan, 1978); and Howard Norton and Bob Slosser, *The Miracle of Jimmy Carter* (Plainfield, NJ: Logos International, 1976). Kucharsky emphasizes Carter's quest for a revival of old values. Nielsen maintains that Carter's faith was a mixture of southern evangelicalism, eighteenth-century religious pluralism, and more recent sophisticated Christian political realism. Pippert argues that the central theme of both Carter's faith and political philosophy is his belief that individuals and nations are fallible and sinful and require forgiveness. Also useful on Carter's civil religion is Richard V. Pierard and Robert D. Linder, *Civil Religion and the Presidency* (Grand Rapids, MI: Academie Books, 1988). Pierard and Linder attribute Carter's drive for excellence to his Christian mind-set and his experience working for Admiral Hyman Rickover.

A number of books also have chapters that furnish important insights into Carter's character and beliefs. Among these are William R. Leuchtenburg, *In the Shadow of FDR: From Harry Truman to Ronald Reagan* (Ithaca, NY: Cornell University Press, 1983); Alonzo Hamby, *Liberalism and Its Challengers: FDR to Reagan* (New York: Oxford University Press, 1985); Barbara Kellerman, *The Political Presidency: Practice of Leadership from Kennedy through Reagan* (New York: Oxford University Press, 1984); and Richard E. Neustadt, *Presidential Power: The Politics of Leadership from FDR to Carter* (New York: John Wiley and Sons, 1980). Leuchtenburg argues that part of Carter's problem as president was his effort to distance himself from the New Deal tradition of Franklin Roosevelt, while Hamby maintains that New Deal liberalism was exhausted by the time Carter took office. On the basis of her analysis of Carter's energy program, Kellerman concludes that the president was a failed politician because he refused to play politics. Finally, Neustadt attributes many of Carter's problems as president to his operational style.

For Carter's political career before running for president, consult the works by Glad, *Jimmy Carter*, and Norton and Slosser, *Miracle of Carter*. Also useful is James Wooten, *Dasher: The Roots and the Rising of Jimmy Carter* (New York: Summit Books, 1978). An important work on Carter's term as governor of Georgia is Gary Fink, *Prelude to the Presidency: The Political Character and Legislative Leadership Style of Governor Jimmy Carter* (Westport, CT: Greenwood Press, 1980), which contends that much of Carter's later difficulties with Congress were foreshadowed by his struggle with the Georgia legislature over the reorganization of state government.

In addition to Anderson's *Electing Jimmy Carter*, there are several books on the 1976 presidential campaign. The most thorough is Jules Witcover, *Marathon: The Pursuit of the Presidency, 1972–1976* (New York: Viking Press, 1977). Hamilton Jordan's plan for winning the Democratic nomination can be found in Kandy Stroud, *How Jimmy Won: The Victory Campaign from Plains to the White House* (New York: William Morrow, 1977). Elizabeth Drew, author of *American Journal: The Events of 1976* (New York: Random House, 1977), is one of the nation's most astute political observers. Drew is critical of candidate Carter, whom she describes as a pragmatic liberal, for being too thin-skinned and not offering voters any vision of the future. In *Running for the President, 1976: The Carter Campaign* (New York: Stein and Day, 1977), Martin Schram makes the point that Carter failed to reestablish the FDR Democratic coalition. In *Dasher*, Wooten remarks that Carter was purposefully enigmatic during the campaign and did whatever was necessary to win the election. A good analysis of the Catholic vote in the election can be found in George Gallup Jr. and Jim Castelli, *The American Catholic People: Their Beliefs, Practices, and Values* (Garden City, NJ: Doubleday, 1987). A discussion of how Carter was able to stop—momentarily, at least—the flight of white voters from the Democratic Party is in William J. Keefe, *Parties, Politics, and Public Policy in America* (Washington, DC: CQ Press, 1988). For campaign speeches by Carter and Ford, consult *The Presidential Campaign 1976*, 3 vols. (Washington, DC: Government Printing Office, 1978).

On the 1980 election, see Andrew E. Busch, *Reagan's Victory: The Presidential Election of 1980 and the Rise of the Right* (Lawrence: University Press of Kansas, 2005), a thorough analysis of the election that emphasizes demographic, cultural, and political patterns; and Jack W. Germond and Jules Witcover, *Blue Smoke and Mirrors: How Reagan Won and Why Carter Lost the Election of 1980* (New York: Viking, 1981), a journalistic interpretation by two political commentators. Also useful is Richard Harwood, ed., *The Pursuit of the Presidency 1980* (New York: Berkley Publishing Company, 1980), which is an account of the campaign by reporters from the *Washington Post*. A group of essays generally critical of the rightward swing of the electorate is Thomas Ferguson and Joel Rogers, *The Hidden Election: Politics and Economics in the 1980 Presidential Campaign* (New York: Pantheon Books, 1981). Ferguson and Rogers develop this theme further in *Right Turn: The Decline of the Democrats and the Future of American Politics* (New York: Hill and Wang, 1986). For an analysis of voting patterns in both the 1976 and 1980 elections, see also Euel W. Elliott, *Issues and Elections: Presidential Voting in Contemporary America—A Revisionist View* (Boulder, CO: Westview Press, 1989). Always insightful are the comments of the dean of presidential campaign historians, Theodore White. See his *America in Search of Itself: The Making of the President, 1956–1980* (New York: Harper and Row, 1982). Useful for anecdotal information is Paul F. Boller Jr., *Presidential Campaigns* (New York: Oxford University Press, 1984).

Although there are no comprehensive histories of the Carter administration, there are a number of general studies. The two most important are Erwin C. Hargrove, *Jimmy Carter as President: Leadership and the Politics of the Public Good* (Baton Rouge: Louisiana State University Press, 1988), and Charles O. Jones, *The Trusteeship Presidency: Jimmy Carter and the United States Congress* (Baton Rouge: Louisiana State University Press, 1988). Both these books are based on the interviews with former administration officials held at the Miller Center. In addition to *The Presidency and Domestic Policies of Jimmy Carter*, Rosenbaum and Ugrinsky edited the Hofstra conference papers and commentaries related to Carter's foreign policy in *Jimmy Carter: Foreign Policy and Post-Presidential Years* (Westport, CT: Greenwood Press, 1994). In addition to the above-mentioned material on Rosalynn Carter, the Rosenbaum-Ugrinsky volumes contain papers on such topics as the Panama Canal treaties, human rights, the Middle East peace process, SALT II, energy policy, labor policy, White House–congressional relations, and Carter's character. Among those who comment on the papers are former Carter administration officials, including Bert Lance, Robert Pastor, Frank Moore, Mary Finch Hoyt, William Quandt, and Stansfield Turner. Another useful collection is M. Glenn Abernathy, Dilys Hill, and Phil Williams, eds., *The Carter Years: The President and Policymaking* (New York: St. Martin's Press, 1984). Three indictments of the Carter presidency are Haynes Johnson, *In the Absence of Power: Governing America* (New York: Viking Press, 1980); Clark Mollenhoff, *The President Who Failed: Carter out of Control* (New York: Macmillan, 1980); and Laurence H. Shoup, *The Carter Presidency and Beyond: Power and Politics in the 1980s* (Palo Alto, CA: Ramparts Press, 1980). Johnson criticizes Carter for his weak leadership, although he also comments that the president did not receive credit for the things he did right. Mollenhoff accuses Carter of hypocrisy and of being too willing to compromise on policy matters—something most other writers have criticized him for *not* doing. Shoup maintains that a small group of the corporate upper class shaped the 1976 presidential campaign and dominated the administration. Both the Mollenhoff and Shoup volumes are unconvincing. A revisionist critique that places the administration in a more positive light is John Dumbrell, *The Carter Presidency, a Re-evaluation,* 2nd ed. (New York: Manchester University Press, 1995). Dumbrell views Carter as driven by a "postliberal" ideology that sought to come to grips with changes in the domestic and international environment. Although the president failed to solve these postliberal difficulties, he accomplished a great deal. An excellent history of the 1970s is Bruce J. Schulman, *The Seventies: The Great Shift in American Culture, Society and Politics* (New York: Da Capo Press, 2001). Also see Peter N. Carroll, *It Seemed Like Nothing Happened: The Tragedy and Promise of the 1970s* (New York: Holt, Rinehart, and Winston, 1982).

Several books and articles deal with Carter's efforts to assemble his administration and his first few months in office. The most comprehensive treatment is Bruce Adams and Kathryn Kavanagh-Brown, *Promises and Performance: Carter Builds a New Administration* (Lexington, MA: D. C. Heath, 1979). For a good discussion of the struggle between Hamilton Jordan and Jack Watson over staffing the White House, see Carl M. Brauer, *Presidential Transitions: Eisenhower through Reagan* (New York: Oxford University Press, 1986). Also useful are Lawrence X. Clifford, "An Examination of the Carter Administration's Selection of Secretary of State and National Security Adviser," in Rosenbaum and Ugrinsky, *Jimmy Carter,* pp. 5–15; James L. Sundquist, "Jimmy Carter as Public Administrator: An Appraisal at Mid-Term," *Public Administration Review* 39 (January–February 1979): 3–8; Richard E. Neustadt, "Staffing the Presidency: Premature Notes on the New Administration," *Political Science Quarterly* 93 (Spring 1978): 1–9, 12–14; Richard E. Neustadt and Ernest R. May, *Thinking in Time: The Use of History for Decision-Makers* (New York: Free Press, 1983); Nelson W. Polsby, "Presidential Cabinet Making: Lessons for the Political System," *Political Science Quarterly* 93 (Spring 1978): 15–25; Leslie Gelb, "Reflections on the Carter Transition," in *History and Current Issues,* ed. Kenneth W. Thompson (Lanham, MD: University Press of America, 1986), pp. 69–86; and Robert Shogan, *Promises to Keep: Carter's First Hundred Days* (New York: Crowell, 1977). Clifford points to the Trilateral Commission's influence on Carter's choices for his top diplomatic aides and on the making of his foreign policy. Sundquist maintains that initially, Carter did not recognize the need for overall management of his administration. Neustadt criticizes Carter for not appointing a chief of staff early in his administration and for making peremptory decisions. Neustadt and May also believe that Carter could have been more effective in gaining public and congressional support for his policies if he had emphasized a few familiar themes after taking office. Polsby contrasts Richard Nixon's effort to control the entire executive apparatus through "political commissars" with Carter's effort to staff his cabinet with "subject-matter" experts. Gelb thinks that Carter should have appointed Paul Nitze rather than Harold Brown as secretary of defense. Shogan maintains that Carter got off to a vigorous but erratic start during the first hundred days in office.

There are numerous books and articles on various aspects of Carter's domestic policies. In addition to Jones, *The Trusteeship Presidency,* and Hargrove, *Jimmy Carter as President,* see Dilys Hill, "Domestic Policy," and Stephen Woolcock, "The Economic Policies of the Carter Administration," in Abernathy, Hill, and Williams, *The Carter Years,* pp. 13–34 and 35–53, respectively. Hill argues that Carter's program was overly ambitious and took too much time to legislate.

Woolcock considers Carter's economic program as a compromise between his conservative preferences and the views of more liberal Democrats in Congress. The most comprehensive treatment of Carter's economic policy, however, is W. Carl Biven, *Jimmy Carter's Economy: Policy in an Age of Limits* (Chapel Hill: University of North Carolina Press, 2002). Based on the major collections at the Carter Library, Biven argues that Carter's economic policies were a reasonable response in an age of limited resources.

On the constraints on Carter's influence over domestic policy, see also Paul Charles Light, *The President's Agenda: Domestic Policy Choice from Kennedy to Carter (with Notes on Ronald Reagan)* (Baltimore: Johns Hopkins University Press, 1982); Ernest S. Griffith, *The American Presidency: The Dilemmas of Shared Power and Divided Government* (New York: New York University Press, 1976); and Michael Nelson, ed., *The Presidency and the Political System*, 2nd ed. (Washington, DC: CQ Press, 1988).

On the management of the Carter administration, consult Larry Berman, *The Office of Management and Budget and the Presidency, 1921–1979* (Princeton, NJ: Princeton University Press, 1979); Colin Campbell, *Managing the Presidency: Carter, Reagan, and the Search for Executive Order* (Pittsburgh: University of Pittsburgh Press, 1986); A. Whitfield Ayres, "The Carter White House Staff," and Donald A. Marchand, "Carter and the Bureaucracy," both in Abernathy, Dilys, and Williams, *The Carter Years*, pp. 144–164 and 192–207, respectively; and Richard Polenberg, "Roosevelt, Carter, and Executive Reorganization: Lessons of the 1930s," *Presidential Studies Quarterly* 9 (Winter 1979): 35–46. According to Berman, one of the obstacles Carter confronted was the fact that the executive office of the president had not historically managed or executed policy directly. Campbell maintains that Carter's much-vaunted cabinet consultation amounted to little more than a ritual. Ayres argues that Carter's staff was inexperienced and ill suited for its tasks. He continues that of all the recent presidents, Carter took the keenest interest in presidential management, but the results of his initiatives were limited. Polenberg observes that efforts at executive reorganization, such as Carter's, have historically been a minefield for the incumbent because of the resistance they encounter. The most recent   and best— discussion of the staffing and operations of the Carter White House is Karen M. Hult and Charles E. Walcott, *Empowering the White House: Governance under Nixon, Ford, and Carter* (Lawrence: University Press of Kansas, 2004).

Carter's rocky relations with Congress have been the subject of considerable scholarship. Mark A. Peterson, *Legislating Together: The White House and Capitol Hill from Eisenhower to Reagan* (Cambridge, MA.: Harvard University Press, 1990), claims that most chief executives have been able to work with Congress. Peterson believes that presidents should be agenda focused; Carter was not, and this was the root of his problems. Nelson W. Polsby, *Consequences of Party Reform* (New York: Oxford University Press, 1983), regards Carter's troubled relations with Congress as one by-product of party reform. Robert L. Beckman, *Nuclear Non-Proliferation: Congress and the Control of Peaceful Nuclear Activities* (Boulder, CO: Westview Press, 1985), details the dispute between the White House and lawmakers regarding how far the United States should go to prevent the spread of nuclear technology. In "Campaign Promises of Jimmy Carter: Accomplishments and Failures," *Presidential Studies Quarterly* 15 (Winter 1985): 136–144, Michael J. Krukones concludes that although Carter fulfilled about 60 percent of his campaign promises, he neglected many of his major ones, such as tax reform and price supports for farmers. Similarly, William F. Mullen, in "Perception of Carter's Legislative Successes and Failures: Views from the Hill and the Liaison Staff," *Presidential Studies Quarterly* 12 (Fall 1982): 522–544, states that Carter's failures on Capitol Hill were of his own doing, since Congress was willing to work with him. For a somewhat different view, see Charles O. Jones, "Carter and Congress: From the Outside In," *British Journal of Political Science* 15 (July 1985): 271–298, and "The Separated Presidency—Making It Work in Contemporary Politics," in *The New American Political System: Second Version*, ed. Anthony King (Washington, DC: AEI Press, 1990), pp. 1–28. In these articles, Jones emphasizes the difficulties every modern president encounters in working with Congress.

One reason given for this legislative stonewall is the power of special-interest groups and political action committees (PACs) on Capitol Hill. Although the huge and growing literature on these entities is beyond the scope of this review, readers can consult the essays in Allan J. Cigler and Burdett A. Loomis, eds., *Interest Group Politics* (Washington, DC: CQ Press, 1983), which collectively present a balanced view of both the benefits of and the dangers inherent in interest-group politics. Also useful are Robert H. Salisbury, "The Paradox of Interest Groups in Washington—More Groups Less Clout," in King, *New American Political System*, pp. 203–229, and Benjamin Ginsburg and Martin Shefter, "The Presidency and the Organization of Interests," in Nelson, *The Presidency and the Political System*, pp. 311–349. For an excellent study of one interest group active on Capitol Hill during the Carter administration, see Edward Tivnan, *The Lobby: Jewish Political Power and American Foreign Policy* (New York: Simon and Schuster, 1987).

An early but still exceptional study of Carter's endeavors on behalf of welfare reform is Laurence E. Lynn Jr. and D. F. Whitman, *The President as Policymaker: Jimmy Carter and Welfare Reform* (Philadelphia: Temple University Press, 1982). On Carter's battle with Congress over the water projects, consult Paul Scheele, "President Carter and the Water Projects: A Case Study in Presidential and Congressional Decision-Making," *Presidential Studies Quarterly* 8 (Fall 1978): 348–364, in which Scheele argues that the eventual compromise was a limited victory for Carter that showed that he could be educated politically. On Carter's urban policy, see Harold L. Wolman and Astrid E. Merget, "The Presidency and Policy Formulation: President Carter and the Urban Policy," *Presidential Studies Quarterly* 10 (Summer 1980): 402–415. On Carter and civil rights, see M. Glenn Abernathy, "The Carter Administration and Domestic Civil Rights," in Abernathy, Hill, and Williams, *The Carter Years*, pp. 106–111, and Steven F. Lawson, *In Pursuit of Power: Southern Blacks and Electoral Politics, 1965–1982* (New York: Columbia University Press, 1985). On Carter's energy program, consult Kellerman, *The Political Presidency*, and J. William Holland, "The Great Gamble: Jimmy Carter and the 1979 Energy Crisis," *Prologue* 22 (Spring 1990): 63–69. Holland discusses the crisis of confidence surrounding Carter's decision to postpone his 1979 speech on energy. Another study of the 1979 malaise and Camp David domestic summit is Robert Strong, "Recapturing Leadership: The Carter Administration and the Crisis of Confidence," *Presidential Studies Quarterly* 16 (Fall 1986): 636–650.

During his four years as president, Carter faced an increasingly critical press. One study of the news media's treatment of the Carter administration argues that the press evaluated Carter on the basis of what it thought a successful president should do rather than on what Carter sought to achieve; see Mark J. Rozell, *The Press and the Carter Presidency* (Boulder, CO: Westview Press, 1989). A somewhat different approach is taken by John William Tebbel and Sarah Miles Watts in *The Press and the Presidency: From George Washington to Ronald Reagan* (New York: Oxford University Press, 1985). Tebbel and Watts argue that Carter and his press secretary Jody Powell overestimated the power of the press.

There has been a dramatic increase in recent years in the number of works on the Carter administration's foreign policy. Gaddis Smith's *Morality, Reason, and Power: American Diplomacy in the Carter Years* (New York: Hill and Wang, 1986) still stands up well. The book's title indicates what Smith believes were the three themes of Carter's foreign policy. Several works have emphasized Carter's failed attempt to develop a foreign policy that downplayed the cold war and containment policy. David Skidmore, *Reversing Course: Carter's Foreign Policy, Domestic Politics, and the Failure of Reform* (Nashville, TN: Vanderbilt University Press, 1996), contends that conservative criticism at home led the White House to fear that not returning to a policy of containment would cost it votes, while Jerel Rosati, *The Carter Administration's Quest for Global Community: Beliefs and Their Impact on Behavior* (Columbia: University of South Carolina Press, 1987), and Richard C. Thornton, *The Carter Years: Toward a New Global Order* (New York: Paragon House, 1991), highlight the Soviet threat as the cause. Each of these authors notes to varying degrees the importance of the Vance-Brzezinski dispute and its impact on administration policy making. Timothy Maga, *The World of Jimmy Carter: U.S. Foreign Policy, 1977–1981* (West Haven, CT: University of New Haven Press, 1994), praises Carter's promotion of human rights but is generally critical of his foreign policy making. Andrew J. Katz, "Public Opinion and the Contradictions of Jimmy Carter's Foreign Policy," *Presidential Studies Quarterly* 30 (December 2000): 662–687, writes that the Carter administration made poor use of polling information to develop a foreign policy acceptable to the public. Another book that is critical of the administration, and that focuses solely on the advisory process, is Jean Garrison, *Games Advisors Play: Foreign Policy in the Nixon and Carter Administrations* (College Station: Texas A&M University Press, 1999). Garrison argues that Carter tried and failed to develop a collegial model of advising. Her work, however, is beset with a variety of errors and poor use of evidence. In more recent years a number of revisionist accounts have appeared that are less critical of Carter than Smith, Skidmore, and Thornton are. Aside from Dumbrell, *The Carter Presidency*, see Robert A. Strong, *Working in the World: Jimmy Carter and the Making of American Foreign Policy* (Baton Rouge: Louisiana State University Press, 2000). Strong uses a series of case studies to show that Carter was neither a weak nor an indecisive president. Rather, the president's vision of world affairs was a pragmatic one that led to improper charges of weakness and vacillation on his part. Anyone working on the administration's foreign policy should also consult biographies of the major figures. David S. McLellan, *Cyrus Vance* (Totowa, NJ: Rowan and Allanheld, 1985), is a laudatory portrayal of the secretary of state. Gerry Argyris Andrianopoulos, *Kissinger and Brzezinski: The NSC and the Struggle for Control of U.S. National Security Policy* (New York: St. Martin's Press, 1991), argues that both NSC advisers had similar foreign policies based on the idea of power politics, but Brzezinski was more supportive of implanting morality into U.S. diplomacy and developing a collegial style of decision making.

No aspect of Carter's foreign policy has elicited more appraisal than the president's commitment to human rights. The literature on the topic is daunting. A critical analysis is Joshua Muravchik, *The Uncertain Crusade: Jimmy Carter and the Dilemmas of Human Rights* (New York: Hamilton Press, 1986). A number of other works, however, take issue with Muravchik's conclusions, including Sandy Vogelgesang, *American Dream, Global Nightmare: The Dilemma of U.S. Human Rights Policy* (New York: W. W. Norton, 1980); Friedberg Pflüger, "Human Rights Unbound: Carter's Human Rights Policy Reassessed," *Presidential Studies Quarterly* 19 (Fall 1989): 705–716; David F. Schmitz and Vanessa Walker, "Jimmy Carter and the Foreign Policy of Human Rights: The Development of a Post–Cold War Foreign Policy," *Diplomatic History* 28 (January 2004): 113–143; and Harold Molineau, "Carter and Human Rights: Administrative Impact of a Symbolic Policy," *Policy Studies Journal* 8 (Summer 1990): 879–885. Some scholars have pointed out how bureaucratic infighting weakened the human rights program, including A. Glenn Mower, *Human Rights and American Foreign Policy: The Carter and Reagan Experiences* (Westport, CT: Greenwood Press, 1987); Victor S. Kaufman, "The Carter Administration and the Human Rights Bureau," *Historian* 61 (Fall 1998): 51–66; Caleb Rossiter and Anne Marie Smith, "Human Rights: The Carter Record, the Reagan Reaction," *International Policy Report* (1984): 1–27; and Lars Schoultz, *Human Rights and U.S. Policy towards Latin America* (Princeton, NJ: Princeton University Press, 1981). For more general treatments of the human rights issue, see also A. H. Robertson and J. G. Merrils, *Human Rights in the World: An Introduction to the Study of the International Protection of Human Rights*, 3rd ed. (New York: St. Martin's Press, 1989); Kenneth W. Thompson, *Morality and Foreign Policy* (Baton Rouge: Louisiana State University Press, 1980); Kenneth W. Thompson, ed., *Moral Dimensions of American Foreign Policy* (New Brunswick, NJ: Transaction Books, 1984); Natalie Kaufman Hevener, *The Dynamics of Human Rights in U.S. Foreign Policy* (New Brunswick, NJ: Transaction Books, 1981); and Peter G. Brown and Douglas MacLean, eds., *Human Rights and U.S. Foreign Policy* (Lexington, MA: D. C. Heath, 1979).

The human rights policy had a significant impact on U.S.-Soviet relations. Robert O. Freeman's *The Soviet Union and the Carter Administration* (Pittsburgh: University of Pittsburgh Center for Russian and European Studies, 1987), is based on the public record, and many of the author's conclusions are, by his own admission, conjectural. For a far better analysis of superpower relations during the Carter era, see Raymond L. Garthoff, *Détente and Confrontation: American-Soviet Relations from Nixon to Reagan*, rev. ed. (Washington, DC: Brookings Institution, 1994). Also useful is Svetlana Savranskaya and David A. Welch, *Global Competition and the Deterioration of U.S.-Soviet Relations, 1977–1980* (Providence, RI: Center for Foreign Policy Development, 1995). Three general studies of the cold war that aided the completion of this book are Walter LaFeber, *America, Russia, and the Cold War, 1945–2002*, 9th ed. (Boston: McGraw-Hill, 2004); Mike Bowker and Phil Williams, *Superpower Détente: A Reappraisal* (London: Sage, 1988); and Ronald E.

Powaski, *The Cold War: The United States and the Soviet Union, 1917–1991* (New York: Oxford University Press, 1998). On the Polish crisis, Douglas J. MacEachin, *U.S. Intelligence and the Confrontation in Poland, 1980–1981* (University Park: Pennsylvania State University Press, 2002), is the best source. However, scholars might also want to look at Thomas M. Cynkin, *Soviet and American Signalling in the Polish Crisis* (New York: St. Martin's Press, 1988), and Patrick G. Vaughan, "Beyond Benign Neglect: Zbigniew Brzezinski and the Polish Crisis of 1980," *Polish Review* 64 (1999): 3–28. On the Soviet brigade issue, see David Newsom, *The Soviet Brigade in Cuba: A Study of Political Diplomacy* (Bloomington: Indiana University Press, 1987). For the U.S. response to the invasion of Afghanistan, Gabriella Grasselli, *British and American Responses to the Soviet Invasion of Afghanistan* (Brookfield, VT: Dartmouth, 1996), is based largely on the public record. Jerry W. Sanders, *Peddlers of Crisis: The Committee on the Present Danger and the Politics of Containment* (Boston: South End Press, 1983), traces the influence of the CPD and its fight against the ratification of SALT II.

Surprisingly, there are no books solely on U.S. relations with the nations of western Europe during the Carter years. Some works that scholars might want to consult are Robert M. Hathaway, *Great Britain and the United States: Special Relations since World War II* (Boston: Twayne, 1990); Hans W. Gatzke, *Germany and the United States, A "Special" Relationship?* (Cambridge, MA: Harvard University Press, 1980); Frank A. Ninkovich, *Germany and the United States: The Transformation of the German Question since 1945* (New York: Twayne, 1995); Jonathan Carr, *Helmut Schmidt: Helmsman of Germany* (New York: St. Martin's Press, 1985); Frank Costigliola, *France and the United States: The Cold Alliance since World War II* (New York: Twayne, 1992); and Seán Cronin, *Washington's Irish Policy, 1916–1986: Independence, Partition, Neutrality* (Dublin: Anvil Books, 1987).

The writings on the Middle East and the Arab-Israel dispute are so numerous as to be beyond the scope of this essay. However, some good, recent overviews of U.S. Middle East policy are H. W. Brands, *Into the Labyrinth: The United States and the Middle East, 1945–1993* (New York: McGraw-Hill, 1994); Burton I. Kaufman, *The Arab Middle East and the United States: Inter-Arab Rivalry and Superpower Diplomacy* (New York: Twayne, 1996); and George Lenczowski, *American Presidents and the Middle East* (Durham, NC: Duke University Press, 1990). Other good overviews are Richard H. Curtiss, *A Changing Image: American Perceptions of the Arab-Israeli Dispute* (Washington, DC: American Educational Trust, 1982); Seth P. Tillman, *The United States and the Middle East: Interests and Obstacles* (Bloomington: Indiana University Press, 1982); T. G. Fraser, *The USA and the Middle East since World War II* (New York: St. Martin's Press, 1989); William Stivers, *America's Confrontation with Revolutionary Change in the Middle East, 1948–83* (New York: St. Martin's Press, 1986); Steven L. Spiegel, *The Other Arab-Israeli Conflict: Making America's Middle East Policy, from Truman to Reagan* (Chicago: University of Chicago Press, 1985); Bernard Reich, *The United States and Israel: Influence in the Special Relationship* (New York: Praeger, 1984); Maya Chadda, *Paradox of Power: The United States in Southwest Asia, 1973–1984* (Santa Barbara, CA: ABC-CLIO, 1986); and Paul Charles Merkley, *American Presidents, Religion, and Israel* (Westport, CT: Praeger, 2004). Spiegel has a chapter on Carter, whose Middle East policy, he concludes, was based on a creative global philosophy that was overtaken by world events. Reich, who examines U.S. policy toward Israel during the Carter and Reagan years, concludes that the use of incentives rather than coercion was the best way to influence Israeli policy. Chadda, who includes Pakistan and Afghanistan in her study, approves of Carter's attempt to develop a liberal internationalist foreign policy and places the blame for his failure on a combination of timing, the manner in which he promoted his agenda, and U.S. domestic politics. Merkley sees religion as having an impact on how presidents view Arab-Israeli relations and charges Carter with having a bias against Israel. Carter's policy of nuclear nonproliferation also had an impact on the United States' relationship with the Middle East. For more on that subject, see Shai Feldman, "Superpower Nonproliferation Policies: The Case of the Middle East," in *The Soviet-American Competition in the Middle East*, ed. Steven L. Spiegel et al. (Lexington, MA.: Lexington Books, 1988), p. 96. Kathleen Christison, *Perceptions of Palestine: Their Influence on U.S. Middle East Policy* (Berkeley: University of California Press, 1999), is an excellent source on the Palestinian question. On the Camp David talks, Tom Princen, "Camp David: Problem-Solving or Power Politics as Usual?" *Journal of Peace Research* 28 (1991): 57–69, views Carter's use of "power politics" as central to the president's success in those talks.

There is also a growing body of literature on relations with South and East Asia during the Carter years. Works on U.S. policy toward Pakistan and India tend to focus on the matters of military aid and nuclear nonproliferation. For more on these subjects, see, in addition to Beckman's *Nuclear Non-Proliferation*, J. Michael Martinez, "The Carter Administration and the Evolution of American Nuclear Nonproliferation Policy," *Journal of Policy History* 14 (2002): 261–292; J. Samuel Walker, "Nuclear Power and Nonproliferation: The Controversy over Nuclear Exports, 1974–1980," *Diplomatic History* 25 (Spring 2001): 215–249; Robert F. Goheen, "U.S. Policy toward India during the Carter Presidency," in *The Hope and the Reality: U.S.-Indian Relations from Roosevelt to Reagan*, ed. Harold A. Gould and Šumit Ganguly (Boulder, CO: Westview Press, 1992); Brahma Chellaney, *Nuclear Proliferation: The U.S.-Indian Conflict* (New Delhi: Orient Longman, 1993); Shirin Tahir-Kheli, *The United States and Pakistan: The Evolution of an Influence Relationship* (New York: Praeger, 1982); Dennis Kux, *India and the United States: Estranged Democracies, 1941–1991* (Washington, DC: National Defense University Press, 1992), and *The United States and Pakistan, 1947–2000: Disenchanted Allies* (Washington, DC: Woodrow Wilson Center Press, 2001); and H. W. Brands, *India and the United States: The Cold Peace* (Boston: Twayne, 1990). There are no books that devote extensive coverage to U.S.-Japanese relations during the Carter years. The best work on this subject is Chae-Jin Lee and Hideo Sato, *U.S. Policy toward Japan and Korea: A Changing Influence Relationship* (New York: Praeger, 1982). Also of use, though based solely on the public record, is Hugo Dobson, *Japan and the G7/8, 1975–2002* (New York: Routledge, 2004). There are numerous works on Sino-American relations, with a focus on the process of normalization. The most comprehensive coverage of this issue can be found in Harry Harding, *A Fragile Relationship: The United States and China since 1972* (Washington, DC: Brookings Institution, 1992); James Mann, *About Face: A History of America's Curious Relationship with China, from Nixon to Clinton* (New York: Vintage Books, 2000); Patrick Tyler, *A Great Wall: Six Presidents and China* (New York: Public Affairs, 2000); and Robert S.

Ross, *Negotiating Cooperation: The United States and China, 1969–1989* (Stanford, CA: Stanford University Press, 1995). Harding sees Sino-American relations marked by cycles of improved ties followed by stagnation. Mann highlights the Carter administration's willingness to downplay human rights in the name of better relations—particularly strategic relations—with Beijing. Tyler emphasizes Brzezinski's role in the achievement of normalization and how the changing political climate in China aided in that effort. Ross explains that despite their differing views over the status of Taiwan, the positions of the United States and China permitted compromise. Also helpful are Qingshan Tan, *U.S. China Policy: From Normalization to the Post–Cold War Era* (Boulder, CO: Lynne Rienner, 1992), and Qinxin Ken Wang, *Hegemonic Cooperation and Conflict: Postwar Japan's China Policy and the United States* (Westport, CT: Praeger, 2000). The desire to normalize relations with China had a direct impact on U.S. policy toward Cambodia and Vietnam. Several works, all critical, on Carter's policy toward Cambodia are Kenton Clymer, *The United States and Cambodia, 1969–2000: A Troubled Relationship* (New York: Routledge, 2004); Christopher Brady, *United States Foreign Policy towards Cambodia, 1977–92: A Question of Realities* (New York: St. Martin's Press, 1999); and Sheldon Morris Neuringer, *The Carter Administration, Human Rights, and the Agony of Cambodia* (Lewiston, NY: E. Mellen Press, 1993). For Carter's Vietnam policy, see Steven Hurst, *The Carter Administration and Vietnam* (New York: St. Martin's Press, 1996). Raymond Bonner, *Waltzing with Dictator: The Marcoses and the Making of American Foreign Policy* (New York: Vintage Books, 1988), provides the most comprehensive coverage available on the Carter administration's Philippine policy. He argues that the White House largely ignored Ferdinand Marcos's repressive government in the name of maintaining good relations with the Philippines.

With regard to Latin America, Robert Pastor's *Whirlpool: U.S. Foreign Policy toward Latin America and the Caribbean* (Princeton, NJ: Princeton University Press, 1992) compares and contrasts the policies of Carter, Ronald Reagan, and George Bush. Of the three, he praises the multilateralist policy of the Carter administration. On the Panama Canal treaties, see Walter LaFeber, *The Panama Canal: The Crisis in Historical Perspective,* updated ed. (New York: Oxford University Press, 1990); J. Michael Hogan, *The Panama Canal in American Politics* (Carbondale: Southern Illinois University Press, 1986); William L. Furlong and Margaret E. Scranton, *The Dynamics of Foreign Policymaking: The President, the Congress, and the Panama Canal Treaties* (Boulder, CO: Westview Press, 1984); Robert Strong, "Jimmy Carter and the Panama Canal Treaties," *Presidential Studies Quarterly* 21 (Spring 1991): 269–284; and Larry Grubbs, "'Hands on Presidency' or 'Passionless Presidency'? Jimmy Carter and Ratification of the Panama Canal Treaties," *Society for Historians of American Foreign Relations Newsletter* 30 (December 1999): 1–17. For U.S. policy toward Central America, see Walter LaFeber, *Inevitable Revolutions: The United States in Central America* (New York: W. W. Norton, 1984), and William M. Leo Grande, *Our Own Backyard: The United States in Central America* (Chapel Hill: University of North Carolina Press, 1998). With regard to Nicaragua specifically, see, aside from Pastor, *Condemned to Repetition,* Morris H. Morley, *Washington, Somoza, and the Sandinistas: State and Regime in U.S. Policy toward Nicaragua, 1969–1981* (New York: Cambridge University Press, 1994), and Robert Kagan, *A Twilight Struggle: American Power and Nicaragua, 1977–1990* (New York: Free Press,

1996). Morley views U.S. policy as being driven by a desire to preserve or develop in other countries institutions that would support Washington's agenda; when the Sandinistas began to threaten the Nicaraguan state, U.S. officials sought to develop new institutions in that country that would protect U.S. interests. Kagan denounces the Carter administration's ambivalent Nicaraguan policy and charges the White House with believing that it was possible to moderate the Sandinistas' pro-Soviet agenda. On the Soviet brigade in Cuba, see David Newsom, *The Soviet Brigade in Cuba: A Study of Political Diplomacy* (Bloomington: Indiana University Press, 1987). An excellent work that covers the Mariel boatlift and its impact is Felix Roberto Masud Piloto, *From Welcomed Exiles to Illegal Immigrants: Cuban Migration to the U.S., 1959–1995* (Lanham, MD: Rowman and Littlefield, 1996). Piero Gleijeses, "Truth or Credibility: Castro, Carter, and the Invasions of Shaba," *International History Review* 18 (February 1996): 70–103, places Brzezinski in the center of the Carter administration's decision to play up what Gleijeses says was actually a nonexistent Cuban role in the two invasions of Shaba.

Three books that deal with Carter's African policy are Gerald J. Bender et al., eds., *African Crisis Area and U.S. Foreign Policy* (Berkeley: University of California Press, 1985); Thomas J. Noer, *Cold War and Black Liberation* (Columbia: University of Missouri Press, 1985); and Zaki Laidi, *The Superpowers and Africa: The Constraints of a Rivalry, 1960–1990* (Chicago: University of Chicago Press, 1990). There is very little on the dispute in the Horn of Africa, but a good place to begin is Paul B. Henze's *The Horn of Africa: From War to Peace* (New York: St. Martin's Press, 1991). On Rhodesia, Mordechai Tamarkin, "Kissinger, Carter, and the Rhodesian Conflict—From the Art of the Possible to Mission Impossible," *Asian and African Studies* 26 (1992): 153–172, states that the administration's attempt to implement a worldview that emphasized human rights and North-South issues did not mesh with the actual situation that existed in southern Africa. The result was a failed Rhodesian policy. For relations with South Africa, see Christopher Coker, *The United States and South Africa, 1968–1985: Constructive Engagement and Its Critics* (Durham, NC: Duke University Press, 1986), and Richard E. Bissell, *South Africa and the United States: The Erosion of an Influence Relationship* (New York: Praeger, 1982). Both note the failure of the Carter administration to bring about reform in that country.

For the U.S. response to the Iranian revolution and the hostage crisis, David Farber's *Taken Hostage: The Iran Hostage Crisis and America's First Encounter with Radical Islam* (Princeton, NJ: Princeton University Press, 2005), and David Harris's *The Crisis: The President, the Prophet, and the Shah—1979 and the Coming of Militant Islam* (New York: Little, Brown, 2004), are vital. Harris, who worked for the *New York Times Magazine*, gives a journalistic account, avoiding the level of analysis provided by Farber. However, Harris was able to interview numerous participants in the revolution and the hostage crisis, on both the American and Iranian sides. Other works of use to scholars are Barry Rubin, *Paved with Good Intentions: The American Experience in Iran* (New York: Oxford University Press, 1980); James A. Bill, *The Eagle and the Lion: The Tragedy of American-Iranian Relations* (New Haven, CT: Yale University Press, 1988); and Ofira Seliktar, *Failing the Crystal Ball Test: The Carter Administration and the Fundamentalist Revolution in Iran* (Westport, CT: Praeger, 2000). Two recent but unconvincing works are Christopher Hemmer,

Which Lessons Matter? American Foreign Policy Decision Making in the Middle East, 1979–1987 (New York: State University of New York Press, 2000), and David Patrick Houghton, *US Foreign Policy and the Iran Hostage Crisis* (New York: Cambridge University Press, 2001). Both argue that administration officials relied on analogies to decide the best response to the hostage crisis. A widely cited account that contains a number of inaccuracies is Michael Ledeen and William Lewis, *Debacle: The American Failure in Iran* (New York: Knopf, 1981). On Carter's decision to let the shah into the United States for medical treatment, see Edward B. McMahon et al., *Medical Cover-ups in the White House* (Washington, DC: Farragut Publishing Company, 1987). On the Huyser mission to Iran, consult Robert E. Huyser, *Mission to Iran* (New York: Harper and Row, 1986). On the failed hostage rescue, see Paul B. Ryan, *The Iranian Rescue Mission and Why It Failed* (Annapolis, MD: Naval Institute Press, 1986), and Charlie Beckwith and Donald Knox, *Delta Force* (New York: Harcourt Brace and Jovanovich, 1983). The excruciating diplomacy leading to the final release of the hostages is covered in Warren Christopher et al., *American Hostages in Iran: The Conduct of a Crisis* (New Haven, CT: Yale University Press, 1985).

There is a growing scholarship on Carter's defense policy. One early study is S. Sarkesian, ed., *Defense Policy and the Presidency: Carter's First Years* (Boulder, CO: Westview Press, 1979). For a general overview, see also Phil Williams, "Carter's Defense Policy," in Abernathy, Hill, and Williams, *The Carter Years*, pp. 84–105. Hill argues that during his first two years in office, Carter and the liberal Democrats basically agreed on defense policy, producing a conservative backlash that damaged him for the remainder of his administration. For a study of the generally strained relations that existed between Carter and the Pentagon, see the pertinent chapter in Dale S. Herspring, *The Pentagon and the Presidency: Civil-Military Relations from FDR to George W. Bush* (Lawrence: University Press of Kansas, 2005). For the dispute over the development and deployment of the neutron bomb, Sherri Wasserman, *The Neutron Bomb Controversy: A Study in Alliance Politics* (New York: Praeger, 1983), is the most extensive review of the topic. For the controversy over the MX missile, see Herbert Scoville Jr., *MX: Prescription for Disaster* (Cambridge, MA: MIT Press, 1981), and Colin Gray, *The MX ICBM and National Security* (New York: Praeger, 1981). Scoville, then president of the Arms Control Association, attacks the idea of deploying the MX, declaring that it would have invited a Soviet nuclear strike. Gray defends the missile system, saying that it was necessary to protect the United States against the Soviet threat and would make Moscow more willing to compromise on SALT. A brilliant study of the politics and diplomacy of the SALT II treaty is Strobe Talbott, *Endgame: The Inside Story of SALT II* (New York: Harper and Row, 1979). For a discussion of organizational change in the NSC and Defense Department, see R. Gordon Hoxie, *Command Decision and the Presidency: A Study of National Security Policy and Organization* (New York: Readers Digest Press, 1977). On PD-59, see Jeffrey Richelson, "PD-59, NSDD-1, and the Reagan Strategic Modernization Program," *Journal of Strategic Studies* 6 (June 1983): 125–126. An excellent study of the B-1 bomber controversy by a Pulitzer Prize–winning journalist is Nick Kotz, *Wild Blue Yonder: Money, Politics, and the B-1 Bomber* (New York: Pantheon Books, 1988).

For Carter's life since he left the presidency, see, in addition to his own works, Douglas Brinkley, *The Unfinished Presidency: Jimmy Carter's Journey beyond the White House* (New York: Penguin, 1998). Brinkley argues persuasively that Carter has used his postpresidential years to continue an agenda that focuses on human rights and world peace, even at the cost of alienating officials in Washington. A similar argument is developed by John Whiteclay Chambers II, "Jimmy Carter's Public Policy Ex-Presidency," *Political Science Quarterly* 113 (Fall 1998): 405–425. For a polemic, see Steven F. Hayward, *The Real Jimmy Carter: How Our Worst Ex-President Undermines American Foreign Policy, Coddles Dictators and Created the Party of Clinton and Kerry* (Washington, DC: Regnery, 2004).

INDEX

that shaped Carter's presidency, from Koreagate and the Cuban boatlift to the Camp David accords and the Iran hostage crisis. They explore bureaucratic infighting over his human rights policies, describing how the administration's position changed with greater emphasis on security issues after 1979; they also examine the issue of arms control in the light of newly opened Soviet archives and argue that the Vance-Brzezinski dispute was more profound than had originally been thought.

In the final analysis, the Kaufmans fault Carter for not crafting a coherent message that would offer the American people a vision on which to build a base of support and assure his success. As his reputation as an ex-president continues to grow, this updated book offers an even better understanding of his White House years.

Burton I. Kaufman is former dean of the School of Interdisciplinary Studies and professor of history at Miami University in Ohio and author of eight other books, including *The Korean War: Challenges in Crisis, Credibility, and Command.* **Scott Kaufman** is associate professor of history at Francis Marion University in Florence, South Carolina, and author of two books, including *Confronting Communism: U.S. and British Policies toward China.*